Gluten-Free Baking FOR DUMMIES®

by Dr. Jean McFadden Layton and
Linda Larsen

WILEY

John Wiley & Sons, Inc.

Gluten-Free Baking For Dummies®

Published by
John Wiley & Sons, Inc.
111 River St.
Hoboken, NJ 07030-5774
www.wiley.com

Copyright © 2012 by John Wiley & Sons, Inc., Hoboken, New Jersey

Published by John Wiley & Sons, Inc., Hoboken, New Jersey

Published simultaneously in Canada

For general information on our other products and services, please contact our Customer Care Department within the U.S. at 877-762-2974, outside the U.S. at 317-572-3993, or fax 317-572-4002.

For technical support, please visit www.wiley.com/techsupport.

Wiley also publishes its books in a variety of electronic formats and by print-on-demand. Some content that appears in standard print versions of this book may not be available in other formats. For more information about Wiley products, visit us at www.wiley.com.

Library of Congress Control Number: 2011941730

ISBN 978-1-118-07773-3 (pbk); ISBN 978-1-118-20610-2 (ebk); ISBN 978-1-118-20611-9 (ebk); ISBN 978-1-118-20612-6 (ebk)

Manufactured in the United States of America

10 9 8 7 6 5 4 3 2

WILEY

About the Authors

If you could find a doctor who truly understands gluten intolerance and celiac disease, what would be your first questions? Better yet, what if she could also serve as a recipe consultant, adapting your favorite family recipes so you can continue to enjoy the foods you love?

Dr. Jean McFadden Layton combines the best of both worlds as she guides her patients and the general public toward an understanding of gluten intolerance and its role in people's health.

Following the premature death of her first husband, Dr. Layton's interest in alternative medicine was launched. "There has to be a better way" became her mantra. She left the world of professional food service to return to school to complete her undergraduate degree, meeting her second husband, Ed, while catering in New York City.

They moved to Portland, Oregon, to complete their respective degrees — hers a doctorate in naturopathic medicine, his a master's in Oriental medicine — and to begin their family. Fiona and Katie were born in the middle of medical school.

Celiac disease and gluten intolerance became a part of their life after moving to Bellingham, Washington, when Ed fractured his femur in an ice-skating accident. He was 48 and had osteoporosis. Research and experience pointed toward a gluten-free diet as a solution, and so it began for him. He now has a bone density that's appropriate for his age.

Dr. Layton discovered that her brain fog, menstrual irregularities, and body temperature fluctuations all improved with a gluten-free diet. Celiac disease and gluten intolerance have a genetic component. Realizing that their daughters' growth had plateaued, the Laytons took gluten out of their daughters' diet. The girls responded by increasing their heights by 1½ inches each within three months of starting a gluten-free diet.

Dr. Layton specializes in celiac disease and gluten intolerance, attracting patients from around Washington State and the lower mainland of Canada. She proudly serves on the board of directors for the Bellingham Gluten Intolerance Group and facilitates the local Healthy Gluten-Free Kids group.

Building on the medical oath she swore to uphold, which includes the concept of *docere* (doctor as teacher), Dr. Layton teaches gluten-free baking and cooking classes with the Community Food Co-op and Whatcom Community College. Conveying the ease and breadth of healthy gluten-free food, Dr. Layton has written her well-known blog, *GFDoctorRecipes,* since 2006. Here, she explores the world of recipe development as well as the current research in gluten intolerance.

As @GFDoctor, Dr. Layton is active in the social media world with thousands of international Twitter followers. Her website, www.gfdoctor.com, and her Facebook sites, GFDoctor and Healthy Gluten-Free Kids, convey even more information to the general public about up-to-the-minute changes in foods and products.

Linda Larsen is an author and journalist who has written 26 books, many about food and nutrition. She earned a BA degree in biology from St. Olaf College and a BS with high distinction in food science and nutrition from the University of Minnesota.

Linda worked for the Pillsbury Company for many years, creating and testing recipes. She was a member of the Pillsbury Bake-Off staff five times, acting as manager of the search team and working in the test kitchens. Linda is the Busy Cooks Guide for About.com and writes about food, recipes, and nutrition. She has written articles for *Woman's Day, Quick & Simple,* and *First* magazines. Her books include *Eating Clean For Dummies, Medical Ethics For Dummies,* and *Detox Diets For Dummies* (all published by Wiley); *Knack Grilling Basics* (Knack); *The Starter Cook* (Lyons Press); *The $7 a Meal Cookbook, The Everything Tex-Mex Cookbook,* and *The Everything Healthy Cooking for Parties Cookbook* (Adams Media).

Dedication

From Dr. Layton: For my husband and daughters, without whom this book would never have been written, at least not by me. They have been my inspiration, cheerleaders, and tasters of everything, good and bad. We're an outstanding team to create the real food that our palates crave.

Fiona, thanks for being the amazingly honest critic that you are. It makes life interesting. I still owe you a gluten-free croissant. It's coming soon.

Katie, you bake an amazing gluten-free brownie, as your blue ribbon from the county fair demonstrates. Collaborating with you in the kitchen is fun!

Ed, our life together for the past 16 years has had so many challenges and joys. I've learned that together, we can do anything. Thanks for covering my back in so many ways. All those late nights of social media swirling are finally worth it.

From Linda: I dedicate this book first and foremost to my husband Doug. Throughout the last 30 years, we've had many adventures in food. Gluten-free foods were new to him, and he was a willing taster for many of these recipes. Through it all, he's been by my side and is my biggest cheerleader and confidant. I'd also like to dedicate the book to my parents, Duane and Marlene Johnson, for their support and encouragement. They always told me I could do anything I attempted and let me cook and bake anything I wanted to.

Authors' Acknowledgments

From Dr. Layton: When you have the chance to thank people for the first time in print, the thank-you list can go on like an Academy Awards speech.

To Linda Larsen, my coauthor, for her humor, knowledge, and guidance of this newbie author. This project would have been impossible with anyone else. To Barb Doyen, our amazing agent, thank you for finding me, believing in me, and giving me the chance to be the teacher of many. And thanks to all the editors, recipe testers, and technical folks who made our words the reality you are holding.

Leading the way to real food recipes we can all enjoy, Shauna Ahern, Ali Segersten, and the rest of my GFGF (Gluten-Free Girl Friends): Thank you all for keeping it real.

Penny De Los Santos, Clare Barboza, and Helene Dujardin: Thank you for showing the way to make a visual story sing.

Finally, thanks to all my patients, Healthy Gluten-Free Kids support group members, fellow naturopaths, Bellingham Gluten Intolerance Group members, Facebook friends, and Twitter followers for inspiring my professional development, continued research, recipe creation, and answer-seeking.

From Linda: I'd like to thank my coauthor, Dr. Jean Layton, first of all, for being such a wonderful friend and guide while working on this book. We have the same sense of humor and the same desire to share this information with the world. She is such a valuable resource for nutrition and medical information.

I'd also like to thank the Department of Food Science at the University of Minnesota for giving me such a strong foundation in science. Thanks to our agent Barb Doyen. She had such confidence in my ability to write this book and encouraged me every step of the way. Thanks to our wonderful editors and recipe testers at Wiley for their support, suggestions, and guidance. And thanks to my friends, especially my Facebook friends, and my faithful family for their support and love as I worked on this book.

Publisher's Acknowledgments

We're proud of this book; please send us your comments at http://dummies.custhelp.com. For other comments, please contact our Customer Care Department within the U.S. at 877-762-2974, outside the U.S. at 317-572-3993, or fax 317-572-4002.

Some of the people who helped bring this book to market include the following:

Acquisitions, Editorial, and Vertical Websites

Senior Project Editor: Tim Gallan

Acquisitions Editor: Michael Lewis

Copy Editor: Todd Lothery

Recipe Testers: Pamela Mitchell, Nicole New, Emily Nolan, and Angela Okragly

Nutritional Analyst: Patty Santelli

Assistant Editor: David Lutton

Editorial Program Coordinator: Joe Niesen

Editorial Manager: Michelle Hacker

Editorial Assistants: Rachelle S. Amick, Alexa Koschier

Art Coordinator: Alicia B. South

Photographer: T. J. Hine Photography, Inc.

Food Stylist: Lisa Bishop

Cartoons: Rich Tennant (www.the5thwave.com)

Composition Services

Project Coordinator: Nikki Gee

Layout and Graphics: Joyce Haughey, Christin Swinford

Proofreaders: Melissa Cossell, Betty Kish

Indexer: Sharon Shock

Publishing and Editorial for Consumer Dummies

    Kathleen Nebenhaus, Vice President and Executive Publisher

    Kristin Ferguson-Wagstaffe, Product Development Director

    Ensley Eikenburg, Associate Publisher, Travel

    Kelly Regan, Editorial Director, Travel

Publishing for Technology Dummies

    Andy Cummings, Vice President and Publisher

Composition Services

    Debbie Stailey, Director of Composition Services

Contents at a Glance

Recipes at a Glance

Table of Contents

Introduction

When Jean's family was diagnosed with gluten intolerance, she became a detective and an investigative baker. She started experimenting with baking and cooking to make sure her daughters would be healthy and could enjoy the joys of childhood. She researched gluten-free baking and found resources that helped her create delicious gluten-free recipes that her husband and daughters love. In fact, her daughters now feel sorry for people who don't enjoy gluten-free cookies, pies, and cakes!

Gluten-free foods are the only way people with celiac disease and gluten intolerance can live healthy lives. Gluten is a protein molecule found in wheat, rye, barley, and triticale. In people who are intolerant to gluten, this protein does a lot of damage.

The medical community has known about celiac disease for a long time. In 1887, a pediatrician described this condition in London. The link with wheat was made in the 1950s by a Dutch pediatrician. More recent research discovered diagnostic mechanisms and a more complete understanding of this condition. In the past ten years, interest in gluten-free baking has skyrocketed. Hundreds of blogs, books, and articles are devoted to the topic, along with some scientific research. And great strides have been made in making light and fluffy gluten-free baked goods.

In this book you discover the scientific reasons for eating gluten-free and ways to bake yummy gluten-free cakes, cookies, breads, and more. We break down the science so it's easy to understand. And we give you many options so you can bake to your (gluten-free) heart's content.

About This Book

The gluten-free lifestyle is unique in that a complex disease can be treated (though not cured) with a special diet. People who must avoid gluten have to be very vigilant in what they eat and how they cook and bake. Baking, of course, is most problematic because gluten, the protein in wheat that provides structure to baked goods, must be avoided. Dedicated bakers have made great strides in this area over the past decade.

This book is arranged in a practical format. First, we look at the basics of gluten-free living and how to adapt to this new lifestyle. We tell you why people eat gluten-free, list the symptoms of gluten intolerance and celiac disease, and tell you a bit about testing options.

Then we delve into baking, first looking at the science of baking with wheat, including how to measure ingredients, mix batters and doughs, bake in a properly calibrated oven, and interpret doneness tests. After you have a pretty good understanding of baking science, we discuss the unique issues of gluten-free baking, including special tips and rules, tools of the trade, and how to handle issues with different types of baked goods.

Next we discuss the flours and starches you use in your gluten-free baking adventure. We list most of the popular flours, starches, and additives, with their protein and fiber content and unique characteristics. Then we look at the structure of dough and why it's been so difficult to get to an airy, mouth-watering loaf of bread with a tender texture.

Nutrition, of course, can't be omitted in any discussion about food. We help you understand what gluten intolerance may have done to your body and how to get yourself back into good health. Casein and lactose are other compounds many celiac patients must avoid; we tell you what they are, where to find them, and some good ideas for workable substitutes.

Next, we tell you how to make your kitchen and your home gluten-free and where to buy the products you need. And we show you how to convert your favorite wheat recipes into delectable gluten-free treats.

Finally, this book has recipes! These recipes will see you through your day from morning to night, with baking mixes, breakfast foods, sweet yeast breads, quick breads, savory yeast breads, brownies, cookies, pies, cakes, doughs, biscuits, pizzas, calzones, and casseroles.

The great thing about *Gluten-Free Baking For Dummies* is that it's so versatile. You can pick and choose the information you need to read and follow our tips for adapting to this new lifestyle. After you start seeing the very real physical changes that accompany eating gluten-free, you can stay on it for life.

Conventions Used in This Book

Like with all cookbooks, we recommend that you read through each recipe before you start making it. If you jump right in, you may not account for the refrigerating time, standing time, or freezing time in your schedule (and, as a result, your recipe may not be ready to eat when you are!). Reading the recipe's directions beforehand also clues you in to any special tools or materials, like food processors or piping bags, you may need to complete that particular recipe.

Here are a few other guidelines to keep in mind about the recipes in this book:

✔ All butter is unsalted. Margarine isn't a suitable substitute for butter unless we state you can use either one.

✔ Unless otherwise noted, all eggs are large.

✔ All milk is organic whole milk unless otherwise specified.

✔ When the recipe ingredients say "sugar" or "granulated sugar" (as opposed to brown sugar or powdered sugar), we use organic cane sugar.

✔ All measurements for flour and flour mixes are given in cups as well as grams. Because precision for flour measuring counts in baking, especially gluten-free baking, *using gram weights gives you the best results.*

✔ All onions are yellow unless otherwise specified.

✔ All salt is sea salt or fine salt.

✔ All pepper is freshly ground black pepper unless otherwise specified.

✔ All dry ingredient measurements are level, but the flours and starches are measured by gram weight.

✔ All temperatures are Fahrenheit.

✔ All lemon and lime juice is freshly squeezed.

✔ All vanilla is vanilla extract unless otherwise defined.

✔ Most pans and baking sheets are prepared by greasing with unsalted butter, solid shortening, or nonstick cooking spray to prevent sticking. We include this information in the recipe directions but not in the recipe ingredients.

The following conventions are used throughout the text to make things consistent and easy to understand:

✔ All web addresses appear in `monofont`.

✔ New terms appear in *italic* and are closely followed by an easy-to-understand definition.

✔ **Bold** is used to highlight keywords in bulleted lists and the action parts of numbered steps.

We include information gleaned from Dr. Layton's practice and years of experience throughout the text. And in the last three chapters, we give you tips on how to bake the best gluten-free products, how to help your child adjust to a gluten-free lifestyle, and some sneaky places gluten can hide.

What You're Not to Read

We've arranged this book so you can find information easily and understand what you find. Each chapter covers one area of gluten-free baking and baking science. But if you don't want to read every word, you can skip the text that's set off from the main information; it's interesting and relevant but stuff you can live without:

✔ **Text in sidebars:** Sidebars are the shaded boxes that give detailed examples or add interesting information that helps enhance your understanding of gluten-free baking.

✔ **Every paragraph:** You don't need to read every paragraph of this book to understand the eating clean lifestyle.

Foolish Assumptions

The following are some things we've assumed about you since you're reading this book:

✔ You've been diagnosed with celiac disease or gluten sensitivity or intolerance, and you don't want to give up bread, pizza, cookies, cakes, and pies.

✔ A family member has been diagnosed with celiac disease or a condition on the gluten intolerance spectrum, and you're in charge of cooking and baking in your house.

✔ You've heard about the wheat-free or gluten-free lifestyle and want to know whether it's a good plan for you.

✔ You want to know more about how food and the body interact. We've tried to avoid using much scientific jargon in this book so anyone can understand it. An interest in the topic is all you really need to find out more.

How This Book Is Organized

This book is divided into five parts. Each part deals with a certain aspect of transforming your life through the gluten-free plan and discusses the relevant issues related to gluten-free baking, including structure, taste, mixing and baking methods, dough science, nutrition, conversion of your own recipes, and lots and lots of scrumptious recipes specifically developed to be gluten-free.

You don't have to read straight through the book; you can pick a chapter of interest and read it to discover all you need to know about that issue.

Part 1: What Is Gluten-Free Baking?

So what is gluten and why is it such a problem for so many people? Avoiding gluten is the only way to control conditions such as celiac disease and gluten intolerance. Because gluten is the plant protein molecule that forms a solid web when mixed with water, you have to find ways to mimic its structure and texture. Before you begin in the kitchen, you should know a little bit about the science of baking. Don't be scared; this isn't rocket science! We tell you how ingredients work in baked goods and then discuss some of the issues of gluten-free baking. We tell you all about the ingredients you need and techniques to use so you can produce wonderful loaves of gluten-free bread, along with cakes, cookies, pies, pizza, calzones, soufflés, casseroles, and pastries.

Part II: The Nuts and Bolts of Gluten-Free Baking

Many of you will begin (or have begun) your gluten-free path for medical reasons. Perhaps you've been diagnosed with celiac disease or gluten intolerance. Or maybe you've heard that wheat and gluten can negatively affect your health and that what you eat has a direct impact on how you feel and you want to eat for more energy and physical fitness. We tell you how to get your health back on track through nutrition, how to keep a gluten-free kitchen, and how to convert old family favorite recipes to the gluten-free lifestyle.

Part III: Sweet Gluten-Free Baking Recipes

Now we get to the recipes. When gluten-intolerant people hear they can't eat wheat, all the treats that are off-limits come to mind. What about pancakes and waffles? Can I ever eat banana bread again? What about chocolate chip cookies, pizza, and apple pie? Well, take heart. With these recipes you can eat all those foods again, and more. This section has recipes for sweet baked goods, including Sour Cream Blueberry Crumb Muffins, Cinnamon Rolls, Thin Mint Cookies, Chocolate Chip Cookies, Butterscotch Brownies, Vanilla Cupcakes, and Pecan Pie.

Part IV: Savory Gluten-Free Baking Recipes

This part focuses on savory baked goods. If you're craving a savory pizza with a crisp yet tender crust, this is the part for you. If you want to toast some English muffins and fill their crevices with melting butter and jam, you'll find a recipe for them here. Then we get into recipes for crepes, pot pies, quiches, casseroles, and soufflés. There's really no food that you can't adapt to gluten-free baking! Try Ham and Cheese Muffins, Sourdough Bread, Pepperoni Pizza, Vegetable Cheese Calzone, Classic Chicken and Dumplings, and Soft Egg Bread.

Part V: The Part of Tens

Finally, we look at some ways to help you make the transition to your gluten-free diet as easy as possible and how to keep it up for life. We start with ten important gluten-free baking tips and end with ten (or so) sneaky places gluten can hide.

Icons Used in This Book

To make this book easier to read and simpler to use, we include some icons that can help you find and fathom key ideas and information.

Whenever you see this icon, you know that the information that follows is so important that it's worth reading twice. Or three times!

This icon appears whenever an idea or information can help you in your quest for better health or in your progress in the eating clean lifestyle.

This icon highlights information that's important and that can be dangerous to you if you don't heed it.

Where to Go from Here

This book is organized so that you can go wherever you want to find complete information. Want to know more about cleaning your kitchen to make it free from gluten? Check out Chapter 8. Do you need to know how to convert Grandma's recipe for Snickerdoodles into a gluten-free treat? Flip to Chapter 9. And if you want recipes, Chapters 10 through 21 give you lots of choices for treats, meals, and snacks. You can also use the table of contents to find broad categories of subjects or use the index to look up specific information. If you're not sure where to start, read Part I. It gives you all the basic information you need to understand the gluten-free lifestyle and tells you where to get the details.

Part I
What Is Gluten-
Free Baking?

The 5th Wave   By Rich Tennant

RICHTENNANT

"See? Living gluten-free isn't that hard. Now,
let's try living goatee-free."

In this part . . .

Gluten-free living boils down to one simple fact: You must avoid gluten for the rest of your life. But why? What is gluten, and what foods have it? How do you read a label to determine whether the product contains gluten? And how can you possibly change your whole life to accommodate your condition? In this part, we look at the basics of gluten and why you should eat gluten-free, and we tell you a bit about the rules of baking. We also examine the issues and problems of gluten-free baking and tell you how to build baked goods with wonderful flavor and structure — and without gluten.

Chapter 1

The Challenges and Rewards of Gluten-Free Baking

In This Chapter
▶ Understanding the basics about gluten
▶ Taking steps to remain gluten-free
▶ Embracing the gluten-free lifestyle

Gluten has been in the news a lot recently. Many celebrities are choosing a wheat-free and gluten-free life. And gluten-free bakers and bloggers are becoming famous. But what is gluten? Where is it found? Why do some people choose to avoid it, and why do others have to avoid it?

Gluten is a protein molecule found in wheat and other grains such as rye, barley, spelt, and triticale. This particular molecule affects certain people with a condition called *celiac disease* as well as other conditions that range from *gluten sensitivity* to *gluten intolerance.* (Gluten intolerance is also called *nonceliac gluten sensitivity.*)

The gluten protein causes an *autoimmune reaction* in gluten-responsive people. Your body perceives the gluten molecule as some type of alien space invader and attacks the molecule with everything in its extensive arsenal. This reaction causes all sorts of unpleasant side effects that range from digestive problems to skin rashes to malnutrition to more serious diseases and ailments such as cancer, chronic fatigue, diabetes, migraines, thyroid problems, ulcers, seizures, depression, and osteoporosis.

But unlike most other conditions that hurt your body, you have only one way to treat celiac disease and gluten intolerance: avoid gluten. Period. Avoid gluten and your life will change: Your energy will return, you won't have digestive problems, and you won't feel sick or bloated or have skin rashes and dental problems. All from just eliminating a tiny protein molecule from your life! That's the good news.

Sounds simple, doesn't it? Well, yes and no. And that's the bad news. Gluten can hide in the most unlikely places (think lipstick and marshmallows). And giving up foods like pizza, brownies, cookies, cakes, pies, and soufflés — foods that make life worth living! — is no fun.

So for the best news of all: You don't have to give up those foods! This book contains recipes for all those formerly wheat-based goodies. And they're easy to make and delicious. In fact, you may actually feel sorry for your friends who still depend on wheat.

The Basics of Gluten-Free Baking

Baked goods evolved around wheat. The agricultural revolution allowed for the spread of civilization. No longer did people have to spend 90 percent of their time hunting and gathering food. Huge farms could grow all the food so others could devote their time and energy to writing books, building cities, and inventing.

No doubt some intrepid bakers in the 17th and 18th centuries tried to make baked goods without wheat. And they most likely failed because baking without wheat is tricky. In this section we tell you all about the gluten molecule and what foods contain it. We also talk about ways to bake scrumptious and nutritious foods without that pesky molecule.

What is gluten, and where does it lurk?

Gluten is a molecule unique to certain plants. It consists of two smaller proteins called *glutenin* and *gliadin*. When mixed with water, these two proteins combine to form gluten. Gluten is a stretchy substance that holds carbon dioxide in baked goods and gives these goods their texture and structure. For more about the ins and outs of gluten, see Chapters 2, 5, and 6.

Gluten is found in these products:

- Barley
- Bulgur
- Durum
- Einkorn (a wild wheat species)
- Hand lotion
- Kamut (an ancient relative of wheat)
- Paste glue
- Play-Doh
- Prescription medicines

✔ Rye

✔ Semolina

✔ Spelt (an ancient species of wheat)

✔ Triticale (a hybrid of wheat and rye)

✔ Wheat

✔ Wheat pasta

Wait a minute! Hand lotion, Play-Doh, and prescription medications? What's going on here? Well, although the grains in this list naturally contain gluten, the gluten protein molecule can easily be removed from those grains and used in other products. In fact, gluten is used in many consumer goods as well as foods. This perniciousness is why those on the gluten intolerance spectrum (those with celiac disease, people who are gluten intolerant, and those who are sensitive to gluten) have to be so careful about reading labels, what they buy, what they eat, and how they live their lives. Gluten sneaks into lots of products.

And then there's the issue of cross-contamination. Oats don't contain gluten, but if they're grown in a field next to a wheat field or processed in the same plant that processes wheat into flour, gluten can sneak into oatmeal and oat flour. If a bakery makes wheat bread and then makes gluten-free breads, the mixer, pans, spoons, cutting boards, rolling pins, measuring cups, and knives can carry gluten molecules into the (supposedly) gluten-free bread.

The world is gradually becoming more accepting of the need for gluten-free products. Many companies are converting their factories to be gluten-free, dedicating mills and bakeries to keep them free of gluten and gluten products, and searching out gluten certification for their products. But there's still a long way to go. And the best way to keep gluten out of your life and your body is to bake and cook at home.

Why gluten and baking used to be inseparable

Have you ever tried to make a loaf of bread with cornstarch? If you have, you know what I'm going to say next. If you haven't, here's what you end up with: a dense brick with no texture and no flavor. That's because cornstarch has no gluten.

A lot of other flours lack gluten, too, and that's why wheat and baked goods used to go hand in hand. Gluten is the only protein that forms a stretchy web strong enough to trap and hold air and tender enough to produce a light and airy crumb. These characteristics are unique to the gluten molecule.

But take heart! Notice the phrase "used to." Intrepid and creative bakers have been working on making perfect gluten-free baked goods for years. They've tried every flour, starch, and attitude known to man. And they've succeeded! Chewy and soft sourdough bread, crisp and airy popovers, light sandwich bread with a crisp crust, dense and delectable whole-grain breads, perfect chocolate chip cookies, and flaky and light pie crusts are all now available in gluten-free form. For more about these success stories, see the recipe chapters in this book.

How you can bake without gluten

So what's the secret? Through lots of trial and error, a few successes, and many more failures, gluten-free bakers have learned that combining flours and adding special ingredients to some recipes can make gluten-free baked goods that are very similar to wheat baked goods.

Here are the breakthroughs in gluten-free baking over the last decade:

- ✔ Additives were the secret to better gluten-free baked goods until the last few years. Xanthan gum and guar gum, in particular, were used in almost every gluten-free baking recipe.

  But then some people started noticing that those gums led to physical reactions such as bloating, gas, and diarrhea. Turns out that some people are sensitive to those gums. And those products, especially xanthan gum, are very expensive and can be difficult to find.

- ✔ At first, many bakers tried to make their doughs look and act like wheat-based doughs. They wanted dough they could knead and shape by hand. But gluten-free flours simply don't behave like wheat flours in any way. They're denser, so they need a smidge more liquid, and they absorb that liquid more slowly than wheat flour. Successful gluten-free doughs are more like thick cake batters. And you don't knead most of them.

- ✔ The final breakthrough was the notion of using a combination of flours and starches. This technique seems to work best because all the gluten-free flours have different protein and starch amounts — and different proteins and starches! These compounds work together to give doughs and batters, and the resulting baked goods, a structure similar to wheat baked goods.

This evolution took place over time, but ever since the secrets were revealed (mainly on the Internet), the popularity of gluten-free baked goods has exploded. Bloggers share tricks and recipes, and as more and more people jump on the bandwagon, gluten-free baking will only get better over time.

One interesting fact is that there hasn't been a lot of scientific research into the molecular structure of gluten-free baked goods or how gluten-free flour proteins work together in batters and doughs. This will change as the scientific community catches on to the fact that gluten-free baking isn't going away. So stay tuned!

What Gluten-Free Means

Removing gluten from your life doesn't just mean that you don't eat foods made with wheat, barley, or rye. Gluten has found its way into many man-made products. And even if gluten hasn't been deliberately added to a product or food, it can find its way into your life through cross-contamination.

In this section we explain how those on the gluten intolerance spectrum can be as gluten-free as possible. Reading labels, decoding safe foods, and identifying forbidden and questionable foods are key to staying healthy and feeling good.

Reading labels

Labels are the holy grail for those who must avoid gluten. Fortunately, manufacturers of all kinds are starting to come around to the fact that those on the gluten intolerance spectrum are demanding transparency in product labeling.

To see a list of terms indicating that gluten may be in a product, see Chapter 8. You can also do some research online. Dr. Jean's website, www.gfdoctor recipes.com/2011/08/gluten-free.html, has a complete list of the terms and fancy names gluten can hide behind. She updates the list quarterly to reflect current understanding of gluten-free products.

You can also turn to organizations dedicated to the gluten-free lifestyle for more help. The Gluten Intolerance Group is a nonprofit organization that inspects products for gluten and gluten only. This company verifies manufacturers' claims that a product is gluten-free. The group isn't a government organization, and the certification is voluntary. But until the government manages to set the standards, go to www.gluten.net for more information.

So labels are the gluten-intolerant person's best friend. But the thing about labels is that they can change. Manufacturers change products all the time, without warning. And they should note those changes on the label. So every time you buy a product with a label, you must read that label to make sure it's still gluten-free and safe for you to eat. If you have any doubts or questions about an ingredient on a label, call the manufacturer to check.

What's on a label

The eight main food allergens, as classified by doctors, are wheat, milk, eggs, tree nuts, peanuts, fish, shellfish, and soy. These foods were chosen because they cause 90 percent of all food allergies. Government rules state that manufacturers must label foods containing these ingredients with a clear warning. The problem is, gluten isn't one of these eight allergens.

If a product is made of wheat, the label must say so. That's a plus for those who must avoid gluten. But gluten itself isn't considered an allergen. In fact, celiac disease isn't an allergy! So until things change at the government level, you're pretty much on your own when it comes to ferreting out gluten. That may change in the next few years, as gluten is on the radar of more and more people.

For more about gluten-free products, reading labels, and specific terms and words to look for on ingredient lists and product labels, see Chapter 8.

Finding safe foods

Fortunately, you can find a lot of safe, gluten-free foods on the market. Good sources for these foods, especially the more unusual ones, are health food stores and the Internet. If you can't find xanthan gum at your local grocery store, you can order it from Amazon.com, along with light bulbs and diamonds!

After your house is a safe zone (see Chapter 8 for more information about this task), you'll want to venture out into the world. Eating at food trucks, fast food joints, and fancy restaurants are some of the joys of life. And eating at a friend's house ranks right up there! But if you must avoid gluten, those joys contain pitfalls.

To stay healthy, you must become something of a detective. Question waiters, ask to speak to the chef, demand labels from places that serve food, and ask about possible cross-contamination. Don't be shy about asking questions; this is your health we're talking about. Being polite is certainly necessary, but don't let anyone tell you that his food is "perfectly fine" unless you're sure he understands the possible ramifications of being wrong. Be polite yet firm. After all, you have to live with the consequences of what you eat.

You must be an advocate for yourself and your family. And you can do some proactive things to make eating out and traveling safer. These websites offer guides to safe restaurants and grocery stores in the United States and around the world:

✔ The Gluten-Free Restaurant Awareness Program (www.glutenfree restaurants.org) lists safe gluten-free restaurants by state. This guide is especially helpful when you're traveling.

✔ The Gluten-Free Registry (www.glutenfreeregistry.com) lists gluten-free restaurants, grocers, bakeries, and caterers by state.

✔ Celiac Travel has printable gluten-free restaurant cards (www.celiac travel.com/cards) you can carry with you when you travel. Available in 51 languages, these cards detail what you can and can't eat. Print them out and take them with you on your trip to increase your odds of avoiding gluten wherever you are.

✔ The Gluten-Free Travel Site (www.glutenfreetravelsite.com) has reviews of gluten-free restaurants, along with hotels, resorts, and cruise ships.

✔ For the smart phone set, www.urbanspoon.com has a helpful gluten-free application.

Armed with this information, you can relax and enjoy your adventures outside your safe, gluten-free home. After all, life is meant to be lived as an adventure! But a gluten-free lifestyle does have some complications. Turn to Chapter 24 to discover some sneaky places that gluten can hide, and flip to Chapter 8 to find out what foods you can keep in your kitchen and what foods you should toss.

Just remember to stay on your toes. Although you'll relax as you become more accustomed to sniffing out gluten, you can never completely let your guard down. Keep reading labels and stay informed about progress in gluten-free cooking and baking. Lobby your legislators for more labeling laws. And write to manufacturers and request gluten-free foods, gluten-free certification, and more dedicated mills and manufacturers. The number of gluten-free people is growing. Make your voice heard!

Getting Excited about the Gluten-Free Lifestyle

Many people don't understand how anyone could get excited about having to forgo an entire class of food. Won't you feel deprived? Won't you feel singled out?

Well, feeling sorry for yourself is easy when you have to give up gluten forever. But you can look at it another way: Eliminating gluten from your life means you'll regain your health and energy. And nothing's more important than that. Changing your diet and the way you cook seems like a small price to pay for increased vitality and the ability to enjoy life again!

In this section we tell you how to boost your spirits about living gluten-free and how to help your gluten-free child navigate the big world. We also help you set realistic expectations and give you tips to make living the gluten-free life simply wonderful.

Gluten-free doesn't mean flavor-free

Admittedly, the first forays into gluten-free baking weren't promising. Gluten-free bakers were really trying to replicate the look, taste, texture, and flavor of wheat breads. And that's pretty impossible.

So instead of focusing on what gluten-free baked goods aren't, focus on what they *are!* The flavors of rice flour, sorghum flour, buckwheat flour, almond flour, and millet flour are unique. Each one allows you to build a flavor profile that fits your taste buds perfectly. Try that with boring old wheat.

And if you don't love the taste of one gluten-free flour, use another as a substitute. You can find more than a dozen different varieties of gluten-free flour. Just substitute as we tell you in Chapters 5 and 9. As long as you use a combination of flours and use starches and additives such as gums judiciously, you should have success.

Of course, some gluten-free flours are more suited to certain baked goods. The flours with a higher percentage of protein do better in yeast breads and pizza doughs. The flours with a lower percentage of protein do better in cakes, cookies, and soufflés. (See Chapter 5 for a list of alternative gluten-free flours and their protein content.) Just use some common sense and have fun experimenting!

Here are some other tricks for adding more flavor to gluten-free baked goods:

- ✔ Substitute fruit and vegetable purées for some of the liquids in the recipe.
- ✔ Increase the amount of extracts you use (be sure they're gluten-free!). More vanilla or some almond extract can help add lots of flavor.
- ✔ Increase the amount and number of spices you use. If a recipe calls for ½ teaspoon of cinnamon, double it, and then add a bit of nutmeg and cardamom for a more complex flavor.
- ✔ Use brown sugar, especially dark brown sugar, in place of some of the granulated sugar in a recipe. Brown sugar contains molasses, which adds flavor and moistness.

Raising kids to love the lifestyle

Removing wheat and gluten ingredients from a child's diet is probably one of the most challenging things you'll do. When your child learns that she won't be able to share pizza with her best friend at the bowling alley or that cupcakes at the next birthday party are verboten, she'll probably break down in tears.

That's where you come in. Your attitude is crucial to making your celiac child's life better. You must be the gatekeeper. But this is also an incredibly important learning experience. Your child watches everything you do, so adopt a positive attitude and look for the good in a diagnosis on the gluten intolerance spectrum.

Getting your child involved in choosing foods, helping her learn to bake, teaching her which foods she can and can't eat, and then baking special treats she loves (and taking them to that birthday party) are the crucial steps to getting her to love her new lifestyle. Check out Chapter 23 for more tips and tricks.

The most important part of a child living gluten-free is that she can be a child again. Nothing's more painful than watching your child suffer physically and emotionally. The act of giving up gluten, which may seem overwhelming at times, is a small price to pay for better health. When your child hits a home run or wins a swimming competition, she'll know that her gluten-free diet is the reason her body is powerful once more.

Setting realistic expectations

Although many gluten-sensitive people feel better immediately when they eliminate gluten from their diets, you may not be so fortunate. Depending on the severity of your condition and how long you suffered undiagnosed, you may take months to see the true results of a gluten-free diet.

Sure, immediately being able to run a marathon would be wonderful, but be realistic! Your body has to heal itself. Your body is a complex organism, and you may have to consider other variables. You may have developed other allergies or intolerances because of the damage done to your intestinal tract. You may have to eliminate casein and/or lactose from your diet to feel better (see Chapter 7 for information about casein and lactose intolerance).

If your child needs to be gluten-free, be realistic about recovery. If your child is older than 5 or 6, he may never completely catch up on the growth charts because of the damage that's been done. But that doesn't mean he can't live a happy, healthy, and fulfilling life. Stress feeling good. Don't stress about not being 6'3" and a football star.

The point is, healing takes time. Be gentle with yourself during the transition to a gluten-free lifestyle. Eliminate all gluten immediately, of course, but still eat your favorite foods. Don't hide in your house. Go out to restaurants. Travel. Bring gluten-free treats with you to parties and events.

And learn to love life again, because you're going to feel great!

Chapter 2

Why Bake Gluten-Free?

*B*ecause you're reading this book, you're interested in baking without gluten. But why do people want to avoid this protein? Are there reasons other than gluten sensitivity for avoiding gluten? What are the symptoms of gluten sensitivity, gluten intolerance, and celiac disease, and why is gluten such a problem?

In this chapter we look at the basics of the *gluten sensitivity spectrum* (the overarching term for several conditions) and its different manifestations. We also explain why many people who don't have celiac disease or gluten intolerance are avoiding gluten. Getting a diagnosis for one of these conditions can be difficult. We talk about testing options and what happens when someone who should avoid gluten eats it, either deliberately or accidentally.

Avoiding gluten certainly takes practice, especially at first. But with some diligence, a bit of kitchen science knowledge, and a few basic baking skills, you can enjoy delicious baked goods without gluten. And you'll feel much better, too!

Why People Eat Gluten-Free

In the last decade, many people have begun to follow a gluten-free diet. Some must avoid gluten for specific health reasons; others do so because they think gluten consumption aggravates another medical condition such as irritable bowel syndrome, rheumatoid arthritis, or asthma. Still other people avoid gluten simply because they feel better without it.

In this section we discuss the different medical conditions that necessitate a gluten-free diet and the differences among them. We also look at why people may want to avoid gluten even if they don't have a medical condition that demands doing so. Whether you're diagnosed with celiac disease, are gluten intolerant, have nonceliac gluten sensitivity (NCGS), or just want to avoid gluten for general health reasons, you must be vigilant about staying gluten-free for the best health.

Understanding celiac disease

First the good news! If you have celiac disease, you can get rid of symptoms and avoid complications just by eliminating gluten from your life. Your body will begin to heal itself immediately, and your digestive system will soon function well. All the nasty side effects and symptoms will go away, and your future will look rosy.

But the key to all these good outcomes is an early diagnosis. Some people who are diagnosed with celiac disease after years of having the disease never completely recover, although they feel much better on a gluten-free diet. So the motto for this disease is, "early diagnosis, excellent outcome."

Celiac disease is sometimes called *celiac sprue, coeliac disease* (the British spelling), *nontropical sprue, gluten-sensitive enteropathy,* or simply *CD.* Celiac disease isn't an allergy and it isn't a sensitivity to gluten. This disease is an autoimmune condition where your body's immune system literally attacks the gluten molecule. The body treats gluten as an alien invader and sets out to destroy it with antibodies. This reaction happens in the small intestine. Unfortunately, while your antibodies are attacking gluten, they're also attacking the wall of the small intestine, causing extensive damage over time.

Your small intestine has lots of small protrusions or hairlike cells called *villi* that increase its surface area so it can absorb lots of nutrients. When a person has celiac disease, those villi are damaged or blunted (this is called *villous atrophy*), and the body loses its ability to absorb many nutrients. Villous atrophy is a gradual process that occurs over years. The longer a gluten-intolerant person is undiagnosed and continues to eat gluten, the more extensive and severe the damage becomes.

If celiac disease is untreated or if a gluten-sensitive person cheats on his or her diet, the person can develop many more diseases. Diseases of malnutrition, including osteoporosis, can occur, along with cancer, depression, seizures, and ulcers of the small intestine, although it can take decades for these conditions to develop.

Scientists think that 1 in 133 people around the world have this disease, although it's more common among northern European citizens and their descendants. It's a genetic disease, meaning that you inherit it from one of your parents. The only treatment is to completely avoid gluten in your diet. But if you eliminate gluten from your life, the good news is that your symptoms will disappear and you can live a normal life.

Celiac disease has many symptoms, both gastrointestinal (stomach- and intestinal-related) and nongastrointestinal, such as headaches, a skin rash, and general weakness. That's one of the reasons this disease is so difficult to diagnose. Because the symptoms of all three members of the gluten sensitivity spectrum (gluten intolerance, gluten sensitivity, and celiac disease) are so similar, we list them here. These lists aren't complete, but they do highlight the most common symptoms of the gluten sensitivity spectrum.

These are some of the classic gastrointestinal symptoms of celiac disease, as well as gluten intolerance and nonceliac gluten sensitivity:

- Abdominal bloating
- Abdominal pain and cramps
- Bloody stools
- Chronic diarrhea
- Gas and flatulence
- Greasy, smelly stools
- Nausea
- Vomiting
- Weight gain
- Weight loss

The nongastrointestinal symptoms of celiac disease, gluten intolerance, and nonceliac gluten sensitivity include

- Dental problems
- Dermatitis herpetiformis
- Eczema
- Fatigue
- Headaches
- Joint or bone pain

- ✔ Lactose intolerance
- ✔ Respiratory problems
- ✔ Rosacea
- ✔ Seizures
- ✔ Tingly sensation in hands and feet
- ✔ Vitamin and mineral deficiencies
- ✔ Weakness
- ✔ Weight loss

Whew! With lists like these, with such conflicting, sometimes vague, and common symptoms, you can see how a diagnosis of celiac disease can be so hard to come by. Some people go for years with no diagnosis. And in those years, lots of damage can be done to your health.

To make things even more complicated, some people with celiac disease have no symptoms at all but aren't diagnosed until another, more acute disease develops. And things can get fuzzier because people with celiac disease can also suffer from other autoimmune diseases, such as type 1 diabetes, rheumatoid arthritis, and autoimmune thyroid disease.

For information about testing for this disease and how to get an accurate diagnosis, see the section "Exploring Testing Options" later in this chapter.

What's a prolamin?

This is going to be confusing and may sound strange, but using the word *gluten* to describe gluten sensitivity and gluten intolerance is technically incorrect. *Gluten* is the overarching term we use when we talk about these conditions and celiac disease. But gluten isn't the true culprit. The technically correct term for the protein that causes all the trouble is *prolamin,* a type of protein found in different grains. In wheat, the prolamin is gliadin. In rye, it's secalin. In barley, the prolamin is hordein. Corn and rice have prolamins too, but they don't cause an autoimmune response. These proteins in wheat, rye, and barley have two specific amino acids, called *glutamine* and *proline,* that scientists think cause the autoimmune reaction.

Because the term *gluten* is so strongly identified with these conditions and because it's so widely used, that's the term we use in this book. But if you're ever at a party discussing trivia, you can become the center of attention by telling people about this little quirk in the gluten-free world!

Living with gluten intolerance

Some specialists estimate that as many as one in three people around the world may have gluten intolerance. Because many of these people have mild symptoms or no symptoms at all, they're never diagnosed with a gluten intolerance or sensitivity.

The symptoms for gluten intolerance are generally the same as for celiac disease. Even though the treatment for gluten intolerance is the same as for celiac disease, these two conditions aren't the same. Gluten intolerance isn't an *autoimmune disease;* in other words, you don't have an antibody reaction when you ingest gluten. Gluten intolerance doesn't result in small intestine damage and poses no risk for the serious complications that can occur with celiac disease.

Gluten intolerance is often used as a broad term that includes celiac disease and nonceliac gluten sensitivity. Technically, though, gluten intolerance is simply a nonautoimmune and nonallergenic condition that creates uncomfortable symptoms when the person consumes gluten. People with gluten intolerance can still feel miserable. And, as you saw in the preceding section, all these conditions share many of the same symptoms.

If you have these symptoms, visit your doctor. If you take a blood test for celiac disease and it comes back negative, don't assume you can continue to eat gluten. Many people who test negative for celiac disease yet still experience these symptoms when eating gluten-containing foods may be gluten intolerant. An elimination diet may be your best bet for a diagnosis; more about that later in this chapter.

Some people have what's called *subclinical gluten intolerance.* That means that they experience no symptoms or the symptoms are so mild that they're just dismissed as the "24 hour flu" (even though the flu lasts for years) or as mild food poisoning. But the damage is being done, even though symptoms aren't alarming enough to seek medical attention. Some doctors and specialists think that the vast majority of people in the world have subclinical gluten intolerance and that most people should avoid gluten as a matter of public health.

If you feel better when you don't eat gluten, then just avoid it. You don't have to be as scrupulous about eliminating gluten from your life as someone who has celiac disease or NCGS, but the choice is yours. Though eliminating gluten isn't easy, doing so becomes easier with practice. And wouldn't you rather feel better with a little more effort?

What about wheat allergies?

Wheat is one of the eight most common allergens. Celiac disease, gluten intolerance, and nonceliac gluten sensitivity aren't the same as a wheat allergy. People who are allergic to wheat have a different immune response, called an *IgE mediated response,* to the proteins in wheat. Gluten isn't the only protein in wheat. Symptoms of wheat allergies are typical of other allergy symptoms, including swelling, itching, hives, nasal congestion, cramps, vomiting, diarrhea, difficulty breathing,

and, in severe cases, anaphylaxis. People who are allergic to wheat can still eat rye, oats, and barley, although cross-contamination can be a problem.

And an allergy can sometimes resolve itself all on its own, but sensitivity to gluten is a lifelong condition. Many people outgrow food allergies, and food allergies can suddenly develop at any time throughout life. A person with celiac disease is born with that condition and never outgrows it.

Dealing with nonceliac gluten sensitivity

The third type of gluten problem, nonceliac gluten sensitivity, may be much more common than first believed. In fact, some studies indicate that one in seven people worldwide may have NCGS. This condition can be very difficult to diagnose. Many people with NCGS have negative blood test results so they don't have an intestinal biopsy. But that doesn't mean they don't have a problem.

A lot of overlap exists between these three classes of gluten problems, so you can see why a definitive diagnosis is difficult. But a diagnosis is important, simply because the sooner you start avoiding gluten, the sooner your body can start to heal. And you'll prevent some very serious medical conditions that can develop after years of your body reacting to gluten.

Like celiac disease, nonceliac gluten sensitivity is an autoimmune disorder, in which antibodies attack the wall of the small intestine when you eat gluten. But the atrophy of the villi in the small intestine isn't apparent in those with nonceliac gluten sensitivity, so they can't be diagnosed with celiac disease.

The antibodies that your body produces in reaction to gluten may be produced only in the small intestine and don't show up in the bloodstream. (Your intestine is actually part of your immune system, so this is certainly possible.) If that's the case, a blood test won't show the presence of these antibodies even though your body is making them.

Doctors think that in patients with nonceliac gluten sensitivity, the damage occurs in the overall functioning of the intestine and other tissues and organs in the body. Some doctors who specialize in gluten sensitivity and celiac disease also believe that only people who've been suffering from gluten sensitivity for a long time actually have positive test results; this means that a lot of damage has been done by the time the patient is diagnosed.

An incorrect diagnosis can have serious consequences. If someone has NCGS but isn't diagnosed, continuing to eat gluten-containing foods can lead to some irreversible conditions, including diabetes, osteoporosis, brain impairment, cancer, inflammatory bowel disease, and skin diseases.

Here's the short answer about nonceliac gluten sensitivity: If your tests for celiac disease are negative and other diseases have been ruled out but you're still experiencing the aforementioned symptoms, try an elimination diet. If you feel better when you eliminate gluten from your diet (and we mean a complete elimination), then you probably have nonceliac gluten sensitivity.

The longer people who are sensitive to gluten eat gluten, the more damage occurs. And the longer this goes on, the more likely the damage will be permanent. The sooner you can eliminate gluten from your diet, if it's the cause of your distress, the better you'll feel and the less damage your body will suffer.

Unraveling symptoms in kids

Diagnosing one of the gluten sensitivity spectrum conditions in children can be difficult. But the earlier the disease is diagnosed, the better the chance for a long and healthy life.

Adults and children usually have different symptoms of this disease. Gastrointestinal symptoms are more common in children. Children can have very specific symptoms of celiac disease, gluten intolerance, and nonceliac gluten sensitivity, including

- ADD/ADHD
- Autism
- Behavioral problems
- Canker sores
- Delayed growth
- Delayed puberty
- Dental caries or soft teeth
- Failure to thrive
- Nosebleeds
- Short stature
- Weight loss

Dermatitis herpetiformis

This complicated name that's difficult to pronounce is one of the signatures of gluten sensitivity. (This rash isn't related to the herpes virus, despite the name similarity.) Your skin and the lining of the intestine have very similar cells, which is why this condition so often affects celiac patients: Antibodies are attacking these kinds of cells. Dermatitis herpetiformis, or DH, is an itchy rash that also forms small blisters. If you develop this skin condition, you almost certainly have celiac disease. The rash usually develops on the knees, elbows, and buttocks, and less commonly on the face, scalp, shoulders, and back. If you develop this rash, your doctor should test your blood for the presence of tissue transglutaminase antibody. If the test is positive, get a skin biopsy for a definitive diagnosis.

Symptoms of celiac disease, gluten intolerance, and nonceliac gluten sensitivity can occur any time during the life span. But when infants or children show symptoms, an accurate diagnosis is crucial. Failure to thrive, delayed growth, and weight loss have lifelong consequences, even after gluten is eliminated from the diet.

To minimize the risk of developing any of these conditions, don't introduce gluten to your child until he or she is six months old. Between six and seven months of age, gluten introduction has a lower chance of triggering one of these conditions. That is, of course, if you decide to introduce gluten at all. If celiac disease is present in your family, you may want to avoid gluten in your child's diet altogether.

If your child is older and has learned about all the different foods in the world, including pizza and doughnuts, your task of eliminating gluten is more difficult. That's where this book comes in handy. Jean's daughters have celiac disease, and they actually feel sorry for other kids who have to eat "ordinary" Girl Scout cookies and pizza! Stressing how much better homemade baked goods are can be a crucial way to make your child feel special instead of picked on. Keep a positive attitude, involve your child in baking (it's a life skill everyone should learn), and you can start him or her on the road to a healthy life. (Chapter 23 has ideas on how to boost your gluten-free child's spirits.)

When a child is diagnosed with one of these conditions, you have to decide whether to turn the whole family into a gluten-free group or let some family members eat gluten. Turn to Chapter 8 for more information about transitioning to a gluten-free kitchen and sharing space with gluten eaters.

What about autism?

Some people in the autism community think that gluten may be the culprit in this devastating condition. Many food allergies and sensitivities are associated with autism, which is classified as a developmental disability. The medical community is conflicted over whether a link exists between the gluten sensitivity spectrum and autism.

One study, in the medical journal *Pediatrics*, found that mothers with celiac disease are more than three times as likely to have an autistic child. A study at the University of Alberta, Canada, found that the malabsorption of nutrients common in celiac patients may be a trigger for autistic behaviors. Malnutrition, from any cause, can lead to nervous system dysfunction.

If a child has symptoms that mimic or overlap with gluten sensitivity spectrum symptoms, medical tests for celiac disease may be in order. Failure to thrive, dental problems (including tooth growth issues), and short stature may indicate a need for these tests. And if an autistic child has relatives with celiac disease, tests are definitely in order. But before you place your child on a gluten-free diet, consider having him or her tested for gluten sensitivity. The presence of gluten in the body is necessary for accurate test results, and a false negative test result can be discouraging and harmful in the long run.

Should You Be Gluten-Free?

What if you don't have celiac disease, gluten intolerance, or nonceliac gluten sensitivity? Should you be avoiding gluten too? These questions have several answers. Many people believe that gluten isn't good for the human body, period.

In this section we address the problems gluten and wheat can cause in the human body in the absence of the gluten sensitivity spectrum. We also examine the link between gluten and behavioral problems and gluten's role (or lack thereof) in nutrition.

Wheat is not your friend

The human body didn't evolve to eat grains. Our hunter-gatherer ancestors ate meat, nuts, vegetables, fruits, and berries. In fact, eating wheat and other grains didn't become common until 4,000 B.C. And wheat wasn't developed into its present form by selective breeding until the beginning of the 20th century.

Brownies made from the Brownie Mix recipe in Chapter 10; Butterscotch Brownies from Chapter 14.

Chocolate Chip Cookies along with cookie sandwiches made with Vegan Cookie Filling (both from Chapter 13); in the background, Cookie Mix without Gums (Chapter 10)

Madeleines from Chapter 13 and Rugelach from Chapter 15.

Clementine Cake (Chapter 16) and a Galette Pie Crust filled with fruit (Chapter 17)

Herbed Cream Biscuits from Chapter 18 and dumplings in chicken broth from the Dumpling Batter recipe in Chapter 1.

The bottom line is that if you feel better without gluten in your life, eliminate it. Gluten isn't necessary for good health, and wheat doesn't provide essential nutrients.

Gluten and behavior problems

Gluten has been accused of causing many health problems, and behavior issues are one of the latest hot-button causes. Many people think that gluten may cause everything from attention deficit disorder (ADD) to autism to "fuzzy brain," which manifests as difficulty thinking clearly and concentrating.

Because gluten causes nutrient deficiencies, it may have a direct effect on the brain and therefore on mood and behavior. After all, your brain depends on everything in your body working in good harmony. Even slight vitamin and mineral deficiencies can cause problems in brain development, brain function, and behavior. Celiac disease, especially, is *multisystemic,* meaning that it affects every part of the body, including the brain and central nervous system.

These behavior problems may be associated with gluten consumption:

- ✔ **ADD/ADHD:** Quite a few studies have found improvement in ADD and ADHD symptoms when patients have eliminated gluten. Celiac disease is positively associated with disruptive behavior disorders, according to a study published in 2006 in the *Journal of Attention Disorders.*

- ✔ **Anxiety and panic attacks:** Many patients report that their anxiety and crippling panic attacks subside or completely disappear when they go on a gluten-free diet. Serotonin, the chemical in your brain that calms mood, is produced in the intestines. So if your intestines are damaged, your brain is probably deficient in this critical chemical.

- ✔ **Autism spectrum:** Some people on the gluten sensitivity spectrum literally turn gluten into a drug; in other words, they literally get "high" from eating gluten-containing foods. Eliminating gluten can improve autistic behaviors, and some people have completely recovered when they eliminate gluten from their lives. In some people, a gluten-free and casein-free diet (GFCF) can produce dramatic results. (See Chapter 7 for info on casein.)

- ✔ **Depression:** If the gluten sensitivity spectrum doesn't actually cause depression or other mood disorders, it can certainly exacerbate them. Gluten's inflammatory tendencies can initiate depression, which is a brain disorder. Depression is more common in people with celiac disease than in the general population.

- ✔ **Fuzzy thinking:** While this isn't a technical medical term, many people who are on the gluten sensitivity spectrum report feeling "foggy" or "fuzzy" and find it hard to concentrate. These symptoms improve when the patient embarks on a gluten-free diet.

✔ **Sleep disorders:** Many patients with celiac disease suffer from sleep disorders before diagnosis. In fact, even after following a gluten-free diet, some people continue to suffer from sleep problems. A study published in *Alimentary Pharmacology and Therapeutics* in 2010 found that gluten-intolerant people, even after eliminating gluten, scored higher on the Pittsburgh Sleep Quality Index (PSQI) scale.

Gluten and nutrition

Gluten, and wheat for that matter, isn't necessary for a balanced diet. In fact, wheat, barley, rye, and oats contain no nutrients that you can't get in other foods. So eliminating gluten from your diet isn't going to demand that you scrutinize the rest of your diet for nutrients or take special vitamins or minerals.

Many people who are sensitive to gluten are also sensitive to *casein,* the protein in milk products. If you find that your health improves avoiding gluten but you still don't feel completely better, you may want to eliminate casein from your diet, too. (See Chapter 7 for more on casein.)

You can find many vegan alternatives to dairy products, such as vegan cream cheese, rice milk, almond milk, and soymilk, that are delicious and easy to find in regular grocery stores.

People who are on the gluten sensitivity spectrum are often allergic to or sensitive to other foods, such as *lactose,* the sugar found in milk. In fact, lactase, the enzyme that lets your body digest lactose, is produced at the tips of the villi in your small intestine. As the villi are damaged and flattened, your body loses its ability to produce this enzyme. (See Chapter 7 for info on lactose.)

Following a gluten-free diet means that you can continue to eat a good variety of whole foods, which is the key to good health in the first place. Avoiding gluten-containing foods with the help of the recipes in this book means that you don't have to feel deprived, you can continue to eat the types of foods you love (although they'll be modified), and you can eat nutritious, delicious foods like everyone else. For more information about gluten and nutrition, turn to Chapter 9.

Exploring Testing Options

Many different tests and series of tests check for gluten intolerance, celiac disease, and nonceliac gluten sensitivity. In fact, an entire book can be written on those tests!

In this section we look at the different types of medical tests to diagnose celiac disease, gluten intolerance, and nonceliac gluten sensitivity. Blood tests, biopsies, stool tests, and other tests are all available to help pinpoint the exact problem.

But sometimes these tests produce false positives and false negatives. Here's the bottom line: If you've been through extensive testing for gluten sensitivity and the tests have come back negative but you feel better avoiding gluten, avoid it. But don't self-diagnose until you've been tested. A clear diagnosis is the best way to go forward in life, if you can get it.

Medical tests for gluten sensitivity spectrum

So how are celiac disease, gluten intolerance, and nonceliac gluten sensitivity (NCGS) diagnosed? If you ask ten people with the disease, you'll probably get ten different answers. Many people are misdiagnosed simply because these symptoms are common to many other diseases and conditions. For instance, inflammatory bowel disease, diverticulitis, chronic fatigue syndrome, and iron-deficiency anemia share the same symptoms with celiac disease.

The gold standard diagnosis method is a combination of blood tests and an intestinal biopsy. When you have celiac disease or NCGS, your body produces antibodies against gliadin, one of the two molecules that make up gluten. This antibody is called *antigliadin IgA*.

The blood test is conducted first, simply because it's less invasive. People with celiac disease have high levels of certain types of antibodies, called *tTGA, IgA, IgG,* and *EMA*.

If a blood test shows the presence of these antibodies, a biopsy, which looks at the condition of the small intestine wall, is performed. The correct way to perform this type of biopsy is by threading an instrument through your mouth down to your small intestine to take at least six to eight samples for examination. A biopsy for celiac disease isn't performed with a colonoscopy; this test can result in false negatives. If the correctly performed biopsy shows intestinal damage, celiac disease is confirmed.

If you get a positive diagnosis, the next step is to remove all gluten from your diet. The symptoms should go away within a few days to a week. You typically get follow-up blood work done six to eight months later, and if you've stayed away from gluten and the test results are normal, then you have absolute confirmation of the disease.

The problem with taking intestinal biopsies is that damage can be patchy or can occur farther down in the small intestine than instruments can reach. Because the small intestine, laid out flat, is the size of a football field, you can understand why it can be easy to miss patchy damage.

One problem many celiac patients have is that their IgA levels are naturally very low. If this is the case, the test for IgA levels may show a "normal" reading. But because the IgA levels are so low to begin with, a "normal" reading actually means elevated levels! For the most accurate test, ask for a *total* IgA profile.

Other tests exist for the gluten sensitivity spectrum. Some naturopathic doctors use a stool analysis to test for celiac disease. An upper GI (gastrointestinal tract) series and bone density tests can show damage caused by a gluten response, but they're not considered diagnostic for celiac disease. Of course, the ultimate test is seeing symptoms disappear when gluten is completely eliminated from the patient's diet.

If your tests are negative but you feel better when eliminating gluten, think about having another test done in a few months. You may be just at the very beginning of celiac disease or NCGS, and your blood may not have enough antibodies or your intestine may not be damaged enough for a positive result.

If a member of your family has celiac disease, consider being tested even if you don't show any symptoms of the disease. Studies show that one in three blood relatives of gluten-intolerant people have the disease. And years of undiagnosed illness, even if symptom-free, can lead to serious medical conditions.

The elimination diet

Most *elimination diets* are used to detect food allergies. The patient is put on a diet of very simple foods, such as fresh fruits, vegetables, meats, water, juices, and rice. After a few weeks on this regimen, foods are added back into the diet, one at a time, and the patient is monitored for symptoms.

When symptoms reappear, the food that was most recently reintroduced is usually the culprit, and the patient can then avoid that food. If allergies or sensitivities to more than one food are suspected, additions to the diet are continued until all options are exhausted. Keeping a close record of reactions to foods, as well as which foods are introduced at which times during the diet, is crucial.

The gluten elimination diet is a bit different. Just eliminate all gluten-containing foods and products from your life! This isn't as easy as it sounds. For more information about creating a gluten-free kitchen, see Chapter 8, and to discover how to convert your favorite recipes to gluten-free versions, see Chapter 9.

Facing the Inevitable Consequences of Cheating

As a rule, human beings don't adjust well to strict regimens. More than 90 percent of all dieters eventually gain back the weight they've lost. Anyone who has tried a fad diet understands how difficult it is to eliminate certain foods. But if you must live gluten-free, your condition is different, and you must take it very seriously.

Many people on the gluten sensitivity spectrum say they didn't realize how sick they were until they got rid of gluten. When you're used to feeling run-down and slightly ill, slogging through your day can become the norm. The days when you bounded out of bed and had unlimited energy to do anything you wanted may seem to have disappeared forever. Perhaps you just chalked this up to getting older. But after you try a gluten-free diet, you'll be amazed at how much better you feel.

In this section, we cover the consequences of cheating on a gluten-free diet. Although vegetarians may occasionally sneak a bite of chicken and teetotalers may have a sip of wine now and then, gluten-sensitive people simply can't afford to eat gluten. The potential damage to your health is too severe, and the associated conditions and diseases that can develop when you cheat are serious.

Compromised health

Over time, people with celiac disease suffer severe damage to their intestines. Because your intestines are the place where your body absorbs nutrients so your body can function well, heal from illness, and repair damage, things can go downhill quickly when the damage has been done. Poor diet and nutrient deficiencies can cause many common diseases, as diverse as cancer, heart disease, and osteoporosis.

Even if your symptoms are mild or if you're *asymptomatic* (without symptoms), the damage is occurring. You just aren't getting the nutrients you need for good health. And over time, this lack of nutrients can develop into serious diseases.

The sooner you're diagnosed with a condition on the gluten sensitivity spectrum, the better. Because the disease can develop at any point during your life span, you must be on the lookout for symptoms. Don't be afraid to talk to your doctor about the possibility of celiac disease, gluten intolerance, or nonceliac gluten sensitivity. Your doctor's job is to listen to you and help you live the best life you can.

Unpleasant associated conditions

Some diseases and disorders are associated with undiagnosed or untreated celiac disease and other gluten-related disorders. Some are autoimmune diseases; these conditions tend to go hand in hand. Others are the result of years of malnutrition and poor nutrient absorption.

If you or a family member suffers from one of these conditions, you may want to talk to your doctor about testing for gluten sensitivity. Many people with these conditions improve on a gluten-free diet even if they aren't sensitive to gluten. And if they are, eliminating gluten from the diet may alleviate some symptoms of these conditions.

These are conditions that can occur when people on the gluten sensitivity spectrum are untreated:

- ✔ ADD/ADHD
- ✔ Addison's disease
- ✔ Anemia
- ✔ Cancer
- ✔ Crohn's disease
- ✔ Depression
- ✔ Gallbladder disease
- ✔ Neuropathy
- ✔ Osteoporosis
- ✔ Scleroderma
- ✔ Systemic lupus
- ✔ Thyroid disease
- ✔ Type 1 diabetes
- ✔ Ulcerative colitis

If that list isn't enough to convince you to go gluten-free, perhaps the promise that you'll feel better and be able to live a more active life will do it! Remember, when you eliminate gluten, healing begins on day one. Your health can only get better from this point.

Chapter 3

Understanding the Rules of Baking

. . . .

In This Chapter

▶ Understanding structure in the science of baking

▶ Making sure you measure ingredients correctly

▶ Knowing when your baked goods are done

▶ Cooling your creations properly

. . . .

*B*aking is thought of as an art, but it's actually a science. Baking requires you to follow very specific rules or your baked goods will fail. Baking recipes are designed to create a structure that's supported by proteins and starches, rises because of chemical reactions, and is flavored and made tender with sugar and fat.

Before you begin baking, you need to understand a few rules about how to measure both wet and dry ingredients, the order in which you add ingredients to recipes, and what pan types to use. Then, placement in the oven and cooling methods are also critical to the success of baked goods. We cover all these important topics in this chapter.

The challenge of baking with gluten-free flours is that gluten is the main structure builder in baked goods. It forms a web that traps air so the baked goods rise. It keeps the structure from collapsing as it cools. You need to carefully develop gluten-free baked products to mimic gluten's function.

That doesn't mean you can't have fun too! Baking can be one of the most soul-satisfying activities in life. Nothing matches the aroma of delicious baked goods wafting through your home, and nothing beats presenting a scrumptious, gluten-free birthday cake to a little girl who thought cakes were verboten because of a gluten allergy.

The Basic Science of Baking

When you think of a fluffy cake, a chewy brownie, or bread with a crisp crust and chewy crumb, you're thinking about gluten. And when you can't eat gluten, you need to come up with something else that provides structure to those baked goods. Without structure, you wouldn't be able to tell a cake from flatbread!

In this section we look at how structure is developed and formed in baked goods. Though gluten plays a significant role, starches, eggs, and proteins in other flours, along with combining flours with different protein levels, can make up for the lack of gluten. Before you bake with gluten-free flours, you should understand gluten's role; how other ingredients work together in pies, cakes, cookies, and breads; how recipes for different baked goods work; and some ways to troubleshoot recipes.

Decoding recipe ingredients

The individual ingredients that make up baked goods all have specific roles. You must understand these roles to be a good baker. This section does delve a little bit into food science, but don't be scared! We're not going to talk about shear levels, denaturation, or transesterification (don't ask!).

The main ingredients in baked goods include flour, sugar, fat, eggs, liquid, and flavorings. Each of these components is necessary for good results. Gluten, of course, is the protein we're trying to avoid.

But before you can replace gluten in baked goods, you need to understand how it works and how other ingredients interact with it. Here's a rundown of how ingredients work in baking:

- ✓ **Flour:** Wheat flour provides gluten, which is made up of two molecules: glutenin and gliadin. When the flour comes into contact with a liquid, these molecules connect. Stirring, beating, and kneading makes these molecules form into a stretchy net that traps air. When the product is baked, the net sets, which creates the light structure of breads, cakes, and cookies.

  Different flours contain different amounts of protein. Bread flour is made from hard wheat that has about 12 to 14 percent protein, so it contains a lot of gluten to form the bread structure. Cake flour is made from soft wheat with 8 to 10 percent protein, so it's best used in delicate recipes like angel food cake. All-purpose flour is a combination of soft and hard wheat, so it's right in the middle, with 10 to 11 percent protein. It makes more tender cookies, cakes, and quick breads. The flours in gluten-free baking, quite obviously, don't contain this particular protein. But those flours do have other proteins that help build structure. We talk more about the flours used in gluten-free baking in Chapter 5.

Different gluten-free flours have different amounts of protein. Though those proteins don't act exactly the same as gluten proteins, they still build structure and can create a fine crumb. Working with these different protein amounts in different flours is what makes gluten-free baking so satisfying.

Flour also contains starches, which set up as the product bakes to support the structure of the baked good. When starches are combined with water and heated, they gelatinize. This structure helps interfere with the gluten structure, which keeps the baked goods tender. At the end of baking time, when the structure is setting in the oven, the starch stabilizes the crumb, or texture, so the cake doesn't collapse as the crumb is set. And starches help make the crumb of the cakes, bread, and cookies finer.

✔ **Sugar:** Sugar plays a crucial role in baking. It's *hygroscopic,* which means it attracts water. This keeps baked goods moist for a longer period of time and helps keep water away from gluten, which prevents overdevelopment. Sugar, obviously, also provides lots of flavor. And it helps baked goods brown by reacting with protein in flour, eggs, and milk when heated.

✔ **Fat:** Butter, margarine, and shortening, which are solid fats, help form the structure in breads, cakes, and cookies. When sugar is mixed with flour, the sugar crystals cut tiny holes into the butter. These holes become surrounded with starch and gluten and form the product's crumb.

Fat also provides lots of *mouth feel,* which is how the food feels when you chew on it. A product made with the correct amount of fat is tender and moist. Fat interferes with gluten production because it coats the gliadin and glutenin proteins so they can't bind as easily. This helps keep the baked product more tender.

Finally, fat tastes good! It carries flavors (which is why nonfat foods usually don't have the best flavor) and makes your baked goods taste rich.

✔ **Eggs:** The structure of many baked goods depends on eggs. Egg whites can form a foam, or web, that traps air in the batter. That air expands in the heat of the oven, which makes the product rise. That's how a soufflé becomes light and airy. Eggs also act as an emulsifier, binding together liquid and fat.

As the proteins in eggs set in the heat of the oven, they help to form and stabilize structure. And eggs add fat to baked goods, keeping them moist and tender.

✔ **Liquid:** Water, milk, cream, buttermilk, and juices are the liquids typically used in baking. They perform several functions. They turn flour into a dough, activating the gluten and turning the starch into a gel. Some liquids add flavor and fat to the product. And they turn baking powder and baking soda into carbon dioxide gas that leavens breads, cookies, and cakes.

✔ **Leavening agents:** Three specific ingredients make a baked product rise: baking soda, baking powder, and yeast. Each performs a different function. Baking soda and baking powder add carbon dioxide to the holes already formed in batters because of a property called *pH*. This is a scale that measures ingredients on the basis of acidity and alkalinity. It ranges from 1 to 14. Acidic ingredients, like lemon juice and vinegar, are low on the pH scale. The main alkaline ingredient in baking is baking soda. The pH of batters and doughs need to be near neutral, or 7, to rise and develop the proper texture.

- **Baking soda:** Always known as *sodium bicarbonate* (or *bicarb* in Britain), baking soda has a pH of 8.2 This mild alkalinity is used in recipes that have other acidic ingredients, like lemon juice, buttermilk, brown sugar, cocoa powder, or vinegar. The baking soda not only produces carbon dioxide when it reacts with the acidic ingredients but also brings the pH of the batter closer to 7, which is neutral. A neutral batter has a fine crumb, even texture, and good flavor.

- **Baking powder:** This mixture is a combination of baking soda, which is alkaline (high pH), and an acid, with a low pH. The dry ingredients are inert until they're mixed with a liquid. Then they react and create carbon dioxide, which makes the bubbles already formed in batters and breads larger. Look for double-acting baking soda in the supermarket. This product creates CO_2 when you mix it with liquid and again when you put the batter in the oven. This makes your baked goods very light and fluffy.

You can make your own baking powder. Just combine 2 teaspoons baking soda with 4 teaspoons cream of tartar (not tartar sauce!). Use as a one-to-one substitute for regular baking powder.

Be careful when adding baking powder and baking soda to batters and doughs. If you add too much, the batter will expand too much, the structure will weaken, and the whole thing will collapse. And make sure that your baking powder and soda are fresh. Mix a bit of baking powder with hot water; it should bubble immediately. Mix a bit of baking soda with vinegar; it should bubble. If the mixture doesn't bubble, discard the baking powder or soda and buy a new box.

- **Yeast:** Nothing can replace yeast when making fluffy white bread. Yeast is a living, single-celled organism that reproduces as long as it has water and food; sugar, in this case. As it grows and reproduces, it releases carbon dioxide, which makes the bread rise. But it has another function: As it grows it produces alcohol, which adds flavor to slow-rising bread. That's one of the flavors in sourdough bread.

Yeast comes in three types: dry, pressed, and wild. Dry yeast is the kind found in little packets. The yeast is still alive, but it's in a form of suspended animation. Add water and it will bloom, bubble, and be ready for use. Pressed yeast, also called cake yeast, is really alive. It's sold in the refrigerated section of the supermarket and is fairly hard to find. But it does make wonderful breads. It requires a lower water temperature than dry yeast to dissolve. Wild yeast is just floating in the air. The more bread you bake in your home, the more wild yeast you'll have. Sourdough starters capture wild yeast for tasty bread flavors and wonderful texture.

✔ **Salt:** This ubiquitous product adds flavor to baked goods. Salt is needed even in sweet recipes like cookies and cakes because it enhances overall flavor. Salt also controls the growth of yeast in bread so that it doesn't grow too fast, which would over-stretch and compromise the bread structure. At the same time, salt strengthens the molecular bonds of gluten so that the bread has an even and fine crumb.

Other ingredients in baked goods provide color, nutrition, and flavor. Solid chocolate, cocoa, chopped nuts, coconut, lemon peel, extracts, spices, and different flours are used to change baked goods into something special. Those ingredients do have an effect on the structure; they interfere with it. Whole-grain flours also interfere with the structure of baked goods. The bran and germ of the flour that's milled into whole-wheat flour gets in the way of the gluten strands as they form.

That's desirable if you're making a cookie or quick bread but not so much with a yeast bread. Recipes are developed to compensate for these ingredient quirks, which is why tampering with a baking recipe isn't a good idea unless you're very experienced!

Light and fluffy (or flaky) instead of flat and dense: Getting the right structure

Some baking recipes are supposed to be flat and dense (see the recipe for Decadent Chocolate Torte in Chapter 15, for instance). A loaf of whole-wheat bread is denser than white bread, and that's considered a good characteristic. But it still needs some lightness, an even crumb, and moisture. Most baked goods should be tender and, if not fluffy, a bit airy.

To make delectable, gluten-free baked goods, you need to look at how structure is built as batters and doughs are made. Each type of baked good uses a different method to produce the desired results. Cakes are light and fluffy. Cookies are moist and tender, crisp, or chewy. Quick breads are tender and soft. Pie crusts and biscuits are flaky and tender. And yeast breads have a fine crumb, crisp or chewy crust, and are tender.

Each of these structures depends on gluten, the protein in flour, for its formation. Even when you leave gluten out of the equation, you still need to understand how these products are built. When you need to control gluten in a recipe, gluten-free flours have an advantage. If gluten is the main structural component in a recipe, you need to compensate for its lack with a combination of gluten-free flours and some gums and other ingredients. The following sections look at some baked goods and explain how their structure is formed.

Cake structure

Gluten is an important component in cakes. You need to understand how gluten works in cakes so that you can substitute for it. Cakes are made using either the traditional method or the one-bowl method. Both work equally well to create a cake with a fine crumb, moistness, and even texture.

- **Traditional method:** Butter and sugar mixed together start the structure. You beat eggs into this mixture to add protein, flavor, and fat to the cake and to help the fat combine with the liquid. Then you add flour and liquids alternately, which helps build the structure as the flour proteins and starch form a web around the holes the sugar has made in the butter. And the liquid helps the gluten form and the ingredients blend together. You don't mix the batter much after you add all the ingredients, because otherwise, the gluten overdevelops and the cake will be tough. If you added all the flour at the same time, the batter would be too thick to add the liquid and the structure built by the butter and sugar would be smothered.

  This method, although time-consuming, produces cakes that are quite fluffy and light, with a very fine crumb and tenderness. The cakes have a very even texture and are moist.

- **One-bowl method:** This method was developed in the 1950s. You add all the ingredients to the bowl at once. You beat the mixture for several minutes — much longer than cakes made using the traditional method. This longer beating time is necessary for two reasons. First, air needs to be incorporated into the batter to create the holes for the gluten to form around. And the flour needs to be manipulated with the liquids so the gluten forms and the starch gelatinizes.

  These cakes are very tender and velvety but have lower volume and aren't as fluffy as the traditional method cakes. But unless you're comparing them side by side, you'd be hard-pressed to tell the difference!

Cookie structure

Cookies are usually made from doughs that are stiffer than cake batters (although there are exceptions, such as the Madeleine). Because cookies are less complicated and delicate than cakes, they aren't as fussy to make.

Chewy, cake-like, or crisp?

Everyone has his preference: Do you like your cookies soft and chewy or crisp? And how do you make a cookie that's chewy or one that's crisp? The answer lies in the amount of moisture and fat in the dough. Chewy cookies have more egg, more moisture, and less flour. For chewy cookies, you can use brown sugar instead of granulated sugar because brown sugar is moist. Using butter instead of shortening also makes cookies chewy. And chill the dough before you bake it. You bake chewy cookies at a higher temperature for a shorter time and remove them from the oven just as they're done. In fact, they should still be light-colored in the center when you take them out.

Cake-like cookies have much more liquid than chewy or crisp cookies and more flour. You usually need to make them in a mold, like a muffin tin or a cookie mold, so they hold their shape while baking. That extra liquid makes more gluten form, which holds in the moisture so the cookies steam as they bake.

Crisp cookies contain more fat, less moisture, and less (or no) egg. They use granulated sugar, which is drier than brown sugar. Shortening helps make cookies crisp. You bake crisp cookies at a lower temperature for a longer period of time, until they're light golden-brown.

When you make cookie dough, all the ingredients should be at room temperature. That means the butter should stand at room temperature for an hour or two before you start baking. Warm the eggs by placing the whole eggs in a bowl of warm water for 10 to 15 minutes before you add them to the dough.

Cookies are usually made like cakes, but they have more flour and less liquid. The gluten in the flour develops to hold the cookies together. The one-bowl method is usually used to make cookies, just because it's easier, and cookies aren't as delicate as cakes. Just combine all the ingredients in a bowl and beat until everything is combined. Hold out the extras — like chopped nuts, coconut, and chocolate chips — until the dough is mixed, and then stir them in.

The traditional method for making cookies is just like the traditional method for making cakes, with one exception. You mix the butter with the sugar, then beat in the eggs, and then add the liquids. You add the flour at the end, and you mix the dough just until combined. Cookies need less gluten formation than cakes, so you don't mix them as much.

Quick bread structure

Quick breads are called "quick" because they're leavened with baking powder and baking soda, not yeast. These are usually the first foods that beginning bakers attempt. And they're the easiest foods for you to make on your gluten-free adventure. Just some simple measuring, a bit of stirring, and baking and you'll be able to enjoy delicious muffins and quick breads. But first, we discuss their structure.

Like cakes, you can make quick breads using two methods. The traditional method in this case makes a quick bread that's slightly rough in texture but tender and moist. The cake method for making quick breads uses the traditional cake method.

- ✔ **Traditional quick bread method:** For this method, you combine all the dry ingredients — flour, baking powder, baking soda, sugar, and spices — in a large bowl. You combine the wet ingredients — eggs, milk or buttermilk, extracts, and oil or melted butter — in a small bowl. Then you pour the wet ingredients into the dry ingredients all at once and you stir the mixture *just* until the two mixtures combine.

  These products are lower in fat than cakes, so the gluten has more chance to develop. That's why you stir the batter so briefly; you want as little gluten formation as possible; just enough to develop the structure.

- ✔ **Cake quick bread method:** You make these quick breads exactly like cakes. They have more fat, and the fat is usually butter or another solid, so there's less gluten development. One difference in making quick breads using this method is that you add flours all at once instead of adding them alternately with the liquid.

True quick breads have larger air pockets and a rougher crumb. Overmixing produces tunnels in the product, which are indicative of too much gluten formation. Cake-like quick breads are moister but denser than traditional cakes because they usually have more fat.

Pie crust structure

You make pie crusts by "cutting" fat into flour. That means that you use your fingers, two knives, or a pastry blender to manipulate the fat until it's coated with flour. Then you add liquid to form a dough. Gluten-free pie crusts can be a challenge to make, but making them isn't impossible! Here's how they're formed.

The aim is to create layers of fat surrounded by the flour. If the fat stays in fairly large pieces, the crust will be flaky. If you cut the fat into the flour too much, the crust will be mealy and crumbly. Most pie crust recipes call for the fat to be cut into the flour until the fat is the size of peas. This creates a "short" pie crust (one that has a high proportion of fat to flour; see the nearby sidebar for more). In the oven, the fat melts and releases a little steam, which makes the pie crust flaky.

When you combine the fat and flour, you add the liquid. This develops the gluten in the flour so the dough holds together. You use much less liquid than when making cookies, cakes, or quick breads. The dough is more elastic, and you can manipulate it by rolling with a rolling pin.

Handle and work the pie crust dough as little as possible. And keep the dough as cold as possible so the fat doesn't soften or melt.

Here are some problems with pie crusts and their solutions:

- **Tough pie crust:** Too much flour, too much handling, and not enough fat make a tough pie crust. Follow recipes exactly, measure carefully and accurately, and don't handle the dough too much. Failing to keep the crust cold as you work with it is another cause of tough pie crusts. If the fat softens too much, it mixes with the flour, creating more gluten.

- **Mealy pie crust:** If you cut the fat into the flour until it becomes as fine as breadcrumbs, the dough will be dense and the crust will be mealy. A mealy crust still tastes good, but if you want a flaky crust, don't cut the fat into the flour until it disappears. A mealy pie crust has one advantage; it absorbs less moisture from liquid fillings than a "short" pie crust. This crust is sturdier, with more gluten formation, so it holds up to quiches, fruit pie fillings, and custard fillings.

- **Pie crust tears:** Don't worry if the pie crust tears; just patch it together again and press gently. You can sprinkle the torn area with a tiny bit of water to help it seal.

- **Pie crust is difficult to roll out:** When you first make a pie crust, the gluten is very elastic and the dough can be very springy. Let the pie crust dough rest in the refrigerator, well covered, for an hour or so to let the gluten structure relax.

- **Pie crust shrinks during baking:** When you place the pie crust dough in the pie pan, don't pull or stretch it. That makes the crust shrink when it's exposed to heat. And handle the dough gently. Too much gluten formation in the dough can make the crust shrink when it bakes. Adding ½ teaspoon of vinegar to any pie crust dough can help prevent shrinking because it makes the gluten molecules weaker.

- **Soggy pie crust:** Very moist fillings can cause a soggy pie crust. To prevent this, bake the pie on the lowest rack in the oven so the heat is closer to the bottom of the pie. You can also brush the bottom crust with a little egg white before adding the filling. Some recipes call for prebaking the pie crust before adding the filling; don't skip this step.

Biscuit structure

Biscuits should be light, flaky, and fluffy, with a crisp crust and a soft interior. Like pie crust, biscuits are best when you handle the dough very little. Biscuits form very much like pie crusts, but with less fat and more liquid. The method for making them is just like making pie crust.

What's a "short" dough?

You may have heard the term "short" dough. That doesn't mean a dough that isn't tall! A short dough is one that has a high proportion of fat to flour. The dough is tender and slightly crumbly, with a texture that melts in your mouth.

Shortbreads come to mind; they're the original short dough. Most pie crusts have a little less fat and a little more flour than shortbread so they can be rolled thinner and are easier to handle.

As with pie crust, the larger the pieces of cold fat when you add water, the flakier the biscuits will be. And the colder you keep the dough, the flakier the biscuits will be.

Biscuits come in two kinds: drop biscuits and rolled biscuits. You handle drop biscuits much less. When you form the dough, you just drop it onto a cookie sheet and bake it. With rolled biscuits, you pat them or roll them out and then cut them with a knife or a cookie cutter. They're flakier and less tender than drop biscuits.

Making a good biscuit takes practice and a light hand. Some problems with biscuits and their solutions include

- **Tough biscuits:** These are caused by overworking the dough so the gluten forms too much or letting the dough get too warm so the fat melts. That destroys the layered structure that flaky biscuits depend on, and you end up with a tough biscuit. One way to keep the fat really cold when making biscuits is to freeze it and then grate it into the flour. Work just a little with your hands or a pastry blender so the fat stays cold.

- **Twisted biscuits:** Despite the fact that that phrase sounds like the name of a rock band, twisted biscuits are caused by rotating the biscuit cutter as you cut through the dough. This twisting action also seals the biscuit edges, which stops them from rising. Cut straight down into the dough with the cutter or use a very sharp knife and cut quickly and firmly.

- **Biscuits not flaky:** The fat has been cut in too much. The dough should have large pieces of fat, which melt in the heat of the oven. This releases steam and creates the flakes so desirable in a good biscuit. You need fats that are solid at room temperature. Some biscuit recipes call for slightly kneading the dough. This also helps create flaky layers by, well, layering the dough before it's formed and baked.

Yeast bread structure

It seems that yeast bread is the holy grail in gluten-free baking. When people are first told they need to avoid gluten, they automatically think of the delicious breads they can't eat. Well, that's not true anymore. Gluten-free flours in judicious combinations, along with some use of gums and emulsifiers, can make fluffy breads, dense breads, or any kind of bread you want.

Yeast breads have very complicated structures. Strong gluten development is necessary to hold the structure together and create the fine crumb so desirable in breads. But you must use ingredients that keep the bread moist and tender enough to eat. That's where ingredients like fat, sugar, milk, whole grains, and different flours come in.

Yeast has to have time to rehydrate, eat simple sugars from the flour and sugar in the dough, reproduce, and emit alcohols and carbon dioxide that makes the bread rise. The time that the bread spends rising is called *proofing time*. Some recipes simply tell you to "proof the yeast." That means to dissolve it in liquid with a tiny bit of sugar to get it started.

Gluten is the star of bread recipes. It forms a stretchy web that traps the carbon dioxide that yeast produces as it ferments. But gluten isn't the only player in bread structure. If it was, bread would be so dense you couldn't bite into it!

Starch is an important part of bread structure, too. Starch holds onto water, interferes slightly with the gluten development, and gelatinizes when it comes into contact with water. This gel helps stabilize the bread structure.

So those are the two big structural ingredients in bread. Gluten-free flours have a lot of starch, and they also have varying amounts of protein (see Chapter 12 for more information about this). You have lots of ways to mimic gluten structure in gluten-free breads. But before we talk about that, you need to know the different methods for making bread.

Bread doughs are formed in several different ways:

- **Dissolved yeast method:** This is also called the *straight dough* or *traditional* method. You first dissolve yeast in a warm liquid and then you add it to flour. You may add other ingredients, including fat and eggs, to make the dough more tender. You knead the dough to develop the gluten structure, evenly distribute the yeast throughout the dough, and help form the tiny air holes that become the crumb of the bread. Then it rises, is formed, may rise again, and is baked.

- **Batter method:** You combine yeast, flour, eggs, and liquid and beat them vigorously to start gluten production. Because this is a batter and not a dough, kneading isn't possible. This is the easiest bread method.

- **Sponge method:** In this method, you combine yeast and water with some of the flour used in the recipe and beat them until smooth. You then allow this sponge to rise. You then add the rest of the ingredients, form the dough, allow it to rise, and then shape and bake it. These breads have more fermented flavor because the yeast has time to develop alcohols and other byproducts that give the bread a tangy flavor. And the bread will have more oven-spring and a lighter texture because enzymes released during the fermentation process relax the gluten.

✔ **One-bowl method:** You combine yeast with the flour in this method instead of mixing it with water by itself. The liquid temperature must be higher (120 to 130 degrees) in this method because the flour mitigates the water's temperature.

✔ **Sourdough method:** Instead of using dry packaged yeast, true sourdough captures wild yeast from the air. You make a starter by combining flour, water, and sometimes sugar, and you leave the mixture open to the air. The mixture will bubble after a few days. You use the starter to make the bread by removing half of it and adding flour and other ingredients. You "feed" the remaining half fresh flour and water. Sourdough starters can last, and have lasted, for hundreds of years.

You can use dry or fresh yeast to make sourdough starters. And you can make starters by starting with potato water or immersing organic, unwashed grapes in the flour mixture.

✔ **New "no knead" method:** Jim Lahey invented a new way to make bread in 2006 that was published in *The New York Times*. He discovered that bread actually "kneads itself" when it's allowed to stand for a significant period of time. This molecular kneading produces a loaf with outstanding texture, taste, and crust.

In this method, you combine flour, yeast, and salt with water and stir. You let the sticky dough stand for 18 hours at room temperature. Then you fold the dough a few times (you don't knead it) and shape it into a rough ball. You preheat a heavy pot in the oven and gently plop the dough into the pot. Cover the pot and bake the bread at 450 degrees. This unusual method was a breakthrough in bread baking, and it's how many gluten-free breads are made.

When you have problems with bread, there are usually reasons. To troubleshoot issues with homemade bread, look through this list.

✔ **The bread is tough.** This usually happens when you add too much flour to the bread or knead the bread too much. Weighing or properly measuring ingredients is the best way to ensure success. Don't knead longer than the recipe instructs. And if the recipe doesn't call for kneading, don't do it!

✔ **The bread is heavy.** If this happens, the yeast may have been past its expiration date or may have been killed somewhere along the line. You may want to proof the yeast before baking just to make sure it's alive and in good condition.

- ✔ **The bread falls.** Structural failure is usually caused by the bread rising too much. This can happen to gluten-containing breads, so you must be even more careful with gluten-free breads. The structure is stretched too much by excessive gas from the yeast, and it collapses. Fallen bread can also be caused by not using enough flour, which makes the dough structure weaker.

- ✔ **The bread has an uneven texture.** This is usually caused by not mixing the flours together well or not mixing the dough or batter enough. Or the dough rose in an environment that was too warm. Doughs should rise in temperatures around 80 degrees.

- ✔ **The dough doesn't rise.** When this happens, the yeast didn't survive. Either it was too old and past the expiration date or it was killed by the liquid being at too high a temperature. In an unfortunately misguided effort to help bread rise, some new bakers put their dough in the oven and heat it for a bit. This can kill the yeast. Only put dough into an oven with a pilot light if you want a warm place for proofing.

- ✔ **The bread has coarse texture.** Too much yeast can cause a coarse texture. Of course, in some breads, like focaccia or ciabatta, a coarse texture is desirable. Measure yeast carefully and don't add more than the recipe specifies.

- ✔ **The bread is dry.** Dry bread has usually been overbaked. Learn doneness tests and follow them carefully. Other reasons for dry bread include using too many dry ingredients or letting the dough rise or proof too long.

Oven spring

The best bread recipes experience something called *oven spring*. This is a rapid expansion of the bread dough in the oven during the first few minutes of baking, before the structure sets in the heat. This makes breads light and fluffy with a wonderful crumb. Getting your bread to experience oven spring seems to be more an art than a science. The yeast should be active when you put the bread in the oven. If the yeast has been allowed to grow too long (called *over-proofing*), the bread won't rise more in the oven.

Oven spring ends when the internal temperature of the dough reaches 140 degrees. At that temperature, the yeast dies and no longer produces carbon dioxide. The gluten coagulates and can no longer stretch, and the starch gelatinizes and starts to set.

One thing you can do to help create oven spring is to add moisture to the dry baking environment. A pan containing about an inch of hot water, placed on the rack below the bread, creates steam. This helps keep the dough moist longer, so the air has more of a chance to expand before the structure sets. And don't let yeast doughs rise beyond the recommended times. Over-proofed dough is weakened dough, and oven spring can make the structure collapse.

Baking at high altitude

Baking is tricky enough. Baking gluten-free products adds another layer of complexity. Now what happens if you live at a high altitude? Higher altitudes are problematic for baked goods because air pressure decreases as the altitude increases. These effects become noticeable at 2,000 feet above sea level.

What does this mean for your baking?

- ✔ Lower air pressure has a profound effect on baked goods. Gases expand much more quickly, so quick breads and yeast breads overexpand and then collapse in the oven.

- ✔ Higher altitudes drop the boiling point of water. In fact, the boiling point of water drops one degree for every 500 feet in altitude increase. Water boils at 194 degrees at an altitude of 10,000 feet. Water boils faster the higher you go. When the boiling point of water changes, there are profound changes in the oven. Water leaves baked goods more easily, which weakens the structure and leaves a coarse texture.

- ✔ Air is drier at higher altitudes. You may need more liquid than in recipes that are developed at lower altitudes. Faster evaporation also affects how food bakes and can be a factor in faster staling.

Unfortunately, no single overriding principle creates success in every single baked good made at high altitudes. Until you're more experienced baking at high altitudes, rely on recipes specifically developed for those conditions. Still, here are some general rules to follow to help you achieve more success:

- ✔ **Decrease baking powder.** Omit ⅛ teaspoon of baking powder for each 3,000 feet of altitude so cookies, cakes, pies, and quick breads don't rise too much.

- ✔ **Decrease yeast.** Reduce the amount of yeast called for in bread products. Because doing so reduces the bread's flavor, let the dough rise twice.

- ✔ **Reduce rising times.** Lower air pressure means that doughs rise faster than in recipes developed at sea level.

- ✔ **Reduce sugar.** Remove 1 tablespoon of sugar per cup for each 3,000 feet of altitude. Because more evaporation occurs at higher temperatures, sugar concentrates in the product. This changes the flavor and can also weaken the structure.

- ✔ **Add more flour.** More flour provides more structure to the baked good. Flour absorbs more liquid at high altitudes and can become damp; store it in airtight containers.

✔ **Decrease baking time.** Baked goods are usually done sooner at high altitudes. Check the food's progress a few minutes before the minimum baking time.

✔ **Increase oven temperature.** You want to get the structure of the baked good to set and firm quickly before gasses inside the product can expand too much.

With practice and experience, trial and error, you'll become more proficient at high-altitude baking. The best information usually comes from a county extension agency in your area. They have lots of information about how to successfully bake at high altitudes, along with many tested recipes.

Measuring Ingredients for Best Results

Measuring ingredients correctly is one of the most crucial components to baking. When I was first learning how to bake, I made date bars from a mix. The filling didn't seem wet enough, so I added more water. Result: date bar soup!

Baking recipes are scientific formulas developed for specific results. If you add too much rice flour to a bread, it will be heavy. If you don't add enough sugar to a cake, it will be tough. And the way you measure ingredients is crucial, too.

You can measure all ingredients in two ways: by weight or by volume. In this section we tell you how to measure ingredients so you can produce perfect baked goods every single time.

Measuring dry ingredients

Measuring dry ingredients correctly is crucial in achieving baking success. In European cookbooks, most dry measures are given in grams; in other words, they weigh ingredients by weight. In the United States, this method isn't as popular, although it's the method that professional bakers use. And the method is changing.

Gluten-free bakers are embracing the weight method of measuring. Every person measures ingredients differently when using the volume method: cups, tablespoons, and teaspoons. In fact, while studying food science, Linda learned this firsthand in an experimental foods class. Everyone measured a cup of flour, and then all the cups were weighed. Every single one was different; some higher, some lower.

When measuring dry ingredients, especially flours, for gluten-free baking, we strongly recommend weighing them. Kitchen scales aren't expensive, and they're easy to use with a little practice. All-purpose regular flour weighs 125 grams per cup. Gluten-free flours all weigh different amounts per cup. The best way to get the best results is to substitute flours by weight. If a recipe calls for 1 cup of all-purpose flour but you want to substitute a gluten-free baking mix, substitute 125 grams of the baking mix, not 1 cup.

If you don't want to measure by weight, that's okay too. You then need to know how to measure each ingredient used in baking. Here's how to measure dry ingredients by volume:

- ✔ **Flour:** You should stir flour and then spoon it into the calibrated measuring cup. Add enough flour so the cup overflows. Then use the back of a knife to level off the flour even with the top edge of the cup. Measure flour mixes this way too.

   Never scoop the measuring cup into the flour or you'll add too much flour to the recipe. And don't pack the flour down or pat it down with your fingertips. I see this all the time on television baking shows. It's the wrong way to measure flour.

- ✔ **Granulated sugar:** Scoop the measuring cup into the sugar to overflowing and then level it off with the back of a knife.

- ✔ **Brown sugar:** Because brown sugar has so much moisture, you measure it differently. Pack the sugar into the cup until it's level with the top edge. The brown sugar should hold the shape of the cup when you turn it out into the mixing bowl.

- ✔ **Powdered or confectioners' sugar:** You should sift this fluffy sugar before measuring, simply because it so often has lumps that can ruin your frosting or other recipe. Spoon it into the measuring cup and level it off with the back of the knife, just as you do flour.

- ✔ **Baking powder and soda:** Use proper calibrated measuring teaspoons for these ingredients. Dip them into the box and then level them off with the back of a knife.

- ✔ **Cocoa powder:** Spoon it into the measuring cup until overflowing and then level off with the back of a knife. You may want to sift cocoa before measuring, simply because it often has rather tough lumps.

Measuring liquid ingredients

For liquid ingredients, purchase a couple of glass Pyrex measuring cups. These have cup and milliliter markings on the side, with a spout for pouring the ingredients into the mixing bowl.

Proper measuring tools

If you don't want to measure by weight, you need proper measuring tools. Never measure ingredients using coffee spoons or a soup cup. Some popular cooking shows tell you to eyeball ingredients. That may be fine for cooking recipes, like soups or stews, or for sautéing vegetables in extra virgin olive oil. But you must measure ingredients when baking.

You need to measure dry ingredients with calibrated measuring cups. These are usually nested and come in sets that range from ¼ cup to 1 cup. You need to measure wet ingredients with their own calibrated measuring cups. These glass cups have markings on the sides and a spout for pouring. Even when you're measuring small amounts, like a teaspoon or ½ teaspoon, use measuring spoons. Baking recipes are precise formulas. Adding ½ teaspoon too much baking soda, for instance, can ruin a cake.

To measure liquid ingredients properly, put the cup on the counter and get down so you're at eye level with the cup. Slowly pour the liquid ingredient into the cup until it reaches the mark of the measurement you want. Don't hold the cup in the air and pour, and don't measure by looking down into the cup.

Speaking of looking down into cups to measure, a new gizmo is on the market for measuring liquids. It's called an *angled* measuring cup, and it looks very strange. But you can measure liquid ingredients by looking down into the cup from above. Give it a try!

Measuring everything else

You need to measure everything else in a baking recipe, too! Some ingredients are more difficult to measure than others. But these ingredients aren't quite as critical to baking success, as long as you don't add twice what the recipe calls for.

A comma in a recipe ingredient plays an important role in measuring everything else. Where it's placed in the ingredient list means something. For instance, if a recipe calls for "1 cup nuts, chopped," that means you measure 1 cup of whole nuts and then chop them. But if the recipe says "1 cup chopped nuts," you should chop the nuts and *then* measure them.

Here are the ways to properly measure several other baking ingredients:

- **Nuts:** Chop nuts if the recipe calls for it and then place them into dry measuring cups up to the top of the cup.

- ✔ **Fruit:** You measure some fruit by whole amounts, as in "1 apple, chopped." In that case, the amount of apple isn't crucial to the recipe success, and a little more or less won't hurt. Just don't add 2 apples! If the recipe calls for "1 cup chopped apple," measure in a dry measuring cup.

- ✔ **Coconut:** Place coconut loosely in a dry measuring cup up to the top edge of the cup.

- ✔ **Honey or syrup:** You can measure these ingredients in dry measuring cups or liquid measuring cups. If the recipe has more than one liquid, including honey or maple syrup, first measure the liquid. Then add enough honey or syrup to fill the cup to the correct amount.

- ✔ **Solid shortening:** Press this into a dry measuring cup to make sure it has no air pockets, and then level off the top. You can also measure shortening with the *displacement method:* Put ½ cup cold water into a glass liquid measuring cup and then add enough shortening to raise the liquid level to 1 cup. Remove the shortening, which will be ½ cup, and use it in the recipe.

- ✔ **Butter or margarine:** Sticks of butter or margarine have a little measuring ruler on the side of the paper wrapping. Each stick is equal to 4 ounces or ½ cup; a ½ cup equals 8 tablespoons.

- ✔ **Chocolate:** You usually chop chocolate before adding it to a recipe. Chop using a large chef's knife and then measure in a dry measuring cup. You can also measure by ounces. Many recipes call for "8 ounces chopped chocolate," which would be eight 1-ounce squares.

- ✔ **Shredded cheese:** Shred cheese and place it in a dry measuring cup; don't pack the cheese down. Use a box grater or a food processor to shred the cheese.

- ✔ **Breadcrumbs:** Scoop dry breadcrumbs into dry measuring cups and level them off. Spoon fresh breadcrumbs, which are made from fresh soft bread, into dry measuring cups and level them off.

- ✔ **Herbs and spices:** Measure dry herbs and spices using dry measuring spoons. You usually chop or mince fresh herbs before measuring. To substitute dry herbs for fresh, use ⅓ of the fresh amount. And to substitute fresh herbs for dry, use 3 times the amount called for in the recipe.

Measuring sticky ingredients

Sticky ingredients can pose a special measuring challenge. How do you get all the honey, corn syrup, or peanut butter out of a measuring cup? Here's a trick: Lightly oil the spoon or measuring cup, or spray it with cooking spray before you add the sticky ingredient. Then measure properly, and the honey or peanut butter will come right out. You can also rinse the measuring cup with warm water and not dry it before measuring these sticky foods. Just be sure to measure accurately.

Testing for Doneness

The next to last step in baking is to take the food out of the oven when it's done. But when is it done? You can judge doneness in several ways; each requires a bit of experience and knowledge.

In this section we look at how to test doneness of baked goods using three methods: observation, touch tests, and internal temperature. Some recipes require the use of only one of these tests; you can use all three for some. But without accurate doneness tests, your cakes will fall, your brownies can burn, your cookies will become dry, and your breads may overbake.

Using your eyes: Doneness observations

The oldest way to test for doneness is to simply look at the product. It sounds simplistic, but when many baked goods are done, they *look* done. You can do two kinds of observation doneness tests: simply looking at the product and noting changes, and the toothpick test. For the toothpick test, insert a clean toothpick into the center or near the center of the product. It should come out clean or with just a few moist crumbs clinging to it. If the toothpick has wet batter on it, the product isn't done.

And don't forget about *residual cooking!* When you remove baked products from the oven and don't immediately transfer them from the hot pan to a cooling rack, they continue to cook for a few minutes. The residual heat from the pan causes this. As you become a more experienced baker, you'll learn to recognize just when your food is done.

These are some common observation tests for baked goods:

- ✔ **Cakes:** A cake will be an even, light-golden brown color all over its surface. The cake will also be just starting to pull away from the sides of the pan, which means that it doesn't need the support of the pan to hold its shape. A toothpick inserted in the center of the cake will come out with a few moist crumbs attached to it.

- ✔ **Cookies:** Cookies are golden-brown around the edges when they're done. But different cookies have different observation doneness tests. For chewy cookies, remove them from the oven when the center is still fairly pale. For crisp cookies, remove them from the oven when the center is light golden-brown. Drop cookies are done when they're evenly spread out and puffed. Cutout cookies are done when they're light golden-brown around the edges. Bar cookies are done when they're golden-brown around the edges and don't jiggle when you move the pan. There really isn't a toothpick test for cookies.

- ✔ **Pies:** Most pies are done when the pie crust is golden brown. Fruit pies are done when the juices bubble in the center. Quiches are done when they're puffed and starting to brown in spots on the top. Toothpick tests aren't commonly used on pies.

- ✔ **Quick breads:** Quick breads are done when they're golden-brown on top. They'll also just start to pull away from the sides of the pan. Most quick breads have a center crack from CO_2 escaping through the relatively weak structure; that's normal. The crack shouldn't look wet, but it shouldn't be golden-brown either. A toothpick will come out with a few moist crumbs attached.

- ✔ **Brownies:** Because brownies are moist and fudgy, telling when they're done is difficult. The most accurate doneness test is to observe a dry and shiny crust. The center of the brownie may wiggle a bit when you gently push the pan, but it shouldn't be loose.

- ✔ **Muffins:** Muffins will be golden brown, nicely rounded, and won't jiggle when you move the pan. The edges may be slightly darker. A toothpick inserted in the center will come out clean or with a few moist crumbs attached.

- ✔ **Yeast breads:** Yeast breads are done when they're golden-brown, start to pull away from the pan sides, and sound hollow when you lightly tap them with your fingers.

Trying touch tests

For touch doneness tests, you, well, touch the product! When baked goods are done, they spring back when lightly touched with your finger. Don't press down on the product. Touch tests are most commonly used for quick breads, cakes, and muffins, because those products are softer than yeast breads and pies when they're done.

When do you test for doneness? When you're trying a recipe for the first time, check the food at a few minutes less than the shortest baking time. Even though you've made sure your oven is properly calibrated, all ovens are different. If the product isn't done at the first test, put it (carefully!) back into the oven and set the timer for a few more minutes. Keep checking until the food tests done according to the recipe instructions.

The product will also feel done when it's done. It shouldn't feel hard but firm and springy. If it's very soft or loose, return it to the oven and continue baking. Check every 3 to 4 minutes to make sure you don't overbake the product.

Oven calibration

In order to follow a recipe correctly and get a successful result, your oven needs to be accurate. Without an accurate oven, you can't rely on the recipe for accurate timing. Follow the manufacturer's instruction booklet to make sure the oven is properly calibrated. And always use an oven thermometer to test for temperature accuracy. If you can't regulate the oven temperature, have it checked out by a qualified technician.

Taking the temperature

The final, and most accurate, way to test for doneness is to take the internal temperature of the product. We're used to taking the temperature of meat to check when it's safe to eat, but baked goods also have their own guidelines.

These are internal temperature doneness points for baked goods:

- ✔ Yeast breads are done when the internal temperature measures 200 to 210 degrees.

- ✔ Quick breads are done when the internal temperature is around 203 to 205 degrees.

- ✔ Clear pies, like pecan pies or chess pies, are done when the internal temperature reads 200 degrees.

- ✔ Quiches and other egg pies are done when the internal temperature reaches 160 degrees.

- ✔ Cakes are done when their internal temperature reaches 195 to 200 degrees.

Cooling Down and Chilling Out

The final step in baking is cooling. Though it may seem simplistic to include this as a baking step, how you cool these foods is crucial to success. If you cut into a baked good before it's cool, you'll have problems. In this section we look at what happens when a baked good cools and the different ways you should cool foods.

When you take a baked good out of the oven, it cools down gradually. The starch, which has gelatinized in the moisture of the formula and the heat of the oven, starts to set as heat escapes. Egg proteins and flour proteins set. The product gradually becomes drier as moisture escapes.

Though eating a warm cookie is one of life's pleasures, it's not a good idea to cut into cakes, breads, and pies before they've cooled completely. Slicing into hot bread, quick breads, or cakes compresses the structure before it has completely set, and it won't be as light and fluffy.

Different kinds of pans have different effects on cooling. If the baked good is left in the pan to cool, a glass pan holds residual heat longer and may cause overbaking. Metal pans cool down more quickly. If a recipe calls for the food to be cooled in the pan, choose a metal pan over a glass pan.

You should never rush cooling. Don't place hot baked goods in the fridge or outside on a cold day. Cooling too fast can make baked goods shrink. And always use a cooling rack. If you put a hot baked good on a solid surface, moisture condenses on the bottom as it cools, leaving a soggy mess or a mushy bottom. Air must circulate around the product as it cools for best results.

These are specific ways to cool baked goods:

- **Layer cakes:** You cool layer cakes, which you bake in 8-inch or 9-inch pans, by letting them stand in the pan for 5 to 10 minutes so the structure firms. Then you remove the cakes from the pans by turning them onto a cooling rack.

- **Sponge and chiffon cakes:** These cakes are very delicate, and their structure is easily compressed. Many are turned upside down to cool, so the web of egg proteins, flour proteins, and starch stays stretched while it cools. This prevents sagging.

- **Angel food cakes:** You cool light and airy angel food cakes the same way as sponge cakes. That's also why you don't grease the pans for these types of cakes — because they'd slide right out of the pan while cooling!

- **Sheet cakes:** You typically cool these cakes in the pan. It's best to bake sheet cakes in a metal pan because it holds less residual heat than a glass pan.

- **Cookies:** You cool most cookies on the cookie sheet for a few minutes and then remove them to a wire rack to cool completely.

- **Bar cookies:** Cool this product in the pan. Again, use a metal pan for bar cookies instead of a glass pan so they don't overbake from residual heat.

- **Breads:** You usually remove breads from the pan right away. Shake the pan gently to make sure the bread is loose and then turn out the bread onto a wire rack to cool completely.

Chapter 4

Unique Issues of Gluten-Free Baking

In This Chapter

▶ Discovering some tips for gluten-free baking

▶ Being prepared with the proper tools and supplies

▶ Making the best quick breads and yeast breads

▶ Creating great pie crusts and cakes

▶ Baking cookies, both chewy and crisp

Gluten-free baking has special issues that are distinct from the issues and rules of baking with wheat products. How do you build structure yet keep baked goods tender without the helping hand of gluten? Are there special methods that can "trick" a bread or cake into acting like gluten is part of the structure? And what about taste?

You can build structure and flavor without gluten. Special methods do exist, and they aren't difficult; they just take a bit of extra time and skills that are easy to learn. In this chapter we look at the tricks of gluten-free baking for each category of recipe, because each type of baked good has its own characteristics that you want to emphasize.

Tricks and Traps

Gluten is the stretchy protein that forms when wheat flour is exposed to water and is manipulated, either through beating or kneading. This protein forms a literal web that traps air, creating the *crumb,* or texture, of breads, cookies, cakes, and pastries.

In this section we tell you how to build structure, keep baked goods tender, and create the distinctively nutty taste of wheat flour without using the gluten found in wheat flour. It is possible!

Measuring, proportion, and mixing

When gluten-free products were first developed decades ago, they had many problems. Breads tended to be dense and tough and usually were crumbly and flavorless. Cakes weren't tender or fluffy but had a tough crumb and were heavy. Cookies crumbled or were sticky and dense. Things have changed in the past few years, as intrepid bakers became determined to buck these disasters and make gluten-free baked goods that are just as good as those made with wheat.

Two of the essential steps in baking are key to delicious, gluten-free baked goods: measuring and mixing. Because gluten-free flours are heavier than wheat flours, weighing them (grams) instead of measuring by volume (cups and tablespoons) was a breakthrough. Here are some other points to keep in mind regarding measuring, proportion, and mixing:

- ✔ For the best results with gluten-free ingredients, you should weigh the flours, not measure them by volume. Use a scale set to gram weights and measure each flour you use. Be sure to zero out the scale after each measurement. (By the way, measuring in ounces is called *imperial weights* while measuring in grams is called *metric weights.* Just another cocktail party tidbit for you!)

- ✔ The proportion of flours to liquid is different in gluten-free baked goods. Doughs are rare; most of the recipes, even for yeast breads, are batters. Gluten-free flours are heavier and absorb more moisture than wheat flours, so they need a bit more liquid for the baked goods to be tender and moist.

- ✔ If you do measure by volume, be especially careful with flour and mixes. To measure flour with cups, tablespoons, and teaspoons, always spoon the flour into the measuring cup or spoon and then level off with the back of a knife. Never pack the flour, shake the cup, or press on the flour. Don't scoop the flour out of its container or bag with the measuring cup or you'll end up with too much flour and your products will be heavy and dry.

- ✔ You usually chill batters and doughs before baking. This gives the flour proteins and starches time to absorb the liquid in the recipe, which helps develop structure and flavor.

- ✔ When substituting flours in gluten-free breads, *always* substitute by weight. Don't substitute cup for cup or you'll end up with a disaster. If a recipe calls for 1 cup of potato starch, which weighs 190 grams, and you want to use tapioca starch, you need to add 190 grams of tapioca starch, not 1 cup — because a cup of tapioca starch (also called tapioca flour) weighs 125 grams! Substituting cup for cup just doesn't work. Use that scale and substitute gram for gram! For guidance, see the chart in

Chapter 5. For example, if you want to substitute corn flour for ¾ cup of brown rice flour, the chart in Chapter 5 tells you that ¾ cup of brown rice flour weighs 101 grams. So you need to substitute 101 grams of corn flour, which is ¾ cup (87 grams) plus 2 tablespoons (14 grams). Of course, not all conversions are that precise. Try to get within 4 grams of the total amount.

✔ Mixing, especially for yeast breads, is very different when you use gluten-free flours. First of all, you must mix together the different flours thoroughly before you add them to batters. Gluten-free flours are all different colors. The best way to make sure the flours are well-mixed is to stir them together with a wire whisk until the mixture is one color. Then, you use a stand or hand mixer to thoroughly mix the dry ingredients with the wet ingredients. You really can't overmix gluten-free batters or doughs because they have no gluten to overdevelop, so beat to your heart's content!

Fixing the lack of structure

Gluten-free baking has evolved over the past few years, ever since dedicated bakers discovered new tricks. Because gluten plays such a critical role in the structure of baked goods, replacing it is difficult. But bakers have discovered many ingredients for gluten-free recipes that help replicate gluten's function in baked goods:

✔ **Agar-agar:** Commonly used in processed foods, this vegan alternative to gelatin is made from seaweed. Agar-agar is very high in fiber. Using too much of this ingredient can make baked goods soggy, so measure carefully. Use about a teaspoon of agar-agar powder for each cup of liquid in a recipe.

✔ **Chia seeds:** These are the same seeds from that cheesy commercial that usually runs the day before Christmas (this may be the world's most perfect ear worm: "chi-chi-chi-chia!"). Like flaxseeds, chia seeds form a gel when mixed with boiling water. They're a good substitute for xanthan and guar gums.

✔ **Eggs:** The protein in eggs forms a web that traps air and water when beaten. Eggs are an easy way to add structure to any gluten-free baked product. However, if you're allergic to eggs, you can substitute a gel made from flaxseeds or chia seeds in many recipes.

✔ **Expandex:** This product, which is uncommon in retail markets, is modified tapioca starch. It forms a web with water, so it really mimics gluten's structure with no added taste because it's flavorless. You add from ¼ to ¾ cup of Expandex to bread recipes in place of some of the flour.

- ✓ **Gelatin:** This ingredient is used to make doughs more pliable. When mixed with water, gelatin forms, well, a gel that helps trap water and makes doughs stretchier. Use the unflavored variety only; your breads don't need to be strawberry-flavored!

- ✓ **Ground flaxseed:** Flaxseed, when ground, absorbs water and becomes a gel. You grind the seeds first and then combine them with boiling water to form a thick mixture. Flaxseed is very high in fiber and omega-3 fatty acids, so it's good for you. Do yourself a favor and use only golden flaxseeds. The brown ones contain a bit of chlorophyll, and you may end up with green-tinged bread.

- ✓ **Guar gum:** This gum is made from a legume plant. It's less expensive than xanthan gum but has incredible thickening power. It makes breads that are less "gummy" than breads made with xanthan gum. Both xanthan gum and guar gum have laxative properties, which can cause digestive distress in some people.

- ✓ **Pectin:** Pectin is a complex carbohydrate used to thicken jams and jellies. Dried pectin, which can be difficult to find, helps provide structure for breads and cakes. It absorbs moisture, which helps keep baked goods from drying out and keeps them soft.

- ✓ **Xanthan gum:** Older gluten-free recipes relied heavily on gums. Xanthan gum is made from corn. You use only a tiny bit in recipes — usually a teaspoon. If you use too much the product can become heavy or slimy.

  Gums form a stretchy web when mixed with water, which replicates gluten's structure. But xanthan gum is expensive, and some people who are sensitive to gluten are also sensitive to xanthan gum. Some people can taste the gum in baked goods.

The latest incarnations of gluten-free breads, cakes, and cookies use no gums, gelatin, or artificial structure-makers at all. How is this possible? Gluten-free bakers have found that using a combination of high-protein, high-starch, gluten-free flours helps mimic the structure provided by wheat flours. This knowledge, combined with new weighing and mixing methods, has revolutionized the gluten-free baking world.

We should note that some of these new recipes do use a little bit of gums, especially for yeast breads with little fat, such as French bread. Yeast breads generally need some type of addition to re-create the classic wheat-bread texture. Chia seeds or flaxseeds are preferred over gums, gelatin, or artificial ingredients.

If you want to avoid gums or other artificial add-ins, you need to combine gluten-free flours and starches. No single gluten-free flour has the characteristics, protein content, and starch content to singlehandedly replicate wheat flour.

Getting the ratios right

The newest thing in the gluten-free baking world is called the *ratio*. Recipes for everything from scones to cakes to breads are based on a ratio of gluten-free flours to sugar, liquids, eggs, and fat. If you follow these ratios, you have a better chance of getting the result you want with gluten-free flours. Ratios of ingredients are what make a cookie different from a cake and a scone different from a pancake.

Ratios aren't new in the baking world. For example, people have been making pound cakes for centuries using 1 pound each of butter, flour, eggs, and sugar. Most commercial bakers use ratios for measuring, and if you go to the Culinary Institute of America or the Cordon Bleu School in France to take baking classes, you're taught to measure by weight and to create recipes with ratios.

When you bake using ratios, you can double or triple a recipe with ease. Remember, you still need to weigh the dry ingredients! You may want to weigh the other ingredients, such as milk and sugar, just to make sure you're following the ratio as closely as possible. After all, the biggest variable in every single recipe is the cook. Standardizing how you measure by using grams instead of cups is one way to take one variable out of the baking equation.

When you make a recipe using ratios, you need to establish the base ingredient. This can be any of the ingredients. Most bakers use eggs as the base because eggs are the least variable of all the ingredients. A large egg weighs 2 ounces, or 56 grams. If your recipe calls for 3 parts flour to 3 parts liquid to 1 part egg, you need 168 grams (3×56) of flour and liquid.

Of course, you can use the liquid for the base ingredient and simply crack, beat, and measure the eggs. Just keep the ratios consistent and weigh every ingredient and your gluten-free baked goods will be delicious.

With these ratios, you can substitute teff flour for sorghum flour and almond milk for buttermilk without worry. You can change the flavor of a recipe from sweet to savory and vice versa with the confidence of knowing that scones will be flaky and crumbly, cakes will be tender, and breads will have a lovely, airy crumb.

You can find many formulas for baked goods, depending on the result you want. For instance, the ratio for angel food cake is different from the ratio for a shortening cake. Try to keep your ratios within 5 to 10 percent of the recommended numbers for each particular baked good and you should have success.

Table 4-1 lists some of the basic ratios for common baked goods. Remember that these ratios are measured by weight, not by volume.

These scoops are handy for gluten-free baking in several ways. First, because the batter or dough tends to be sticky, you can quickly form cookies, cupcakes, and muffins without getting your hands dirty. The release lever also helps you make sure that each cookie or cupcake is the same size because it releases all the batter or dough into the cup or onto the pan. And your cupcakes and cookies will all bake through at the same time because they're all exactly the same size. For muffins, the scoop shapes the muffins perfectly.

Buy the best ice cream scoops you can afford, and they'll last a lifetime. Stainless steel ice cream scoops are affordable and clean well in the dishwasher. To prevent sticking, dip the scoop into hot water occasionally or spray it with nonstick cooking spray.

Ice cream scoops come in several different sizes. Check out the list in Table 4-2. The smaller the number, the bigger the scoop! Traditionally, the size is equivalent to the number of scoops in one quart of ice cream (that's another cocktail party tidbit!).

Table 4-2	Ice Cream Scoop Sizes		
Scoop Size	*Fluid Ounces*	*Grams of Batter*	*Approx. Volume*
Number 100	⅓	9½	2 teaspoons
Number 70	½	14	1 tablespoon
Number 40	⅞	24	A bit less than 2 tablespoons
Number 30	1¼	35	7½ teaspoons
Number 24	1½	43	3 tablespoons
Number 20	1¾	50	10½ teaspoons
Number 16	2	57	¼ cup
Number 10	3½	99	6 tablespoons (about ⅓ cup)
Number 8	4	113	½ cup
Number 6	5¼	149	⅔ cup
Number 4	8	227	1 cup

To use these measurements, follow the recipe directions. For instance, because a standard 12-cup muffin tin holds 3½ ounces in each cup, use a number 24 or a number 20 ice cream scoop to fill that cup ½ to ¾ full. For large cookies, use a number 70 scoop; for regular-size cookies, use a number 100 scoop.

Piping bags

You use *piping bags* to form cookies, biscuits, and rolls. Most piping bags are made of coated cloth to prevent sticking. You can find them in most large supermarkets and at kitchen supply stores. You can also find single-use piping bags at these stores.

To use a piping bag, drop a coupler (a plastic ring with threads that holds the piping top) into the bag, screw a tip onto the outside of the coupler that pokes through the bottom hole, and then fold back the bag top. Add batter or dough to the bag, fold the top back, and shake the bag lightly to settle the batter at the bottom. Twist the open top of the bag to close it and then squeeze the bag with your dominant hand while you guide it with your non-dominant hand.

You can make your own piping bag by using a heavy-duty zip-lock disposable plastic bag. Just fill the bag ½ to ⅔ full and then snip off a tiny piece of the corner. Force the batter or dough through the bag out the opening. You can also use parchment paper to make a piping bag. Simply roll a large piece of parchment paper into a cone, fold down the large end once to hold the cone in place, fill it, and squeeze the batter through the small end.

Scales

A scale is the most important tool in gluten-free baking. Gluten-free flours are all different weights, so if you substitute one for another by volume (cup for cup), you're going to run into trouble. A cup of wheat all-purpose flour weighs 125 grams. If you substitute a cup of sweet rice flour, which weighs 155 grams, your baked good will be dry and heavy. *Always* try to substitute by weight. The correct substitution for 1 cup of wheat all-purpose flour is 125 grams of sweet rice flour.

Scales are common and easy to find. Get one with a digital readout for best accuracy. To use a scale, follow these steps:

1. **Turn on the scale.**

2. **Place the container you're using for the ingredient on the scale.**

   The scale will register a weight.

3. **Zero out the scale (this is also called *taring*) by pressing the "Tare" or "Zero out" button.**

   The scale will read "0."

4. **Add the ingredient you're measuring until the scale reads the correct number.**

5. **Remove the ingredient to a separate bowl, add the container, zero out the scale, and measure another ingredient.**

Or you can continue adding ingredients, adding up the total number. This takes some math skills! Or to keep it simple, keep the container on the scale, zero it out again, and add another ingredient until it reaches the number you want.

Weighing ingredients may feel a bit awkward at first, but you'll get the hang of it quickly. It makes cleanup easier too because you have to use only one bowl. And after you see how good your gluten-free baked goods are, you'll never go back to measuring flours by volume! And remember to check if your scale turns off if you haven't added ingredients after a minute or two. Stir the mixture in the bowl if this happens, to keep the scale "awake"!

Thermometers

Two kinds of thermometers are crucial to gluten-free baking: an oven thermometer and an instant-read thermometer. You use the first to make sure that your oven temperature is accurate so that baking times are accurate. You use the second to measure the baked good's doneness.

Oven thermometers

You need to monitor your oven's temperature no matter how new, expensive, or sophisticated the oven is. Over time, temperature sensors can get a little wonky, and if you're baking something that requires a temperature of 350 degrees but your oven is 360 degrees, you'll overbake the food.

Get the best oven thermometer you can buy. Most supermarkets carry thermometers but they aren't very accurate. Buy a good one and keep it in your oven. Thermometers that hang off the bottom of a rack, so they're in the middle of the oven, are the best choice. That's where the temperature should be measured, and in that location the thermometer won't get in the way of pans in the oven.

If your oven is off, check the owner's manual to see whether you can manually adjust the thermometer or temperature. If you can, fiddle with it until the temperature is correct. If not, call a qualified technician and have him or her regulate the temperature.

Instant-read thermometers

When baked goods are done, most of the liquid has evaporated from the batter or dough, and the temperature rises to a certain point. You can use instant-read thermometers to take the temperature of your food. They measure the temperature within 3 to 5 seconds (hence the "instant" moniker) and are quite accurate. Baked goods all have different temperature doneness points. For more information about the doneness temperature of different types of baked goods, see Chapter 3.

Quick Bread Issues

Quick breads are breads that are leavened with baking powder or baking soda. These breads don't need to take time to rise; in fact, the faster you can get the batter into the oven, the better! You don't use yeast in quick breads. Quick breads are usually made of batters, not doughs. Muffins are included in the quick bread category.

In this section we look at the issues behind some quick bread failures and ways you can make the most tender and moist quick breads, even with gluten-free flours and starches.

Keeping it tender when you convert

The main issue with wheat-based quick breads is that you have to mix them as little as possible so a lot of gluten doesn't form. So you're automatically one step ahead, because gluten-free flours don't have gluten! Many gluten-free quick breads tend to crumble when you slice them, and grittiness is a problem. Some people miss the flavor that wheat flours provide, but we can solve those issues! Remember that for the recipes in this book, don't make these changes. These tips are to help you convert wheat-based recipes into gluten-free treats.

To keep gluten-free quick breads tender and moist, follow a few rules. Use these tips when you're altering a wheat flour quick bread recipe to the gluten-free standard.

- ✔ Combine flours for best results. No gluten-free quick bread recipe is made using just one flour.
- ✔ Consider grinding flours in a food processor to make them finer, or look for extra-fine gluten-free flours.
- ✔ Measure flours by weight, not by volume.
- ✔ Make sure you mix the flours together really well before combining them with any of the other ingredients.
- ✔ Use a larger amount of oil and liquid than you would with most standard quick breads. Remember, these flours soak up more liquid than wheat flours.

- Add yogurt or sour cream to the batter in place of water or juices to help make the structure more tender.

- Add nutrition and flavor to gluten-free quick breads using fruit purées.

- Soak dried fruit in some of the liquid used in the recipe before adding it to the batter.

- Toast nuts before adding them to quick breads. This adds flavor and also helps a bit with the structure.

- Increase the amount of baking soda or baking powder by ½ teaspoon. Gluten-free flours are heavier than wheat flours, so a little bit more leavening helps create a good texture.

- When you combine the flours, make a hollow in the center. Combine all the wet ingredients and beat well. Add the wet ingredients to the flours and mix until combined.

- Use the correct size pan and grease it well according to the recipe. You may want to use a smaller pan size. Pans that are 8-x-4 inches or 6-x-3 inches may work better than the standard 9-x-5-inch loaf pan. Fill the loaf pan about ⅔ full for best results. You may have some batter left over; use it to make two or three muffins.

- Bake at the correct temperature for the right amount of time. Be sure that your oven is properly calibrated.

- Understand doneness tests. Quick bread doneness tests include observing a brown crust with a crack down the center, an internal temperature of about 200 degrees, and a firm texture. You can also check doneness with a toothpick; it should come out moist, with just a few crumbs sticking to it.

- Let the bread cool completely before cutting it. Cutting warm bread is just asking for trouble; it will crumble and fall apart.

- Gluten-free quick breads may become dry and taste stale more quickly than wheat-based quick breads. So eat them within a day or two, or freeze them when they've cooled completely.

Building structure in quick breads

Quick breads should have an even crumb, but more open, with larger air holes than yeast breads. The top should be bumpy. The crust should be moist and rich, not hard or dry. You can experiment with lots of different types of flours in your quick breads or you can add other ingredients to help keep the structure firm but tender.

To build structure in quick breads, follow these tips:

- ✔ Use flours with high protein and flours with low protein. A good mix of different flours helps compensate for lack of gluten.

- ✔ Flours that are high in fiber, like coconut flour and brown rice flour, help add strength to the structure without making the bread tough or dry.

- ✔ Mix flours and starches. A combination of flours, like coconut or sweet rice flour, mixed with starches like cornstarch or potato starch give the bread good structure.

- ✔ Add gums. Use xanthan gum or guar gum in small quantities to add structure to quick breads. Use a little less than ½ teaspoon per cup of flour in quick bread recipes.

- ✔ You may want to add another egg to a quick bread recipe you're converting to gluten-free. Egg proteins help provide structure in any baked good, and especially in quick breads. Be sure to reduce the liquid in the recipe by 2 tablespoons if you add another egg.

- ✔ Get the quick breads into the oven as soon as possible. Gluten-free bread structure is more fragile than wheat bread structure, and you want to hold on to all those bubbles you worked so hard to create.

- ✔ Make sure that your oven temperature is accurate. If the oven temperature is too high, the outside of the bread will brown and set before the inside is done.

For more information about flours and starches and which ones are best to use in different recipes, see Chapter 5. After you've worked with these flours and understand what a quick bread batter should look like, the sky's the limit! Invent your own quick bread recipes using the ratios in Table 4-1, earlier in the chapter.

Yeast Bread Issues

Ah, yeast bread. There's nothing like the aroma of baking bread wafting through your home. And the tender but crunchy crust, the soft crumb, the wonderful chewiness; will you ever be able to taste that again?

Of course! Would we tease you like that and not solve the problem of making gluten-free yeast breads? In this section we tackle the flavor and texture issues in gluten-free yeast breads, including why gluten-free batters are different from wheat batters and doughs and how to get the perfect crust.

Understanding the basics of gluten-free yeast breads

Making gluten-free yeast breads is very different from making wheat-based yeast breads, although the goal is to achieve the same texture and flavor. Because ordinary yeast breads use gluten for structure, you have to come up with another way to build that structure without gluten.

Here are some basic rules and methods for making the best gluten-free bread with the texture you find in wheat breads:

- ✔ You make gluten-free yeast breads with thick batters. You may find some gluten-free doughs floating around (or thudding around), but generally they produce very heavy, dense breads. Because gluten-free flours are heavier than wheat flour, without proper structure they can't hold the air that the yeast produces, and you end up with something resembling a doorstop. And because gluten-free flours are drier than wheat flour, they need more liquid. Making gluten-free yeast breads out of batters instead of doughs makes them more tender.

- ✔ Mix the flours together very well before you add any liquid ingredients. The combination of flours, with their different protein and starch contents, is what provides the structure in these breads.

- ✔ Choose gluten-free flours that are high in protein for better structure and more stability. These proteins may not have exactly the same characteristics as gluten, but they can come pretty close.

- ✔ Beat the doughs with a stand mixer for five to ten minutes. This helps work air into the dough and ensures that all the ingredients are well-mixed. It also gives the flour time to absorb liquid and helps the eggs form the structure. You can't knead the batters, so this step helps to form the structure with the proteins and starches in the flour as they hydrate.

- ✔ Gluten-free breads only rise once. If you stir or punch down the dough for a second rise, you'll destroy the delicate structure. You just mix these breads and pour them into a pan, and then they rise and bake. Enjoy the freedom of less work for great breads!

- ✔ You need to use pans to form gluten-free breads. Use muffin tins for rolls and loaf pans for breads. You can find specialty loaf pans, such as pans for French bread loaves, that you can use to shape gluten-free yeast breads.

- ✔ Don't let the batter rise too long! Because the structure of gluten-free yeast breads is more delicate than that of wheat yeast breads, if the yeast overdevelops it forms acid, which can ruin the structure. And too much carbon dioxide produced by the yeast can overwhelm the structure, and the bread will collapse.

Here are several ingredients you can use to get a tender, even crumb in gluten-free yeast breads:

- **Carbonated water:** Use this to add more air to gluten-free yeast breads. Anything you can do to add bubbles is good!

- **Chia and flaxseed slurries:** These are wonderful ways to add structure to these bread recipes. They add fiber and nutrition, too.

- **Dry milk or whey:** These also improve the structure of gluten-free yeast breads. They add protein and nutrition, too.

- **Eggs:** Use eggs to add texture and structure to these breads. If you're sensitive to eggs, use a flaxseed slurry instead. Combine 1 tablespoon ground golden flaxseeds with 2 tablespoons water. Heat until thickened. Use this amount to replace one egg.

- **Xanthan gum and guar gum:** Use these in gluten-free yeast breads to provide structure. This addition also helps keep the bread from crumbling and makes it less grainy.

Building flavor in gluten-free yeast breads

The nutty flavor of wheat flour is hard to replicate. But by using the right types of gluten-free flours, you can get pretty close. Obviously, the flavor of the yeast is paramount in any yeast bread. But flavors and textures of flours play an important part.

Gluten-free flours all have different flavors and characteristics. For specifics, flip to Chapter 5. For making yeast breads, these are the flours that add a wheaty, nutty flavor. Be sure to always substitute by weight, not by volume.

- **Almond and nut flours:** Well, nut flours have a nutty flavor! Almond meal or flour adds delicious flavor to yeast breads. Chestnut flour has a strong nutty flavor too.

- **Amaranth flour:** This flour is nutty and sweet. It makes a thick and chewy crust on yeast breads. Don't use it as the main flour in bread recipes, but you can use it for about ¼ of the total flour amount.

- **Buckwheat flour:** Despite its name, this grain doesn't contain gluten. It has a very strong, earthy flavor when roasted.

- **Garfava flour:** This combination of fava bean and garbanzo bean flours has a bean flavor and lots of protein. It also adds fiber to bread recipes.

- **Rice flour:** Brown rice flour adds a nutty and sweet flavor to breads. If you can find wild rice flour, add it for a nutty flavor. Sweet rice flour is more neutral.

- **Sorghum flour:** This flour has a wheat taste and doesn't have a gritty texture. It's also very high in protein, so it helps with the bread's structure.

✔ **Soy flour:** This flour has a strong flavor, so use it sparingly. It helps bread brown quickly and is high in protein.

✔ **White bean flour:** This is a high-protein flour with a mild taste. If you don't like the taste of soy or garfava, this light-colored flour is a good substitute.

One way to build flavor in gluten-free yeast breads is to add other ingredients. Here are some options:

✔ **Finely grated cheese:** This is a wonderful flavor addition to many yeast breads. Cheeses also add protein and more nutrition.

✔ **Fruit juices or vegetable juices:** You can use these for part of the liquid in bread recipes. They add a sweet flavor or a savory flavor to many breads.

✔ **Gluten-free beer:** Gluten-free yeast breads rise only once, so the yeast flavor may be less pronounced. Beer can add a yeasty flavor to any bread recipe; use it in place of some of the liquid.

✔ **Herbs and spices:** These are good ingredients to add more flavor. You can use fresh or dried herbs. Use three times the amount of fresh herbs, simply because they're less potent.

✔ **Seeds and nuts:** These can add great flavor, along with texture, to gluten-free yeast breads. Toast the seeds and nuts before adding them to the batter to help bring out the flavor.

✔ **Sourdough:** This is the ultimate yeast bread flavor. See Chapter 19 for info about sourdough starters and how to make your own.

Pie Crust Issues

Pie crust is all about the fat and the flour. Pie crust doesn't need much leavening; what you want is tender flakiness. You create that characteristic by the way in which you combine the ingredients and by the ratios of fat to flour to liquid.

In this section we tell you how to make a perfect gluten-free pie crust that has all the texture and flavor of a wheat pie crust. With a few tips and tricks, you can make delicious gluten-free pie crusts with ease.

Building a tasty pie crust structure

When bakers make wheat pie crusts, they battle gluten. When pie crust has too much of that stretchy and pliable protein, it becomes tough and doughy, not flaky and tender. So, just as with quick breads, you're ahead of the game when making pie crust with gluten-free flours.

A combination of flours is the best way to get a tender and flaky pie crust that holds together when you cut it and that doesn't crumble or taste gritty. Here are the ingredients to use when making a gluten-free pie crust:

- **Cold butter or fat:** For best results, make sure that the fat you use is very cold. The fat has to keep its shape as you blend it with the flour. Then, when the crust bakes, the layers of fat melt, creating the flaky layers you want in your pie crust.

- **Cold liquid:** Because the fat needs to be cold, the liquid should be cold too! Most pie crust recipes use cold water. To make sure it stays cold, fill a small bowl with cold water and add ice. Then measure the water for the crust directly from the bowl of ice water.

- **Cream cheese:** This ingredient used to be very popular in pie crust recipes. It helps make the crust very tender. To use it, blend together the cream cheese and butter or other fat and then add the flours. With a cream cheese pie crust, you don't need any added liquid.

- **Eggs:** Eggs can help keep the flour moist and hold the pie crust structure together. If you're avoiding eggs, try using a vegan egg replacer.

- **Leaf lard:** Leaf lard is pork fat, but it's a special type that's more expensive (and more difficult to find) than ordinary lard. Leaf lard really makes your pie crusts flaky because it resists blending with the flour. The lard stays in nice layers, creating beautiful flaky layers in the finished crust.

- **Superfine flours:** Ordinary gluten-free flours, such as rice flour, tend to be gritty. You want a very fine flour so it blends well with the fat. If you can't find superfine flours, grind any type of gluten-free flour in a coffee grinder until it's powdery.

- **Xanthan or guar gum:** Some pie crust dough recipes do add these gums to help build structure and prevent the crumblies. But if you're sensitive to these ingredients, use flaxseed or chia seed slurries instead.

When you're making a gluten-free pie crust, follow these tips for making and handling the dough for best results:

- Try using a food processor instead of making the dough by hand. This machine mixes the ingredients very quickly, which is the best way to keep the ingredients cold.

- Combine the flour and fat until the fat is the size of small peas. The fat should be visible in the flour. This keeps the pie crust tender and helps build the layers.

- Check the dough consistency several times while you mix it. Remember, these flours need a lot of liquid. You may need to add more water to make a dough that holds together. But don't add too much water! The dough should be crumbly but hold together when pressed.

✔ Handle the dough as little as possible. We're not concerned about the overdevelopment of gluten in these recipes; we just want to keep the dough cold!

✔ Let the dough rest before you roll it out. This gives the flour time to absorb the liquid so the pie crust won't be crumbly or gritty.

✔ Use waxed paper or parchment paper to roll out the dough. Gluten-free doughs are usually stickier than wheat doughs. These papers make it easier to handle the dough.

✔ Bake the pie crust at a high temperature. You want the crust to bake really quickly so the fat melts and the structure sets at about the same time. This preserves those flaky layers you've worked so hard to build.

Getting a flaky or mealy texture

People use lots of words to describe pie crust. The most common are "flaky" and "mealy." But what do they mean? Do you sometimes want a flaky crust or a mealy crust? Here's how:

✔ You make flaky pie crusts with larger pieces of fat. These larger pieces leave larger holes when the fat melts, creating more layers. When your fork hits those layers as you eat the pie, they break apart, creating the flaky sensation.

✔ You make mealy pie crusts with smaller pieces of fat. For a mealy crust, cut the fat into the flour until the pieces of fat are small. This makes a dough that's denser, with fewer layers.

So would you ever want a mealy pie crust? Surprisingly, yes! If you're making a fruit pie or a pie with a wet filling, a mealy bottom crust is the way to go. It absorbs less moisture from the filling as the pie bakes and won't crumble or fall apart.

Cake Issues

Everyone wants a light and fluffy cake with a soft and tiny crumb. For gluten-free cakes, you're in luck! This is another product where you want to minimize gluten and its effects. Most cakes are built on egg protein. The flour is just there to stabilize the batter and add some starch for tenderness.

In this section we cover building tender and even cake structure, adding moistness to the gluten-free cakes you bake, and adding flavor to any cake recipe.

Keeping tenderness and moistness

Think about the best cake you ever ate. Chances are it was very tender and moist, with an even, almost velvety texture. In cakes, you want a fine crumb, which means very tiny air holes. And the cake should be moist, not dry. You want to add ingredients that attract moisture and hold it in the structure.

Here are several ways of getting a tender, fine crumb in cakes:

- ✔ Add a little extra leavening. Gluten-free flours are heavier and grab more moisture than wheat flours. Adding a little bit more baking soda and baking powder can give the cake batter the extra lift it needs for a fine and tender crumb.

- ✔ Beat well. You need to aerate these batters. And because you don't have to worry about gluten, you can beat the batters for a fairly long period of time — usually three to five minutes. This adds air to the batter. The protein and starch in the flour and eggs will form around the air bubbles.

- ✔ Use flours with a low protein content. A 50:50 split of flours and starches gives the cake enough structure but keeps the texture fine. See Chapter 5 for info about lower-protein gluten-free flours.

- ✔ Substitute sparkling water or soda pop for some of the liquid. This adds more air to the batter, which helps get the lift you want in any cake.

- ✔ Add some finely divided solids, such as ground chocolate or cocoa powder. That's a food science term for ingredients that are chopped very finely.

- ✔ Use brown sugar. Brown sugar has more moisture than white sugar (which is why you have to pack it into the cup to measure it), so it makes the cake crumb more tender and moist.

- ✔ Use more sugar. Sugar adds tenderness to cakes, and it's *hygroscopic,* which just means that it attracts water. So more sugar means a more tender cake with a finer crumb.

Adding more flavor

Most cake recipes are designed to be full of flavor. Chocolate cakes should taste rich and full of, well, chocolate. Fruit cakes should taste of the fruit and be very moist. Vanilla cakes should have a strong vanilla flavor. You get the idea!

If you find a recipe that has a wonderful texture but the flavor isn't quite there, try these tricks:

✔ Add fruit purées in place of some of the liquid. Applesauce, pear purées, or any other puréed fruit really helps cakes stay moist and tender.

✔ For cake recipes that use cocoa powder, bloom the powder in some hot water first. *Bloom* just means to enhance the flavor in some way. When you mix cocoa with hot water, the flavor is accentuated.

✔ Use another type of liquid instead of milk or water. Coffee adds great depth of flavor to chocolate cakes.

✔ Add more spices. Cinnamon, nutmeg, and cloves are classic cake spices. A tiny bit adds flavor and interest to just about any cake recipe.

✔ Use real extracts. Real vanilla or real almond extract adds more flavor than imitation extracts. And you can add a bit more than the recipe calls for. In fact, double the vanilla extract in any cake recipe for fabulous flavor.

Cookie Issues

Cookies are easy to make and mouth-watering. Because they're so small, building structure in them is easier than in other baked goods. Cookies are a balance among flour, fat, egg, and sugar, with flour the largest amount, fat the second, and sugar the third.

The only issue with gluten-free cookies is choosing the type of texture you want. Do you want a crisp cookie or a chewy one? And how do you make cookies that are tender and moist? In this section we explain the methods for making the kind of cookie you want and ways to use gluten-free flours for the best results.

Making the best gluten-free cookies

A combination of gluten-free flours and starches is the best way to make the best cookies. In fact, an even proportion of flours to starches is the best way to make tender cookies. Gluten-free cookie batters and doughs are softer than wheat-based cookie doughs because more liquid is needed to hydrate the flour.

To make the best gluten-free cookies, use these tips:

✔ Let the dough rest. Resting time, preferably in the refrigerator, gives the flour enough time to absorb the liquid and set the cookie's structure. Chilling also solidifies the fat so that the cookies hold their shape in the oven.

✔ Reduce the oven temperature. Overbaking cookies makes them hard and tough. A longer bake at a lower temperature lets the cookies bake through before the edges get hard or overbrown.

✔ Try freezing the dough before you bake it. Then let the dough thaw in the fridge until you can handle it and form and bake the cookies. This helps the cookies keep their shape.

✔ If your cookies are thin and flat and you want thicker cookies, substitute solid shortening for some of the butter.

✔ Use finely ground flours. Cookies don't have a lot of ingredients, and using a fine flour helps prevent grittiness.

✔ Use parchment paper, plastic wrap, or waxed paper to roll out the dough. Gluten-free doughs are stickier than wheat-based doughs, so these products help you shape cookies with less fuss and mess.

✔ Make sure the cookie sheet is completely cool before you add another batch of cookie dough. Warm cookie sheets make the dough spread before it even gets into the oven, which weakens the structure.

Deciding between crisp and chewy

Cookies come in two basic types: crisp and chewy. Everyone has his favorite type, and each type of cookie should have a certain texture. How do you make a chewy cookie? And what ingredients make a cookie crisp?

Chewy

To make a chewy cookie, your dough needs more moisture. More high-protein flour, eggs, and sugar help keep a cookie chewy. For chewy cookies, follow these rules:

✔ Solid shortening makes a chewier, thicker cookie. This type of fat doesn't spread as much as the cookie bakes.

✔ Chewy cookies have more moisture in the batter or dough.

✔ More eggs typically means the cookie will be chewy. Add an egg yolk to add more fat to the dough; this helps make the cookies chewy.

✔ Use brown sugar. This sugar has more moisture than granulated sugar, so the cookies will be chewier.

✔ Use flour with a high protein content. Because you don't have to worry about gluten developing in these cookies, more protein makes the cookie structure stronger.

✔ Underbake the cookies a little bit. They should still be done, but less baking makes a chewier cookie.

Crisp

Crisp cookies have less liquid and more fat. To make a crisp cookie, follow these rules:

- ✔ Use butter or margarine. These fats spread more in the oven, allowing more moisture evaporation, which makes the cookies crisper.

- ✔ Choose low-protein flours. They make the cookies spread out more as they bake, which makes them crisper.

- ✔ Use less liquid. Crisp cookies shouldn't have much, if any, liquid.

- ✔ Use granulated sugar rather than brown sugar for crisp cookies.

- ✔ For crisp roll-out cookies, refrigerate the cookies right on the cookie sheet before you bake them.

Chapter 5

Building Flavor and Structure without Wheat

. . . .

In This Chapter

▶ Building structure without using gluten

▶ Emulating the taste of wheat

▶ Surveying the range of alternative flours

▶ Understanding the role of starches

▶ Making use of additives in baked goods

. . . .

So gluten is out. This protein forms the main structure in many baked goods, such as bread, cookies, cakes, pie crust, pizza dough — okay, everything! But with a little knowledge and some flour and starch combinations, you can bake without gluten and never miss it.

So how does gluten work in baked goods? What's the science behind this phenomenon? And does wheat add more than just structure to baked goods?

In this chapter we tell you about gluten-free flours that are alternatives to wheat flours. We discuss their flavor, protein, and fiber and starch components and amounts. We show you how to use them to make the best gluten-free baked goods possible. Because the gluten-free products with the most tender yet strong structure are made with a combination of flours, understanding the flavor and protein content of each flour makes you a better baker.

Finally, we take a look at additions to baked goods that help mimic gluten's structure. Gums, gels, certain flours, starches, whey, and some protein powders can build the structure that some gluten-free baked goods lack.

Mimicking Gluten's Structure

Gluten is comprised of two molecules: glutenin and gliadin. Those fancy names are just two proteins that fuse together in the presence of liquid.

When kneaded or beaten, the gluten strands form a web that's incredibly strong and elastic. That's why you can make wheat bread with just flour, water, and yeast.

You must use alternative flours to mimic gluten's strength and elasticity, so in this section you discover ways to build a nice structure in your baked goods without one speck of gluten. Along the way, you want your baked goods to be delicious, so mimicking the nutty, sweet flavor of wheat is another goal. And because gluten plays a part in staling and retaining the freshness of baked goods, we look at ways to achieve these characteristics in gluten-free products.

Remember that we've developed the recipes in this book to retain freshness and deliver the proper structure. Use these tips when converting your own recipes to gluten-free.

Developing structure and strength

Scientists say that gluten has "viscoelastic properties." *Viscoelastic* means that the web of gluten stretches like elastic and has the viscosity of gums. This web is called a *protein network*. To re-create the texture and structure of gluten in gluten-free products, you need to do a little work, but it is possible!

Most gluten-free flour blends use a ratio of about 70 percent high-protein flours to 30 percent lower-protein or high-starch flours. This ratio makes a flour blend that acts pretty much like all-purpose wheat flour in baking recipes.

These are the flour components used to develop structure in baked goods:

- **Protein:** High-protein gluten-free flours are useful for making products that need a strong structure, such as popovers, yeast breads, and pizza crusts. Low-protein gluten-free flours work well in more delicate recipes such as cakes and cookies.

- **Starch:** When starch is combined with water and heat, it *gelatinizes,* or forms a web. That's just what you want! Unfortunately, starch webs are much weaker than protein webs. Starch can do some of the heavy lifting in gluten-free baked goods, but it needs help from protein.

- **Lipids:** All flours contain lipids, or fats. In fact, high-fat flours can become rancid when the fat oxidizes, which is why many flours are stored in the fridge or freezer. Lipids add flavor and help keep the flour's protein structure from overwhelming the product.

For the strongest structure, choose a combination of high-protein gluten-free flours. Most recipes should also include some starch to add a pleasing mouth feel. More delicate recipes can use low-protein flours and more starches. You may have to experiment before you decide which flours work best for your recipes and which flours you prefer for their flavor.

Wheat products use different flours

Here's one way to look at the gluten-free baking challenge. You're probably used to baking with wheat flours. You need different types of wheat flour to make different types of foods. If you tried to make a cake with high-protein bread flour, the cake would be heavy and dense. If you tried to make French bread with low-protein cake flour, the bread structure would collapse and the crumb would fall apart. You must use different types of wheat flour for wheat baking. The same principle holds true with gluten-free flours. The different protein content, starch content, flavors, and properties of gluten-free flours are uniquely suited to different types of baked goods.

Retaining freshness

As baked goods age, they can become stale. Everyone has eaten a piece of stale bread! The tender crumb becomes tough and the bread is stiff. Many people think that the bread has simply dried out, but that isn't what happens. When bread stales, the starch in the bread *retrogrades,* meaning that the starch molecules rearrange as the bread ages, forming a crystalline structure that's unpleasant to eat.

Wheat gluten, unfortunately, is a key component in preventing staling. Choosing higher-protein flours can retard staling. Here are other ways to make your gluten-free baked goods taste fresh longer:

✔ Freeze the bread or rolls soon after baking. Freezing stops starch retrogradation. Thaw the products at room temperature, but be sure to thaw only the amount you're going to eat immediately.

✔ Use a bit of fat in the recipe. A tablespoon of oil or melted butter in a recipe for French bread can help reduce staling.

✔ Don't store your baked goods in the refrigerator. The dry atmosphere and cool temperatures in the fridge encourage retrogradation.

✔ Add a little bit of vinegar to each recipe. This adds a pleasing sour taste to plain breads and helps retard mold growth.

✔ Add a little bit of ascorbic acid (vitamin C) to your breads. This also adds a pleasant slight sour taste and increases the nutrition of your breads.

You can use staleness to your advantage. Stale bread is excellent in bread puddings and stratas and is tasty when toasted. Heating rolls and whole loaves of bread can help re-gelatinize the starch for a very short period.

Of course, the best way to avoid staling is to eat your gluten-free products quickly! Your family will be so pleased by your baking that you probably won't have to worry about your baked goods sitting around long enough to go stale.

Mimicking Wheat's Flavor

Gluten doesn't have a flavor, but wheat flour does. It has a unique nutty, earthy, sweet flavor that's difficult, but not impossible, to duplicate. It's very present in yeast breads but not so much in cookies and cakes.

All gluten-free flours have different flavors. Some are mild; some are strong. You may not like the taste of all gluten-free flours. And you want to use different flours for baking a cake than for making a dark brown bread. In this section we look at how to add nutty, earthy, and sweet flavors to your delicious gluten-free baked goods.

 No gluten-free flour tastes exactly like wheat flour. Though you can get close, you'll never be able to perfectly mimic the nutty, sweet flavor of wheat flour, so you probably have to adjust your expectations. But this can be a good thing! Gluten-free flours have a wider variety of flavors than plain old wheat flour. You can enjoy experimenting with these different flours and creating your own special blends.

Adding nuttiness

Many of the alternative gluten-free flours are already nutty, so mimicking this flavor is easy. Nut flours are obvious choices for this characteristic, but if you're allergic to nuts, you can use other gluten-free flours with a delectable nutty taste, including

- Almond and other nut flours
- Amaranth flour
- Brown rice flour
- Buckwheat flour
- Quinoa flour
- Sorghum flour
- Teff flour

Developing sweetness

Some gluten-free flours, such as coconut and buckwheat flours, have naturally sweet tastes. But some flours can have strong or beany flavors and aftertastes. You can add some extra flavor extracts, such as lemon or vanilla extract, to sweet recipes to help mask those undesirable flavors. Choose recipes that are naturally more flavorful, such as chocolate cakes or nut cakes, to hide the gluten-free flour flavor you may not like.

These are some of the sweeter gluten-free flours:

- ✔ Almond flour
- ✔ Amaranth flour
- ✔ Raw buckwheat flour (the raw part is important because roasted buckwheat flour is far from sweet)
- ✔ Coconut flour

Key Alternative Flours

Certain flours are most often used in gluten-free baking because they work well, especially in combination. Just like baking with wheat flour, you choose gluten-free flours based on the product you're making.

In this section we cover the different gluten-free flours and their characteristics, the type of crumb they produce, and their protein, fiber, and carbohydrate content. Study these lists to find out about the flours that are going to become a part of your kitchen. The more you know about them, the better gluten-free baker you'll be!

We include the fiber content of these flours because many people are trying to increase the fiber in their diet. Fiber can help reduce the risk of certain diseases, lower cholesterol, and improve digestive function. For more information about nutrition and the gluten-free diet, see Chapter 6.

Flours for delicate baked goods

When you're making delicate, gluten-free baked goods, you're starting out ahead. In these types of recipes — for cookies, cakes, muffins, and quick breads — you don't want a lot of gluten formation. The flours you choose should be fairly low in protein with a mild flavor. And you want to add some starch to balance the product structure. Remember to follow the basic 70 percent protein flour/30 percent starch ratio for the best baked goods.

What follows are some of the best flours to use for delicate baked goods, in order of increasing protein content.

White rice flour

This flour, made from white rice, is white and basically flavorless. Like brown rice flour, it provides crunch unless it's very finely ground. It has 2.4 grams of protein, 1 gram of fiber, and 31.7 grams of carbohydrates per ¼ cup. You almost always want to combine it with other gluten-free flours in baking recipes. Try it in shortbread for a wonderfully crumbly texture. Look for superfine white rice flour in specialty stores, Asian markets, and online.

Coconut flour

This flour is white and slightly sweet tasting, yet mild. It's made from dried and ground coconut. It's high in healthy monounsaturated fats and works best in recipes with eggs. This flour is also very absorbent and needs a lot of liquid. In fact, many recipes with coconut flour call for using a 1:1 ratio of flour to liquid. It has 3 grams of protein, 12 grams of fiber, and 6 grams of carbs per ¼ cup.

Almond flour

This flour, sometimes called almond meal, has a wonderfully nutty yet mild and slightly sweet taste. The flour is white or ivory and produces a tender, moist crumb, very similar to wheat flour. It's high in fat, but like coconut flour, the fat is of the healthier monounsaturated variety. Also like coconut flour, almond flour works best in recipes with eggs (to provide more structure). It has 6 grams of protein, 3 grams of fiber, and 6 grams of carbs per ¼ cup. Because it's high in fat, store it in the fridge or freezer. Bring the flour to room temperature before using in a recipe.

Cashew flour

This flour has a naturally nutty and sweet taste and produces soft and tender baked goods because it's made from dried, ground cashews. It's a good choice for mimicking the flavor of wheat flour. Try this flour in chocolate chip cookies or brownies. Cashew flour has 10 grams of protein, 2 grams of fiber, and 16 grams of carbs per ¼ cup.

Flours for yeast breads and rolls

Yeast breads and rolls need more structure than delicate baked goods, so you should use higher-protein flours to make them. You also want more flavor in these breads because the flavor of wheat breads is, well, mostly of wheat. The combination of these flours produces some very yummy bread. After you've tried these flours, you'll feel sorry for people who only eat wheat breads!

This section presents the best flours to use for yeast breads and rolls, in order of increasing protein content.

Corn flour

Corn flour is yellow because it's made from dried and ground corn. It adds strength to doughs and batters and a nice depth of flavor. It tastes sweet, slightly nutty, and, well, a little bit like corn! Corn flour contains 2 grams of protein, 6 grams of fiber, and 22 grams of carbs per ¼ cup.

Brown rice flour

Brown rice flour, made from unhulled rice grains, has a medium protein content and a nutty taste, but it's pretty bland and mild. Unless it's finely ground, the flour provides some crunch to baked goods. Look for superfine brown rice flour at stores. It has 2.9 grams of protein, 2 grams of fiber, and 30 grams of carbs per ¼ cup.

Buckwheat flour

Buckwheat flour is confusing at first. Because its name includes "wheat," many people think it has gluten. But the buckwheat plant isn't a grain; it's a fruit seed that's related to rhubarb. This seed is very good for you; it can help reduce the risk of diabetes and control blood pressure.

Store-bought buckwheat flour is roasted before grinding, creating a lovely dark brown color and an earthy flavor. It produces a tender and sweet crumb that's firm because of high protein content. Buckwheat flour has 3.8 grams of protein, 6 grams of fiber, and 21.2 grams of carbs per ¼ cup.

Raw buckwheat flour can be difficult to find, but you can make your own flour from raw (green) buckwheat groats. Just grind the groats in a coffee grinder or mill. It has a naturally sweet flavor. See the section "Using Additives to Achieve Tender Baked Goods," later in the chapter, for more information on the uses of buckwheat flour.

Sorghum flour

Sorghum is a cereal grain, but it contains no gluten. It was used for years as animal feed, but it's very nutritious. This flour has the most wheat-like taste and a very high protein and insoluble fiber content. It's a pale brown flour with a dark brown fleck. Often used in flour blends, sorghum flour produces a firm but tender structure. It contains 4 grams of protein, 3 grams of fiber, and 25 grams of carbs per ¼ cup.

Quinoa flour

The quinoa plant is an ancient cereal grain. Quinoa is unusual because it's one of the only plants that provides 100 percent of all the amino acids the human body needs. The brown seed is coated with a bitter substance called *saponin* that must be rinsed off before using. The flour has the saponin removed.

Other gluten-free flours

You can find a host of other gluten-free flours that aren't as commonly used. After you're comfortable working with the flours listed in this chapter, you may want to branch out to others. Hemp flour gives foods a nice, nutty taste (and doesn't affect your, um, mood as you may expect), but it can be difficult to find guaranteed gluten-free. Montina is made from a grass seed. This flour is high in protein and fiber and has a nutty flavor. Oat flour is nice for cookies and quick breads if you can find it certified gluten-free. And chestnut flour is obviously nutty. Use it to add a rich flavor to baked desserts and pastries.

This flour is pale brown with a strong flavor, so add only small amounts unless you really enjoy the taste. It can be bitter and tastes quite nutty. It adds great strength to batters and doughs. It contains 4 grams of protein, 4 grams of fiber, and 21 grams of carbs per ¼ cup.

Amaranth

Amaranth is actually an herb. Its seeds are dried and ground to make flour. Amaranth flour is brown with a nutty but mild flavor. It adds an earthy and grassy taste to baked goods and strength to doughs and batters. Amaranth flour has 4 grams of protein, 3 grams of fiber, and 20 grams of carbs per ¼ cup.

Always cook amaranth grains before you eat them because, in a raw state, amaranth has compounds that block the absorption of nutrients.

Teff flour

Teff is another ancient, nutritious grain. Teff is native to Ethiopia, and the flour comes in two colors: dark brown and ivory. It's very high in fiber and contains a good amount of iron, calcium, and B vitamins. Teff flour produces a tender crumb and adds moisture to gluten-free baked goods. The dark brown teff flour has a nutty taste reminiscent of cocoa powder. Ivory teff flour has a much lighter flavor. Teff flour contains 5 grams of protein, 6 grams of fiber, and 32 grams of carbs per ¼ cup.

White bean flour

This flour is made from white beans. You can also find black bean flour, but it's usually used to make bean dips and fillings. White bean flour is white or ivory, produces a tender crumb, and has a mild flavor. It's very high in protein, with 7 grams per ¼ cup. It has 8 grams of fiber and only 20 grams of carbs per ¼ cup.

Fava (or garfava) flour

This flour is a blend of garbanzo bean flour and fava bean flour. Garbanzo beans, also known as chickpeas, are a legume with a sweet flavor. Fava beans, used mostly in Italian cooking, are an ancient pea. This flour blend has a strong taste often described as "beany" and a high protein content. It's usually used in small quantities because of its strong taste. It has 9 grams of protein, 3 grams of fiber, and 23 grams of carbs per ¼ cup.

Soy flour

This flour is made from roasted soybeans and is high in protein. Because it's also high in healthy fats, you should store it in the fridge or freezer. It has a mild and nutty flavor but can also taste beany. It adds tenderness and moistness to baked goods. It helps baked goods brown; in fact, you should watch foods made with soy flour to prevent over-browning. This flour has 12 grams of protein, 5 grams of fiber, and 10 grams of carbs per ¼ cup.

Flours for quick breads

Quick breads need more structure than cakes and cookies but less structure than yeast breads and rolls. Though you still want to maintain the 70 percent flours with protein to 30 percent flours with starch ratio, you can choose flours with a lower protein content for quick breads and muffins.

The following are the best flours to use to make the best gluten-free quick breads and muffins, in order of increasing protein content.

Millet flour

You may think of millet as bird food, but it has been nourishing populations for generations. The tiny seed has a nutritional profile similar to wheat. Millet flour is soft with a low protein content. It has a light ivory color, so it's a good choice for light-colored baked goods, and it produces a soft crumb, so it's a good choice for tender quick breads. Millet flour has a slightly sweet flavor. It has 3 grams of protein, 4 grams of fiber, and 22 grams of carbs per ¼ cup.

Sweet rice flour

Sweet rice is also known as *glutinous rice*. The flour doesn't contain any gluten; this name just refers to the rice's stickiness. This flour is bland and mild. It works very well when combined with brown rice flour because it's more finely ground, and the sweet rice flour creates a sticky structure that helps tender quick breads hold together. It contains 3 grams of protein, 1 gram of fiber, and 24 grams of carbs per ¼ cup.

Flour weight chart

One of the key methods for successful gluten-free baking is substituting flours by weight, not by volume. If you've baked a lot in the past, you're used to measuring flours by volume; that is, by cups and tablespoons. One cup of all-purpose wheat flour weighs 125 grams. Gluten-free flours, however, weigh anywhere from 112 to 160 grams per cup.

That difference in weight doesn't sound like a lot, but baking experts have found that a few grams more or less of any one flour makes a huge difference in the end product. When bakers discovered that measuring flours by weight and not by volume was the key to delicious breads, cakes, and cookies, the world of gluten-free baking changed forever.

While researching this book, Linda and Jean found that there really aren't standardized gram measurements for these alternative flours. For instance, some sources claim that millet flour weighs 120 grams per cup. Others said it weighs 140 grams, and another claimed 125 grams. We wanted this book to be perfectly consistent, so we weighed these flours over and over again to arrive at a consistent amount. We feel confident that these weights are accurate. Whether you use gram weights or cups to measure flour for these recipes, you will achieve good results.

If you're a stickler for math, you'll find that in the conversion of grams to cups or vice versa, there will be differences of up to 2 grams. This occurs because we developed the recipes with grams, then converted to cups. Rounding, because scales can't measure less than 1 gram, create these tiny differences. That amount of flour (equivalent to the weight of two small paper clips, or about $1/_{14}$ of an ounce) won't make a difference in the recipes. These recipes are as finely tuned as we could get them!

And here's something to remember if you measure using grams. The two types of scales Linda has worked with shut off if you don't add anything to the bowl within one minute, which means your work will be lost. Get all of the flours lined up before you begin measuring so you don't lose time hunting for a specific flour. Then weigh them quickly before the scale turns off.

To successfully work with gluten-free flours and starches, you must weigh them. And you need to know how much each of these flours (and starches) weighs. When substituting one flour or starch for another, always substitute by weight. That means that if a recipe calls for 140 grams of millet flour, which is 1 cup, you don't use 1 cup of brown rice flour. You use 140 grams of brown rice flour.

Table 5-1		Flour Weights				
Flour	*1 Cup*	*¾ Cup*	*½ Cup*	*⅓ Cup*	*¼ Cup*	*1 Tbsp.*
All-purpose wheat flour	125 grams	94 grams	62 grams	42 grams	31 grams	8 grams
Blanched almond flour	112 grams	84 grams	56 grams	38 grams	28 grams	7 grams
Amaranth flour	120 grams	90 grams	60 grams	42 grams	30 grams	8 grams
Brown rice flour	135 grams	101 grams	68 grams	45 grams	36 grams	9 grams
Roasted buck-wheat flour	120 grams	90 grams	60 grams	42 grams	30 grams	8 grams
Cake wheat flour	114 grams	85 grams	57 grams	38 grams	28 grams	7 grams
Coconut flour	112 grams	84 grams	56 grams	38 grams	28 grams	7 grams
Corn flour	116 grams	87 grams	58 grams	38 grams	28 grams	7 grams
Garfava flour	120 grams	90 grams	60 grams	42 grams	30 grams	8 grams
High-Protein Bread Flour Mix*	131 grams	99 grams	66 grams	43 grams	33 grams	8 grams
Millet flour	125 grams	94 grams	62 grams	42 grams	31 grams	8 grams
Oat flour	120 grams	90 grams	60 grams	42 grams	30 grams	8 grams
Quinoa flour	120 grams	90 grams	60 grams	42 grams	30 grams	8 grams
Sorghum flour	123 grams	92 grams	62 grams	42 grams	30 grams	8 grams

(continued)

Table 5-1 (continued)

Flour	1 Cup	¾ Cup	½ Cup	⅓ Cup	¼ Cup	1 Tbsp.
Soy flour	112 grams	84 grams	56 grams	38 grams	28 grams	7 grams
Superfine brown rice flour	160 grams	120 grams	80 grams	53 grams	40 grams	10 grams
Sweet rice flour	155 grams	116 grams	78 grams	53 grams	39 grams	10 grams
Teff flour	120 grams	90 grams	60 grams	42 grams	30 grams	8 grams
White bean flour	128 grams	96 grams	64 grams	43 grams	32 grams	8 grams
White Flour Mix*	148 grams	111 grams	74 grams	49 grams	37 grams	9 grams
White rice flour	160 grams	120 grams	80 grams	53 grams	40 grams	10 grams
Whole-Grain Flour Mix*	135 grams	101 grams	68 grams	45 grams	34 grams	9 grams

*These mixes appear in Chapter 10 of this book.

For a chart with the weight measurements of starches, see the next section.

Adding Starches

Starches are important in baking. So what are they? Starches are carbohydrates — links of simple sugars that are tasteless and odorless. In baked goods, starches *gelatinize;* that is, they form gels with water to help support structure and to make the structure more tender.

Starch doesn't work in baked goods all by itself, except in very specific recipes. It must be combined with protein-containing flours. But in most baked goods, the texture of the crumb comes from starch. The starch granules swell; its molecules unwind from their crystallized structure and absorb water when heated. As the product bakes, this structure sets and helps form the crumb of the bread, cake, or cookie.

You can substitute starches for one another without any problem. If a recipe calls for potato starch, for instance, and you only have cornstarch on hand, the recipe should still work. Remember to substitute them by weight, though, and not by volume.

Starches play a critical role in making the best gluten-free breads, cakes, cookies, pies, and desserts. In this section we look at the different starches used in gluten-free baking, how they're used, and which ones are best for different products.

Arrowroot

Arrowroot, sometimes called arrowroot flour, is usually used as a thickener for sauces and puddings. It's made from the root of the arrowroot plant, logically enough. This perennial herb is a *rhizome* — a plant that reproduces with creeping roots, such as ginger and peanuts. It's a good substitute for cornstarch if you're allergic to corn. Many people find arrowroot easy to digest. It's a very pure food that needs minimal processing.

Arrowroot is tasteless, and the white powder turns clear when it's cooked, which is good for sauces but not as important in baked goods. This starch is used to lighten gluten-free baked goods and provide a soft and tender crumb. Arrowroot has 2 grams of fiber and 50 grams of carbohydrates per ¼ cup. This starch doesn't have any protein.

Cornstarch

Cornstarch is made from highly processed corn. It's tasteless and white, with the same thickening ability as arrowroot and tapioca starch. This starch makes finely textured gluten-free baked goods. It's used to make cookies, bars, cakes, and quick breads.

Cornstarch isn't the same as corn flour, so don't confuse the two. Cornstarch doesn't contain any protein or fiber; it has 52 grams of carbs per ¼ cup.

Tapioca starch/flour

Tapioca starch is also called tapioca flour. It's a common ingredient in many gluten-free flour blends. Tapioca starch is made from the cassava root, a potato-like tuber also known as yucca or manna. Tapioca is also formed into tiny beads called *pearls* and is used to make tapioca pudding. Don't confuse tapioca pearls with tapioca starch!

This white starch/flour produces a soft, slightly crisp crumb. It thickens doughs and batters very well. It has no protein, 0.3 grams of fiber, and 26 grams of carbs per ¼ cup.

Potato starch

Potato starch is made from ground potatoes that are washed, removing the protein. The residual starchy liquid is then dried. Don't confuse potato starch with potato flour, which is a very heavy flour made of ground and dried potatoes with a strong potato taste. Most gluten-free baking recipes don't use potato flour because it makes heavy and dense baked goods.

Potato starch is white. It adds tenderness, lightness, and moistness to quick breads and helps create a crumb that glides over your tongue. It has no protein, no fiber, and 40 grams of carbs per ¼ cup.

Starch weight chart

If you're going to create your own gluten-free baking mixes and flour blends, you need to know the weights of starches, too. Even though you weigh these ingredients, sifting starches before using them in recipes or mixing them into baking mixes is a good idea. And remember to substitute starches by weight, not by volume.

Table 5-2	Gluten-Free Starch Weights					
Starch	*1 Cup*	*¾ Cup*	*½ Cup*	*⅓ Cup*	*¼ Cup*	*1 Tbsp.*
Arrowroot	128 grams	96 grams	64 grams	43 grams	32 grams	8 grams
Cornstarch	130 grams	98 grams	65 grams	43 grams	33 grams	8 grams
Potato starch	165 grams	124 grams	83 grams	54 grams	41 grams	10 grams
Tapioca starch (flour)	125 grams	94 grams	62 grams	42 grams	31 grams	8 grams

Using Additives to Achieve Tender Baked Goods

When gluten-free baking became popular years ago, the first efforts turned out bread that was more like bricks and cookies that crumbled at the slightest touch. The first intrepid bakers in this territory discovered that additives could help improve the quality of gluten-free baked goods so that they turned out more like products made with wheat.

Xanthan gum and guar gum, gelatins, and egg and milk proteins were the first additives that helped make gluten-free baked goods less crumbly and more like traditional wheat products. But as time went on, other pioneers discovered that a combination of flours and slurries of certain foods did a better job at creating tender yet strong structures — and without the expense of gums and additives or the uncomfortable dietary side effects! Still, some recipes do better when you use some type of additive.

In this section we discuss how and when to use these additives. Using all the tools at your disposal is the best way to get the best results in gluten-free baking.

Gums

Xanthan gum and guar gum are the two gums most commonly used in gluten-free baking. Each has desirable qualities. They're most often used when a strong structure is really needed in a baked product, such as popovers, breads, and pie crusts.

Gums and other additives keep the starch in baked goods in suspension so it doesn't clump up and so it can absorb water evenly. This keeps the air cells you work so hard to create stable until the starch gelatinizes and the proteins denature, setting the structure of the cake, cookie, or bread.

Though these gums were almost always used in the early years of gluten-free baking, lots of bakers have turned away from them. The gums are very expensive (xanthan gum can cost $16 to $20 per pound), and many gluten-intolerant people have found that both kinds of gums upset their digestive systems. Gluten-free flour and starch combinations have proven just as effective as gums in most recipes.

These gums can also be difficult to find. Some health food stores carry them, but your best source may be online shopping. Amazon.com carries both xanthan gum and guar gum.

Xanthan gum

This gum is a polysaccharide derived from bacteria that ferments with corn sugar. That just means it's a string of sugars held together in a branched structure. When mixed with water, it forms a gel. This gel helps mimic the structure of gluten in baked goods by binding proteins together. Too much xanthan gum can create a product that's very heavy and dense. Bakers use very small amounts — usually a teaspoon or less for an entire recipe — although in the past, they used up to a teaspoon of xanthan gum per cup of starch.

Xanthan gum also acts as an emulsifier that can blend disparate ingredients such as water and oil into a cohesive blend. It's also used as a thickener in ice creams and some salad dressings.

When you add xanthan gum to a recipe, be sure to mix it with the flours and starches before you add water. When water comes into contact with xanthan gum, it immediately becomes incredibly sticky and hard to handle. Mix the dry ingredients (the gum is a powder) with a wire whisk before adding any liquids.

Unfortunately, anyone with an allergy to corn can have problems with this gum. And, as we mention before, it's quite expensive. Many gluten-sensitive people can have digestive problems when they consume products with xanthan gum. Guar gum is a good substitute.

Guar gum

You can use guar gum instead of xanthan gum, but it can have laxative properties. Guar gum is hard to find, but it's a lot cheaper than xanthan gum. It's used to make commercial ice cream because it helps stop ice crystals from forming. In gluten-free baked goods, it helps create the elasticity that gluten provides in wheat products.

This gum is made from the *endosperm,* or coating around the seed, of guar beans. Like xanthan gum, guar gum is a highly branched polysaccharide. It has a very high fiber content. If you need more fiber in your diet, you can add a tiny amount, usually less than 1 teaspoon, to baked goods.

Whichever gum you use, be sure to measure it accurately. Adding just a tiny bit more gum than a recipe or flour mix calls for can create a heavy, gummy, or slimy texture in the product. And that's not what you want!

Gelatin

Gelatin is a protein made from the collagen of animal products. It's been used for centuries in baking and cooking and is an important ingredient in many commercially prepared foods. Everyone has had a gelatin salad! But the type of gelatin we're talking about here is unflavored gelatin, a white powder with no colorings, sugar, or flavorings. Gelatin is on the Food and Drug Administration's GRAS list (generally recognized as safe) and is considered a food, not an additive. Because it's colorless and flavorless, it's a good choice for delicately flavored gluten-free baked goods.

Gelatin forms a thick solution with water, so you can use it in gluten-free baked goods to add structure and moistness to the crumb. It helps hold these products together. Add about a teaspoon of the unflavored (*not* Jell-O!), powdered gelatin to the dry ingredients, just as you would xanthan or guar gum. You can use gelatin in addition to gums for even more structure strength. Doughs made with gelatin are denser and more firm than those made with gums.

Vegan gelatin alternatives

Vegetarians and vegans usually prefer not to use gelatin because it's derived directly from animal products. You can find some vegan versions of gelatin and other alternatives you can use. Agar-agar is made from seaweed. It stabilizes mixtures and thickens sauces and puddings. It comes in flake form, and you should dissolve it in water before adding it to a recipe. Carrageenan is another product from the sea. It's similar to agar-agar and is used in many milk alternatives, such as soymilk, to help thicken and emulsify the product.

One word of warning: Gelatin can create a brittle baked good. That's desirable in some products, such as pizza crust and pie crust, but not in a softer recipe such as a quick bread or a cake. Think about the final structure of the recipe you're making before deciding which additive to use.

Egg protein

Eggs are crucial to many baking recipes, whether gluten-free or not. They add flavor, provide structure because they're high in protein, keep baked goods moist, and help baked goods brown. You can purchase regular eggs, egg substitutes, powdered egg whites, and frozen egg whites for use in baked recipes.

These are the ways egg proteins are useful in gluten-free baking:

- Egg proteins form a web that can trap air and water. The proteins strengthen the structure of baked goods, helping mimic the function of gluten.

- Eggs act as *emulsifiers,* which are molecules that attract and hold water and oil at the same time. They can bind ingredients together and hold them in suspension until the product is baked and the structure sets.

- Egg whites can form foams, adding air to baked goods. When egg whites are whipped, the proteins *denature* (unfold), stretch, and recombine to form a web that traps air. This helps make baked goods light and fluffy.

- Eggs are a leavening agent. Beaten eggs hold air very well. In fact, you can beat whole eggs to a thick foam that holds a lot of air. Beat the eggs, usually with some sugar, for five to ten minutes on high speed until they become thick and very light yellow in color.

- Eggs add moisture and tenderness to baked goods. Egg yolks are high in fat. Fat is important in many baked goods because it helps retain moisture and creates a pleasant mouth feel, in addition to creating a tender product.

✔ Eggs add color and a rich flavor to baked goods. The protein in eggs combines with the sugar and starches in baked goods and browns in the heat of the oven. Unbrowned baked goods just aren't as appetizing as those that are a rich golden-brown color.

Many products, particularly cookies and cakes, are made mostly of eggs, held together by some flours and starches. Other foods, such as pie crusts and breads, use fewer eggs, but adding eggs to these foods can help create a strong yet tender structure without gluten.

Chia and flaxseeds

Chia seeds are an important ingredient in gluten-free baking. And yes, they're the same seeds from the infamous commercial ("Chi-chi-chi-chia!"). Chia seeds can grow on just about anything, creating a green "hairy" object. But they make an excellent slurry that improves the structure and mouth feel of gluten-free baked goods. Golden flaxseeds make a good slurry, too, and are very good for you.

Chia seeds

Most varieties of chia seeds are black; the Salsa brand available in Canada is ivory. These tiny seeds are full of omega-3 fatty acids and antioxidants, which are important to heart health. But that's not why they're used in gluten-free baking, although they're a great addition to any diet (see Chapter 6 for more information about nutrition and the gluten-free diet). Chia seeds are very high in soluble fiber. When mixed with water, chia seeds form a slurry that acts like eggs do in baked products.

Chia seeds are flavorless, which makes them a great addition to delicate baked recipes. They help retain moisture, which prevents premature staling of breads, cakes, and cookies. Chia flour is a newer product that's gluten-free. Not many recipes have been developed with this product because it's so new.

Vegan egg substitutes

Vegan egg substitutes are available. They're usually made out of starches and cellulose (gums). Ener-G Egg Replacer is a reliable brand; this product is used only in baking. Other ingredients you can use as egg substitutes in baking include about 3 tablespoons of mashed banana, soft or silken tofu, applesauce, or plain yogurt. Or use chia or flaxseed slurries (see the nearby "Chia and flaxseeds" section for more information).

To use chia seeds, just soak the seeds in some cool water for 10 to 15 minutes. Doing so forms a gel. Before adding the gel to the recipe, blend this slurry in a blender or food processor. This helps add air to the recipe too and turns the seeds into a light brown mixture. Then stir the mixture in along with the liquid ingredients.

Chia seed slurry makes a great egg replacer, and you can use it in place of xanthan and guar gums in just about any recipe. The slurry really mimics the texture and structure of gluten.

Flaxseeds

Flaxseeds come from the linseed plant. They come in two colors: brown and yellow (also called golden). These tiny seeds are very high in fiber and nutrients, especially those valuable omega-3 fatty acids. The seeds, when ground and mixed with water into a slurry, are another excellent substitute for eggs in baked goods. In fact, they can make gluten-free baked goods fluffy! The seeds have a wonderful nutty taste, which is great for mimicking the taste of wheat.

When using flaxseeds, use 2 teaspoons of ground golden flaxseed for each ½ teaspoon of xanthan or guar gum in any recipe. The brown flaxseeds have far more chlorophyll and can inadvertently turn your bread green. Just remember to remove 2 teaspoons of flour to keep the totals right. For an egg replacer, use 2 tablespoons of ground flaxseed plus 1 tablespoon water for each egg.

Grind the flaxseeds in the spice grinder or coffee grinder and then mix the seeds with an equal amount of water or other liquid from the recipe. Stir until the gel forms and then proceed with the recipe.

Raw buckwheat flour

You can use raw buckwheat flour to replace some of the gums in a recipe because a paste of raw buckwheat flour and water is very gel-like. Mix it with warm water and it works very well to replace gums. But you must use raw buckwheat flour! Roasting or toasting the buckwheat reduces this characteristic of the seed.

Buckwheat helps pizza crust stay thin and crisp and hold together. It holds moisture and makes the structure of the baked goods stronger. And its nutty taste is a definite advantage. It's good for you too! Buckwheat is very high in fiber, it contains all eight essential amino acids that humans need, it has lots of phytochemicals that can help prevent disease, and it's high in minerals.

Keeping flaxseeds fresh

Flaxseeds are high in fat, which means they can become rancid fairly easily. Grind flaxseeds just before use for this reason. Fats become rancid through a process called *oxidation,* which means exposure to the oxygen in air. The seeds are more stable while they're whole; in fact, they'll stay fresh for a year when stored in a cool place in an airtight container. Store the whole seeds in the refrigerator or freezer for longest life. Use a spice grinder or a coffee grinder to pulverize the little seeds just before you're ready to add them to the recipe.

Jean started using raw buckwheat flour instead of gums or other additives because her husband reacts poorly to gums. For best results, grind your own buckwheat flour. Purchase raw buckwheat groats and grind them in a clean coffee or spice grinder. Keep the flour in the fridge until you're ready to add it to the recipe. Use about 2 tablespoons (20 grams) of raw buckwheat flour per 1½ cups of other gluten-free flours.

You can find out more about buckwheat flour in the section "Flours for yeast breads and rolls," earlier in the chapter.

Sweet whey

Whey is a byproduct of cheese-making. It's very high in protein and adds a slightly sweet flavor to baked goods. This product helps baked goods retain moisture, builds structure, makes the crumb softer, and adds to the elasticity and sponginess of pancakes, breads, and cakes.

You can use instant nonfat dry milk as a substitute. Organic Valley makes a dried milk/buttermilk combination that has a wonderful flavor and works very well. Whey protein is mild tasting, white, and easily digestible because it's such a natural product. Make sure that the whey protein isolate, sweet whey, or nonfat dry milk product is certified gluten-free.

The proteins in sweet whey powder are more globular in shape than the proteins in alternative flours, so they add a new dimension to the structure of baked goods. Add about ⅓ cup of sweet whey to bread recipes for every 3 cups of gluten-free alternative flours. Blend well with a wire whisk and continue with the recipe.

Chapter 6

Understanding Dough

· ·

In This Chapter

▶ Breaking down the components of gluten-free dough

▶ Comparing gluten-free doughs to wheat doughs

▶ Handling gluten-free doughs

· ·

Doughs are the holy grail for gluten-free bakers. If you've baked using wheat flour, you know that dough is the basis for breads, pies, cookies, and many desserts. Bakers' first forays into gluten-free baking tried to replicate the characteristics of wheat doughs — and met with failure.

The breakthroughs came when gluten-free bakers started measuring by weight and understanding that gluten-free flours naturally need more time to absorb liquid. This led to light and airy breads, delicate cakes, and delicious pizza and pie crusts.

In this chapter, we look at dough structure and what makes it sturdy yet tender. We examine the differences between wheat protein and gluten-free proteins. We discuss why resting time can make such a big difference in making the best doughs. And we tell you how to shape gluten-free doughs for beautiful and evenly baked gluten-free treats.

Understanding Basic Dough Structure

Dough looks simple, but it's actually quite complex. The simple act of combining flour with water creates a network of starch and protein that separates bubbles of carbon dioxide. Dough has a delicate balance among starch, protein, fat, sugar, and air. Too much of any of these components and the whole structure will collapse.

In this section, we look at how proteins and starches react with water to create dough. We explore how protein, starch, fats, and enzymes contribute to the development of doughs and batters. And we explain how additional ingredients are important to the development of the whole system. Dough has a lot going on at the microscopic level that helps bakers make a great loaf of gluten-free bread, delicious cakes and cookies, crisp pizza crusts, and flaky pie crusts.

Gluten's magical secrets

Gluten is unlike every other plant protein in the way it can organize itself. In the Peanuts cartoon, one strip shows Lucy making her hand into a fist. Linus looks at his fingers and says, "Why can't you guys get organized like that?" In a nutshell, that's the difference between wheat protein and all other cereal, nut, pseudo-grain, and grain proteins.

Many people are working at labs and universities around the country to help make gluten-free products as close to wheat-based products as possible. Food scientists talk about *shear rate* and *viscosity* and use tools such as thermal conductivity detectors and refractive index detectors to learn about gluten and how to replicate its function and structure.

But one of the strange things about doughs and batters is that even with this equipment and all the experiments and theories in the world, no one is 100 percent sure how doughs and batters work.

That's why gluten-free baked goods have gone through such an evolution in real-life kitchens. Food scientists are learning more and more about the science of doughs and batters, but the best laboratory in this particular science is a real-life kitchen. When someone bakes a perfectly tender, crusty, and airy loaf of gluten-free bread and can make that loaf again and again, that's a breakthrough for gluten-free baking and for science.

The components of gluten

So what's known about wheat flours and gluten-free flours? First of all, all flours, even gluten-free flours, are made of about 70 percent starch and 20 percent protein. About 70 to 80 percent of that protein in wheat flour is gluten. (Flour has other proteins too: leucosin, albumin, and proteose.) The remaining 10 percent of flour includes fat, water, sugar, gums, enzymes, vitamins, and minerals.

Although both starch and protein are important dough components, protein gets the most attention because it can form a stretchy web. If you made a loaf of bread with pure starch, it wouldn't rise high, it would be almost too delicate to handle, and it would crumble when sliced.

The most important protein in wheat flour is gluten. Gluten is made up of two proteins: *glutenin* and *gliadin*. In the wheat kernel, these two molecules and starch granules are separated. When the wheat kernel is processed, proteins and starches are mixed together. And when water is added, glutenin and gliadin come together to form gluten.

- ✔ **Gliadin** looks like a ball with little hooks all over it. This molecule makes the dough stretchy, a characteristic called *elasticity*.

- ✔ **Glutenin** is a protein that looks like a long, coiled spring. This molecule makes the dough strong, a characteristic called *plasticity*.

This proportional mixture is why hard winter wheat is stronger than soft wheat and creates better wheat yeast breads. It's also the reason that soft wheat is used for cakes; it's more tender.

The network of glutenin and gliadin is formed when the long glutenin molecules cross-link with the hooks on the globular gliadin molecules. This network is very stretchy and pliable, and this stretchiness lets the dough structure hold on to carbon dioxide, produced by yeast or baking powder, and form the *crumb,* or texture of the bread. The plasticity helps the dough retain its shape.

Water starts the gluten-forming process, but actual manipulation of this protein is what creates the web or net. Gluten is a long protein that's folded in on itself and tangled up. Beating and kneading literally unknots gluten molecules and aligns them to form a net.

How no-knead breads work

Though kneading dough is the most common way to form the gluten network, microscopic kneading is also taking place. Doughs and batters may look calm on the surface, but a lot is going on at the microscopic level. Yeast is a living creature. As it reproduces and grows in a dough, the carbon dioxide it produces literally stirs and kneads the protein molecules. This tiny kneading action takes a lot longer than physical manipulation, which is why no-knead bread recipes call for long standing times.

Enzymes in flour also get into the act in a process called *autolysis,* literally "self breakdown." Enzymes break down long gluten molecules into smaller molecules that then recombine with one another to form a web.

Gluten-free bread doughs work essentially the same way. A long rise time literally "kneads" the proteins in gluten-free flours using the action of yeast and autolysis, forming a network that gives the bread that desirable crumb typical of wheat breads.

How other elements work with gluten

When you bake dough, the gluten web stretches in the heat of the oven as the air expands; this is called *oven spring.* As the dough continues to heat, the protein molecules set in a process called *coagulation.* Water is squeezed out between gluten molecules and is taken up by starch granules. The gluten becomes rigid, and that sets the structure of the bread.

Other components in baked goods affect gluten:

- ✔ Enzymes in the flour break down some of the gluten molecules so they don't overwhelm the structure. These enzymes are *denatured,* or lose their power, when heated.

- ✔ Water can actually weaken a gluten structure. Lots of water overwhelms the gluten web and helps starch molecules dominate.

- ✔ Fats interfere with gluten formation by literally coating protein molecules so they have a harder time combining into a web. This is one reason that fats in gluten-free baking are reduced and the doughs are chilled for rich pastries. The weaker protein structure in gluten-free breads just can't hold the fats in place.

- ✔ Other components in flour, such as the endosperm and bran, physically get in the way of gluten formation. That's why highly processed all-purpose and bread flours are used for yeast breads. You can use whole-grain flours to make yeast breads, but you must usually add processed flours for good structure or these breads end up very dense.

- ✔ Sugar also interferes with gluten formation by attracting and holding on to water molecules. If sugar hogs water, less water is available for gluten formation.

The role of starch

But don't forget about starch! Though gluten is important in bread structure, starch is equally important. A dough made up of just protein is so tough and stretchy that it can't be manipulated. Starch molecules interfere with some of the gluten structure and help hold air in suspension as the bread bakes.

Flours are 70 percent starch, so that component is important in dough formation, too. Starch granules are mixed in with protein molecules in flour. When mixed with liquid in a dough, starches and proteins form two independent structures that intermingle. In other words, starch granules and molecules are embedded in the gluten structure around air pockets. That's how the crumb, or texture, of the baked good forms.

Starch contains two basic kinds of molecules:

- ✔ **Amylose:** A molecule in the form of a long, fairly straight chain. Starches contain about 10 to 20 percent amylose. Amylose forms a firm and heavy gel that's thicker when cold than it is when heated.

- ✔ **Amylopectin:** A highly branched molecule. Starches contain about 80 to 90 percent amylopectin. Amylopectin thickens mixtures but doesn't gel. It's the same thickness whether the mixture it's in is hot or cold.

When starch mixes with water, it hydrates, or swells, and holds water to form a web or gel. That's the primary function of starch in batters and doughs (and why starch is used as a thickener in sauces, soups, and gravies). Starch also acts as a food for yeast. Enzymes in flour and in yeast break down starch molecules into sugar molecules, which feed the yeast so it grows and produces carbon dioxide.

When the hydrated starch is heated as the dough bakes, it *gelatinizes,* or creates a web of structure that expands rapidly, capturing water that the proteins give off as they coagulate. The structure of a good bread is actually an interaction between protein and starch, but in the oven, starch is a much more important player.

Starch doesn't gelatinize completely in baked goods; some of it remains in suspension with water. That's why breads, cakes, and cookies can still be soft even though the protein in the structure has completely coagulated.

What causes bread to go stale?

When you take a bite of a piece of stale bread or cake, you know it. Stale baked goods are hard, with a strange crystal-like mouth feel and a dry texture. The key to staling is starch. When starch has been hydrated and gelatinized in baking, it forms a three-dimensional network. As time goes on, that network starts to crystallize. This process is called *retrogradation.* Scientists have found that amylopectin, the highly branched starch molecule, is responsible for most of the crystallization and staling in breads.

Water is squeezed out of the starch in the center of the bread, making it dry, and migrates to the crust, making it tough and leathery.

You can reheat bread to the gelatinization point of starch, 140 degrees, to make it taste soft and fresh again. That's why reheating breads, in the microwave or oven, makes them fresher. But you can only do this once because the reheated starch molecules crystallize more quickly the second time around.

How Gluten-Free Doughs Are Different

In this section, we look at how gluten-free doughs are different from wheat doughs. We also discuss the ingredients and additives you can use to make gluten-free doughs and batters as close to wheat doughs as possible.

The preceding sections in this chapter help you understand how gluten and starch work in wheat flours so that you can replicate their function in gluten-free doughs. Now that you know that for the best breads you don't need 100 percent gluten development and that starch is almost as important as gluten in dough formation, choosing flours with the right protein content and adding certain ingredients can create a loaf of gluten-free bread very similar to wheat bread.

The proteins in rice flour, amaranth flour, sorghum flour, and other gluten-free flours just don't act like the proteins in wheat flour. They do provide structure, but gluten is a unique molecule with unique properties that's pretty hard, if not impossible, to duplicate.

The first gluten-free baked goods tried to replicate wheat flour by using just one type of flour as a substitute. Those early attempts failed miserably, even with the addition of gums. Combining flours to add as many different protein molecules and starch types as possible was the breakthrough for creating delicious, gluten-free baked goods.

But flour protein isn't all that's important in gluten-free doughs and flours; starches, gels, and proteins from other sources make a huge contribution. All these components together form the structure of doughs, which hold air and then set to form breads, cakes, cookies, and crusts.

Gluten-free doughs are more like thick batters. The flour needs a higher hydration level to perform well in baked goods. The reason so many early gluten-free breads, cookies, and cakes were tough is that bakers were trying to replicate the dough and batter, not the final product.

After you realize that your gluten-free doughs and batters aren't going to look like yeast-based doughs and batters, your baking will be transformed. We're not concerned about replicating the dough and batter texture; we want the texture of the final product to be light, fluffy, airy, and tender!

The components of gluten-free dough

So what components of gluten-free doughs can replicate the stretchy, weblike characteristics of gluten?

- **High-protein flours:** Though the proteins in gluten-free flours never act exactly like gluten, they can come pretty close. Choose high-protein flours to make yeast breads and pizza doughs. Different proteins from different flours make a structure that's pretty close to the unique structure of gluten.

- **Tapioca starch:** This starch, also called tapioca flour, has a strong elastic quality that replicates the springiness of gluten.

- **Egg proteins:** Egg proteins, when beaten, align and form a weblike structure very similar to gluten. This manifests in the form of a foam, which provides the small air cells that contribute to bread's crumb structure.

- **Milk proteins:** The proteins and fat in milk products can also form a foam that creates a fine crumb structure. Think about whipped cream; proteins and fat in that product create a web that holds air.

- **Gums, gelatin, and pectin:** Xanthan and guar gums add plasticity and elasticity to gluten-free doughs that mimic gluten's structure and function. You can use gelatin to create some of this weblike structure, too. Pectin, a compound found in fruit, also forms a gel that replicates gluten's structure.

- **Flaxseed and chia seed:** These slurries are a good substitute for gums and eggs in gluten-free doughs. They form gels that, again, trap air and create a smaller crumb for nice texture.

Structural differences

Besides the different protein structure in gluten-free doughs, they have one more important difference. Gluten-free doughs can hold only so much carbon dioxide before the structure collapses. That's why you need to get gluten-free quick bread doughs into the oven quickly after they're shaped.

Gluten-free yeast breads need rising time for the flour to absorb all the moisture and for the yeast to grow and create carbon dioxide. But even though gluten-free yeast doughs rest before you bake them, they have only one rise time because of the weaker structure.

These doughs are much more liquid than wheat bread doughs because the gluten-free flours take longer to absorb liquid. If you add more gluten-free flours, the resulting bread is extremely dense and tough.

Adding starches, gums, flaxseed slurries, and egg proteins to gluten-free recipes can help strengthen the gluten-free dough structure, which makes a better texture and a more tolerant dough that's easier to work with.

Dough versus batter: What's the difference?

The main difference between doughs and batters is the amount of liquid in the formulation. Batters have much more liquid than dough by weight. In baking, *hydration* is the proportion of flour to water. A dough that's 100 percent hydrated has a ratio of 1 part flour to 1 part water by weight. Most doughs perform best when the hydration ratio is between 70 and 90 percent. This difference in liquid amount completely changes how starch and protein act and interact.

But there's more to a firm dough than just less liquid. Doughs also have fewer ingredients that interfere with protein development and structure. With less fat, sugar, and other flour components, the proteins are free to combine and form a firm structure.

In a practical sense, you can manipulate doughs by hand and they can hold their shape without a pan or mold, but you need to contain batters in pans or molds and you must work them with a spoon. Doughs and batters also have different hydration percentages:

✔ Doughs that you can knead and shape by hand usually range from 50 to 60 percent hydration.

✔ When a dough's hydration percentage reaches 66 percent, the dough becomes much softer and harder to handle.

✔ No-knead doughs have a hydration percentage of 75 to 80 percent.

✔ Batter hydration levels start at about 80 percent and go up to 100 percent.

✔ Pancakes recipes have 100 percent hydration.

✔ Cake batters are typically 125 to 130 percent hydration.

The drier the dough, the less activity in it. That's why no-knead bread doughs are so liquid; in order to move around and align, the protein molecules need a more fluid environment. Gluten-free doughs are less firm than wheat-based doughs because gluten-free flours need more liquid to fully hydrate.

Batters usually have more ingredients that interfere with protein development, so starch is the main structural component. Fats, liquids, and sugars work well with starch, so cakes, cookies, and quick breads have a structure that's strong but tender.

Starches

Starches are more important in gluten-free doughs and batters than they are in wheat doughs and batters. Remember, gluten-free doughs and batters need to have more water than wheat doughs and batters because those flours are more difficult to hydrate. That weakens protein strength, so starch has to take up the slack.

The functions of starches in gluten-free breads, cakes, cookies, and pie crusts are to

✔ Provide structure. In cakes and cookies, starch forms the majority of the structure. Proteins assist this structure but play a minimal role.

✔ Provide moistness. Starch naturally holds on to water so it makes any baking recipe moist.

✔ Provide mouth feel. Starch adds a tender mouth feel to any baked good. Products made with starch are softer and easier to eat.

✔ Provide tensile strength. Even though a dough or batter is soft, it needs to have strength to hold together.

Working with Gluten-Free Doughs

Several methods of making doughs and batters are used in gluten-free baking, and you usually need to corral the doughs and batters in some way so they turn out like you want them to.

In this section, we look at the mixing methods gluten-free bakers use and how they develop structure. We also talk about shaping these doughs and how to freeze them.

Understanding mixing methods

Making gluten-free dough — or any dough — involves three basic methods. The method you use depends on the type of baked good you want to make. Remember to follow the recipe carefully and use the mixing method that the recipe calls for.

Beginning bakers may think that to make a bread, cookie, or cake, all you do is dump the ingredients into a bowl and mix them. Actually, the straight or one-bowl method of mixing is relatively new. Until the 1960s, all cakes were made with the creaming or foam methods, and the one-bowl method was actually quite a breakthrough.

Straight dough

In this method, sometimes called the *one-bowl method,* you thoroughly mix together the dry ingredients — flour, yeast or baking powder, salt, and dry additives — in one bowl. You mix together the wet ingredients — eggs, milk or water, and usually sugar — in another bowl, and then you combine the two mixtures. This is the method used for most gluten-free doughs, such as the yeast bread recipes in this book. It's also the easiest method.

Creaming method

You begin the *creaming method* by beating together butter and sugar. This forms small air holes in the fat that become the crumb of the baked good. You add eggs, and then you add flour and liquid alternately. This is the old-fashioned method of making doughs and batters and was discarded in favor of the straight dough method for most baked goods when bakers discovered the straight dough method produces almost the same result.

Cold foam method

Angel food cakes, soufflés, and sponge cakes are made with the *cold foam method,* which depends on an egg white foam for its structure. You beat egg whites until they're stiff and form a foam with lots of air. Then you add starches and flours for strength. This method is unique; you can't replicate the texture of these foods using the other two methods.

Decoding free-form doughs

Gluten-free yeast doughs are never as dry or stiff as wheat yeast doughs, simply because gluten-free flours are heavier and need more time to absorb liquid and form the type of structure you want. That means you need to corral the doughs in some way.

Almost all gluten-free bread recipes call for some type of pan. Make use of loaf pans, baguette pans, pie pans, pizza pans, rings, muffin tins for rolls, and cake pans to give the dough support as it rises and bakes.

Some gluten-free doughs for bagels and pretzels are piped using a piping bag. This gives you more control over the dough so you can shape it. And you can make your own molds by using heavy-duty foil, folded over several times and formed into the shape you want.

Where does your flour come from?

Believe it or not, where the grain your flour is made from was grown, the conditions under which it was grown, its processing, and its storage conditions all influence how much liquid you need in a recipe. Some flours hold more water than others. Even though you may measure accurately by weight, sometimes you need to add more flour or more liquid to a recipe to get the correct dough or batter consistency. As you become more experienced at baking, this will become easier and eventually become second nature. To help keep flour's moisture levels consistent, always store flour in an airtight container, whether you keep it in the pantry, refrigerator, or freezer.

Part II

The Nuts and Bolts of Gluten-Free Baking

The 5th Wave   By Rich Tennant

In this part . . .

Because celiac disease and gluten intolerance are such serious conditions, they can affect every part of your life. You need to rebuild your health after a diagnosis, and we tell you how to do that. We help you clean out your kitchen and get rid of all gluten (or show you how to keep a "separate and equal" kitchen with gluten products), and we help you shop for gluten-free products. Finally, we take a look at ways to convert your own favorite recipes to gluten-free treats. (The recipes in this book have already been converted, so they don't need changing!)

Chapter 7

Nutrition, Health, and the Gluten-Free Lifestyle

. . . .

In This Chapter

▶ Making sure you get the nutrients you need

▶ Dealing with casein sensitivity

▶ Tolerating lactose intolerance

▶ Taking care of nutritional deficiencies

▶ Losing and gaining weight

. . . .

*I*f you've been diagnosed with celiac disease or the gluten intolerance spectrum, you may have been pretty sick for a while. Unfortunately, lots of damage to your digestive track and your health may have been done by the time a diagnosis was made. You may have lost a lot of weight or developed nutrient deficiencies because of a damaged gastrointestinal tract.

And that damage can cause sensitivities and allergies to other foods. Many gluten-reactive people are sensitive to *casein,* the protein in dairy products and cheeses. And many in this same group are intolerant of *lactose,* the sugar found in milk products.

In this chapter, we look at how people who eat gluten-free can get the most nutrition out of their diet. We discuss the link between celiac disease and other food allergies and sensitivities. What key nutrients may you be missing when eating a gluten-free diet and how can you compensate for them? Finally, we talk about weight issues and offer some solutions.

Staying Healthy When You're Gluten-Free

Gluten isn't necessary for a healthy diet. In fact, gluten isn't an essential nutrient! It's not one of the eight (or nine) essential amino acids that human beings need to thrive. And in fact, many people who don't have celiac disease or gluten intolerance feel better and are healthier when they eliminate wheat products and gluten products from their diets.

In this section, we look at the link between nutrition and health. We also offer hints and tips that those on the gluten intolerance spectrum may need to consider for optimum health and well-being.

The nutritional impact of celiac disease and gluten intolerance

The saying "you are what you eat" is true. That doesn't mean you'll turn into a Snickers bar if you eat a lot of them. But the compounds and chemicals in that Snickers bar will become part of your cells and organs. And if those compounds aren't what your cells need, your health suffers.

Vitamins and minerals have a direct impact on your health. Your body is constantly changing and growing, repairing injuries and damage, and fighting the results of pollution, stress, and aging. Vitamins and minerals help your body use proteins, fats, and carbohydrates to build new muscles, blood cells, nerves, and tissues.

Because gluten damages your small intestine, where your body absorbs most nutrients, even if you have the most perfect diet in the world, your body just isn't able to absorb the nutrients you need when gluten is on your plate. (See Chapter 2 for more information about the mechanism of gluten damage.)

This inability to absorb nutrients, called *malabsorption,* means that your cells, tissues, and organs aren't getting what they need to perform well. These are the nutrients that gluten-intolerant people can be deficient in:

- ✔ B vitamin complex, especially folate
- ✔ Calcium
- ✔ Iron
- ✔ Magnesium
- ✔ Vitamin A

✔ Vitamin D

✔ Vitamin E

Here's the good news: Now that you've been diagnosed, your body will begin to heal. Even people who've been undiagnosed for years can return to a fairly normal digestive tract. Some people may never regain perfect health status, but most people with a disease on the gluten intolerance scale feel much better when they avoid gluten.

Even though gluten isn't a necessary nutrient, the grains that contain gluten do provide nutrients. Gluten-free grains are usually lower in iron and B vitamins than wheat, barley, and rye, so some supplementation may be necessary. Concentrate on eating lots of fresh fruits and vegetables, especially dark-colored produce and green, leafy veggies.

Here are some diseases that gluten-sensitive people are more prone to because their small intestines are damaged:

✔ Anemia

✔ Cancer

✔ Crohn's disease and inflammatory bowel disease

✔ Depression

✔ Diabetes

✔ Osteoporosis

✔ Rheumatoid arthritis

Watching for symptoms of these diseases after a diagnosis is a good idea. Another good idea is to have a complete blood test and other tests done to check for nutritional deficiencies. Though finding out you're deficient in some nutrients and you're at a higher risk for some serious diseases may be scary, you can start to fix deficiencies and lower your disease risk with a healthy diet of whole foods and supplementation.

Getting enough nutrients when you're gluten-free

When you're gluten-free and your body has repaired itself, getting enough nutrients depends on your diet. Though everyone needs to eat a healthy diet, getting lots of vitamins, minerals, fiber, protein, and phytochemicals is more critical for anyone with a chronic illness.

Why is wheat flour more nutritious than gluten-free flours?

Wheat isn't inherently more nutritious than millet, sorghum, or rye flour. But because wheat is such a common grain and is such a large part of the American diet, wheat flours are routinely fortified with vitamins and minerals. For instance, wheat flour has B vitamins — especially folate, iron, and vitamin D — added to it (although processed flours never have as many nutrients as the original grain does). Gluten-free grains aren't fortified as a matter of course. That may change as more and more people ditch wheat and gluten. And remember that minimally processed gluten-free flours always have more nutrients than white, heavily processed, all-purpose wheat flours.

To make sure you're getting enough nutrients on a gluten-free diet, focus on these foods:

- ✔ **Fruits:** Fruits, especially dark-colored and brightly colored fruits, are critical to any healthy diet. Fruits are a good source of vitamin C, minerals, fiber, and *phytochemicals* — antioxidants and other nutrients that reduce inflammation and help reduce the risk of disease.

- ✔ **Good fats:** You may be surprised to see fats on a list of nutritious foods, but healthy fats are an important part of your diet plan. Your body can't absorb fat-soluble vitamins such as A and D without, well, fat. Omega-3 fatty acids and other fatty acids are important to heart health. And monounsaturated fats can lower cholesterol levels and are an important source of quick energy.

- ✔ **Leafy greens:** Spinach, kale, and other dark, leafy greens are a great source of minerals and vitamin K. They also contain lots of phytochemicals, which protect your body from diseases such as osteoporosis, macular degeneration, and diabetes.

- ✔ **Lean meats:** Protein is an important nutrient for everyone, but it's especially important for gluten-reactive people. In fact, eating some protein when you eat carbohydrates — such as putting peanut butter on a gluten-free cracker or adding chicken to toasted, gluten-free bread — helps slow down carbohydrate digestion.

- ✔ **Legumes:** Legumes and lentils are important sources of complex carbohydrates, protein, vitamins, and minerals. These little nutrition powerhouses have lots of potassium, folic acid, calcium, the B vitamin complex, and antioxidants.

✔ **Vegetables:** These foods provide lots of fiber, vitamins (particularly vitamin A), minerals, and phytochemicals. Try to eat a variety of both cooked and raw vegetables. The lycopene in tomatoes, for instance, is more available to your body when it's cooked.

✔ **Whole grains:** Now that you know the grains (and pseudo grains) you can eat, enjoy them! Make whole-grain breads and rolls using the recipes in this book. Serve quinoa pilaf, cooked amaranth, and brown rice risotto. Grains provide lots of fiber and those B vitamins that everyone needs.

The most important advice for celiac patients is to eat a wide variety of the foods you can tolerate. Build a colorful plate every time you sit down to a meal. Eat lots of fresh produce and lean meats. Enjoy baked goods from the recipes in this book, focusing on whole grains and foods with lots of fiber and nutrients.

You or your doctor may want to try specialized diets, such as the Paleo diet or a low carb/high protein diet. Those decisions are up to you. Just remember that any diet that completely eliminates an entire class of food is difficult to sustain in the long run and is deficient in some nutrients.

You may want to consider taking a good multivitamin supplement, especially when you begin a gluten-free diet. (Make sure your diet really is gluten-free; see Chapter 24 to find out about sneaky places that gluten can hide.) Many people find that eating enough foods to supply them with the right amount of nutrients, such as vitamin D and the B complex, is difficult. And while your body is healing, it needs more nutrients to help repair cells and tissues.

And remember that as long as you eat a good mix of whole and healthy foods, you can enjoy treats and desserts, too. We developed the recipes in this book to work with gluten-free flours; they range from easy casseroles and quiches to brownies and pies. Just exercise some common sense and remember: moderation in everything, including moderation!

Casein Issues

Many gluten-reactive people are sensitive to *casein,* a protein found in milk products. Some people develop an intolerance or sensitivity to casein as a result of the damage to their intestinal lining. Or they may have had a problem with casein all along. Some studies estimate that 50 percent of gluten-reactive people are also sensitive to casein.

In this section we examine the connection between gluten sensitivity and problems ingesting casein. We list the foods and ingredients you need to look for and avoid, and we discuss alternatives you can use in recipes.

The link between gluten intolerance and casein sensitivity

Questions about the connection between gluten intolerance and casein sensitivity may seem like the question about the chicken and the egg: Which came first? The answer is: No one really knows.

The casein and gluten molecules are very similar in structure, so in some people, they may cause the same type of damage. Both the gliadin protein and the casein protein can pass through the cells in your small intestine. After they're in those cells, they're broken down into peptides that cause an allergic reaction, which then damages the *villi,* or projections, in the small intestine.

A sensitivity or allergy to casein is an autoimmune reaction. Your body thinks that the casein protein is a harmful alien and releases chemicals that attack the molecule. When you're sensitive or intolerant to casein and you eat dairy products, you experience many of the same symptoms you experience when you eat gluten. These symptoms include gastrointestinal problems, swelling of the mouth, hives, a rash, wheezing, and, in the most severe cases, anaphylaxis.

Or the damage caused by gluten may make your body more sensitive to the casein molecule. When the villi in your intestines are damaged, the enzymes your intestines produce can decrease markedly, which means you can't digest casein.

Avoiding casein in your diet

The diet that people who must avoid both gluten and casein follow is called the *gluten-free casein-free* (GFCF) diet. On this diet, you must be doubly aware and alert. Add the foods and ingredients on the following lists to your list of the foods and ingredients that contain gluten.

Although milk is one of the eight main allergens, along with wheat, products that contain milk or wheat must list that fact on the label. But those who are sensitive to casein and gluten need to watch out for other label terms that seem to have nothing to do with either protein. Like gluten, casein can be extracted from milk products and added to foods.

These are the foods you must avoid on a casein-free diet:

- Butter
- Cheese
- Chicken broth and bouillon
- Cottage cheese
- Cream
- Fast food
- Half and half
- Lunch meats
- Margarine
- Milk and buttermilk
- Milk chocolate
- Most baked goods
- Nondairy whipped topping
- Sausages and hot dogs
- Self-basting poultry
- Sour cream
- Soy cheese
- Yogurt

And these are the terms on labels that indicate a food contains casein:

- Artificial butter flavor
- Calcium casein
- Caseinates
- Hydrolysates
- Lactoglobulin
- Lactose
- Milk protein
- Milk solids
- Naturlose
- Sodium lactylate
- Whey

If you're not sure whether a food is casein-free, you have to be a detective, just like you've been with gluten. Call the manufacturer and ask whether the food is casein-free. Read labels every time you buy a product. And remember that alternatives to casein-containing products exist that you can use in cooking and in recipes (see the next section).

Finding alternatives to casein-containing foods

If you're sensitive to casein, you can find several alternatives to dairy products that taste good and are relatively easy to get.

Remember that all milk products, even those from goats and sheep, contain casein. Goat's milk and sheep cheese aren't casein-free alternatives, because casein is found in all products made from mammals.

These are some casein-free products you can use in cooking and recipes: almond milk, casein-free yogurts such as wholesoy and silk, hemp milk, rice cheese, rice milk, soy cheese, soymilk, tofu, vegan margarines, and vegetable oils.

Dairy-free doesn't mean *casein-free!* Products that contain dairy must be labeled "contains milk" or "may contain milk" because milk is one of the eight major allergens, so some people may think that this label means the food is casein-free too.

Lactose Intolerance

Many people on the gluten intolerance spectrum have trouble digesting lactose too. *Lactose* is the sugar in milk products. The human body uses the enzyme *lactase* to digest this sugar. Those who are lactose intolerant can't digest significant amounts of lactose, more than 8 fluid ounces of cow's milk.

In this section we look at gluten's role in lactose intolerance and give you ideas on how you may be able to eat milk products again after a diagnosis of celiac disease. We also offer suitable substitutions for lactose-containing products you can use in the recipes in this book.

Gluten's role in lactose intolerance

Scientists have found that people with lactose intolerance, which is the inability to digest the sugar in milk, have a higher incidence of celiac disease. And many gluten-sensitive people are lactose intolerant. No one is quite sure which comes first.

The place in the small intestines where lactase, the enzyme that digests lactose, exists is in the very tips of the intestine's microvilli. In fact, the enzyme-producing cell layer is only one cell thick. Damage from gluten affects those cells first, so it makes sense that while you're still eating gluten, lactose is more difficult to digest.

When lactose is undigested, it passes farther on into the intestines, where natural gut bacteria ferment it. This is what causes the gas, nausea, bloating, cramps, abdominal pain, and diarrhea. This condition isn't as dangerous as gluten intolerance because the body doesn't suffer the extensive damage, but the symptoms are very uncomfortable and distressing. If you're lactose intolerant, and some 40 million Americans are, the symptoms make themselves known within 30 minutes to 2 hours of eating something containing lactose.

When you go on a gluten-free diet and your intestines heal, you may be able to digest lactose again. Some people never recover those cells that produce lactase, but some may be able to eat lactose by adding lactase enzymes to the diet. Add some of the enzymes, which are available without a prescription, to milk or other liquids. These products reduce the lactose content of milk by 70 percent if added to cold milk or up to 90 percent if the milk is heated first.

Or you can take supplements that contain lactic acid bacteria, which go by the names of *lactobacillus acidophilus, lactobacillus reuteri,* or *streptococcus salivarius.* Others find relief by eating yogurt that contains live and active bacteria.

Uncovering lactose's hiding places

Like casein and gluten, lactose can hide in some pretty unlikely places. If eating lactose makes you feel sick, the best thing to do is avoid it. Even with over-the-counter enzymes, you may not feel 100 percent if you eat dairy products. And because you've worked so hard to feel better, why spoil it with a sugar that isn't even necessary to good health?

These are the places lactose can hide:

- Baked goods and breads
- Baking mixes
- Breakfast drinks
- Candies
- Coffee creamers
- Lunch meats
- Margarine
- Nondairy whipped toppings
- Over-the-counter medications
- Prepared potato products
- Prescription drugs
- Salad dressings
- Snack foods
- Soups

Because milk is one of the eight allergens, its presence is listed on food labels. But lactose is not. Being vigilant and staying on top of what you eat and drink may seem overwhelming at times, but the good health and vitality that results when you do so is worth it.

Making substitutions

When you avoid lactose, cow's milk, goat's milk, and sheep's milk are automatically off the table, so to speak. But some people who are lactose intolerant can consume regular cheeses because, during the cheese-making process, lots of lactose is lost.

Here are some good substitutions for lactose-containing foods: almond cheese, almond milk, earth balance margarines, rice cheese, rice milk, soy cheese, soy milk, tofu products, and vegan "dairy" products.

Remember, a food that's lactose-free isn't necessarily casein-free. If you need to avoid both, be sure to examine all labels to make sure the product is free from both lactose and casein.

Replacing Key Missing Nutrients

A gluten-free diet may, and we stress the word *may,* be deficient in some nutrients commonly found in wheat products: folate or folic acid, fiber, iron, and other B vitamins. But you can make up for these deficiencies with a little bit of research and effort.

Simply eliminating gluten from your diet automatically makes you healthier because your intestines heal and your body is able to absorb the nutrients you need. The damage caused by gluten reduces your body's ability to absorb nutrients. So by following the recommendations in this book and making these delicious recipes, you're already one step ahead of the game!

In this section we discuss how you can add these nutrients to your diet while still avoiding gluten. After you understand which safe foods have these nutrients, eating and enjoying them becomes second nature.

Finding folate

Folate, also known as *folic acid,* is vitamin B9. You must consume some of this water-soluble vitamin every day. Folate deficiency is common in gluten-reactive people because of intestinal inflammation. Folic acid is especially important for women in their childbearing years. A deficiency in this vitamin can cause serious birth defects, including spina bifida.

Foods high in folate include asparagus, avocados, beans, broccoli, dark, leafy, green vegetables, legumes, liver, and whole gluten-free grains.

Adding fiber

Whole grains are an important part of any diet. Wheat, barley, rye, and other grains are off your diet. These foods are good sources of fiber, a compound that helps maintain regularity, can reduce blood cholesterol levels, and reduces the risk of developing many diseases, including diabetes. Fiber also helps you feel full and stay satisfied longer, which is important for people who are trying to lose weight.

Fiber comes in two kinds: soluble and insoluble. Insoluble fiber doesn't dissolve in water. It's found in whole grains, vegetables, and nuts. It moves food through your digestive tract so you stay regular. Soluble fiber dissolves in water. It binds to cholesterol and helps remove it from your body.

To add more fiber of both kinds to your diet, just read Chapter 5! There, we list the gluten-free grains you can eat, along with their protein and fiber content. Whole grains aren't off your diet; just certain ones. Dozens of delicious and healthy gluten-free whole grains have just as much fiber as wheat.

You can cook and eat whole grains as breakfast cereals. You can make pilaf or risotto from just about any grain. Add whole grains to soups and stews or mix them into meatballs and meatloaf.

Add these gluten-free whole grains to your diet for fiber: amaranth, brown rice, flax, gluten-free whole-grain breads, popcorn, quinoa, and wild rice.

Getting your B vitamins

The B vitamin complex is a group of water-soluble vitamins that your body can't make. Because these vitamins are water-soluble, your body excretes them through your kidneys and in your urine every day.

The B vitamins include thiamine (B1), riboflavin (B2), niacin (B3), pantothenic acid (B5), pyridoxine (B6), biotin (B7), folic acid (B9), and cyanocobalamin (B12). Your body uses these vitamins to create energy from food and to make and repair cells and tissue. The best way to get B vitamins is naturally, through whole foods.

The best food sources of B vitamins include eggs, fatty fish, leafy green vegetables, legumes, liver, milk, poultry, red meat, whole grains.

Adding iron

Anemia is a deficiency of *hemoglobin,* the molecule in blood that carries oxygen to your cells and tissues. Many gluten-sensitive folks are iron-deficient because the intestine's inability to absorb nutrients is so reduced. In fact, a diagnosis of iron-deficiency anemia may be how your gluten intolerance is diagnosed.

About 12 percent of anemia patients have anemia of chronic inflammation, associated with a long-standing condition or inflammation. Your body's immune reaction to gluten can literally interfere with your body's red blood cell production. Symptoms of anemia include weakness, shortness of breath, feeling cold, dizziness, and fatigue.

Iron supplements for children, young men, and women of childbearing years may be necessary to overcome iron-deficiency anemia or anemia of chronic inflammation. Talk to your doctor about adding a supplement to your diet. If you don't actually need iron based on blood tests, you can cause harm by taking an iron supplement.

You can add these iron-rich foods to your diet to help: artichokes, beans and lentils, dark leafy greens, dried fruit, eggs, liver, and red meat.

Eating foods rich in vitamin C at the same time that you eat iron-rich foods helps your body absorb more iron.

Managing Weight Issues

More than 60 percent of all Americans struggle with weight issues. And things are just getting worse with time. Those on the gluten intolerance spectrum are no different.

Something other than overeating may be going on in America's obesity epidemic, including viruses and food additives. But you can control lots of factors. In this section we talk about tools you can use to lose weight if you're overweight or gain weight if you're underweight. Many gluten intolerant people lose weight when they remove gluten from their diets; others gain needed weight when they begin to absorb food adequately. Consult your doctor for guidance.

Losing weight

Some people find that when they go on a gluten-free diet, they tend to gain weight. Here are a few reasons for this phenomenon:

✔ You can enjoy your food now! After a diagnosis, you may be tempted to eat a lot simply because food doesn't make you feel sick anymore. Many people lose weight, usually too much weight, before a diagnosis, so gaining some weight may be a good thing.

✔ Some gluten-free grains are low in fiber, so you can eat more without feeling full. If this is a problem, look for gluten-free grains that are higher in fiber (see Chapter 5 for this information), and include more fiber in your diet from other sources.

✔ Now that you can eat delicious, gluten-free baked goods using this book, you may be tempted to bake all the time. Remember that, even though these recipes are gluten-free and scrumptious, most are still meant as a treat, not as a regular part of your diet.

✔ Portion control may be a problem. Most people don't realize that a serving of bread is one slice. A serving of cake is a piece about 2 by 3 inches. Because you're so happy you can eat treats on a gluten-free diet, overindulging can be easy.

✔ You may consume the same number of calories as before your diagnosis but still gain weight. That's because your body is now absorbing nutrients! Many people who must avoid gluten need to reduce their caloric intake after removing gluten from their diet.

One of the best things about being on a gluten-free diet can help you manage your weight better than just about any diet or weight-loss plan: exercise! And now that you feel so much better and have so much more energy, exercise can be a joy again. Find some type of exercise you enjoy: walking, bike riding, swimming, or some sport. Then practice it regularly to lose and control weight.

Gaining weight

When people on the gluten intolerance scale are diagnosed, chances are pretty good that they're underweight. Damaged intestines and the body's inability to absorb needed nutrients, along with all the gastrointestinal symptoms, take their toll. Clinically, Jean sees a lot more people who lose weight after diagnosis. The autoimmune reactions can cause water retention that's quickly lost when the causative agent is removed.

If you need to add weight, you're in luck! The recipes in this book should all be on your plate. Though it's tempting to eat tons of brownies, cookies, cakes, pies, and desserts of all kinds, keep moderation in mind. After all, after you put weight on, it's very easy to go overboard.

To add 1 pound a week, you need to consume 3,500 extra calories; that works out to 500 calories per day. That's one serving of Cornmeal Pancakes (Chapter 11) or one serving of French Onion Soufflé (Chapter 21). In other words, even when you need to gain weight, you can't eat five or six servings of high-calorie foods a day!

So enjoy higher-calorie foods in moderation. And be sure to check in with your doctor if you aren't regaining needed weight after a few months on a gluten-free diet.

Chapter 8

Keeping a Gluten-Free Kitchen

. . . .

In This Chapter

▶ Examining food labels for hidden gluten

▶ Establishing a safe, gluten-free kitchen

▶ Taking steps to avoid cross-contamination

▶ Knowing where and how to buy gluten-free products

. . . .

When you want to rid your life of gluten, the kitchen is the obvious place to start. In this chapter, we guide you through a kitchen transformation.

First you find out how to read a label to unearth gluten, identify ingredients that may be contaminated with gluten, and spot ingredients that indicate hidden gluten. After you understand ingredient labels, you discover what to toss from your kitchen and what to keep. Then you have to decide whether to make your kitchen completely or only partially gluten-free. A thorough kitchen cleaning is the next step to remove any lingering gluten particles from work surfaces, drawers, cupboards, appliances, and utensils. Then we help you avoid cross-contamination, discuss how to shop for gluten-free products, and tell you where to find specialty ingredients.

These steps may sound daunting, but they're essential. A severe gluten allergy can be life-threatening, and making your kitchen gluten-free (or gluten-safe) is an important first step to a healthier life.

Decoding Cryptic Labels

When someone in your family has a problem with gluten, you need to become a detective. And yes, you need the traditional magnifying glass and a notebook (or iPad!) for recording clues and crucial information. (The funny hat and curved pipe are optional.) You'll find yourself calling manufacturers to verify ingredients in their foods.

Some hidden sources of gluten include proteins made with spelt, kamut, triticale, farro, and durum. All these names are just varieties of wheat; tasty ones, but wheat nonetheless. Don't fall for the wheat-free claims that occasionally appear on products made from these grains.

In this section we discuss how to read food ingredient labels to ferret out hidden gluten. We list terms that need further investigation and tell you how to make sure that a food labeled gluten-free or one that seems gluten-free is, in fact, free of gluten. Or as free as it's possible to be!

Understanding label jargon

Every food in the supermarket that contains more than one ingredient must have a label that lists all the ingredients, along with nutrition information and some specific warnings and health claims. These labels are one line of defense against gluten, but they aren't the holy grail. You may need to do some research before you can confidently buy and eat products that are safe for you.

If only avoiding gluten was as easy as simply avoiding wheat pasta, breads, and flour! Gluten can hide in foods as diverse as salad dressing and low-fat sour cream. (Gluten can even be present in non-food items; see *Living Gluten-Free For Dummies* [Wiley] for more information.)

The government is helping you out a bit with label warnings. The Food Allergen Labeling and Consumer Protection Act (FALCPA) took effect in 2006. More than 160 foods are identified as allergens, but 90 percent of all food allergies are caused by just eight of them. The FALCPA requires that any product that contains one of the eight major allergenic foods clearly list that allergen on the label. Wheat is one of the eight allergens.

Coming soon: A gluten-free label

As of the publication of this book in late 2011, manufacturers will soon be able to put an FDA-sanctioned, gluten-free label on products that have tested gluten-free in an accredited lab, using the ELISA-based testing method. Right now, companies can add a gluten-free label to any product, but that claim isn't certified by the U.S. Food and Drug Administration. Certification is currently granted by the Gluten-Free Certification Organization (GFCO), part of the Gluten Intolerance Group. You can trust products with labels certified by this organization.

The proposed standard for the amount of gluten in a product labeled *gluten-free* is 20 parts per million (ppm). This number was set by the Codex Alimentarius Commission of the World Health Organization. Some companies and advocates want to see a limit of less than 10 ppm gluten. The most accurate test can detect 5 ppm at this time. Part of the controversy continues to rage because the evaluation is based on the amount of gluten per serving. If you eat several products containing small amounts of gluten over the course of a day, each one below 20 ppm, you can easily rise above the level of gluten that causes damage and you may experience painful symptoms.

These limits may be too high for many people who have celiac disease or are gluten intolerant. Here's the lesson in all this: "Gluten-free" doesn't mean "no gluten at all." There's simply no way to guarantee zero gluten in any one product, unless you buy an apple or lemon that hasn't been coated with a wax or solution that contains gluten. Or unless you grow your own food!

When the standards for the gluten-free label are finalized, the inclusion of the FDA-sanctioned statement on labels will make a difference to most people who need to avoid gluten. You'll be able to buy more products, confident that they're as free of gluten as possible. Pressure from consumers may encourage manufacturers to follow the government's guidelines and use this statement. Companies know that in these days of instant news on the Internet, if a company labels its product gluten-free and it isn't, the company's reputation will be hurt, and quickly.

Cross-contamination issues

Manufacturers don't have to mention possible cross-contamination, which is a big issue when dealing with gluten. If a manufacturer processes soy flour in the same plant that it processes wheat flour, cross-contamination can easily occur.

On products made with flour or other grains, look for this statement on the label: "Processed in a dedicated mill." A *dedicated* mill specifically processes only one particular grain.

Rye and barley

Rye and barley, two grains that contain gluten, aren't included in label regulations because they aren't major allergens. Rye is fairly easy to avoid because it's usually only listed as "rye" on labels, but barley can hide behind the generic term "natural flavors" and many others. If you see vague or generic terms on a product label, contact the manufacturer to find out exactly what ingredients are in that food.

Barley malt, especially, is in many commercially prepared products. That ingredient is the reason Rice Krispies cereal isn't gluten-free. But there is hope! Many manufacturers are realizing that simple changes will let them market their products as gluten-free. What it really comes down to is this: Read every label, every single time, before you buy.

Avoiding suspect ingredients

Dozens of ingredients contain gluten. Some are obvious, like "bran" and "graham," but others are vague and nonspecific. Without some special knowledge, few people would know that "emulsifiers" can mean that gluten lurks in that product or that "vegetable protein" is a flashing red alarm for those who must avoid wheat.

You have to learn some technical terms that are used to describe gluten or that gluten can hide behind and look for them on every product you consider purchasing.

Here are just a few of the ingredients to look for on food products when you need to avoid gluten. Don't buy products with these terms:

- Bran (rice and corn bran are safe)
- Coloring
- Couscous
- Graham
- Hydrolyzed
- Kamut
- Malt (corn malt is safe)
- Natural flavors
- Soy sauce (unless specifically labeled wheat-free)
- Spelt
- Starch
- Vegetable protein

The following baking products may contain gluten. Read the label carefully before you buy them, and if any terms aren't clearly defined and identified, contact the manufacturer and find out whether the product is gluten-free. Manufacturers must list contact information on all their products.

- Cocoa and chocolate products
- Commercial dairy products
- Malted drinks and powders
- Marzipan
- Packaged bread mixes
- Packaged cake mixes
- Packaged frosting mixes

✔ Pastry fillings

✔ Pie fillings

✔ Seasoning mixes

✔ Some baking powders

✔ Some cake decorating products like sprinkles

Making Your Kitchen Safe

Before you bring gluten-free foods into your home, you have to clean the kitchen to remove anything that may contain gluten. Remember, even a tiny crumb or some flour dust can contaminate gluten-free products. And crumbs and dust fly everywhere in the rough-and-tumble world of the kitchen.

In this section we point out the foods you should discard and the products you can keep. We also tell you how to clean your kitchen, including cleaning a few places that many people don't think about cleaning.

What to toss

To clean out your kitchen, start by taking everything out of the pantry, fridge, and freezer — but clean out only one area at a time! Don't leave chilled and frozen items out of the fridge and freezer for more than two hours for food safety reasons. The key to this step is organization. You don't want to get overwhelmed by the process; you want to know what's in your kitchen and make sure every item has a designated home.

Carefully read every label, looking for the terms that indicate gluten (see the preceding section). And remember the phrase, "When in doubt, throw it out!"

The baking products that can contain gluten and that you should discard or isolate include

✔ **Baking powder:** This product often contains an ingredient that helps absorb moisture so the baking powder doesn't clump. Some brands use wheat starch as that ingredient. Gluten-free baking powders include Rumford, Clabber Girl, Featherweight, and Bakewell Cream. Or you can make your own baking powder by combining 1 part baking soda with 2 parts cream of tartar.

✔ **Baking sprays made with flour:** Cooking sprays are made with oil, but some have added flour and are marketed for baking. Make sure you use a pure oil spray.

✔ **Cornstarch:** Cornstarch doesn't contain gluten, but it may be contaminated with gluten if it isn't produced in a dedicated mill. If the product in your pantry doesn't say "gluten-free" or "produced in a dedicated mill," it may not be gluten-free.

✔ **Flour and flour blends:** Until you stock your kitchen with gluten-free flours and mixes, you should toss or isolate all products like these that are now in your kitchen.

✔ **Malt or malt flavorings:** Malt flavoring is made from barley, which is a no-no for anyone allergic to gluten. Other products using malt may be made from corn, but product labels don't have to specify whether corn is used. Contact the manufacturer to ask about the ingredients.

✔ **Oats and oatmeal:** Although oats don't contain gluten, they're often grown in a field next to wheat or processed in the same mill used to process wheat. Throw out oats that don't have the "dedicated mill" label or clearly mark them as "not gluten-free."

✔ **Soy sauce:** Though soy sauce is made with wheat, the natural fermentation process can destroy gluten. Kikkoman's soy sauce tests gluten-free, but the only brand that guarantees its claims of gluten-free is San-J.

✔ **Spices:** Some spices and spice blends (like curry powder) may contain an anticaking agent that contains gluten. As an alternative, you can dry your own spices or look for gluten-free brands in specialty stores or online. You can make your own curry powder using one of many recipes on the Internet.

✔ **Vanilla:** Though vanilla can be made from distilled alcohol that comes from grains, it's most likely gluten-free. If you're concerned about the tiniest possible amount of gluten, you can make your own vanilla by steeping whole vanilla beans in a small bottle of potato vodka for a few weeks. It's then ready to use in any recipe.

✔ **Vinegars:** Malt vinegar isn't gluten-free. Most vinegars made in the United States come from corn, potatoes, or, as unappetizing as this sounds, wood. Some flavored vinegars aren't gluten-free, and vinegar made outside the U.S. may contain gluten. We have to say it again: Read labels and call the manufacturer if you're unsure!

✔ **Wheat germ oil:** This product, obviously, is derived from wheat grains. The gluten level can vary from very little to a lot, depending on the production methods, so to be safe, just avoid it. Other oils, like sesame oil and nut oils, are good alternatives.

In the section "Coming soon: A gluten-free label" earlier in the chapter, we talk about the 20 parts per million number. How much gluten is that? In an average diet of 2,400 calories a day, that number equates to about 4.5 milligrams of gluten, which is the equivalent of 0.001 teaspoon.

That sounds like a teeny amount, doesn't it? But some people are so sensitive to gluten that they can't tolerate even the smallest amount. If that's the situation you're facing, be more vigilant about purchasing gluten-free products or consider making your own products.

What to keep

After you sort through all the products in your kitchen and toss the suspected culprits, read the labels of every other product. Toss or give away anything that may contain gluten or put it in a separate area until you decide whether your kitchen is going to be completely gluten-free or not.

Many products are naturally free of gluten, although cross-contamination is an issue with every food until you clean and reorganize your kitchen. These are the foods you can keep:

- ✔ **Baking soda:** This product doesn't contain gluten, but if you've been using a box for a while, it may be contaminated with gluten from flour products or baking powder. After all, not many people use separate measuring spoons for baking soda and baking powder!

- ✔ **Chocolate:** Pure chocolate, like baking chocolate and semisweet chocolate, is gluten-free. Cocoa powder may not be, and products made with chocolate, like chocolate chips, pudding mixes, and chocolate drink mixes, may contain gluten. Read labels and contact the manufacturer before you use them.

- ✔ **Dairy products:** Most dairy products are safe, although low-fat sour cream, eggnog, and cream cheese may be made with stabilizers or emulsifiers that contain gluten. Read that label!

- ✔ **Eggs:** Eggs are gluten-free, and because they come in a nice little package, they're rarely contaminated.

- ✔ **Fresh meats:** Processed meats may contain gluten, but ordinary chicken breasts and ground beef are considered gluten-free. You don't want to create a delicious, gluten-free pizza crust and then top it with pepperoni that contains wheat flour!

- ✔ **Fruits and vegetables:** You may want to peel fruits and veggies before eating them because some are coated with a wax or solution that can contain gluten. Otherwise, whole fresh fruits and vegetables in their original peels are fine for a gluten-free diet. Watch out for frozen vegetable and fruit combinations that may contain seasonings or a sauce mix.

- ✔ **Honey and corn syrup:** These products are gluten-free, although you may want to check with the manufacturer of corn syrup to make sure there's no possible contamination.

 ✔ **Nuts:** Nuts are naturally gluten-free but are often processed in a nondedicated facility. If you're very sensitive, be safe and only purchase nuts processed in a dedicated gluten-free plant.

 ✔ **Yeast:** Yeast cakes are usually safe, although you may want to call the manufacturer to make sure. Dried yeast doesn't contain gluten.

Although examining all these products sounds daunting, remember that you only have to go through this process once. You're radically changing your lifestyle, and although doing so entails a lot of work, the peace of mind (and body) that comes with a safe kitchen is worth it.

Many "safe food" lists circulate around the Internet. The biggest problem with these lists is accuracy. Some of the lists continue to label safe foods as "unsafe" and vice versa. So always read the label of any processed food, contact the manufacturer if you have any questions, and keep a good record of all safe foods for yourself and your family.

How to clean the kitchen

If you're an experienced baker, you know that keeping a kitchen clean is a challenge. You need to clean many places that beginners just don't think about, like sink plugs and cupboard handles! And gluten can hide in lots of places.

Whether your kitchen is completely gluten-free or you compromise and keep a few foods made with gluten, you need to thoroughly clean every single surface after you sort through food, utensils, and cookware. A single bread or cracker crumb contains a lot of gluten molecules.

For your kitchen to be a safe haven for gluten-intolerant people, you must wipe down every surface and clean it with soap and water before you restock the pantry, fridge, and freezer. Baking uses a lot of powders (flour, baking powder, spices, and so on) that can drift in the air and land on just about every available surface.

A thorough kitchen cleaning takes some time, so don't try to rush this process. Ordinary household dust is different in the kitchen; it can contain gluten from wheat flour, slicing breads, and cookies and cakes. Though keeping your kitchen dust-free is impossible, make a clean start and get rid of as much dust and grime as possible before you reorganize and restock the shelves and cupboards.

When you're deciding what to clean, remember that grease attracts and holds dust. Any surface that's even slightly greasy is a possible source of gluten. So clean everything using gluten-free cleaners (yes, these products are important too — try Mrs. Meyer's household cleaners), rinse with water, and dry thoroughly before reassembling your now-spotless kitchen.

For a really thorough kitchen decontamination, you should clean

- ✔ **Cabinet and drawer faces:** Wiping off obvious drips and spills from cabinet faces is easy, but over time, a thin layer of grease accumulates on these surfaces, and flour dust can stick to that grease. Wash down with a mild soap solution, rinse, and dry.

- ✔ **Ceiling fan blades:** Just think of all the gluten particles a ceiling fan can fling around the room! Wash the fan blades and the light fixture, and wipe down the fan casing.

- ✔ **Cookware and bakeware:** Scrub all utensils free of crumbs, baking spray residue, and grease residue. Be especially careful with items that have cracks or crevices.

- ✔ **Cupboard and drawer handles:** Handles are easily contaminated by sticky fingers. Wash every handle carefully.

- ✔ **Floors and countertops:** Obviously! Also wipe down baseboards and windowsills.

- ✔ **Garbage disposal:** Clean this by running ice and cut-up lemons through it. Then run water for a few minutes through the disposal while it's turned on.

- ✔ **Inside all drawers:** Silverware drawers, especially, can hang on to crumbs and flour dust. Take all items out of the drawer, run them through the dishwasher or wash them by hand, and then wipe down the cupboard and let it dry.

- ✔ **Light fixtures:** Dust can accumulate in light fixtures. Take the fixture down or take it apart and thoroughly clean every piece before reassembling it.

- ✔ **Sink strainers and sink plugs:** These items can hold a lot of gunk from everyday use. In fact, buy a new sink strainer and plug for your disposal. Most hardware stores stock them.

- ✔ **Toaster and toaster oven:** Crumbs can lurk in the cracks and crevices of these appliances. Clean them according to the manufacturer's directions and wipe down the entire appliance.

- ✔ **Tops of kitchen cupboards:** This is another place where dust and crumbs can accumulate. If you keep plants or decorative items on top of cupboards, take them down and clean them, too.

After reading a list like this, which really drives home the potential for cross-contamination, many people choose to keep their kitchens completely gluten-free. But that's a decision only you and your family can make.

Dealing with Cross-Contamination

Cross-contamination can occur with the tiniest bread crumb or bit of flour dust. If your gluten allergy or sensitivity is severe, you may react to a minute amount of gluten. Keeping your kitchen gluten-free really does minimize cross-contamination risk. But if gluten-containing foods are sharing the space, some special consideration is needed.

In this section we show you how to reduce cross-contamination in your kitchen, whether you choose to go gluten-free or not. We discuss utensil and equipment use, along with the items you may want to duplicate if your kitchen isn't completely gluten-free. We also look at the best storage containers for your kitchen.

Thinking like a crumb to avoid crumbs

Cross-contamination is the corruption of gluten-free products with gluten. This term doesn't mean accidentally using wheat flour when you're making pancakes. Cross-contamination can occur when you use the same spatula that flipped a whole-wheat grilled cheese sandwich to remove gluten-free cookies from a cookie sheet. Or a gluten-free biscuit can be contaminated with a knife that you just used to spread butter on a whole-wheat muffin. It's all kind of mindboggling, isn't it? You really have to start thinking about food at the crumb level.

Now you have a decision to make. Are you going to get rid of all the gluten-containing products in your kitchen and home? Or, if some members of your family aren't sensitive or allergic to gluten, will you keep some gluten-containing foods on hand?

If you don't get rid of all the gluten-containing foods in your kitchen, you have to institute a strict system to minimize cross-contamination. You may want to keep one cupboard, shelf, or drawer completely gluten-free. Or you can declare the kitchen mostly gluten-free and designate one cupboard or drawer for gluten-containing foods and baking equipment. Or you can mark products clearly, writing "gluten-free" or "warning: contains gluten!" on them. We call a kitchen where gluten-containing and gluten-free products coexist a *mixed kitchen*.

Separating utensils and equipment

Dedicated spaces for utensils and baking equipment are the key to reducing cross-contamination in a mixed kitchen. Think about people who keep kosher. They must have separate dishes for certain occasions. That's the type of organization you need to implement in your kitchen.

For a mixed kitchen, you should have two of each of these appliances, equipment, and utensils or be willing to deep clean each item every single time it's used:

- ✔ Baking pans
- ✔ Bread machine
- ✔ Cookie cutters
- ✔ Cookie sheets
- ✔ Cooling racks
- ✔ Cutting boards
- ✔ Kitchen towels
- ✔ Knives
- ✔ Measuring cups and spoons
- ✔ Mixing bowls
- ✔ Rolling pins

- ✔ Sifters
- ✔ Spatulas
- ✔ Spoons
- ✔ Stand and hand mixers
- ✔ Strainers and colanders
- ✔ Toaster
- ✔ Toaster oven (can be used for gluten-containing items if the food is put on foil)
- ✔ Whisks and beaters

You can clean equipment after each use and not resort to keeping separate equipment and utensils, but you need to be a neat freak to keep gluten-containing crumbs, dust, and residue at bay. If you feel you can keep this system running efficiently and safely, have at it!

Keeping "twin" foods

You need to keep many food products "separate but equal" as well. Think about the number of times you dip a knife into peanut butter and spread it on bread. Every time the knife is put back into the peanut butter, it's carrying gluten with it, and the whole jar is contaminated. Any food product you serve with gluten-containing foods should have a "twin" that's specifically labeled for gluten-free use only.

Training your family

After you clean and separate everything, you have to train your family to make sure they understand your system and how to keep these items separate. Training can take some time, especially if you have young children. Using colorful stickers can help warn little fingers to stay away from certain products. You may have to put locks on drawers or cupboards to keep small children away from products they shouldn't eat.

After you sort the products and clean the kitchen, put your feet up, sip some gluten-free tea (yes, some tea products contain roasted barley to replicate a coffee-like flavor), and enjoy a gluten-free snack! Then put food products, utensils, and cookware away. Make sure everything has a home it can return to after you use it. If you aren't creating a gluten-free kitchen, designate a special shelf or drawer for baking ingredients and baking equipment.

Storing food safely

Storing gluten-free and gluten-containing items in the same kitchen can be quite the balancing act. If you empty out a plastic container that contained bars made with gluten, wipe it out with a damp cloth, and add some gluten-free cookies, are those cookies still gluten-free? The answer? No!

Storage containers in your kitchen should be made of glass or ceramic. Plastic containers can hold on to greasy residue that attracts gluten, from crumbs or dust. Metal containers can have seams that trap flour and crumbs. Glass and ceramic are easy to clean and sterilize. You can run them through the dishwasher and eliminate all traces of grease or gluten. They don't hold on to grease, sticky substances, crumbs, or dust. They look nicer than plastic, they last longer, and you don't have to worry about materials from plastic leaching into your food!

But what if you want to freeze your gluten-free baked goods? Although you can find freezer-safe glass containers, most glass isn't a good candidate for freezing because the shock of extreme temperature changes can make it crack. (I've shattered a few Pyrex pie plates by moving them from the freezer to the countertop.) Instead, use freezer wrap to store gluten-free baked goods in the freezer. It's specially marked and can be found in any grocery store.

Chapter 9

Converting Favorite Recipes to Gluten-Free

*A*fter you discover how to bake tender and delectable gluten-free products using the recipes in this book, you'll naturally be curious about transforming your own favorite recipes into safe and healthy foods you can enjoy. Everyone has a favorite bread, cookie, cake, or pie that Grandma or Mom used to make.

In this chapter you find out how to convert your favorite traditional, wheat-based recipes for baked goods into gluten-free delights. First, try some of the recipes in this book just so you understand how gluten-free baking works. There's nothing like hands-on experience to make you a better baker.

When you feel comfortable with the process, tackle a simple recipe. And as your confidence grows, you'll be able to convert more of your old-fashioned wheat recipes into yummy gluten-free treats.

Adjusting the Dough or Batter

Converting traditional wheat-based recipes isn't difficult, but you do need knowledge of dough structure (see Chapter 7), familiarity with alternative flours and starches (see Chapter 5), and practice with the mechanisms, unique issues, and procedures of gluten-free baking (see Chapter 4). Read through those chapters before you attempt a conversion.

In this section we look at how to convert traditional recipes into gluten-free baked goods step by step by using baking mixes and containing, baking, and cooling the product.

When you're converting a traditional wheat recipe into a gluten-free recipe, be sure to read the traditional recipe carefully. Make note of the types of flour used and any other possible gluten products or ingredients called for, and list alternatives you can use.

Then jump right in, following these tips and tricks. With time, you'll be turning out delicious recipes from your past, altered to fit your new gluten-free lifestyle.

Converting traditional dough and batter recipes to gluten-free

You can make lots of easy changes to a traditional recipe to convert it to a desired gluten-free treat. You just need some knowledge about the chemistry of the recipe, a little practice, and a lot of patience.

Remember that we've already adjusted the recipes in this book to make them gluten-free. You can change them by substituting other flours (gram for gram) or by using casein-free or lactose-free ingredients. Most of the recipes have tips to vary the recipe if you'd like.

Here are some important points to keep in mind when converting a traditional wheat batter or dough to a gluten-free batter or dough:

- ✔ Always weigh your flours. Remember that a cup of all-purpose flour weighs 125 grams. If a recipe calls for a cup of all-purpose wheat flour, substitute 125 grams of an alternative flour. That means that sometimes you'll use less than a cup, sometimes more. Weighing is crucial.

- ✔ Always combine alternative flours. Don't substitute all-brown rice flour for all-purpose wheat flour, for instance. A combination of different flours provides the best results.

- ✔ When substituting flours, use higher-protein flours for bread recipes, pie crusts, and pizza crusts. Use lower-protein flours and more starches for cookies, cakes, dumplings, and soufflés.

- ✔ Remember the 70 percent protein flour to 30 percent starch flour ratio. This is a general guide for any gluten-free baked good. The protein provides the structure, and the starch provides tenderness and a fine crumb.

- ✔ Follow the ratios in Chapter 4 for different baked goods. If your traditional recipe doesn't quite follow the ratio, adjust the flour, sugar, fat, and liquid amounts so it does. This takes a little bit of work with a calculator, but you can do it!

- ✔ Many recipes taste better with brown sugar instead of granulated sugar. Honey is a good addition to use; replace some of the liquid in the recipe with honey or maple syrup.

✔ Add more liquid to the wheat recipe you're converting. Start out with a couple of tablespoons of extra liquid. After you make the recipes in this book, you'll know what a good gluten-free batter should look like. Measure the ingredients carefully and write down what you added, along with the quantities.

✔ Add a tiny bit of an acidic ingredient such as vitamin C powder, sour cream, or buttermilk. Gluten-free flours aren't as acidic as wheat flours, so baking soda doesn't work quite as well. Vitamin C powder is a good choice for those who can't use cow's milk in recipes.

✔ Baking powder can make some gluten-free baked goods taste a little tinny. Look for baking powders made with calcium, not aluminum. And try to find double-acting baking powder, which creates carbon dioxide when mixed with water and also when heated, which means your baked goods get a lift when the batter is mixed and in the oven! Always make sure that your baking powder and baking soda are labeled gluten-free. Consider making your own baking powder by combining equal amounts of gluten-free baking soda and cream of tartar.

✔ You may want to increase the leavening. Add a bit more baking powder, baking soda, or yeast to the traditional wheat recipe. Start by adding 25 percent more.

✔ Use yogurt or buttermilk to replace some of the liquid in the traditional recipe. Doing so helps make gluten-free baked goods, especially cakes and quick breads, fluffier.

✔ Think about using carbonated water in recipes. Doing so helps give the texture an extra boost without adding any more leavening, which can make baked goods bitter or sour.

✔ Puréed fruits and vegetables help add flavor and also add *pectin,* a natural substance found in produce that thickens liquid. Like gelatin, pectin increases moisture, too. Substitute these products for some of the liquid in a traditional wheat recipe.

✔ Add an extra egg, egg white, or egg replacer. The protein in the egg helps build the structure along with the gluten-free flours. In fact, you can replace some of the liquid in the traditional recipe with egg whites. One egg white is about 2 tablespoons.

✔ Increase flavorings. Double the vanilla and add more of any extract called for, and increase the amount of spices slightly. Just don't go overboard! Increase by 10 percent at first. If you like the results, you can add more the next time.

✔ Flavorful liquids can improve gluten-free breads, cakes, and cookies. Use cold coffee, molasses, fruit juice, honey, coconut milk, vanilla soy milk, nut milks, and vegetable juices to replace some or all of the liquid in a wheat recipe.

✔ Think about including an additive in your gluten-free doughs and batters. For more information about the best additives and how they work, see Chapter 5. Xanthan or guar gum, gelatin, sweet whey, eggs, raw buckwheat flour, chia slurries, and flaxseed slurries are excellent additions that can give your baked goods more structure and a better, finer crumb.

You may have to try several times before you successfully convert your favorite recipe into a gluten-free treat. Just remember that experimenting in the kitchen is a learning experience and can be fun when you approach it with a light attitude. Think of it as exploring a new world, and you're in charge. The more you learn, the easier converting recipes is!

Mixing gluten-free batters

You make most gluten-free recipes the same way as traditional wheat recipes, although you can skip some steps. For instance, adding liquid and flour alternatively to a creamed butter and flour mixture isn't necessary. You can just combine all the ingredients and beat for a few minutes. That saves you lots of time and work in the kitchen.

Keep these points in mind when mixing gluten-free doughs and batters:

✔ Always stir the flours, starches, gums, salt, and yeast or baking powder together until they're one color so that everything is evenly distributed before proceeding with the recipe. Use a wire whisk to make sure the dry ingredients are well combined. No one wants to bite into a cookie and get a chunk of sorghum flour or xanthan gum!

✔ Beat the batter longer than the traditional recipe suggests. Because the recipe has no gluten to overdevelop, you don't have to worry about creating a tough product. But these flours need a little extra time to absorb water and hydrate properly so they form a nice crumb. And beating adds air to your recipes, which creates the airy texture you're looking for.

✔ You mix most gluten-free quick breads like wheat quick breads — just until the ingredients are combined.

✔ You usually beat cookie doughs and batters for a minute or two to hydrate the dough and form the crumb structure.

✔ Beat cakes for a minute or two. Folding in beaten egg whites can help make the cakes fluffier and lighter.

✔ Beat bread doughs and yeast breads with a mixer, using the paddle attachment, for several minutes to add air and develop the protein structure. You don't knead gluten-free bread doughs, because they're soft and sticky.

✔ For pie crust, you may need to add more flour until a soft dough forms. Chill the dough before rolling it out.

✔ A food processor can help mix doughs thoroughly and in little time. Process the ingredients until they're well mixed. Add a few more seconds of processing time if the recipe tells you to beat by hand or with a mixer for a few minutes.

Using baking mixes

Baking mixes are a great choice for gluten-free baking. Having a mix on hand means you'll be more likely to make cookies or a cake because you can just reach for a mix instead of hauling out three or four bags of gluten-free flours.

This book has recipes for lots of gluten-free baking mixes. Two of them, White Flour Mix and Whole-Grain Flour Mix (both in Chapter 10), are used in many of the recipes. Jean and I suggest that you make up a batch of each of these mixes to make gluten-free baking much easier. You can make your own mixes after you get more experience in the kitchen. Just follow the 70 percent protein flour to 30 percent starch flour rule, measure by weight, and mix the ingredients really well before storing.

You can find lots of commercial gluten-free baking mixes on the market, too. Most work very well. Before you buy a commercial gluten-free mix, be sure to read product reviews from Amazon.com or other online stores. Avoid mixes with poor reviews to save time and money.

Keep a pen in the kitchen

Always, always write down your discoveries and changes as you work. Nobody can remember that baking at a lower temperature and using one more egg white transformed your grandmother's pie crust into a gluten-free winner! Most experts tell bakers, whether they're using wheat flour or amaranth flour, to write changes, observations, and baking times down on every single recipe. Make sure to write notes on the recipe about exactly what flours you use, in what weights, and any changes in dough appearance.

In fact, when Linda worked in the Pillsbury test kitchens, writing down baking times, observations, and recommendations was expected! When you're converting recipes, get in the habit of keeping a pen in the kitchen right next to your scale and parchment paper. After all, you're acting like a scientist!

You can use many of the baking mixes in Chapter 10 — including Cookie Mix without Gums, White Flour Mix, Quick Bread Mix, High-Protein Bread Flour Mix, Light Cakey Corn Bread Mix, Hearty Corn Bread Mix, and Whole-Grain Flour Mix — to substitute for flours in any recipe. For instance, use the Light Cakey Corn Bread Mix in your grandmother's recipe for corn bread baked in a cast-iron skillet. Use the High-Protein Bread Flour Mix in your mom's recipe for Parker House rolls. And use the Cookie Mix without Gums in your aunt's recipe for sugar cookies.

If you don't keep a 100 percent gluten-free kitchen, using baking mixes helps you avoid cross-contamination. (For more on cross-contamination, see Chapter 8.) Think about making wheat-based baking mixes, too, on a different day from your gluten-free baking. Flour dust can hang in the air for 24 to 48 hours after use, so spread out the different types of baking. Never bake a gluten-free recipe and a wheat recipe on the same day, unless, of course, you bake the gluten-free recipe first and remove it from the kitchen while you bake the wheat product. But remember, your cleanup must be impeccable!

Handling and Baking the Dough

After you adjust your gluten-free dough or batter ingredient list, you need to mix the dough, shape it, bake it, and cool it. You handle gluten-free baked goods a bit differently from wheat-based baked goods.

In this section we discuss handling the doughs, shaping them, choosing products to help form the doughs, setting baking times and temperatures, and knowing the best ways to cool and store your delicious gluten-free baked goods.

Working with gluten-free doughs

Gluten-free doughs are much softer and stickier than wheat doughs, and they need a little help to form. Fortunately, regular supermarkets have all the supplies you need to handle your doughs and batters with ease.

Here are some tips for handling gluten-free doughs:

✔ Chill cookie doughs before you bake them. We recommend doing so even for wheat cookies; in fact, pastry chef and cookbook author David Lebovitz has a wheat-based recipe that rests for 36 hours! The rest time helps the dough firm up so it's easier to shape and holds its shape in the oven. And it gives the flour more time to hydrate so the cookie is more tender.

✔ Grease pans or cookie sheets well and flour them with a tiny bit of gluten-free flour or starch. Or you can use parchment paper or Silpat liners to line cookie sheets and baking pans. Gluten-free doughs are stickier than wheat doughs so they can use the extra help.

✔ Piping bags can be your best friend in the kitchen. Because gluten-free doughs are much softer and stickier than wheat-based doughs, using a piping bag can help you form breadsticks, cookies, and rolls with ease.

✔ Ice cream scoops are another wonderful appliance to help you handle gluten-free doughs. See Chapter 4 for more information on which scoops to stock in your kitchen.

✔ Plastic wrap and parchment paper are also your friends in the gluten-free kitchen. You use these products to shape doughs and wrap them for chilling in the fridge.

✔ Because they're about the consistency of thick cake batter, you need to place gluten-free doughs and batters into pans and forms before you bake them. The pans give the dough structure and help hold it in the correct form while the structure sets. Have fun with your gluten-free recipes by choosing pans with unusual or fun shapes.

✔ Use a smaller pan than the one called for in the traditional recipe. Make two breads in 5-x-3-inch pans rather than one large loaf in a 9-x-5-inch pan. Make sure that you fill the pan with the same proportion of batter or dough as called for in the original recipe.

✔ Don't use dark-colored or Teflon pans. These types of pans hold more heat than shiny light metal or glass baking pans, and the bottoms and sides of your beautiful creations may burn before the inside is done.

Baking and cooling doughs

When you're ready to bake, be sure that your oven is properly calibrated before you begin. This is an essential step whether you're baking with wheat or gluten-free flours. An oven temperature that's off by 25 degrees or more can ruin your breads, cakes, cookies, and pies. Follow the manufacturer's instructions to calibrate your oven.

For the best gluten-free baked goods, try these tips for baking methods, times, and temperatures:

✔ Use the middle oven rack unless the recipe tells you to bake on a higher or lower rack. On the middle rack, the oven heat circulates evenly around the pans.

✓ As a general rule, don't bake more than one pan at a time. If you stack cookie sheets on two racks in a conventional oven, the top sheet will have underbaked bottoms, and the bottom sheet will have underbaked tops. You can rotate pans after half of the baking time has elapsed if you're in full Christmas cookie production! However, you can stack sheets or pans in a convection oven because the fans in that type of oven circulate the air more efficiently.

✓ Preheat pizza stones and cast-iron pans before you add your gluten-free doughs and batters. In fact, bread recipes turn out with a wonderful crust and light interior when you use a heavy pot with a lid. See Chapter 19 for detailed instructions.

✓ Brush your gluten-free creations with milk or eggs (if dairy or eggs aren't a problem) to help them brown just before you put them into the oven. Olive oil helps baked goods brown, too.

✓ You bake most gluten-free baked goods at the same temperature as wheat products. If you find that your breads or cakes aren't quite done inside, lower the temperature by 25 degrees and increase the time by five minutes or so.

✓ Don't overbake gluten-free products. They don't brown quite the same as wheat products. Use touch and temperature tests to judge doneness.

✓ Set the timer for a few minutes less than the baking time calls for in the traditional wheat recipe. Check the food for doneness according to directions in Chapters 3 and 4.

✓ Remove the baked goods from the pans quickly so the breads, cakes, and cookies don't steam. Cool them on a wire rack.

✓ For a nice, crisp crust on yeast breads, after you remove the bread from the pan, put it back in the oven, directly on the rack, for a minute or two. This helps drive off excess moisture in the crust and also browns the bread evenly.

✓ Angel food cakes and sponge cakes are cooled in a specific way: hung upside down like a bat! These cakes have very delicate structures. Cooling them upside down helps stretch the protein and starch web as it cools so it doesn't shrink and collapse. Place a funnel or glass pop bottle on the counter and carefully balance the tube pan upside down.

✓ Cool baked goods completely before you wrap and store them. If you wrap a bread or cake before it's cool, water collects on the product's surface, making it soggy.

Storing baked goods

Storing gluten-free baked goods isn't very different from storing wheat-based baked goods. Store these products as the recipe directs. If a recipe contains a perishable ingredient (meat, cheese, eggs, dairy, and so on), you need to store it in the refrigerator. Because the fridge is such a dry place, always store foods well-covered. Most baked goods are stored in airtight containers at room temperature. Home-baked goods, whether made from wheat or gluten-free flours, go stale more quickly than commercial products. Freeze baked goods within a couple of days (if there's anything left!).

Managing Expectations

When you find out that you must avoid gluten for the rest of your life, you may think that biting into a slice of tender bread with a crisp crust and a fluffy texture is a sensation you'll never experience again.

With the tips and tricks in this book, you *can* have that experience again. But no matter how good a gluten-free recipe is, it will never be the same as a wheat recipe. It can be even better! Jean's daughters have found that they feel sorry for people who eat only wheat-based cookies and cakes. Nothing beats homemade treats. Making them healthy is a bonus.

In this section we discuss flavor differences, texture differences, and visual differences between wheat-based and gluten-free baked goods. At first the change may take some adjustment, but you'll soon learn to love the taste, texture, and look of gluten-free cakes, cookies, pies, and desserts.

Flavor differences

Wheat flour is known for its consistency; it's consistent in the way it behaves in recipes, consistent in its look, and consistent in taste. That's where gluten-free flours have an advantage: They all have a different taste!

When you transition to a gluten-free diet, the number of alternative flours and starches can seem dizzying. Read through Chapter 5 carefully; it lists the most common flours and their characteristics, including color, texture, taste, protein content, and the best ways to use them. As you bake, you'll discover the flours and starches you like best.

Some flours are naturally sweet, others are nutty, and others have a strong flavor. When you're just getting started baking gluten-free, try as many as you can. And keep notes about which flours you like and which you don't.

The point is to be flexible. No gluten-free recipe ever tastes exactly the same as a wheat flour recipe. But remember that homemade gluten-free baked goods taste better than anything made in a factory, mass-produced, or made in a supermarket bakery.

Texture differences

Texture is the elephant in the room for gluten-free baked goods. Huge improvements were made when flour combinations and additives were added to the mix. Measuring according to weight instead of volume represented the next step forward. Even with these changes, gluten-free baked goods don't have quite the same texture as wheat-based products. To get the best texture from your gluten-free baked products, try these tips:

- ✔ Eat breads and rolls warm. Of course, nothing's better than eating these products warm from the oven, but you can reheat breads and rolls before serving for better texture. Microwave rolls for 8 to 10 seconds apiece on high power. Wrap breads in foil and reheat them in a 350 degree oven for 9 to 12 minutes. But don't try this more than once! Reheating makes starch go stale faster, so multiple reheating creates a tough and dry bread or roll.

- ✔ Some gluten-free flours have a slightly gritty texture, especially brown rice flour. Sweet rice flour from Asian markets is incredibly fine textured. But corn flour, teff flour, and quinoa flours are all a bit gritty. Use less of these flours or grind them in a food processor for a finer texture.

- ✔ Some gluten-freed baked goods can be denser than their wheat cousins, although many of the newer gluten-free recipes are wonderfully light. To adjust to this fact, bake recipes that are naturally denser. A whole-grain bread will always be denser than a white bread. It's also better for you, with more fiber and vitamins.

- ✔ If your breads aren't as soft or tender as you'd like, toast them. Nothing's better than toasted homemade bread spread with a little softened butter or whipped honey.

- ✔ If you're not completely happy with the texture of your gluten-free baked goods, freeze them. Freezing firms structure and can help keep products moist for a longer period. In fact, some products, such as brownies and soft cookies, taste delectable when frozen and partially thawed.

Visual differences

Finally, many gluten-free baked goods look a little different from wheat baked goods. The breads may not rise quite as high, and cookies and pastries may be flatter. Browning is a little different, too. But you may be surprised at how appetizing these gluten-free treats look. The crumb of gluten-free breads and cakes is very similar to wheat products. Pie crusts are just as flaky, and cookies can be crackled and golden-brown. Here are some ways to improve the look of your gluten-free baked goods:

- ✔ You can get a more evenly browned look by brushing doughs and batters with a beaten egg or any kind of milk before you put them into the oven.

- ✔ Use muffin tins or baking rings when making rolls and biscuits to help the softer batters and doughs hold their shape.

- ✔ Use piping bags and ice cream scoops to shape cookies and rolls. A thicker batter or dough produces a puffier product.

Part III
Sweet Gluten-Free Baking Recipes

"What a wonderful swirled icing effect! How ever did you do it?"

In this part . . .

Now it's time for recipes! These seven chapters cover baking mixes, breakfast foods, cookies, brownies and bars, pies and pastries, and cakes and frosting recipes. No matter what you want to bake in the kitchen, we have a recipe for it here. Follow the recipes carefully, using the ingredients, tools, and tips in this book, and you'll turn your kitchen into a gluten-free bake shop.

Chapter 10

Gluten-Free Baking Mixes

In This Chapter

▶ Using baking mixes

▶ Getting familiar with several mix recipes

*O*ne of the best and most efficient ways to bake gluten-free is to make some mixes with a combination of gluten-free flours and starches. Then all you need to do is add some water, milk, and sometimes an egg or some oil; stir; and bake cakes, cookies, brownies, or breads.

With mixes in your pantry, you don't need to feel stymied by a recipe that requests five different flours, four starches, and a gum or two. You can use these mix recipes on their own and in many recipes in this book. The basic instructions for using each mix, along with how much mix and additional ingredients you need, are in each recipe.

And best of all, you totally eliminate possible cross-contamination using mixes, especially if you don't have a dedicated gluten-free kitchen!

In this chapter, we offer some recipes for baking mixes, including mixes for cakes, cookies, quick breads, and a couple of different mixes for yeast breads and general baking.

Getting Started with Easy Baking Mix Recipes

Baking mixes, like baking recipes, are scientific formulas. You must measure carefully and accurately for best results. You measure many baking recipes using weights (see Chapter 4 for information on weighing ingredients), and mixes are no exception. In fact, in nonmix recipes in this book, we ask you to weigh the flours and starches, but with mixes, you really should weigh every ingredient.

You've no doubt used mixes in the past, so you're familiar with the process; you just dump the mix into a bowl, add other ingredients, stir, pour the batter or dough into a pan, and bake.

Here are a few rules to follow when you're creating your own mixes.

- **Measure using a scale.** Be sure that you weigh each flour ingredient separately for the most accurate results. Always zero out the scale after the bowl is on the scale, before you add each ingredient. If you don't use a scale, always measure by spooning the flour or flour mix lightly into a measuring cup and leveling off the top with the back of a knife. See Chapters 4 and 5 for more info on measuring by weight and volume.

- **Be sure all your ingredients are fresh.** Baking powder, baking soda, and yeast all have expiration dates, beyond which they just don't work as well. There's no point in making all this effort and spending all this money on a mix, only to have it fail because your ingredients are too old.

- **Try to use the exact ingredients the mix calls for.** You can make some substitutions for food allergy reasons or if you can't find a certain flour. For instance, you can substitute a flour with a similar protein content for another (see Chapter 5 for a chart that lists the protein content of different gluten-free flours). When you make a substitute, be sure to do so by weight, not by volume. Try to weigh all flours, always!

- **Always label the mixes.** After mixes are mixed and stored in your pantry, you won't be able to differentiate between the Cookie Mix and the High-Protein Bread Flour Mix. Mark the name of the mix, the date you made it, and instructions for use directly on the bag or container.

- **Store the mixes in airtight containers in a cool, dry place.** Flours are very absorbent and absorb excess moisture from the air when it's very humid. And heat may affect the leavening properties of the baking soda or baking powder. Finally, some high-fat flours can become rancid in the presence of high heat and moisture.

White Flour Mix

Prep time: 10 min • **Yield:** 18⅓ cups

Ingredients	Directions
5½ cups (685 grams) tapioca flour (also known as tapioca starch)	*1* In a very large bowl, combine all ingredients and blend using a wire whisk until they're a single color.
8⅓ cups (1,370 grams) potato starch	*2* Store in an airtight container and use in recipes. 1 cup weighs 148 grams.
4½ cups minus 1 tablespoon (685 grams) sweet rice flour (glutinous rice flour)	

Note: For accuracy and best results, weigh out the flours for this mix and weigh the mix when you use it in recipes. 1 cup of this mix weighs 148 grams.

Note: This mix is used as a flour substitute in many recipes in the book, especially cake, bar cookie, and cookie recipes. It's a good substitute for all-purpose white flour in any recipe that you want to convert to a gluten-free recipe. For tips on converting recipes, see Chapter 9.

Tip: You can find glutinous rice flour at local Asian markets.

Whole-Grain Flour Mix

Prep time: 10 min • **Yield:** 14 cups

Ingredients	Directions
4½ cups minus 1 tablespoon (600 grams) brown rice flour	**1** In a large bowl, combine all ingredients until the mixture is one color. Use a wire whisk to stir for best results.
4¾ cups plus 2 tablespoons (600 grams) sorghum flour	
3¼ cups minus 1 tablespoon (400 grams) millet flour	**2** Store in an airtight container and use in baking recipes in place of flour.
1¾ cups (275 grams) sweet rice flour	

Note: Weigh these flours instead of measuring them by volume. You end up with much better results, and you find that with a little experience, weighing is faster than measuring by cups. 1 cup of this mix weighs 135 grams.

Note: This flour mix is used in a lot of bread recipes in this book. It's a good substitute for whole-wheat flour in many recipes.

Cookie Mix without Gums

Prep time: 20 min • **Yield:** 11 cups

Ingredients	Directions
4 cups sugar	**1** Combine the sugar, baking soda, baking powder, and salt in a large, sealed, plastic bag or container, stirring until the sugar is well-coated in the baking soda, powder, and salt. This step is essential to eliminate tiny pockets of bitterness in your cookies.
2 tablespoons baking soda	
3 tablespoons baking powder	
1 tablespoon sea salt	
2 cups minus 2 tablespoons minus 1 teaspoon (250 grams) regular grind brown rice flour	**2** Add all the remaining ingredients and mix well to combine completely and thoroughly.
1 cup (160 grams) regular grind white rice flour	**3** Store in an airtight container at room temperature. Use this mix in any recipe as a substitute for a cookie mix, or use it in the recipes in Chapters 13 and 14. Spoon this mix into a measuring cup and level off the top before adding it to the recipe.
1 cup minus 1 teaspoon (160 grams) potato starch	
2 cups (246 grams) sorghum flour	
1 cup minus 1 tablespoon (116 grams) tapioca flour	

Note: This is a good base for making lots of cookies. It's easier to stir up a big batch of this mix than to drag out and measure all the different flours many times. If you don't want to use one of these flours, refer to the chart in Chapter 5 and choose a flour that's similar in protein, fat, and carbohydrate content. Recipes using this mix need an overnight rest in the refrigerator to let the flours rehydrate and the sugars dissolve. And if you prefer a sweeter cookie, you can add up to 1 more cup of sugar to the mix.

Vary It! You can use a fine grind of flour for these cookies. Substitute the fine grind for the regular grind by weight. In other words, if you want to use fine grind brown rice flour, use 250 grams of it, not 2 cups minus 2 tablespoons minus 1 teaspoon. The texture of cookies made with fine grind flour changes. As a bonus of using fine grind flours, you can mix the cookie dough and bake it immediately rather than waiting while the batter rests overnight.

Cake Mix

Prep time: 20 min • **Yield:** Six 9-inch round cake layers, or 48 servings

Ingredients	*Directions*
6 cups sugar	*1* In a large bowl, combine the sugar, White Flour Mix, Whole-Grain Flour Mix, baking powder, and salt; mix until they're a single color.
5¾ cups (852 grams) White Flour Mix (see page 153)	
2⅓ cups plus 1 tablespoon (324 grams) Whole-Grain Flour Mix (see page 154)	*2* Using a mixer or a pastry blender, blend the butter into the flour mixture until the mixture looks like sand.
2 tablespoons baking powder	*3* Divide the mixture into six portions and place each portion in a glass storage container or a heavy-duty Ziploc plastic bag.
1 teaspoon salt	
3 cups unsalted butter	

Note: Everyone deserves a homemade birthday cake! Keep this simple mix in the fridge or freezer and you're ready to prepare a cake at a moment's notice. You can store this mix in the fridge for three weeks or freeze it for up to three months.

Preparing cake pans

Properly preparing any cake pan when you're baking is very important, but even more so for gluten-free cakes. Because the structure is more delicate, you should grease the pans well with unsalted butter, solid shortening, or cooking spray (with no salt, because salt makes batters stick to the pan) and then dust the pans with a little gluten-free flour. Knock the excess flour out of the pan and add the batter. This gives the delicate batter something to hold on to as it rises in the oven and climbs the sides of the pan. Be especially careful with Bundt cake pans because they can be tricky to grease. Take extra time and make sure that you grease and flour every crease and crevice.

Cake Mix Cake

Prep time: 10 min • **Cook time:** 48–50 min • **Yield:** 6–8 servings

Ingredients	Directions
1 portion (2 cups) Cake Mix (see page 156) **2 eggs, separated** **½ cup milk** **1 teaspoon vanilla** **⅛ teaspoon salt**	*1* Allow the Cake Mix to come to room temperature. Preheat the oven to 350 degrees and grease a 9-inch cake pan with unsalted butter. *2* In a large bowl, beat the Cake Mix, egg yolks, milk, and vanilla for 3 minutes. *3* In a small bowl, beat the egg whites until soft peaks form. Add the salt and beat until stiff peaks form. *4* Fold the egg whites into the batter gently. Pour into the prepared pan. Bake for 48 to 50 minutes, or until the cake is golden-brown and starts pulling away from the sides of the pan. *5* Cool the cake in the pan for 5 minutes and then move it to a wire rack to cool completely.

Per serving: Calories 250 (From Fat 107); Fat 12g (Saturated 7g); Cholesterol 99mg; Sodium 149mg; Carbohydrate 34g (Dietary Fiber 0g); Protein 4g.

Quick Bread Mix

Prep time: 20 min • **Yield:** 3 standard loaf pans; 18 servings

Ingredients	Directions
4½ cups minus 1 tablespoon (600 grams) Whole-Grain Flour Mix (see page 154)	**1** Combine all ingredients in a large bowl and mix until they're one color.
2½ cups minus 1 tablespoon (360 grams) White Flour Mix (see page 153)	**2** Divide the mixture into three batches. Store the batches in airtight, heavy-duty plastic bags or plastic containers.
1 cup plus 3 tablespoons packed brown sugar	
1 cup granulated sugar	
3 tablespoons baking powder	
4½ teaspoons baking soda	
1½ teaspoons salt	

Note: You can store Quick Bread Mix at room temperature for about a month. For longer storage, freeze it for up to three months.

Tip: Weighing the flours will give you the best results. But if you need to measure this mix by volume, just be sure to stir the flour first and then spoon it into the measuring cup and level off with the back of a knife. Just a little extra flour in each cup makes the overall mix heavier and creates denser baked goods.

Vegan Applesauce Quick Bread

Prep time: 10 min • **Cook time:** 45–48 min • **Yield:** 8 servings

Ingredients	*Directions*
⅓ **recipe Quick Bread Mix (see page 158)**	*1* Preheat the oven to 350 degrees. Grease an 8-x-4-inch loaf pan with unsalted butter or solid shortening.
1 cup applesauce	
1 teaspoon vanilla	*2* In a medium bowl, combine the Quick Bread Mix, applesauce, vanilla, and oil and beat until well mixed. Pour into the prepared pan.
¼ **cup vegetable oil**	
	3 Bake for 45 to 48 minutes, or until a toothpick inserted in the center comes out clean. The internal temperature should be 190 to 200 degrees.
	4 Cool the bread in the pan for 10 minutes and then move it to a wire rack to cool completely.

Per serving: Calories 277 (From Fat 69); Fat 8g (Saturated 1g); Cholesterol 0mg; Sodium 573mg; Carbohydrate 52g (Dietary Fiber 2g); Protein 2g.

Brownie Mix

Prep time: 15 min • **Yield:** 8 cups

Ingredients	Directions
1 cup minus 2 teaspoons (142 grams) White Flour Mix (see page 153)	**1** In a large bowl, combine all ingredients and mix until they're one color. Divide the mixture into four containers and store at room temperature.
1¼ cups minus 1 teaspoon (165 grams) Whole-Grain Flour Mix (see page 154)	
5 cups sugar	
1 cup cocoa powder	
2 teaspoons baking powder	
1 teaspoon salt	

Tip: This mix works well as a basic chocolate brownie, somewhere between cakey and chewy. You can easily bend the results toward your favorite texture by varying the amount of butter and cooking time. More butter and a shorter cooking time make a chewier brownie. Less butter and a longer cooking time make a more cake-like brownie.

Is it really done?

Though the internal temperature of a baked good is the best indicator of doneness, you also have to rely on visual cues. For instance, a loaf of bread may test 200 degrees, which is the correct doneness temperature, but it may not have finished browning. And a browned loaf of bread is most visually appealing. So use the instant-read thermometer but also make sure that your baked goods are evenly browned, but not burned, before you take them out of the oven.

Brownies

Prep time: 15 min • **Cook time:** 48 min • **Yield:** 16 servings

Ingredients	Directions
1 bag Brownie Mix (see page 160)	*1* Preheat the oven to 350 degrees. Grease a 9-inch square cake pan with unsalted butter or solid shortening.
6 ounces dark chocolate, melted and cooled	
½ cup softened butter	*2* For chewy brownies, combine 1 bag Brownie Mix, chocolate, butter, vanilla, and eggs and beat until combined. For cakey brownies, reduce the chocolate amount to 3 ounces. Mix and bake both types of brownies as directed.
2 teaspoons vanilla	
3 eggs	
	3 Pour the batter into the prepared pan and bake for 48 to 50 minutes, or until the brownies are set and have a shiny crust. Cool completely before cutting.

Per serving: Calories 203 (From Fat 90); Fat 10g (Saturated 6g); Cholesterol 55mg; Sodium 87mg; Carbohydrate 29g (Dietary Fiber 2g); Protein 3g.

Note: If you like fudgy or chewy brownies, more chocolate makes the brownies moister. For cake-like, lighter brownies, use less chocolate.

Vary It! You can embellish this basic brownie easily by adding chocolate chips, melted chocolate, or dried fruits to the batter; by layering with different frostings; or by stirring in ¾ cup chopped walnuts per batch.

Light Cakey Corn Bread Mix

Prep time: 10 min • **Yield:** 6–7 cups

Ingredients

3 cups yellow or white cornmeal

1¾ cups plus 3 tablespoons (284 grams) White Flour Mix (see page 153)

1¼ cups minus 1 teaspoon (165 grams) Whole-Grain Flour Mix (see page 154)

½ cup sugar (optional)

5 teaspoons baking powder

1 teaspoon baking soda

1½ teaspoons salt

¾ cup butter, buttery sticks, or coconut oil (optional)

Directions

1 Combine the cornmeal, White Flour Mix, Whole-Grain Flour Mix, sugar (if desired), baking powder, baking soda, and salt in a large bowl and stir well with a wire whisk until the mixture is all one color.

2 Add butter, buttery sticks, or coconut oil (if you're going to use the mix just for corn bread and not for cornmeal pancakes) and cut the fat into the flour until the mixture resembles sand.

3 Divide into four equal portions, about 1½ cups each, and place in glass jars or plastic freezer bags.

Note: People from the southern United States are usually horrified at the thought of sugar in corn bread, while those from the North (including Jean and Linda) like sugar in this quick bread. So to keep the peace, the sugar in this recipe is optional. This recipe makes light and cake-like muffins and corn bread.

Note: Store Light Cakey Corn Bread Mix in the refrigerator for three months or in the freezer for six months.

Light Cakey Corn Bread

Prep time: 15 min • **Cook time:** 25 min • **Yield:** 9 servings

Ingredients	*Directions*
2 eggs	*1* Preheat the oven to 350 degrees. Grease a 9-inch square pan with unsalted butter or solid shortening.
1 portion Light Cakey Corn Bread Mix (see page 162)	*2* In a medium bowl, beat the eggs until fluffy. Add Light Cakey Corn Bread Mix, milk or buttermilk, and oil; mix well.
1½ cups milk or buttermilk	
¼ cup vegetable oil	*3* Pour into the prepared pan. Bake for 25 to 28 minutes, or until the bread sets and turns light golden-brown. Serve warm. If you'd rather bake muffins, reduce the baking time to 20 to 22 minutes.

Per serving: Calories 187 (From Fat 108); Fat 12g (Saturated 4g); Cholesterol 61mg; Sodium 169mg; Carbohydrate 17g (Dietary Fiber 1g); Protein 4g.

Hearty Corn Bread Mix

Prep time: 15 min • **Yield:** 6–7 cups

Ingredients	Directions
4 cups yellow or white cornmeal	**1** In a large bowl, combine the cornmeal, Whole-Grain Flour Mix, White Flour Mix, sugar (if desired), baking powder, baking soda, and salt and mix well with a wire whisk until the ingredients are well-blended and all one color.
1¼ cups minus 1 teaspoon (165 grams) Whole-Grain Flour Mix (see page 154)	
1 cup minus 2 teaspoons (142 grams) White Flour Mix (see page 153)	**2** Add the unsalted butter, buttery sticks, or coconut oil (if desired) and blend the fat into the flour until the mixture resembles sand.
½ cup sugar (optional)	
5 teaspoons baking powder	**3** Divide the mix into four equal portions and place them in glass jars or plastic freezer bags.
1 teaspoon baking soda	
1½ teaspoons salt	
¾ cup unsalted butter, buttery sticks, or coconut oil (optional)	

Note: Store Hearty Corn Bread Mix in the refrigerator for three months or in the freezer for six months.

Hearty Corn Bread

Prep time: 15 min • **Cook time:** 25 min • **Yield:** 9 servings

Ingredients	Directions
2 eggs	**1** Preheat the oven to 350 degrees. Grease a 9-inch square pan with unsalted butter or solid shortening.
1 portion Hearty Corn Bread Mix (see page 164)	
1½ cups milk or buttermilk	**2** In a medium bowl, beat the eggs until fluffy. Add Hearty Corn Bread Mix, milk or buttermilk, and oil; mix well.
¼ cup vegetable oil	
	3 Pour into the prepared pan. Bake for 25 to 28 minutes, or until the bread is set and turns light golden-brown. Serve warm.

Per serving: Calories 282 (From Fat 96); Fat 11g (Saturated 2g); Cholesterol 53mg; Sodium 37mg; Carbohydrate 41g (Dietary Fiber 5g); Protein 8g.

Note: This corn bread is grainier and heavier than the Light Cakey Corn Bread. Use it when you want a dense and well-textured corn bread to serve with chili in the fall and winter.

High-Protein Bread Flour Mix

Prep time: 20 min • **Yield:** 15 cups

Ingredients

4⅓ cups (583 grams) brown rice flour

4¾ cups (583 grams) sorghum flour

4½ cups plus 2 tablespoons plus 2 teaspoons (583 grams) millet flour

1¼ cups minus 2 teaspoons (155 grams) white bean flour

½ cup plus 2 tablespoons (74 grams) garfava flour

Directions

1 In a large bowl, combine all ingredients and mix until they're one color.

2 Store in a large container at room temperature for no longer than one month.

Note: Gluten-free folk have a true problem re-creating the structure and function of the protein gluten. Some people use lots of xanthan and guar gum to mimic the stickiness and stretchiness of gluten molecules. But breads made with these ingredients can be a bit, well, gummy. This mixture mimics the high-protein content of bread flour.

Bread flour contains 14 percent protein as well as fat and fiber. This mixture creates a lovely loaf of bread that rises high and stays tender. If you're sensitive to bean flours or one of the other flours, substitute another flour (by weight only!) that has a similar protein content.

Note: This mix will keep in the freezer for six months.

Pancake Mix

Prep time: 20 min • **Yield:** 40–50 pancakes

Ingredients	Directions
2 cups minus 2 tablespoons (250 grams) brown rice flour	**1** In a large bowl, combine all ingredients and mix until they're one color.
1 cup (123 grams) sorghum flour	
½ cup minus 1 teaspoon (80 grams) potato starch	**2** Divide into five portions and store in heavy-duty Ziploc plastic bags or plastic containers.
1 cup minus 1 tablespoon (120 grams) cornstarch	
½ cup sugar	
1 tablespoon baking powder	
2 teaspoons baking soda	
1 teaspoon salt	

Note: Store Pancake Mix at room temperature for up to two months or in the freezer for six months.

Pancakes

Prep time: 10 min • **Cook time:** 5 min • **Yield:** 8–10 pancakes

Ingredients	Directions
2 eggs	*1* In a small bowl, combine the eggs, milk, and butter and mix well.
1 cup milk	
2 tablespoons butter, melted	*2* Put the Pancake Mix in a medium bowl, add the egg mixture, and beat until smooth.
1 cup Pancake Mix (see page 167)	
	3 Heat a griddle over medium-high heat. Grease with a bit of unsalted butter or solid shortening.
	4 Drop the batter, by ¼ cup portions, onto the griddle. Cook until bubbles form on the surface and the edges look dry, about 3 to 4 minutes. Turn with a spatula and cook for 1 to 2 minutes on the second side until brown. Serve immediately.

Per serving: Calories 125 (From Fat 49); Fat 5g (Saturated 3g); Cholesterol 65mg; Sodium 185mg; Carbohydrate 16g (Dietary Fiber 1g); Protein 3g.

Vary It! You can dress up these Pancakes with the addition of spices or cocoa powder. Add a teaspoon of cinnamon or a teaspoon of apple pie spice to the basic mix. You can also drop miniature chocolate chips or blueberries onto the pancakes when they're ready to be flipped on the griddle.

Chapter 11

Quick Breakfast Recipes

*Y*ou've most likely heard the saying "breakfast is the most important meal of the day." That's true, and nutritionists are discovering that breakfast is even more important than first thought. Breakfast fuels your body and brain for the rest of the day. People who regularly eat breakfast have fewer weight problems than people who skip it. Children do better at school when they eat a good, nutritious breakfast.

In this chapter we offer some delicious and easy breakfast recipes that range from simple muffins to some special coffeecakes and pancakes. Even on a gluten-free diet, you can still enjoy these foods and tempt recalcitrant appetites with wonderful aromas floating out of your kitchen.

Why Breakfast Is So Important

A good breakfast really sets the tone for the rest of your day. After all, you haven't eaten anything since the night before, at least eight hours ago! Your blood sugar is low, your stomach is rumbling, and your brain doesn't function well unless you feed it. More than half of the people in America skip breakfast. Don't be one of them!

These are the benefits of a healthy breakfast:

- ✔ Breakfast should provide a good amount of the vitamins, minerals, and phytochemicals your body needs to keep going. Without breakfast, you're more likely to be too hungry at lunch, which can result in overeating. And that cinnamon roll in the vending machine will be more tempting.

- ✔ Your brain does better on breakfast. Your brain needs a lot of fuel to perform at peak capacity. Studies show that people who eat a good breakfast are better at tests and performing simple tasks, and those people have better memory recall.

- ✔ Your body goes into fasting mode overnight and burns few calories. You need a good amount of protein, carbohydrates, and fat to get your metabolism going and to rev up your energy levels.

- ✔ Eating breakfast can help control your cholesterol levels and blood glucose levels. Keeping your cholesterol low is good for your heart, and regulating blood sugar makes you less likely to develop type 2 diabetes.

- ✔ People who eat breakfast are more likely to make healthy food choices throughout the day, and those people tend to weigh less than others.

Quick and Easy Breakfast Recipes

The recipes in this chapter are varied, with many different flavors and textures. You can mix and match them to create an interesting breakfast or depend on just one or two to get you through the week. During the week, Granola Bars or Lemon Cranberry Cornmeal Scones are perfect for breakfast on the run. On the weekend, have a leisurely breakfast with Banana Pancakes served with Warm Fruit Sauce.

You can serve several of these recipes at a brunch or breakfast gathering. Make a few muffins and a coffeecake, along with several types of tea and some different sausages. Set a pretty table with your good china and invite friends over for a shower or a party celebrating the beginning of the school year. And remember that you can also serve these recipes any time of the day. Breakfast for dinner is a wonderful concept. These foods are comforting and warming, served on a cold winter night.

If you don't use a scale to measure flours and mixes, always measure by spooning the flour lightly into a measuring cup and leveling off the top with the back of a knife. See Chapters 4 and 5 for more info on measuring by weight and volume.

Banana Pancakes

Prep time: 20 min • **Cook time:** 5 min • **Yield:** 4–6 servings

Ingredients	*Directions*
1 large ripe banana, peeled	*1* In a large bowl, combine the banana, eggs, oil, vanilla, and honey and beat well until the banana is broken into small pieces.
2 eggs	
3 tablespoons vegetable oil	
1 teaspoon vanilla	*2* Add the White Flour Mix, Whole-Grain Flour Mix, baking powder, and baking soda, and stir for 1 minute.
1 tablespoon honey	
1 cup minus 2 teaspoons (142 grams) White Flour Mix (see Chapter 10)	*3* Beat in the buttermilk and stir until the mixture is smooth.
½ cup plus 1 tablespoon plus 2 teaspoons (83 grams) Whole-Grain Flour Mix (see Chapter 10)	*4* Preheat a griddle to 350 degrees. Test for the correct temperature by dropping a bit of water on the hot surface; it should sizzle away within seconds. Lightly coat the griddle with unsalted butter.
1½ teaspoons baking powder	*5* Using a small ladle, pour 2½-inch circles of batter onto the hot griddle.
1 teaspoon baking soda	
1¼ cups buttermilk	
	6 Cook the pancakes on one side until bubbles rise to the top and start to break and the pancake edges look dry, about 2 to 4 minutes.
	7 Flip the pancakes and let them cook for 1 to 2 minutes longer until done. Serve immediately.

Per serving: Calories 402 (From Fat 130); Fat 15g (Saturated 2g); Cholesterol 109mg; Sodium 428mg; Carbohydrate 63g; Dietary Fiber 2g; Protein 8g.

Note: These tender pancakes are very easy to make. Serve them with Warm Fruit Sauce (see page 188) or warmed maple syrup.

Buckwheat Pancakes

Prep time: 20 min • **Cook time:** 5 min • **Yield:** 6 servings

Ingredients	*Directions*
1¼ cups minus 1 teaspoon (165 grams) Whole-Grain Flour Mix (see Chapter 10)	*1* Preheat an electric griddle to 375 degrees or place a heavy griddle on medium heat.
1 cup minus 2 teaspoons (142 grams) White Flour Mix (see Chapter 10)	*2* In a large bowl, combine the Whole-Grain Flour Mix, White Flour Mix, buckwheat flour, brown sugar, baking powder, baking soda, cinnamon, and nutmeg and stir well with a wire whisk until the mixture is one color.
¾ cup minus 1 teaspoon (87 grams) buckwheat flour	
2 tablespoons packed brown sugar	*3* In a medium bowl, combine the eggs, milk, yogurt, vegetable oil, and vanilla and beat well.
1 teaspoon baking powder	
1 teaspoon baking soda	*4* Stir the egg mixture into the flour mixture and beat until combined.
1 teaspoon ground cinnamon	
⅛ teaspoon nutmeg	*5* Grease the griddle with vegetable oil or unsalted butter.
3 eggs	
1½ cups milk	*6* Pour the batter by ¼ cupfuls onto the hot greased griddle. Cook until bubbles rise to the surface and break and the edges look done, about 3 to 4 minutes.
½ cup plain yogurt (any fat content is fine)	
2 tablespoons vegetable oil	*7* Carefully turn the pancakes with a spatula and cook for 1 minute longer.
1 teaspoon vanilla	
	8 Serve immediately.

Per serving: *Calories 325 (From Fat 93); Fat 10g (Saturated 3g); Cholesterol 116mg; Sodium 352mg; Carbohydrate 52g; Dietary Fiber 2g; Protein 9g.*

Note: These pancakes have a lovely color, a nutty flavor, and a tender texture. They're a great choice for breakfast, and they're healthy, too. Serve them with Honey Butter (see page 187), Warm Fruit Sauce (see page 188), or maple syrup.

Cornmeal Pancakes

Prep time: 15 min • **Cook time:** 5 min • **Yield:** 4–5 servings

Ingredients	*Directions*
3 eggs	*1* Preheat the griddle over medium heat.
1 cup buttermilk	
1½ cups Light Cakey Corn Bread Mix without shortening (see Chapter 10)	*2* In a large bowl, beat the eggs until they're light and fluffy and then add the buttermilk, corn bread mix, and oil. Beat until the batter is uniform and all one color. Because this batter has no gluten, the pancakes won't get tough no matter how long you beat!
¼ cup vegetable or light olive oil	
	3 Sprinkle the griddle with a few drops of water. When the water sizzles and disappears quickly, the griddle is ready.
	4 Grease the griddle with unsalted butter. Pour the batter onto the griddle, using a ¼-cup measuring cup.
	5 Cook until the batter rises, the pancake edges set and look cooked, and bubbles form on the surface, about 2 to 5 minutes.
	6 Carefully turn the pancakes with a spatula and cook for 2 minutes longer. Serve immediately.

Per serving: Calories 512 (From Fat 301); Fat 33g (Saturated 11g); Cholesterol 200mg; Sodium 495mg; Carbohydrate 46g; Dietary Fiber 3g; Protein 10g.

Note: You can substitute other types of milk for the buttermilk in this recipe, including almond milk, rice milk, and soy milk. But add a teaspoon of lemon juice to the milk substitute because buttermilk is more acidic than these other milk types.

Whole-Grain Buttermilk Waffles

Prep time: 15 min • **Cook time:** 8 min • **Yield:** 4 waffles

Ingredients	Directions
3 eggs	*1* In a medium bowl, beat together the eggs, butter, sugar, vanilla, and buttermilk until combined.
4 tablespoons butter, melted and cooled, or light vegetable oil	
2 tablespoons sugar	*2* In a large bowl, combine the Whole-Grain Flour Mix, White Flour Mix, baking powder, baking soda, and salt; mix well.
1 teaspoon vanilla	
1 cup buttermilk	*3* Pour the wet ingredients into the dry ingredients and mix just until combined.
1¼ cups minus 1 teaspoon (166 grams) Whole-Grain Flour Mix (see Chapter 10)	*4* Preheat a waffle iron according to the appliance's instructions. The iron has to be hot for the best waffle texture.
½ cup minus 1 teaspoon (71 grams) White Flour Mix (see Chapter 10)	
1 tablespoon baking powder	*5* Spray the waffle iron with nonstick cooking spray.
½ teaspoon baking soda	
¼ teaspoon salt	*6* Add enough batter to evenly cover the bottom waffle surface. The amount you use depends on your waffle iron; follow the instructions. Close the iron and bake until the steaming stops, about 7 to 8 minutes.

Per serving: Calories 398 (From Fat 151); Fat 17g (Saturated 9g); Cholesterol 193mg; Sodium 702mg; Carbohydrate 53g; Dietary Fiber 2g; Protein 11g.

Note: Be sure to read the instructions that come with your waffle iron. All waffle irons cook different amounts of batter and for different times. A general rule is to cook until the steam stops coming out of the sides of the iron.

Note: The first waffle often sticks. If it does stick, use the tip of a knife on the unplugged waffle iron to pry it off. The next waffle should come off clean because the butter in the batter helps to grease the iron as it cooks.

Banana Buttermilk Muffins

Prep time: 20 min • **Cook time:** 30 min • **Yield:** 12 muffins

Ingredients	Directions
2 eggs	*1* Preheat the oven to 350 degrees. Line 12 muffin cups with paper liners or spray with nonstick cooking spray.
3 ripe bananas, peeled and mashed	
⅓ cup brown sugar	*2* In a medium bowl, combine the eggs, bananas, brown sugar, buttermilk, and vanilla and beat well.
½ cup buttermilk	
1 teaspoon vanilla	
1¼ cups minus 1 teaspoon (165 grams) Whole-Grain Flour Mix (see Chapter 10)	*3* In a large bowl, combine the Whole-Grain Flour Mix, White Flour Mix, baking powder, baking soda, and cinnamon. Mix with a wire whisk until the dry ingredients are one consistent color.
½ cup minus 1 teaspoon (71 grams) White Flour Mix (see Chapter 10)	*4* Add the wet ingredients all at once to the dry ingredients. Stir until the batter is smooth with a few lumps; stir in the walnuts.
1 teaspoon baking powder	
½ teaspoon baking soda	
½ teaspoon cinnamon	*5* Spoon the batter into the prepared muffin tins, filling each halfway.
½ cup chopped walnuts	
	6 Bake for 30 to 32 minutes, until golden-brown. With paper liners, you may need to bake for a minute or two longer.

Per serving: Calories 169 (From Fat 42); Fat 5g (Saturated 1g); Cholesterol 36mg; Sodium 109mg; Carbohydrate 30g; Dietary Fiber 2g; Protein 4g.

Note: If you don't have buttermilk, you can easily make a substitute. Put 1 teaspoon of plain vinegar, apple cider vinegar, or lemon juice in a ½ cup measure. Fill the cup up to the top with whole milk or 2% milk. Let stand for 5 minutes and then use in the recipe.

Make-Ahead Muffins

Prep time: 25 min • **Cook time:** 20 min • **Yield:** 18 servings

Ingredients	Directions
¾ cup minus 2 teaspoons (110 grams) sweet rice flour	**1** In a large bowl, combine the sweet rice flour, millet flour, baking powder, baking soda, brown sugar, and salt; mix until the mixture is all one color.
⅓ cup plus 1 teaspoon (46 grams) millet flour	
2 teaspoons baking powder	**2** In a small bowl, combine the buttermilk, egg, vegetable oil, and vanilla; beat with a wire whisk until smooth.
½ teaspoon baking soda	
½ cup packed brown sugar	**3** Pour the wet ingredients into the dry ingredients and mix until combined.
¼ teaspoon salt	
1¼ cups buttermilk	**4** Stir in the cereal flakes and raisins or cranberries. You can bake the muffins immediately at this point or cover and refrigerate the batter for up to three days.
1 egg	
¼ cup vegetable oil	**5** To bake, preheat the oven to 400 degrees. Line six muffin cups with paper liners; spray the liners sparingly with nonstick cooking spray.
1 teaspoon vanilla	
3 cups gluten-free cereal flakes	**6** Scoop the batter into the prepared muffin cups, filling each cup ⅔ full.
1 cup raisins or dried cranberries	
	7 Bake for 16 to 20 minutes, until the muffins are set and light golden-brown.
	8 Cool the muffins in the muffin tins for 3 minutes and then carefully move them to wire racks to cool completely. Serve warm.

Per serving: Calories 136 (From Fat 34); Fat 4g (Saturated 0g); Cholesterol 13mg; Sodium 174mg; Carbohydrate 25g; Dietary Fiber 1g; Protein 2g.

Vary It! Instead of the raisins or cranberries, try using chopped dates, chopped dried apricots, dried blueberries, or dried mixed fruit.

Note: The batter will be good even after three days in the fridge. The muffins will be more dense as the batter sits, but they're still delicious.

Note: Serve these muffins warm from the oven with Honey Butter (see page 187) for an excellent breakfast treat.

Vegan Flax Raisin Muffins

Prep time: 26 min • **Cook time:** 30 min • **Yield:** 18 muffins

Ingredients	*Directions*
1 cup (150 grams) dark raisins	*1* Preheat the oven to 350 degrees. Grease 18 muffin cups or line them with paper liners.
¼ cup golden flaxseeds	
1½ cups plus 1 teaspoon (206 grams) Whole-Grain Flour Mix (see Chapter 10)	*2* Place the raisins in a small bowl; pour hot water over them to cover and soak for 15 minutes; drain.
1 cup minus 2 teaspoons (142 grams) White Flour Mix (see Chapter 10)	*3* Start the food processor and add the flaxseeds through the feed tube while it's running to break them up. You can either grind them to a fine powder or just bread the seed coats to add texture to the muffins.
⅓ cup packed light brown sugar	
2 teaspoons baking powder	*4* Add the drained raisins to the food processor and purée.
1 teaspoon baking soda	
½ teaspoon sea salt	*5* In a medium bowl, combine the Whole-Grain Flour Mix, White Flour Mix, brown sugar, baking powder, baking soda, and salt and mix until the mixture is one color.
⅓ cup light olive oil	
1 teaspoon vanilla	
1⅓ cups applesauce	*6* Add the mixed flours, olive oil, vanilla, and applesauce to the food processor with the raisins and flaxseeds. Process until completely combined.
	7 Spoon the batter into the prepared muffin cups, filling each ⅔ full.
	8 Bake for 28 to 30 minutes, or until the muffins spring back when lightly touched and are golden-brown.
	9 Cool the muffins in the pan for 3 minutes and then move them to a wire rack to cool completely.

Per serving: *Calories 171 (From Fat 45); Fat 5g (Saturated 1g); Cholesterol 0mg; Sodium 182mg; Carbohydrate 31g; Dietary Fiber 2g; Protein 2g.*

Vary It! You can use other dried fruits in place of the raisins; just substitute the same weight. Dried apricots, pears, or mangoes are yummy. Weigh, hydrate, and purée.

Almond Orange Coffeecake

Prep time: 20 min • **Cook time:** 35–40 min • **Yield:** 9 servings

Ingredients	Directions
3 eggs	**1** Preheat the oven to 350 degrees. Grease a 9-inch square pan with nonstick cooking spray and set aside.
½ cup sour cream	
¼ cup oil	**2** In a large bowl, beat together the eggs, sour cream, oil, milk, and almond extract.
¼ cup milk	
1 teaspoon almond extract	**3** In a medium bowl, combine the brown sugar, Whole-Grain Flour Mix, White Flour Mix, baking powder, baking soda, and salt. Stir with a wire whisk until the mixture is one color.
¼ cup brown sugar	
1 cup plus 3 tablespoons (164 grams) Whole-Grain Flour Mix (see Chapter 10)	
⅓ cup (50 grams) White Flour Mix (see Chapter 10)	**4** Stir the dry ingredients into the wet ingredients and mix until combined.
2 teaspoons baking powder	**5** Pour the batter into the prepared pan and spread evenly. Sprinkle with the almonds and then drop orange marmalade by teaspoons over the batter. The marmalade sinks into the batter as it bakes.
1 teaspoon baking soda	
¼ teaspoon salt	
½ cup sliced almonds	
1 cup orange marmalade	**6** Bake for 35 to 40 minutes, or until the cake pulls away from the sides of the pan and the cake springs back when lightly touched in the center.
	7 You can serve this cake warm after cooling it for 15 to 20 minutes or you can cool it completely on a wire rack.

Per serving: Calories 337 (From Fat 125); Fat 14g (Saturated 3g); Cholesterol 77mg; Sodium 343mg; Carbohydrate 51g; Dietary Fiber 2g; Protein 6g.

Note: If you're looking for the perfect Sunday morning coffeecake, this is it. Tender cake, luscious jam, and sliced almonds all come together in a delectable treat. But this recipe also isn't too difficult to stir together in time for a quick treat with afternoon tea. For best results, look for British marmalade, which is more bitter and balanced. But you can use any variety of marmalade or jam you'd like.

Cranberry Pear Bundt Coffeecake

Prep time: 25 min • **Cook time:** 1 hr • **Yield:** 16 servings

Ingredients	*Directions*
2 tablespoons plus 6 tablespoons unsalted butter, melted **¼ cup plus ¼ cup sugar** **1¼ cups plus 1 teaspoon (189 grams) White Flour Mix (see Chapter 10)** **⅓ cup plus 1 tablespoon (54 grams) Whole-Grain Flour Mix (see Chapter 10)** **2 teaspoons baking powder** **1 teaspoon baking soda** **¼ teaspoon ground nutmeg** **¼ teaspoon salt** **2 pears, peeled and diced** **1 cup fresh or frozen cranberries** **4 eggs** **1 cup sour cream** **1 teaspoon vanilla**	*1* Preheat the oven to 350 degrees. Brush a 12-inch Bundt pan with 2 tablespoons melted butter and sprinkle with ¼ cup sugar, coating every crack and crevice.
	2 In a medium bowl, combine the White Flour Mix, Whole-Grain Flour Mix, ¼ cup sugar, baking powder, baking soda, nutmeg, and salt and mix well with a wire whisk.
	3 Use 3 tablespoons of this mixture to toss with the pears and cranberries; set aside.
	4 In a large bowl, beat the eggs with sour cream, 6 tablespoons melted butter, and vanilla until combined. Add the flour mixture and stir until well blended.
	5 Fold in the coated fruits.
	6 Pour the batter into the prepared pan. Place in the oven on the bottom rack.
	7 Bake for 55 to 60 minutes, or until the cake springs back when lightly touched and starts to pull away from the sides of the pan.
	8 Let the cake cool in the pan for 3 minutes and then gently shake the pan to make sure the cake is released. Turn onto a wire rack and let the cake cool completely before storing it in an airtight container.

Per serving: Calories 173 (From Fat 91); Fat 10g (Saturated 6g); Cholesterol 75mg; Sodium 188mg; Carbohydrate 19g; Dietary Fiber 1g; Protein 3g.

Note: This is an excellent breakfast treat for fall mornings. The combination of tart cranberries and sweet pears is special. The cake's flavor develops overnight, so bake it the day before for the best flavor.

Sour Cream Blueberry Crumb Muffins

Prep time: 20 min • **Cook time:** 30 min • **Yield:** 12 muffins

Ingredients	Directions
¼ cup plus 2 teaspoons (41 grams) plus 1¼ cups minus 1 teaspoon (165 grams) Whole-Grain Flour Mix (see Chapter 10)	**1** Preheat the oven to 350 degrees. Spray a 12-cup muffin tin with nonstick cooking spray or line it with paper liners.
¼ cup (36 grams) plus ¾ cup minus 1 teaspoon (108 grams) White Flour Mix (see Chapter 10)	**2** To make the crumb topping, stir together ¼ cup plus 2 teaspoons (41 grams) Whole-Grain Flour Mix, ¼ cup (36 grams) White Flour Mix, almond meal, cinnamon, and brown sugar until combined. Mix in the butter until crumbly and set aside.
2 tablespoons almond meal	
½ teaspoon cinnamon	**3** In a large bowl, beat together the sour cream, eggs, oil, cane sugar, and vanilla.
¼ cup brown sugar	
¼ cup unsalted butter, softened	**4** In a medium bowl, combine 1¼ cups minus 1 teaspoon (165 grams) Whole-Grain Flour Mix, ¾ cup minus 1 teaspoon (108 grams) White Flour Mix, baking powder, and baking soda and stir with a wire whisk until the mixture is one color. Use 3 tablespoons of the flour mixture to coat the blueberries.
½ cup sour cream	
3 eggs	
½ cup vegetable oil	
½ cup organic cane sugar	**5** Combine the wet and dry mixtures with a few quick strokes. Gently fold in the coated blueberries along with the flour mixture used to coat the blueberries.
2 teaspoons vanilla	
1½ teaspoons baking powder	
½ teaspoon baking soda	**6** Spoon the batter into the prepared pans and top each with some of the crumb topping, using it all.
1½ cups blueberries	
	7 Bake for 28 to 30 minutes, or until the muffins spring back when lightly touched in the center. Cool on a wire rack.

Per serving: Calories 301 (From Fat 157); Fat 18g (Saturated 5g); Cholesterol 68mg; Sodium 125mg; Carbohydrate 34g; Dietary Fiber 1g; Protein 4g.

Quick Streusel Coffeecake

Prep time: 20 min • **Cook time:** 25 min • **Yield:** 6 servings

Ingredients	Directions
3 tablespoons butter, softened	**1** Preheat the oven to 375 degrees. Grease a 9-inch square cake pan with nonstick cooking spray and set aside.
6 tablespoons plus ¼ cup packed brown sugar	
1 teaspoon cinnamon	**2** In a small bowl, combine 3 tablespoons butter with 6 tablespoons brown sugar, cinnamon, cardamom, and salt and mix until smooth. Stir in the oats; the mixture will be crumbly.
⅛ teaspoon cardamom	
Pinch salt	
1 cup gluten-free quick oats	**3** In a medium bowl, beat the egg with the milk. Add the cane sugar, ¼ cup brown sugar, and vanilla and beat well until combined.
1 egg	
½ cup milk	
¼ cup organic cane sugar	**4** In a small bowl, stir together the sweet rice flour, almond flour, baking powder, baking soda, and ¼ teaspoon salt until the mixture is one color. Stir into the egg mixture and beat for 1 minute.
1 teaspoon vanilla	
½ cup plus 1 tablespoon plus 1 teaspoon (92 grams) sweet rice flour	
¼ cup plus 2 teaspoons (33 grams) almond flour	**5** Pour the batter into the prepared cake pan and spread evenly. Sprinkle with the oatmeal mixture.
1 teaspoon baking powder	**6** Bake for 20 to 25 minutes, or until the cake is puffed, set, and light golden-brown. Remove the cake from the oven and cool for 15 minutes; then cut into squares to serve.
½ teaspoon baking soda	
¼ teaspoon salt	

Per serving: Calories 304 (From Fat 108); Fat 12g (Saturated 7g); Cholesterol 64mg; Sodium 316mg; Carbohydrate 45g; Dietary Fiber 2g; Protein 5g.

Vary It! If you can't find gluten-free oats or if you don't want to use oats, you can substitute flaked coconut instead. Or use chopped nuts or a combination of nuts and coconut.

Apple Raisin Strata

Prep time: 30 min, plus rest time • **Cook time:** 50 min • **Yield:** 8 servings

Ingredients	Directions
1 recipe Cinnamon Raisin Walnut Bread (see Chapter 12), sliced and cubed	**1** Grease a glass 13-x-9-inch baking dish with nonstick cooking spray. Place half of the bread cubes in the prepared baking dish.
3 apples, peeled and diced (1½ cups)	**2** In a medium bowl, toss together the apples, lemon juice, and raisins; let sit for 5 minutes and then scatter over the bread cubes in the baking dish.
2 tablespoons lemon juice	
⅔ cup raisins	
One 8-ounce package cream cheese	**3** In the same medium bowl, combine the cream cheese, 2 tablespoons light cream, powdered sugar, and cinnamon; beat until smooth. Drizzle over the bread and fruit in the baking dish. Top with the remaining bread cubes and pecans (if desired).
2 tablespoons plus 2 cups light cream or whole milk	
¼ cup powdered sugar	
1 teaspoon cinnamon	
½ cup chopped pecans (optional)	**4** In a large bowl, combine the eggs, 2 cups light cream, honey, melted butter, vanilla, and salt and beat well until combined.
6 eggs, beaten	**5** Pour the egg mixture slowly into the casserole. Cover tightly with foil and refrigerate at least 8 hours or overnight.
⅓ cup honey	
¼ cup butter, melted	
1 teaspoon vanilla	**6** When you're ready to bake, preheat the oven to 350 degrees. Bake the casserole, covered, for 25 minutes.
¼ teaspoon salt	
	7 Remove the foil and bake for 20 to 30 minutes longer, until the casserole is puffed, golden-brown, and set. Let it cool for 10 minutes and then cut it into squares to serve.

Per serving: Calories 607 (From Fat 237); Fat 26g (Saturated 12g); Cholesterol 211mg; Sodium 358mg; Carbohydrate 84g; Dietary Fiber 6g; Protein 15g.

Vary It! You can use almond milk, soymilk, or rice milk in place of the light cream in this recipe if you're avoiding casein, and you can use vegan cream cheese in place of the regular cream cheese.

Lemon Cranberry Cornmeal Scones

Prep time: 25 min • **Cook time:** 23 min • **Yield:** 12 scones

Ingredients	*Directions*
¾ cup whole milk plain yogurt	*1* Preheat the oven to 425 degrees. Line two cookie sheets with Silpat liners or parchment paper.
1 cup dried cranberries	
6 tablespoons unsalted butter, softened	*2* In a small bowl, combine the yogurt with the dried cranberries and set aside to plump for a few minutes.
½ cup sugar	
1 cup plus 3 tablespoons (177 grams) White Flour Mix (see Chapter 10)	*3* In a large mixing bowl, beat the butter until it's light and fluffy. Gradually add the sugar, beating on high, until the mixture is light and creamy, about 3 to 6 minutes.
½ cup plus 2 tablespoons minus 1 teaspoon (83 grams) Whole-Grain Flour Mix (see Chapter 10)	*4* Beat in the White Flour Mix, Whole-Grain Flour Mix, cornmeal, baking powder, salt, and lemon rind. The mixture will be very dry and sandy.
1 cup (142 grams) yellow or white cornmeal	*5* Beat in the eggs and the lemon juice.
1 tablespoon baking powder	
½ teaspoon salt	*6* Add the yogurt and cranberries and beat for 1 minute, until a dough forms.
1 teaspoon grated lemon rind	
2 eggs	*7* Scoop out the batter with a ⅓ cup ice cream scoop (Number 10) and place six on each prepared cookie sheet, leaving plenty of room to spread. Sprinkle with a bit of coarse sugar (if desired).
2 teaspoons lemon juice	
Coarse sugar for topping (optional)	
	8 Place pans in the oven and immediately lower the temperature to 350 degrees. Bake for 22 to 25 minutes, or until the scones are just barely browned. Move them to a wire rack to cool. Serve warm.

Per serving: Calories 274 (From Fat 98); Fat 11g (Saturated 6g); Cholesterol 79mg; Sodium 316mg; Carbohydrate 43g; Dietary Fiber 1g; Protein 4g.

Vary It! If you prefer a different dried fruit, go ahead and use it. Dried blueberries or cherries are good choices; just be sure to rehydrate them in the yogurt before using.

Note: If you don't like the crunch of cornmeal, you can substitute the same weight of corn flour. But don't substitute cup for cup because corn flour weighs much more than cornmeal. You don't want dense and dry pastries, do you?

Cinnamon Apple Fritters

Prep time: 20 min • **Cook time:** 4 min • **Yield:** 8–10 fritters

Ingredients

3 eggs

1 cup minus 2 tablespoons (107 grams) sorghum flour

⅓ cup (55 grams) sweet rice flour

⅓ cup minus 1 teaspoon (41 grams) brown rice flour

1 cup minus 2 tablespoons minus 1 teaspoon (105 grams) tapioca flour

½ teaspoon salt

1 tablespoon plus 1 teaspoon maple syrup

1 teaspoon baking powder

1½ teaspoons cinnamon

⅔ cup minus 1 tablespoon buttermilk

½ teaspoon plus 1 teaspoon vanilla

1 small Granny Smith apple, peeled and minced

2 cups safflower oil for frying

1 cup powdered sugar

1 tablespoon milk

Directions

1 Beat the eggs in a large bowl with a spout. Add the flours, salt, maple syrup, baking powder, and cinnamon and beat for 1 minute.

2 Beat in the buttermilk and ½ teaspoon vanilla. Stir in the apple and let the batter rest while the oil preheats.

3 Heat 2 cups safflower oil or solid shortening in a large frying pan. Line a cookie sheet with a few pieces of newspaper and then top with paper towels.

4 In a shallow bowl, combine the powdered sugar, 1 teaspoon vanilla, and milk and mix until smooth; set this glaze aside.

5 Check the oil temperature; it should be at 365 degrees.

6 Carefully drizzle ¼ cup of the dough into the oil. Drizzle the batter in one direction and then perpendicular to the first layer, leaving holes for the oil to penetrate so the fritter cooks evenly.

7 Fry the fritter for 2 to 3 minutes, until the top edges start to turn brown. Flip the fritter and cook for another minute until browned.

8 Remove the fritter with tongs to the prepared cookie sheet; let it rest for 30 seconds and then flip to drain.

9 Repeat with the remaining batter. As the fritters start to cool, you can dip them into the powdered sugar glaze. Let them stand on a wire rack until the glaze hardens. Store at room temperature for three days.

Per serving: Calories 260 (From Fat 117); Fat 13g (Saturated 1g); Cholesterol 65mg; Sodium 190mg; Carbohydrate 34g; Dietary Fiber 1g; Protein 4g.

Granola Bars

Prep time: 20 min, plus rest time • **Cook time:** 40 min • **Yield:** 60 bars

Ingredients	Directions
1 cup unsalted organic butter	**1** In a large saucepan over low heat, melt the butter, brown sugar, honey, and almond butter, stirring until the mixture has a smooth and even texture.
¾ cup packed brown sugar	
½ cup honey	
12 ounces smooth or chunky almond butter	**2** Remove from the heat and add the rolled oats. Stir until combined.
5½ cups gluten-free rolled oats	**3** Stir in the eggs, baking soda, salt, and vanilla until well-combined.
2 eggs, beaten	
2 teaspoons baking soda	
½ teaspoon salt	**4** Add the fruits, nuts, coconut, and M&Ms. You can use any combination of any of these ingredients as long as they add up to 4 cups.
1 tablespoon vanilla	
4 cups diced dried fruit, chopped nuts, coconut, and M&M candies	**5** Cover the dough and let it chill overnight to let the oats absorb the eggs, butter, and almond butter.
	6 When you're ready to bake, preheat the oven to 300 degrees. Line two cookie sheets with parchment paper. Divide the dough between the cookie sheets and pat it into an even layer about ½-inch thick.
	7 Bake for 20 minutes and then rotate the pans and move them around on the racks. Bake for 20 minutes longer, until the bars are light golden-brown and set.
	8 Cool completely and cut into bars. Store in an airtight container at room temperature.

Per serving: Calories 155 (From Fat 85); Fat 10g (Saturated 3g); Cholesterol 16mg; Sodium 71mg; Carbohydrate 16g; Dietary Fiber 1g; Protein 3g.

Note: These granola bars are delicious as a quick snack or on a road trip. Keep them on your person at all times when you're hungry but can't find a gluten-free food. Try to use only unsulfured organic fruits for the best flavor, texture, and nutrition. A nice combination is dried tart cherries, dried apricots, unsweetened flaked coconut, and dark chocolate M&Ms.

Banana Quick Bread

Prep time: 30 min • **Cook time:** 35 min • **Yield:** 8 servings

Ingredients	Directions
1 cup minus 1 tablespoon (125 grams) Whole-Grain Flour Mix (see Chapter 10)	*1* Preheat the oven to 350 degrees. Grease an 8-x-4-inch loaf pan with nonstick cooking spray or unsalted butter; set aside.
⅓ cup plus 1 teaspoon (52 grams) White Flour Mix (see Chapter 10)	*2* In a medium bowl, combine the Whole-Grain Flour Mix, White Flour Mix, sugar, baking powder, baking soda, cinnamon, and salt. Mix until the mixture is one color.
3 tablespoons organic cane sugar	
¾ teaspoon baking powder	*3* In a small bowl, mash the bananas until they're mostly smooth. Beat in the sour cream, oil, egg, and vanilla.
½ teaspoon baking soda	
¼ teaspoon cinnamon	*4* Add the wet ingredients to the dry ingredients and stir until well-mixed. Pour into the prepared pan.
⅛ teaspoon salt	
2 medium ripe bananas, peeled	*5* Bake for 35 to 38 minutes, or until the bread is golden-brown and springs back when lightly touched with a finger. The temperature of the bread should be 190 to 200 degrees.
6 tablespoons sour cream	
1 tablespoon olive oil	
1 egg	*6* Cool the bread in the pan for 5 minutes and then carefully remove the bread from the pan and cool it completely on a wire rack. Store covered at room temperature up to three days.
1 teaspoon vanilla	

Per serving: Calories 159 (From Fat 45); Fat 5g (Saturated 2g); Cholesterol 31mg; Sodium 165mg; Carbohydrate 27g; Dietary Fiber 2g; Protein 3g.

Vary It! You can add lots of delicious ingredients to this bread. Add ⅓ cup chocolate chips, chopped walnuts, or dried fruit such as dried cranberries or dried cherries. But be sure to limit the additions to only 50 grams or they'll interfere with the bread structure.

Honey Butter

Prep time: 5 min • **Yield:** 16 servings

Ingredients	Directions
½ cup softened butter or Earth Balance Buttery Spread	*1* Combine the butter and honey in a small bowl and beat until smooth and well-blended. Cover and store in the refrigerator.
¼ **cup honey**	

Per serving: Calories 66 (From Fat 51); Fat 6g (Saturated 4g); Cholesterol 15mg; Sodium 1mg; Carbohydrate 4g; Dietary Fiber 0g; Protein 0g.

Note: You can serve this Honey Butter with any type of pancake or waffle, on hot toast, or with corn bread or dinner rolls. You can keep it in the refrigerator for up to a month.

Note: Honey Butter is a great choice for spreading on toast. Gluten-free bread makes excellent toast, and this recipe enhances its flavor with less fat than butter or margarine.

Vary It! Think about making this spread with maple syrup or Lyle's Golden Syrup instead of honey. You can also use a buttery spread for a vegan version. Or add a dash of cinnamon or nutmeg to the mixture for a Spiced Honey Butter.

...Fruit Sauce

Prep time: 10 min • **Cook time:** 3–4 min • **Yield:** 6 servings

Ingredients	Directions
2 tablespoons unsalted butter	**1** In a small saucepan, melt the butter.
1 cup applesauce	
1 large banana, peeled and mashed	**2** Stir in the applesauce, banana, and maple syrup; stir well until combined.
1 tablespoon maple syrup	**3** Warm over low heat until the mixture is hot, about 3 or 4 minutes. Let it cool for a few minutes and then serve it over pancakes or waffles.

Per serving: Calories 95 (From Fat 36); Fat 4g (Saturated 2g); Cholesterol 10mg; Sodium 2mg; Carbohydrate 16g; Dietary Fiber 1g; Protein 0g.

Vary It! You can vary this fruit sauce in many ways. Instead of applesauce, purée some drained canned pears to equal 1 cup. You can add chopped toasted nuts to the sauce or add some dried fruits like dried cherries or cranberries. Serve it over pancakes or waffles or try it as a dipping sauce with toast fingers.

Chapter 12

Sweet Yeast Breads

*O*ne of the pleasures of life is coming into a kitchen where cinnamon rolls have just finished baking. You may think that, on a gluten-free diet, those days are gone forever. Not so! These easy recipes for sweet gluten-free yeast breads are foolproof and delicious.

In this chapter, we offer you recipes for everything from Monkey Bread to Honey Oat Bread to Cinnamon Rolls to Bismarck Doughnuts. These recipes are usually reserved for special occasions, such as a birthday breakfast or a holiday brunch. But you may want to make a Wednesday morning special and serve some sticky buns to your family!

Working with Yeast

Yeast can be a tricky creature. And it is a creature: a one-celled organism that uses sugar and water to multiply fruitfully. As it grows, yeast gives off carbon dioxide, which makes yeast breads rise. The yeast also ferments the sugar in the batter or dough, imparting the distinctive and characteristic flavor that only comes from these types of recipes.

Here are a few rules to follow when working with yeast.

✔ Before you even start mixing the dough, make sure your yeast is fresh. Active dry yeast packets have expiration dates stamped clearly on them. Abide by these dates, as the yeast isn't as lively after the dates have passed.

- ✔ You can depend on those expiration dates, but if you want to make sure, proof the yeast before you start. To *proof* — or reactivate — yeast, mix it with a bit of water or milk from the recipe, along with a pinch of sugar. After about 10 minutes, if the mixture is puffy, then your yeast is active and can be used.

- ✔ Be careful about temperatures when working with yeast. You shouldn't expose active dry yeast to temperatures over 110 degrees. Fresh compressed yeast, which is more difficult to find, must stay below 110 degrees also. When dry yeast is mixed with flour, the temperature of the liquid in the recipe can get to 120 degrees before you run into problems.

- ✔ Because most gluten-free bread doughs aren't kneaded, one rise is all they get. Make sure the breads rise in a warm, draft-free place. If your house is cool, you can put the breads into an oven with a pilot light on. Or turn on the oven for a few minutes, turn it off (be sure to turn it off!), and add the proofing bread dough.

- ✔ Any ingredient in the bread dough or batter other than flour slows down the yeast fermentation. Sugar speeds the process, up to a point. Lots of sugar actually slows yeast growth. Salt is added even to sweet yeast breads to temper the yeast growth. Doughs and batters made with eggs, fat, dairy products, and other ingredients take longer to rise.

Enjoying Easy Sweet Yeast Bread Recipes

Enjoy the process when you're making these breads. There's something very contemplative about working with yeast. Baking yeast breads is an ancient art. And get your family involved in the process, too. Nothing's cozier than baking a sweet yeast bread on a snowy morning. You're teaching your kids a life skill and making their childhood wonderful, too.

Make sure that you measure all the ingredients carefully when making yeast breads. Weighing the flour when working with yeast doughs and batters is particularly important. In most wheat flour–based yeast bread recipes, you knead the dough, which gives you the ability to adjust the flour amounts to the correct point. With these recipes, measuring the flours by weighing is crucial. If you don't use a scale to measure flours and mixes, always measure by spooning the flour lightly into a measuring cup and leveling off the top with the back of a knife. See Chapters 4 and 5 for more info on measuring by weight and volume.

Lemon Cardamom Coffeecake

Prep time: 45 min • **Cook time:** 25 min • **Yield:** 9 servings

Ingredients	*Directions*
¾ cup plus 2 tablespoons milk	*1* In a medium saucepan, warm all the milk over low heat. Pour 2 tablespoons into a small bowl and add the yeast; let stand 10 minutes.
1¼ teaspoons active dry yeast	
2 tablespoons plus 2 tablespoons unsalted butter	*2* Add 2 tablespoons butter, granulated sugar, and salt to the remaining milk in the pan and heat until the butter melts. Pour into a medium bowl and let cool; stir in the lemon peel.
3 tablespoons granulated sugar	
¼ teaspoon salt	
½ teaspoon grated lemon peel	*3* Add the egg yolk to the yeast and milk mixture and beat until smooth.
1 egg yolk	
¼ teaspoon lemon extract	*4* Stir in the lemon extract, ¼ teaspoon cardamom, White Flour Mix, and High-Protein Bread Flour Mix; beat for 1 minute.
¼ teaspoon plus ⅛ teaspoon cardamom	
¾ cup plus 1 tablespoon plus 1 teaspoon (124 grams) White Flour Mix (see Chapter 10)	*5* Grease a 9-inch square cake pan with unsalted butter.
½ cup minus 1 teaspoon (62 grams) High-Protein Bread Flour Mix (see Chapter 10)	*6* Place the batter into the prepared pan.
¼ cup packed brown sugar	*7* In a small bowl, combine the brown sugar, 2 tablespoons butter, and ⅛ teaspoon cardamom; mix well. Sprinkle over the batter in the pan.
	8 Let rise for 30 to 40 minutes.
	9 Preheat the oven to 350 degrees. Bake the coffeecake for 24 to 27 minutes, or until golden-brown, and set. Cool in the pan until warm; cut into squares to serve.

Per serving: *Calories 177 (From Fat 60); Fat 7g (Saturated 4g); Cholesterol 41mg; Sodium 81mg; Carbohydrate 29g; Dietary Fiber 1g; Protein 2g.*

Vary It! Cardamom is a Scandinavian spice that's like nutmeg but milder. You can substitute ground nutmeg for the cardamom in this recipe if you'd like.

Cinnamon Rolls

Prep time: 1 hr • **Cook time:** 35 min • **Yield:** 8 servings

Ingredients	Directions
Dough: **1½ cups plus 2 tablespoons (240 grams) White Flour Mix (see Chapter 10)** **1½ cups plus 1 teaspoon (200 grams) High-Protein Bread Flour Mix (see Chapter 10)** **¼ cup plus 2 teaspoons (40 grams) Whole-Grain Flour Mix (see Chapter 10)** **¼ cup organic cane sugar** **1 tablespoon active dry yeast** **½ teaspoon salt** **½ cup dry milk** **1 teaspoon xanthan gum** **1 egg** **2 egg yolks** **½ cup unsalted butter, softened** **¾ cup plus 1 tablespoon plus 1 teaspoon water** **½ teaspoon vanilla** **Filling:** **¼ cup unsalted butter** **⅔ cup packed brown sugar** **2½ teaspoons ground cinnamon** **½ cup powdered sugar in a sifter or sieve**	**1** In a large bowl, combine the White Flour Mix, Bread Flour Mix, Whole-Grain Flour Mix, cane sugar, yeast, salt, dry milk, and xanthan gum; mix until the mixture is one color. **2** Beat in the egg, egg yolks, and ½ cup softened butter. Add the water and vanilla; beat for 3 minutes. Cover and let rest while you make the filling. **3** Melt ¼ cup butter. In a medium bowl, combine the brown sugar and cinnamon. **4** Grease a 9-x-12-inch pan well with unsalted butter or solid shortening. **5** Place a 16-inch-long piece of plastic wrap on your work surface. Sprinkle heavily with powdered sugar. **6** Place the dough in the center of the powdered sugar and sprinkle the top heavily with more powdered sugar. Cover with another 16-inch piece of plastic wrap. **7** Roll the dough out to a rectangle ½-inch thick that completely fills the plastic. **8** Spread the dough with ¼ cup melted butter. Then sprinkle the dough with the brown sugar and cinnamon mixture, leaving 1 inch at one long end of the dough uncovered.

9 Lift the plastic wrap from the long side completely covered with filling. Let the dough fold toward itself, pulling it tightly into the center. Lift the plastic wrap off as you work and roll toward the other long edge.

10 Cut the dough into 2-inch rounds. Place each roll in a greased pan, cut side down so the spiral of filling shows, leaving space between each roll for rising.

11 Cover the pan with plastic wrap and let rise until doubled, about 30 to 40 minutes.

12 Preheat the oven to 450 degrees. Remove the plastic and place the rolls in the oven. Immediately reduce the heat to 400 degrees and bake the rolls for 20 minutes.

13 Reduce the heat to 350 degrees and bake the rolls for 15 minutes longer, until the rolls are brown and set. The internal temperature of the rolls should be 190 to 200 degrees.

14 Cool the rolls in the pan for 5 minutes and then carefully move them to wire racks to cool completely.

15 Frost the rolls with Cream Cheese Frosting (see Chapter 16) when they've cooled. Store in an airtight container at room temperature for up to two days. If they're frosted, keep them in the fridge.

Per serving: Calories 600 (From Fat 251); Fat 28g (Saturated 16g); Cholesterol 149mg; Sodium 198mg; Carbohydrate 85g; Dietary Fiber 2g; Protein 8g.

Note: Traditional recipes hold the stories of families. As a child, when Jean heard stories of other kids' grandmothers baking cinnamon rolls for holidays, she was sad; her grandparents all passed on before she was born. Her family made the kind of cinnamon rolls that came in a can; that was a story too!

Living gluten-free doesn't mean you lose a desire for gooey good cinnamon rolls. Jean makes these rolls for her family on Christmas mornings or for other celebrations that deserve that warm sweet smell coming from the kitchen.

Hot Cross Buns

Prep time: 40 min • **Cook time:** 30–40 min • **Yield:** 9 servings

Ingredients	*Directions*
½ cup whole milk 1 tablespoon active dry yeast	*1* In a small saucepan, warm the milk to 110 degrees. Stir in the yeast and set aside.
1¼ cups plus 1 tablespoon (196 grams) White Flour Mix (see Chapter 10) 1¼ cups minus 1 teaspoon (165 grams) Whole-Grain Flour Mix (see Chapter 10)	*2* In a large bowl, combine the White Flour Mix, Whole-Grain Flour Mix, xanthan gum, nutmeg, cinnamon, salt, and granulated sugar; mix until the mixture is one color.
½ teaspoon xanthan gum Pinch nutmeg	*3* Beat in the eggs, egg yolk, and vanilla and then add the milk mixture; beat for 2 minutes.
Pinch cinnamon ½ teaspoon salt	*4* Add the butter and beat 1 minute longer. Stir in the raisins and orange peel.
½ cup granulated sugar 2 eggs	*5* Cover the bowl with plastic wrap and let rise for 15 minutes.
1 egg yolk 1 teaspoon vanilla	*6* Grease nine muffin cups with unsalted butter or solid shortening.
6 tablespoons unsalted butter ¼ cup dried currants or raisins	*7* Use a large ice cream scoop to fill the muffin cups. Cover with plastic wrap and let rise for 30 minutes.
¼ cup minced candied orange peel	*8* Preheat the oven to 450 degrees. Uncover the pan and place the buns on the middle rack of the oven.
Icing: ¼ cup powdered sugar 1 drop almond extract 1 tablespoon milk	

9 Immediately reduce the heat to 350 degrees and bake for 30 to 32 minutes, or until the buns are browned. Internal temperature should be 190 to 200 degrees.

10 Cool the buns in the pan for 5 minutes and then turn the buns onto a wire rack to cool.

11 If desired, combine the powdered sugar, almond extract, and milk. Use this mixture to make a cross on top of the cooled buns.

Per serving: Calories 321 (From Fat 93); Fat 10g (Saturated 6g); Cholesterol 93mg; Sodium 159mg; Carbohydrate 55g; Dietary Fiber 2g; Protein 5g.

Xanthan gum: It's the stickiest!

There's a very good reason that bakers add xanthan gum and guar gum to the dry ingredients when they make gluten-free breads. When combined with water, xanthan gum and guar gum are super sticky. In fact, they're so sticky that getting the wet gums off your hands is difficult! So unless you want to spend a lot of time cleaning your hands, always mix gums into the dry ingredients very thoroughly before you add the wet ingredients.

Gooey Orange Rolls

Prep time: 45 min • **Cook time:** 35 min • **Yield:** 8 servings

Ingredients	Directions
Cinnamon Roll dough (see page 192)	*1* Make the Cinnamon Roll dough through Step 2.
¼ cup unsalted butter	*2* Melt the butter. In a small bowl, combine the granulated sugar, 2 teaspoons orange peel, and 2 tablespoons orange juice; mix well.
1 cup granulated sugar	
2 teaspoons plus 2 teaspoons grated orange peel	*3* In another small bowl, combine the powdered sugar, 2 teaspoons orange peel, and 3 tablespoons orange juice; set aside. This is the final glaze for the rolls.
2 tablespoons plus 3 tablespoons orange juice	
⅔ cup powdered sugar	*4* Roll out the dough on powdered sugar–covered plastic wrap, as directed in Steps 4 through 7 of the Cinnamon Roll recipe.
	5 Brush the dough with melted butter and sprinkle with the sugar-and-orange mixture.
	6 Continue with the Cinnamon Roll recipe through Step 13.
	7 When the rolls are done, immediately pour the powdered sugar mixture over them. Let the rolls cool completely in the pan before eating them.

Per serving: Calories 591 (From Fat 200); Fat 22g (Saturated 13g); Cholesterol 134mg; Sodium 190mg; Carbohydrate 95g; Dietary Fiber 2g; Protein 8g.

Note: These rolls should cool completely before you eat them, but if you just can't resist, at least let them get down to "warm" before you devour them.

Sticky Buns

Prep time: 1 hr • **Cook time:** 35 min • **Yield:** 8 servings

Ingredients	*Directions*
Cinnamon Roll dough (see page 192)	*1* Make the Cinnamon Roll dough through Step 2.
½ cup unsalted butter 1 cup sugar	*2* Melt the butter and spread it evenly into a 9-x-12-inch pan, completely covering the bottom of the pan.
2 cups pecan halves or raisins or a combination	*3* Sprinkle evenly with the sugar. Then add the nuts or raisins or both, pressing them down into the sugar and butter.
	4 Continue with the Cinnamon Roll recipe from Steps 3 through 13. When the buns are done, immediately invert them onto a serving plate. If any nuts or raisins stick to the pan or if any of the glaze is still in the pan, carefully scoop them/it out with a spoon (it's hot!) and put on top of the rolls. Serve warm.

Per serving: Calories 763 (From Fat 406); Fat 45g (Saturated 18g); Cholesterol 149mg; Sodium 192mg; Carbohydrate 87g; Dietary Fiber 4g; Protein 10g.

Note: If you're from the Jersey shore, Sticky Buns are another name for Cinnamon Rolls but with one special twist: The rolls are layered with more butter, more sugar, and nuts or raisins, or maybe even both. As the rolls bake, the sugar and butter create a lovely sticky glaze. You turn the buns out hot from the oven so that the glaze trickles down the sides. One bite and you'll be back at Beach Haven! Just skip the Cream Cheese Frosting; no one needs that much sugar at one time.

Bismarck Doughnuts

Prep time: 50 min plus rising time • **Cook time:** 4–6 min • **Yield:** 9 servings

Ingredients	*Directions*
5 eggs	*1* In a large bowl, beat the eggs until they're light, fluffy, and pale yellow, about 5 to 6 minutes.
1 cup plus 3 tablespoons (155 grams) High-Protein Bread Flour Mix (see Chapter 10)	*2* Add the High-Protein Bread Flour Mix, tapioca flour, buckwheat flour, sugar, salt, butter, and yeast and beat for 1 minute longer.
1 cup minus 2 tablespoons (110 grams) tapioca flour	
2 tablespoons (20 grams) raw buckwheat flour	*3* Tear off parchment paper into twelve 4-inch squares. Using an ice cream scoop, scoop the batter onto the center of each parchment paper square. The dough will look very thin and liquid; don't worry about this.
2 tablespoons sugar	
½ teaspoon salt	*4* Let the dough rise for 2 hours. It will still be very thin. When the dough hits the fat, it will puff and become firm.
2 tablespoons unsalted butter, melted	
1 tablespoon active dry yeast	*5* Prepare the Bavarian Cream Filling while the batter rises.
Bavarian Cream Filling (see page 200)	
4 cups safflower oil	*6* Cover a cooking sheet with several pages of newspaper and then cover that with paper towels; set aside.
6 ounces dark chocolate, melted	

7 In a large, deep, heavy frying pan, heat the oil to 365 degrees.

8 Carefully lift up two of the doughnuts, one at a time, still on the parchment paper, and place them into the oil, paper side down. Work quickly but carefully. Don't slide them into the oil or the dough may come off the paper and the doughnuts will be misshapen.

9 Let them fry for 2 to 3 seconds and then flip the doughnuts. Remove the parchment paper using tongs.

10 Let the doughnuts fry for 1 to 2 minutes. Flip the doughnuts again and fry for 1 minute longer. Place them on the prepared cookie sheet to drain. Repeat with the remaining doughnuts.

11 Cool completely. To fill, put the Bavarian Cream Filling in a pastry bag or plastic bag. Cut a slit into the side of each doughnut and pipe the filling inside.

12 Spread the doughnuts with the melted chocolate. Store in the refrigerator up to two days.

Per serving: Calories 546 (From Fat 322); Fat 36g (Saturated 14g); Cholesterol 210mg; Sodium 202mg; Carbohydrate 53g; Dietary Fiber 3g; Protein 9g.

Bavarian Cream Filling

Prep time: 15 min plus chilling time • **Cook time:** 10 min • **Yield:** 2 cups

Ingredients	Directions
¾ **cup heavy cream** ⅔ **cup whole milk** ¼ **cup plus 2 tablespoons sugar** **1 egg** **2 egg yolks** **2 tablespoons cornstarch** **2 tablespoons unsalted butter** **1 teaspoon vanilla**	*1* In a large, heavy saucepan, combine the heavy cream, milk, and sugar. Cook over medium heat until the mixture simmers, stirring occasionally so the sugar dissolves. *2* Meanwhile, in a mixing bowl with the whisk attachment, beat the egg and the egg yolks until they're pale yellow and fluffy. *3* Beat in the cornstarch. *4* When the milk mixture has come just to a simmer with consistent bubbles, pour 2 tablespoons of the milk mixture into the egg mixture and beat. *5* Continue to add all the milk mixture gradually, beating constantly. *6* Turn the egg mixture back into the pan and cook over medium heat until the mixture begins to steam and thicken. This should take less than a minute. *7* Remove from the heat and whisk in the butter and vanilla. *8* If you love perfectly smooth centers to your donut, feel free to strain the mixture through a sieve. *9* Cover the Bavarian Cream Filling with plastic wrap directly on the surface and chill until cold, about 2 hours.

Per ¼-cup serving: Calories 175 (From Fat 118); Fat 13g (Saturated 8g); Cholesterol 94mg; Sodium 38mg; Carbohydrate 13g; Dietary Fiber 0g; Protein 2g.

Note: Because of the eggs, you must refrigerate this mixture. And make sure it's completely cold before you fill the doughnuts. You can use this mixture to fill cakes, too. You should refrigerate any cake filled with this cream as well.

Note: If you have trouble filling the doughnuts with the cream filling, just cut the doughnuts in half, add the cream, and then put the tops back on and frost. You won't have any complaints!

Cinnamon Raisin Walnut Bread

Prep time: 35 min plus rising time • **Cook time:** 65–70 min • **Yield:** 16 slices

Ingredients	Directions
½ **batch Egg-Free Yeast Bread (see Chapter 19)**	*1* Prepare the Egg-Free Yeast Bread dough from the recipe in Chapter 19 as directed. Divide the dough in half and work with one half. (You can use the other half to make Parmesan Lemon Thyme Baguettes; see Chapter 19.)
2 teaspoons cinnamon	
½ **cup raisins**	
½ **cup walnut pieces**	*2* Grease an 8½-x-4½-inch loaf pan with unsalted butter.
1 tablespoon brown sugar	
1 tablespoon (9 grams) Whole-Grain Flour Mix (see Chapter 10)	*3* Combine the cinnamon, raisins, walnuts, brown sugar, and Whole-Grain Flour Mix and mix until well-coated. Stir into the bread batter.
	4 Pour the batter into the prepared pan. Cover with plastic wrap and let rise for 2 to 3 hours, or until doubled in size.
	5 Preheat the oven to 350 degrees. Bake the bread for 65 to 70 minutes, rotating the pan once in the oven to ensure even baking, until an internal temperature thermometer registers 190 to 200 degrees.
	6 Let the bread cool in the pan for 5 minutes and then turn out onto a cooling rack to cool completely.

Per serving: Calories 126 (From Fat 26); Fat 3g (Saturated 0g); Cholesterol 0mg; Sodium 67mg; Carbohydrate 24g; Dietary Fiber 2g; Protein 3g.

Note: Coating the raisins and walnuts in flour helps keep them suspended in the bread so they don't drop to the bottom of the loaf. When using nuts in a yeast dough, never add them whole; always coarsely chop them. Whole nuts act like little anchors to the rising batter and can keep the bread dense and damp.

Vary It! A drizzle of powdered sugar icing is the perfect finishing touch on this bread. Mix 1 cup powdered sugar with 1 to 2 tablespoons of milk and ¼ teaspoon vanilla until smooth. Drizzle over the cooled loaf and let stand until hardened. You can also spread this cooled bread with nut or sunflower butter for a simple and delicious snack that's full of fiber and protein. This is a perfect idea for a hearty breakfast on the run.

Monkey Bread

Prep time: 45 min plus rising time • **Cook time:** 30 min • **Yield:** 12 servings

Ingredients	*Directions*
½ cup milk	*1* In a small saucepan, heat the milk to 110 degrees. Stir in the yeast and set aside.
1 tablespoon yeast	
1¼ cups plus 1 tablespoon plus 1 teaspoon (196 grams) White Flour Mix (see Chapter 10)	*2* In a large bowl, combine the White Flour Mix, Whole-Grain Flour mix, xanthan gum, ½ cup cane sugar, nutmeg, cinnamon, and salt and mix until the mixture is one color.
1¼ cups minus 1 teaspoon (165 grams) Whole-Grain Flour Mix (see Chapter 10)	*3* Beat in the eggs, egg yolk, and vanilla. Stir in the yeast mixture and beat for 2 minutes.
½ teaspoon xanthan gum	
½ cup plus ¼ cup organic cane sugar	*4* Add 6 tablespoons softened butter and beat 1 minute longer.
¼ teaspoon nutmeg	
½ teaspoon cinnamon	*5* Cover the bowl with plastic wrap and let rise for 15 minutes.
½ teaspoon salt	
2 eggs	*6* Melt ½ cup butter and coat a 12-cup Bundt pan completely, making sure to coat the center stem as well. Reserve the remaining butter.
1 egg yolk	
1 teaspoon vanilla	
6 tablespoons plus ½ cup unsalted butter, melted	*7* In a food processor, combine ¼ cup cane sugar, brown sugar, and lemon peel. Start the machine running and add the nuts through the feed tube; process until the nuts are finely ground but not oily.
¼ cup brown sugar	
1 teaspoon grated lemon peel	
1 cup almonds, walnuts, or pecans	*8* Sprinkle the inside of the cake pan with 3 tablespoons of the nut mixture. Place the remaining nut mixture in a shallow bowl.

9 Use a small ice cream scoop to scoop the dough out of the bowl and into the nut mixture. Roll each ball in the nut mixture to coat and place them into the prepared pan. When the pan has one layer of balls, drizzle with 1 tablespoon melted butter.

10 Repeat with the remaining dough, nut mixture, and butter. You should have three layers of dough balls in the pan when you're done.

11 Cover the pan with plastic wrap and let rise for 2 hours, or until doubled in size.

12 Preheat the oven to 450 degrees.

13 Remove the plastic wrap and place the pan on the middle rack of the oven.

14 Immediately reduce the temperature to 350 degrees. Bake the rolls for 30 to 32 minutes, until deep golden-brown. The temperature on an instant read thermometer should be 190 to 200 degrees.

15 Cool the bread in the pan for 5 minutes and then turn out onto a wire rack to cool completely.

16 Serve this bread with tongs so people can pull off one piece at a time.

Per serving: Calories 333 (From Fat 202); Fat 22g (Saturated 10g); Cholesterol 90mg; Sodium 68mg; Carbohydrate 31g (Dietary Fiber 2g); Protein 5g.

Note: We don't know how this pull-apart bread got its jungle-based name. It doesn't have any tropical ingredients; just a bit of cinnamon and nutmeg for sweet spiciness. Maybe it's because we grab a bun?

Vary It! If you can't eat nuts, just grind up some orange peel with the sugars for a nice variation.

Honey Oat Bread

Prep time: 20 min plus rising time • **Cook time:** 60–70 min • **Yield:** 16 slices

Ingredients	*Directions*
2 cups plus 2 tablespoons (290 grams) Whole-Grain Flour Mix (see Chapter 10)	*1* Grease a 9-x-5-inch loaf pan with unsalted butter.
1 cup minus 2 tablespoons (105 grams) gluten-free rolled oat flour	*2* In the bowl for a stand mixer, combine all ingredients. Beat on medium speed for 2 minutes.
⅔ cup gluten-free rolled oats	*3* Pour the mixture into a prepared bread pan. Cover and let rise for 1 to 2 hours, or until the batter has doubled in size and almost reaches the rim of the pan.
2 eggs	
2 tablespoons honey	
¼ teaspoon sea salt	*4* Preheat the oven to 350 degrees. Using a razor blade, make a cut down the center of the loaf for even more oven spring.
1 teaspoon active dry yeast	
½ teaspoon xanthan gum	*5* Bake for 60 to 70 minutes, or until the temperature on an instant read thermometer reads 190 to 200 degrees. The bread will be golden-brown, pull away from the pan sides, and sound hollow when tapped.
1⅓ cups warm water (102 to 103 degrees)	
	6 Cool the bread in the pan for 3 minutes and then move it to a wire rack to cool completely. Cool the bread completely before slicing.

Per serving: Calories 130 (From Fat 17); Fat 2g (Saturated 0g); Cholesterol 27mg; Sodium 45mg; Carbohydrate 25g; Dietary Fiber 2g; Protein 4g.

Note: This bread makes the most amazing toast. The eggs provide a bit more protein to help the structure develop and add great flavor.

Chapter 13

Cookie Recipes

In This Chapter

▶ Some advice for making the best cookies
▶ A collection of scrumptious cookie recipes

*E*veryone loves cookies. In fact, a full cookie jar is emblematic of America! Nowadays, many people think that a good cookie comes out of a package from the supermarket. How wrong they are.

Making cookies is an act of love. Cookies just out of the oven are a real treat. Cookies can celebrate an occasion or soothe a hurt. And just because you have to avoid wheat flour doesn't mean you have to skip cookies!

In this chapter we offer cookie recipes for everything from classic Chocolate Chip Cookies and Oatmeal Raisin Cookies to a variation on a popular Girl Scout cookie. You can make these cookies even more special with any frosting from Chapter 16, or use one of the Six Vegan Cookie Fillings recipes to make some easy sandwich cookies.

How to Make the Best Cookies

Baking cookies isn't very different from any other type of baking, but gluten-free cookies are a bit different. Here are some tips for making the best cookies:

✔ Measure flour carefully. I know we say that every time, but unless you want dense or tough cookies, measure by weight. If you don't use a scale to measure flours and mixes, always measure by spooning the flour or mix lightly into a measuring cup and leveling off the top with the back of a knife. See Chapters 4 and 5 for more info on measuring by weight and volume.

✔ Most gluten-free cookie doughs are chilled before baking. The chilling lets the flour hydrate completely so the structure of the cookies is strong enough to hold their shape but tender enough to be delicious. Always chill the dough as the recipe directs.

✔ Doneness tests are different for cookies than for most other baked goods. You don't need to check the internal temperature or do a toothpick test. Most people simply use the observation test — when a cookie looks done, it's done! You may even want to take cookies out of the oven a few minutes before they're actually browned because they continue to cook on the baking sheet.

✔ Always cool cookies on a wire rack. If you leave the cookies on the cookie sheet, they may stick or overbake. If you cool cookies on a solid surface, their bottoms may become damp, which defeats the purpose of a crisp cookie like Crisp Chocolate Roll Out Cookies.

You can make most cookie doughs well ahead of time and chill or even freeze them until you're ready to bake them. That's a huge time savings in the kitchen. And you impress people who drop by unexpectedly when you whip some just-baked cookies out of the oven.

Easy and Delicious Cookie Recipes

Have fun with the recipes in this chapter, and remember, after you master a cookie recipe, feel free to change it! For instance, add some orange peel to Vanilla Roll Out Cookies and frost them with Buttercream Frosting (Chapter 16) flavored with orange juice. Or use white chocolate to coat Chocolate Lemon Meringue Cookies; substitute pecans or cashews for the almonds in Almond Madeleines; or use dried currants, dried cherries, or dried cranberries instead of raisins in Oatmeal Raisin Cookies. The possibilities are endless! And don't forget that you can frost any cookie or put cookies together into sandwiches using one of the Six Vegan Cookie Fillings.

Chocolate Chip Cookies

Prep time: 20 min, plus chilling time • **Cook time:** 15 min • **Yield:** 48 servings

Ingredients	*Directions*
1¾ cups plus 3 tablespoons (284 grams) White Flour Mix (see Chapter 10)	*1* In a large bowl, combine the White Flour Mix, Whole-Grain Flour Mix, baking powder, salt, brown sugar, and granulated sugar; mix until the mixture is one color.
⅓ cup minus 1 teaspoon (42 grams) Whole-Grain Flour Mix (see Chapter 10)	*2* Add the softened butter and beat until sandy crumbs form.
1 teaspoon baking powder	
½ teaspoon salt	*3* Add the eggs and vanilla and beat until well combined. The batter will be quite soft.
1 cup packed brown sugar	
¾ cup granulated sugar	*4* Add the chips and nuts and stir until well mixed.
1 cup butter, softened	*5* Cover the dough and chill at least 2 hours or overnight. If you can, chill the dough up to 2 days. This rest lets the flours absorb the moisture in the dough and lets the brown sugar create a true caramel undertone in the cookie.
2 eggs	
1 teaspoon vanilla	
2 cups chocolate chips	
1 cup chopped walnuts or pecans	*6* When you're ready to bake, preheat the oven to 350 degrees. Line cookie sheets with parchment paper or grease them lightly.
	7 Drop the dough by teaspoons, 2 inches apart, onto the prepared cookie sheets.
	8 Bake for 15 to 16 minutes, rotating the cookie sheets in the oven halfway through the baking time.
	9 Remove the cookies from the oven, let them cool on the sheets for 2 minutes, and then remove them to wire racks to cool completely.

Per serving: Calories 139 (From Fat 70); Fat 8g (Saturated 4g); Cholesterol 19mg; Sodium 38mg; Carbohydrate 18g; Dietary Fiber 1g; Protein 1g.

Vary It! You can use dark chocolate chunks, dried tart cherries, or any other type of candy in these delicious cookies. Just keep the total weight of the ingredients you add to 510 to 525 grams and you'll have success.

Coconut Macaroons

Prep time: 15 min • **Cook time:** 12–15 min • **Yield:** 30 cookies

Ingredients	*Directions*
½ cup (55 grams) coconut flour 3 cups flaked coconut ⅓ cup sugar ¾ cup light cream 1 egg white 1½ teaspoons vanilla ½ teaspoon coconut extract Pinch salt	*1* Preheat the oven to 350 degrees. Line a cookie sheet with parchment paper or foil; set aside.
	2 In a large bowl, combine the coconut flour, flaked coconut, and sugar and mix well. Add the light cream, egg white, vanilla, coconut extract, and salt and mix until combined. You may need to add more light cream to make a workable soft dough, depending on how much moisture the coconut flour soaks up.
	3 Using a small (1½ inch) ice cream scoop, scoop out the dough onto the prepared cookie sheet. You can spray the scoop with nonstick cooking spray or dip it into cold water before scooping to prevent sticking.
	4 Bake the macaroons for 12 to 15 minutes, or until lightly browned and set. Let them cool 10 minutes on the baking sheet and then move them to wire racks to cool completely.

Per serving: Calories 64 (From Fat 34); Fat 4g (Saturated 3g); Cholesterol 4mg; Sodium 32mg; Carbohydrate 7g; Dietary Fiber 1g; Protein 1g.

Crisp Chocolate Roll Out Cookies

Prep time: 20 min, plus chilling time • **Cook time:** 10–12 min • **Yield:** 48 cookies

Ingredients	Directions
½ cup unsalted organic butter, softened 2½ cups Cookie Mix without Gums (see Chapter 10) ½ cup cocoa powder 1 egg 1 tablespoon milk 1 teaspoon vanilla	**1** Place the butter in a large bowl and beat until light and fluffy. Gradually add the Cookie Mix and cocoa and continue to beat until well blended. **2** Beat in the egg, milk, and vanilla and continue to beat for 1 minute. The batter will be pliable and thick. **3** Cut off a 15-inch piece of plastic wrap and place it on the work surface. Place the dough in a long, even log down one side of the wrap and roll the dough into the plastic. Refrigerate for 3 to 4 hours before baking. **4** To make the cookies, preheat the oven to 350 degrees. Place a large sheet of parchment paper on the work surface. Add the dough and top with another sheet of parchment paper. If the dough is hard or stiff, let stand at room temperature for 30 minutes. **5** Roll out the dough to ½-inch thickness and cut with cookie cutters. Place it on Silpat-lined cookie sheets. (Silpat liner is a reusable sheet made from silicone that prevents baked goods from sticking. If you don't have one or can't find one, use parchment paper.) **6** Bake for 10 to 12 minutes, until the cookies puff slightly and feel slightly firm to the touch. Let them cool on the cookie sheets for 2 minutes and then move them to wire racks to cool completely.

Per serving: Calories 54 (From Fat 20); Fat 2g (Saturated 1g); Cholesterol 10mg; Sodium 145mg; Carbohydrate 8g; Dietary Fiber 1g; Protein 1g.

Note: You can freeze this dough for up to 3 months. Let it thaw in the refrigerator overnight before using. And always use the parchment paper to roll out the cookies because the dough is difficult to handle. These cookies are crisp and tender. For a more cake-like cut-out chocolate cookie, simply add 2 tablespoons of water to the recipe along with the egg and vanilla.

Oatmeal Raisin Cookies

Prep time: 30 min plus chilling time • **Cook time:** 15 min • **Yield:** 24 servings

Ingredients	*Directions*
¼ cup granulated sugar	**1** In a large bowl, combine the granulated sugar, brown sugar, White Flour Mix, Whole-Grain Flour Mix, baking powder, salt, cinnamon, nutmeg, and ginger and mix until the mixture is one color.
1 cup packed brown sugar	
1 cup minus 2 teaspoons (142 grams) White Flour Mix (see Chapter 10)	**2** Add the butter and vegetable oil and beat until the mixture is the texture of wet sand.
½ cup plus 1 tablespoon plus 2 teaspoons (83 grams) Whole-Grain Flour Mix (see Chapter 10)	**3** Add the egg, honey, vanilla, and milk and beat for 1 minute.
2 teaspoons baking powder	**4** Stir in the oats, nuts, and raisins. Cover and refrigerate the dough for at least 2 hours to let the oats absorb the liquid.
½ teaspoon salt	
2 teaspoons cinnamon	
¼ teaspoon nutmeg	**5** When you're ready to bake, preheat the oven to 350 degrees. Line two cookie sheets with Silpat liners or parchment paper.
½ teaspoon ginger	
½ cup unsalted butter, softened	
¼ cup vegetable oil	**6** Drop the dough by spoonfuls onto the prepared cookie sheets, making 24 cookies in all.
1 egg	
2 teaspoons honey	**7** Bake for 13 to 15 minutes, or until the cookies are lightly browned. Let them cool on cookie sheets for 3 minutes and then move them to a wire rack to cool completely.
1 teaspoon vanilla	
⅓ cup milk	
1¾ cups gluten-free rolled oats	
½ cup chopped walnuts	
¾ cup raisins	

Per serving: Calories 126 (From Fat 22); Fat 3g (Saturated 0g); Cholesterol 9mg; Sodium 90mg; Carbohydrate 25g; Dietary Fiber 1g; Protein 2g.

Chocolate Crackle Cookies

Prep time: 20 min plus chilling time • **Cook time:** 10–12 min • **Yield:** 36 cookies

Ingredients	Directions
1 batch Crisp Chocolate Roll Out Cookies (see page 209) **2 tablespoons water** **1 cup powdered sugar**	*1* Prepare the Crisp Chocolate Roll Out Cookie dough as directed, using 2 tablespoons water in place of the milk, and chill for 3 to 4 hours.
	2 Preheat the oven to 350 degrees. Line cookie sheets with Silpat liners or parchment paper.
	3 Break off tablespoons of the dough or use a small cookie scoop to make small balls. Roll the dough between your palms until smooth.
	4 Drop each ball of dough into the powdered sugar, making sure it's well-coated. Place the balls at least 2 inches apart on the prepared cookie sheets.
	5 Bake for 10 to 12 minutes, or until the cookies puff slightly and are firm to the touch. Let them cool on the cookie sheets for 2 minutes and then move them to a wire rack to cool. Store them in an airtight container.

Per serving: Calories 85 (From Fat 27); Fat 3g (Saturated 2g); Cholesterol 13mg; Sodium 194mg; Carbohydrate 14g; Dietary Fiber 1g; Protein 1g.

Note: These little cookies have a crunchy, sweet shell and a tender, dark heart. They make a perfect afternoon snack with a glass of milk. The shaping is so simple that any child can help.

Vary It! You can use a different extract or flavoring for the cookies if you'd like. A drop of orange oil adds a rich taste. Or use ¼ or ½ teaspoon of peppermint extract. You can also roll the dough in finely ground nuts or baking sprinkles for a fun change of pace.

Peanut Cookies with Chocolate Chips

Prep time: 20 min plus chilling time • **Cook time:** 15–18 min • **Yield:** 60 cookies

Ingredients	Directions
2 eggs	**1** In a large bowl, combine all ingredients. Beat them together until the mixture is smooth and blended.
¼ cup water	
1 tablespoon vanilla	
1½ cups peanut butter, crunchy or smooth	**2** Place the dough in a bowl and cover with plastic wrap. Refrigerate overnight, or at least 2 hours.
1½ cups Cookie Mix without Gums (see Chapter 10)	**3** Preheat the oven to 350 degrees. Using a small ice cream scoop, scoop out the cookies and place them on ungreased cookie sheets.
⅓ cup plus 1 tablespoon brown sugar	
⅔ cup semisweet chocolate chips (optional)	**4** Bake for 15 to 18 minutes, or until the cookie edges are just browned slightly. Move them to a wire rack to cool completely.

Per serving: Calories 54 (From Fat 24); Fat 3g (Saturated 1g); Cholesterol 8mg; Sodium 74mg; Carbohydrate 7g; Dietary Fiber 1g; Protein 1g.

Note: These crispy cookies are like old-fashioned peanut butter creams. They aren't crumbly, which is unusual for a gluten-free cookie.

Vary It! If you don't want to use peanut butter, any nut butter will substitute fine. Also, you can sandwich these cookies together using your choice of the Six Vegan Cookie Fillings on page 217.

Vanilla Roll Out Cookies

Prep time: 20 min plus chilling time • **Cook time:** 10–12 min • **Yield:** 48 cookies

Ingredients	Directions
½ **cup organic unsalted butter, softened** **3 cups Cookie Mix without Gums (see Chapter 10)** **1 egg** **1 tablespoon vanilla** **2 tablespoons water**	**1** In a large bowl, beat the butter until it's light and fluffy. Add the Cookie Mix and continue to beat until well-blended. **2** Stir in the egg, vanilla, and water and beat for 1 minute. The dough will be soft and thick. **3** Cut a 15-inch-long piece of plastic wrap and place it on your work surface. Place the dough in a long log down one side of the wrap. Roll the dough into the plastic and refrigerate for 3 to 4 hours. The dough can be frozen at this point for slice-and-bake cookies. **4** When you want to bake the cookies, preheat the oven to 350 degrees. **5** Place a sheet of parchment paper on the work surface and add the dough. Top with another sheet of parchment paper. If the dough is hard or stiff, let stand at room temperature for 30 minutes. **6** Roll out the dough to ½-inch thickness. Cut out using cookie cutters. **7** Place the cookies on ungreased cookie sheets about 2 inches apart. Bake for 10 to 12 minutes, until the cookies puff slightly, the edges are golden-brown, and the cookies feel slightly firm to the touch. Let them cool on the cookie sheets for 1 minute and then move them to wire racks to cool completely.

Per serving: Calories 56 (From Fat 19); Fat 2g (Saturated 1g); Cholesterol 10mg; Sodium 161mg; Carbohydrate 9g; Dietary Fiber 0g; Protein 1g.

Note: To bake the cookie dough when it's frozen, remove the dough from the freezer and slice it ½-inch thick. Place it on ungreased cookie sheets and bake it at 350 degrees for 15 to 20 minutes.

Note: Have fun frosting these cookies during the holidays. Use the Buttercream Frosting recipe in Chapter 16. Divide the frosting into several smaller bowls and tint it using gluten-free food coloring.

Chocolate Lemon Meringue Cookies

Prep time: 15 min • **Cook time:** 40 min • **Yield:** 24 cookies

Ingredients	*Directions*
3 egg whites	*1* Preheat the oven to 300 degrees. Line two cookie sheets with parchment paper and set aside.
⅛ teaspoon salt	
⅛ teaspoon cream of tartar	*2* Place the egg whites in a large mixer bowl and let stand at room temperature for 20 minutes. Add the salt and cream of tartar; beat on low speed until blended.
¾ cup sugar	
¼ cup finely crushed hard lemon candies	*3* Increase speed to high and add the sugar, a tablespoon at a time, until the mixture is stiff and glossy. The sugar should be dissolved; rub a little bit between your fingers. You shouldn't feel any grains of sugar.
1 cup dark chocolate chips	
¼ cup milk chocolate chips	*4* Fold in the lemon candies. Drop the mixture by teaspoons onto the prepared cookie sheets.
	5 Bake for 30 to 40 minutes, or until the meringue bottoms start to turn light golden-brown. The cookies should be firm but not browned.
	6 Remove them from the oven and place the parchment paper, with the cookies, on wire racks. Cool completely and then peel the cookies off the parchment paper.
	7 Place the dark chocolate chips in a small, microwave-safe bowl. Microwave on high for 2 minutes, stirring halfway through the cooking time, until the chips melt. When the chips are melted, stir in the milk chocolate chips until smooth and combined.
	8 Line the cookie sheets with waxed paper. Dip the bottoms of the cooled meringue cookies about ¼ inch into the melted chocolate and place them on waxed paper. Let stand until firm.

Per serving: Calories 76 (From Fat 22); Fat 2g (Saturated 2g); Cholesterol 0mg; Sodium 22mg; Carbohydrate 14g; Dietary Fiber 1g; Protein 1g.

Madeleines

Prep time: 20 min • **Cook time:** 15 min • **Yield:** 12 cookies

Ingredients	*Directions*
½ cup butter, softened	*1* Preheat the oven to 375 degrees. Spray a Madeleine pan with nonstick cooking spray or vegetable oil spray.
⅔ cup sugar	
2 eggs	*2* In a medium bowl, combine the butter and sugar and beat together until fluffy.
1 teaspoon vanilla	
½ teaspoon grated lemon peel	*3* Add the eggs, vanilla, lemon peel, and salt and blend well.
Pinch salt	
½ cup plus 1 tablespoon plus 2 teaspoons (83 grams) Whole-Grain Flour Mix (see Chapter 10)	*4* Stir in the Whole-Grain Flour Mix and White Flour Mix.
½ cup minus 1 teaspoon (71 grams) White Flour Mix (see Chapter 10)	*5* Place the batter into the molds, filling just to the top of the pan. Don't overfill the molds or the Madeleines will run together as they bake.
	6 Bake for 15 to 16 minutes, until the Madeleines start to pull away from the pan at the edges. The upper side will be a soft golden color; the pan side will be golden-brown.
	7 Remove the cookies from the pans immediately and cool them on a wire rack.
	8 Before baking the next batch, wipe out the pans to remove the crumbs.

Per serving: Calories 138 (From Fat 77); Fat 9g (Saturated 5g); Cholesterol 56mg; Sodium 23mg; Carbohydrate 14g; Dietary Fiber 0g; Protein 2g.

Note: Proustian references about these cookies abound, so people think they must be hard to make. Actually, these are one of the simplest cookies imaginable. You need the correct specialized pan — called, obviously, a Madeleine pan — if you want to make the classic shell-shaped cookie, but you can use the same batter to make round cookies. Just use a muffin tin and fill with an inch of the batter. Bake as directed.

Almond Madeleines

Prep time: 20 min • **Cook time:** 12–15 min • **Yield:** 24 cookies

Ingredients	*Directions*
½ cup organic butter, softened	*1* Preheat the oven to 350 degrees. Grease Madeleine pans (shallow pans with indentations that look like scallop shells) with unsalted butter and set aside.
⅔ cup sugar	
½ cup plus 1 tablespoon plus 2 teaspoons (83 grams) Whole-Grain Flour Mix (see Chapter 10)	*2* In a medium bowl, combine the softened butter and sugar and beat well, until the mix is light and fluffy.
¼ cup plus 2 teaspoons (33 grams) almond flour (blanched almonds ground to a flour)	*3* Add the Whole-Grain Flour Mix, almond flour, White Flour Mix, salt, and baking powder. Beat until well-combined.
¼ cup (35 grams) White Flour Mix (see Chapter 10)	*4* Add the eggs and almond extract and beat for 1 minute.
Pinch salt	
¼ teaspoon baking powder	*5* Spoon the batter into the Madeleine pans using a rounded tablespoon for each. Bake for 12 to 15 minutes, or until the cookie edges are light golden-brown and they spring back lightly when touched.
2 eggs	
1 teaspoon almond extract	*6* Use the tip of a knife to gently pry the Madeleines out of the pan and cool them completely on a wire rack.

Per serving: Calories 72 (From Fat 45); Fat 5g (Saturated 3g); Cholesterol 28mg; Sodium 16mg; Carbohydrate 6g; Dietary Fiber 0g; Protein 1g.

Note: Madeleines are a delicate cookie. Don't overbake them, and try to get them out of the pans as quickly as possible. Handle them gently.

Vary It! You can use other nuts instead of the almonds to change the flavor of these cookies. Substitute 3 tablespoons plus 1 teaspoon (33 grams) sweet rice flour in place of the almond flour and use ground pecans or walnuts in place of the almonds. Omit the almond extract and use 1 teaspoon vanilla extract instead.

Note: If you don't have a Madeleine pan, feel free to use a muffin tin and create delicate circular cookies.

Six Vegan Cookie Fillings

Prep time: 10 min • **Cook time:** 3 min • **Yield:** 1 cup

Ingredients	Directions
2 tablespoons boiling water **2 tablespoons organic palm oil shortening** **2 cups powdered sugar** **1 drop vanilla**	*1* In a medium, heat-proof bowl, combine the boiling water and shortening. Let the shortening melt.
	2 Stir in the powdered sugar and vanilla. Beat with a mixer until the mixture is light. The consistency will be plastic and spreadable.
	3 Use the filling to make sandwich cookies. Roll the filling into a ball and place it between two cookies, flat sides together. Gently press down to spread the filling.
	4 Cover the bowl with plastic wrap to prevent drying if you make this filling before the cookies are ready.

Per 1 tablespoon serving: Calories 72 (From Fat 15); Fat 2g (Saturated 1g); Cholesterol 0mg; Sodium 0mg; Carbohydrate 15g; Dietary Fiber 0g; Protein 0g.

Vary It! You can vary this filling in many ways:

1) For **Coconut Cream Filling:** Substitute 2 tablespoons coconut oil for the shortening and coconut extract for the vanilla.

2) For **Fudge Crème Filling:** Reduce the shortening to 1 tablespoon and melt 1 ounce chopped bittersweet or unsweetened chocolate into the shortening and then add the sugar and water.

3) For **Peanut Crème Filling:** Reduce the shortening to 1 tablespoon and add ¼ cup natural peanut butter to the shortening and water mixture.

4) For **Grasshopper Crème Filling:** Substitute 2 tablespoons boiling peppermint tea for the boiling water and mint or peppermint extract for the vanilla. You can tint this green with a drop of food coloring.

5) For **Almond Crème Filling:** Substitute almond extract for the vanilla.

Thin Mints

Prep time: 25 min • **Cook time:** 10–20 min • **Yield:** 48 cookies

Ingredients	Directions
1 recipe Crisp Chocolate Roll Out Cookies (see page 209) **1 recipe Grasshopper Crème Filling (see page 217, variation 4)** **1 pound dark chocolate bar, chopped** **3 tablespoons organic palm oil shortening** **2 teaspoons mint extract**	*1* Prepare the cookie dough as directed. Roll the dough into plastic wrap but don't roll it out between parchment paper. Just slice the dough ¼-inch thick and place it on parchment-lined cookie sheets.
	2 Bake the dough at 350 degrees for 10 to 12 minutes, or until the cookies puff slightly and feel firm to the touch.
	3 Remove the cookies from the cookie sheets and let them cool completely.
	4 Break off 1 teaspoon of the Grasshopper Crème Filling and roll it into a ball. Place the ball on one cookie and use a glass bottom to flatten it. The filling shouldn't reach the edge of the cookie. Repeat with the remaining cookies.
	5 In a medium, heat-proof bowl, combine the chopped chocolate and shortening. Melt over simmering water just until melted. Stir in the mint extract.
	6 Place each cookie on a fork and gently dip it into the melted chocolate mixture, turning it to coat the other side. Then turn it right side up, scoop it out with a fork, tap it on the side of the bowl gently to remove excess chocolate, and place it on waxed paper until firm. Store in an airtight container at room temperature.

Per serving: Calories 136 (From Fat 60); Fat 7g (Saturated 4g); Cholesterol 10mg; Sodium 146mg; Carbohydrate 19g; Dietary Fiber 1g; Protein 1g.

Vary It! You can omit the Grasshopper Crème Filling and just coat the plain chocolate cookies for a more authentic version of the classic Girl Scout cookie.

Note: Girl Scout cookie time is especially poignant for the gluten-free. There are no gluten-free Girl Scout cookies (yet!). And when your child is a Girl Scout and is asked, "What's your favorite cookie?" an upset is guaranteed. These cookies taste even better than the original. Jean's girls, who have been Girl Scouts since kindergarten, feel sorry for the folks who have to buy cookies rather than having this homemade treat! They especially love the cookies frozen.

Chocolate Dipped Double Peanut Cookies

Prep time: 20 min plus chilling time • **Cook time:** 18 min • **Yield:** 36 cookies

Ingredients	*Directions*
½ cup unsalted butter, softened ½ cup crunchy peanut butter 2 eggs 1 teaspoon vanilla 1½ cups Cookie Mix without Gums (see Chapter 10) 1¼ cups (128 grams) peanut flour ⅓ cup plus 1 tablespoon packed brown sugar ¾ cup dark chocolate chips ¼ cup chopped peanuts for decoration (optional)	*1* In a large bowl, combine the butter and peanut butter. Beat in the eggs and vanilla. *2* Add the Cookie Mix, peanut flour, and brown sugar and beat for 1 minute, until the batter is well combined. *3* Form the dough into a long log shape on plastic wrap; wrap well and freeze overnight. *4* When you're ready to bake, preheat the oven to 350 degrees. Line the cookie sheets with Silpat liner or parchment paper. *5* Slice the dough into ⅛-inch slices and place them on the cookie sheets. *6* Bake for 15 to 18 minutes, or until the edges are lightly browned. Cool them on the cookie sheets for 3 minutes and then move them to a wire rack to cool completely. *7* When the cookies are cool, melt all but 2 tablespoons chocolate chips in a glass, microwave-safe measuring cup on high in 30 second intervals, stirring after each interval, until smooth. Stir in the remaining 2 tablespoons chocolate chips until melted and smooth. *8* Dip each cookie halfway into the chocolate, shake off the excess, and place it on waxed or parchment paper to harden. Sprinkle with chopped peanuts, if desired.

Per serving: Calories 108 (From Fat 57); Fat 6g (Saturated 3g); Cholesterol 19mg; Sodium 113mg; Carbohydrate 11g; Dietary Fiber 1g; Protein 3g.

Note: The method of melting part of the chocolate and then stirring in the remainder until melted helps temper the chocolate, arranging the crystals in the chocolate so it hardens without refrigeration. Just keep stirring until the 2 tablespoons of chocolate chips completely melt.

Quadruple Chocolate Cookies

Prep time: 30 min • **Cook time:** 11 min • **Yield:** 48 cookies

Ingredients	*Directions*
4 ounces unsweetened chocolate, chopped	**1** In a heavy, medium saucepan over low heat, melt together the unsweetened chocolate, semisweet chocolate, milk chocolate, and butter. Stir until smooth and then remove from heat.
4 ounces semisweet chocolate, chopped	
4 ounces milk chocolate, chopped	**2** In a large mixing bowl, beat the eggs until they're combined. Gradually add granulated sugar and brown sugar, beating on high speed until the mixture is thick, light, and lemon-colored. This should take about 5 minutes.
½ cup butter	
4 eggs	
¾ cup granulated sugar	
⅔ cup brown sugar	**3** Beat in the melted chocolate mixture.
¼ cup (30 grams) sorghum flour	**4** In a small bowl, combine the sorghum flour, potato starch, tapioca flour, salt, and baking powder and stir with a wire whisk to combine. Add to the batter and mix well, and then stir in the chocolate chips.
1 tablespoon (10 grams) potato starch	
1 tablespoon (7 grams) tapioca flour	**5** Let the batter stand for 25 minutes at room temperature. Preheat the oven to 350 degrees.
¼ teaspoon salt	
¼ teaspoon baking powder	**6** Line cookie sheets with Silpat liners or parchment paper. Drop the batter by spoonfuls onto the prepared sheets, about 3 inches apart.
½ cup mini semisweet chocolate chips	
	7 Bake for 9 to 11 minutes, or until the cookies are just set. Let them cool on the cookie sheets for 2 minutes and then pull the parchment paper with the cookies onto a wire rack to cool completely.

Per serving: Calories 94 (From Fat 51); Fat 6g (Saturated 3g); Cholesterol 23mg; Sodium 21mg; Carbohydrate 11g; Dietary Fiber 1g; Protein 1g.

Chapter 14

Brownies and Bars

In This Chapter

▶ Knowing the keys to making brownies and bar cookies

▶ Checking out tasty recipes for brownies and bars

Brownies and bar cookies are some of the easiest treats to make. You don't have to form individual cookies; you just put batter or dough into a pan and bake. And they're perfect for any occasion.

In this chapter, we present recipes for delicious brownies and bar cookies. These recipes range from the decadent, such as Lemon Truffle Bars, to the simple, such as Granola Bars. We also give you tips for making the best brownies and bar cookies, including doneness tests and the best way to prepare baking pans.

The Keys to Delicious Brownies and Bar Cookies

The most important part of making brownies and bar cookies is doneness. Overbaked brownies are tough and dry, no matter how perfectly you measure the ingredients. And underbaked bar cookies don't hold together, so you can't cut and serve them.

To make the best brownies and bar cookies:

- ✔ Always grease the pan well, using unsalted butter, solid shortening, or nonstick cooking spray. Salted butter makes the cookies stick to the pan, and oil doesn't work very well for greasing.

- ✔ If you don't use a scale to measure flours and mixes, always measure by spooning the flour or mix lightly into a measuring cup and leveling off the top with the back of a knife. See Chapters 4 and 5 for more info on measuring by weight and volume.

- ✔ You may want to line the cake pan or baking pan with foil or parchment paper and then grease the foil if the recipe calls for it. Use enough foil to extend past the pan's edges. Smooth the foil down so it fits closely inside the pan. When you bake the brownies or bar cookies, cool them completely in the pan and then lift them out of the pan using the foil edges. Peel off the foil and cut into bars.

- ✔ If a recipe calls for baking a crust before adding a filling, be sure to bake it until it's done. Crusts get soggy and fall apart if you don't thoroughly bake them before you add a soft or creamy filling.

- ✔ To cut brownies and bar cookies, use a sharp knife. Dip the knife in hot water and wipe it off before each cut for smooth edges and well-defined squares.

Store brownies and bar cookies well covered at room temperature unless the recipes specify otherwise. The cut edges of these foods can dry out if they aren't well covered.

Delicious Recipes for Brownies and Bar Cookies

If you need to serve a crowd or make goodies for a bake sale, brownies and bar cookies are the way to go. A 13-x-9-inch pan of treats serves 24 to 36 people, depending on how small you cut the bars. You should cut some bar cookies, like Double Chocolate Caramel Bars, small simply because they're so rich. You can cut Granola Bars larger because they're a healthier treat.

Enjoy these easy recipes and have fun making your own creations after you understand a recipe. You can substitute different ingredients, such as cashews instead of walnuts or dried cherries instead of chocolate chips. Frost these treats with a recipe from Chapter 16; in fact, layer a couple of frostings for a really decadent dessert.

Tangy Lime Bars

Prep time: 30 min • **Cook time:** 35–45 min • **Yield:** 16 servings

Ingredients	Directions
3 tablespoons unsalted butter, softened	**1** Place the oven rack in the lower third of the oven. Preheat the oven to 350 degrees. Spray a 13-x-9-inch baking pan with nonstick cooking spray and set aside.
⅓ cup plus ⅔ cup sugar	
2 egg yolks	**2** In a large bowl, beat the butter until it's light and fluffy. Add ⅓ cup sugar and beat until creamy. Add the egg yolks, yogurt or vinegar, and vanilla, beating well.
1 tablespoon yogurt or ¼ teaspoon vinegar	
¼ teaspoon vanilla	
1 cup plus 2 tablespoons (165 grams) White Flour Mix (see Chapter 10)	**3** Add the White Flour Mix, Whole-Grain Flour Mix, salt, and baking soda and beat well.
½ cup plus 1 tablespoon plus 2 teaspoons (83 grams) Whole-Grain Flour Mix (see Chapter 10)	**4** Press the dough into the prepared pan and prick all over with a fork.
Pinch salt	**5** Bake 20 to 25 minutes, until the crust is golden-brown.
⅛ teaspoon baking soda	**6** Meanwhile, make the topping. In a medium bowl, combine the eggs and egg whites and beat well.
2 eggs	
2 egg whites	**7** Add ⅔ cup sugar, lime juice, lime zest, and tapioca flour and mix well.
½ cup strained fresh lime juice	
1 teaspoon grated lime zest	**8** Remove the crust from the oven and pour the topping over.
2 tablespoons (16 grams) tapioca flour	**9** Return the crust to the oven and bake for 15 to 20 minutes longer, until the topping is set.
	10 Cool completely and then cover and chill the bars for 2 to 3 hours before serving.

Per serving: Calories 145 (From Fat 32); Fat 4g (Saturated 2g); Cholesterol 59mg; Sodium 36mg; Carbohydrate 27g; Dietary Fiber 0g; Protein 2g.

Note: Either yogurt or vinegar works to create the tang in the crust and add some acidity. Use whichever one you have on hand.

Peanut Butter Chocolate Bars

Prep time: 15 min • **Cook time:** 25 min • **Yield:** 36 bar cookies

Ingredients	Directions
2 cups plus ½ cup creamy peanut butter	*1* Preheat the oven to 350 degrees. Line a 13-x-9-inch pan with foil and set aside.
½ cup packed brown sugar	
½ cup powdered sugar	*2* In a large bowl for a stand mixer, combine 2 cups peanut butter, brown sugar, powdered sugar, granulated sugar, honey, eggs, and vanilla. Beat well until combined.
⅓ cup granulated sugar	
¼ cup honey	
2 eggs	*3* Spoon and spread the mixture into the prepared pan. Bake for 15 to 25 minutes, or until the bars are set and light golden-brown around the edges. Remove them from the oven and place them on a cooling rack.
1 teaspoon vanilla	
One 12-ounce package (2 cups) semisweet chocolate chips	
1 cup chopped peanuts	*4* In a medium, microwave-safe bowl, combine the chocolate chips with ½ cup peanut butter. Microwave on high for 1 minute; remove and stir. Continue microwaving the mixture on high for 1-minute intervals, stirring after each interval, until the mixture is melted and smooth.
	5 Pour the chocolate mixture over the warm bars and spread to cover. Sprinkle with chopped peanuts and let stand until cool. Cut into bars to serve.

Per serving: Calories 209 (From Fat 126); Fat 14g (Saturated 4g); Cholesterol 12mg; Sodium 89mg; Carbohydrate 19g; Dietary Fiber 2g; Protein 6g.

Vary It! You can vary these bars in many ways. Swirl some of your favorite jam into the bars just before baking them or top the finished bars with a thin layer of jam and some ground peanuts. You can also top the bars with chocolate chips, peanut butter chips, or white chocolate chips before baking them instead of frosting them. Enjoy these delicious bars with a big glass of cold milk!

Butterscotch Brownies

Prep time: 15 min • **Cook time:** 35 min • **Yield:** 16 bars

Ingredients	*Directions*
¼ cup unsalted butter	*1* Preheat the oven to 325 degrees. Lightly grease an 8-x-8-inch square baking pan with unsalted butter and set aside.
1 cup packed brown sugar	
1 egg	
1 teaspoon vanilla	*2* In a medium saucepan, melt the butter. Add the brown sugar and heat, stirring, until the sugar is dissolved. Set aside to cool for 10 minutes.
½ cup minus 2 teaspoons (63 grams) brown rice flour	
1 teaspoon baking powder	*3* Beat in the egg and vanilla.
¼ teaspoon salt	
½ cup finely chopped walnuts	*4* In a small bowl, combine the flour, baking powder, and salt. Stir the flour mixture into the butter mixture. Add the nuts, mixing gently.
	5 Pour the batter into a prepared pan and bake for 25 to 33 minutes, until brownies are set and light golden-brown. Cool and cut into bars.

Per serving: Calories 121 (From Fat 51); Fat 6g (Saturated 2g); Cholesterol 21mg; Sodium 70mg; Carbohydrate 17g; Dietary Fiber 0g; Protein 1g.

Vary It! These delicious brownies pack and ship well. You can frost them with a chocolate or caramel frosting. They're also delicious with some butterscotch or chocolate chips (gluten-free, of course) stirred in along with the walnuts.

Lemon Truffle Bars

Prep time: 45 min, plus chilling time • **Cook time:** 20 min • **Yield:** 16 bar cookies

Ingredients	Directions
½ recipe Vanilla Roll Out Cookies (see Chapter 13)	**1** Prepare the Vanilla Roll Out Cookie dough. Divide the dough in half and chill both halves as the recipe directs. Reserve one half for later use.
1 cup sugar	
2 tablespoons (16 grams) cornstarch	**2** When you're ready to bake, preheat the oven to 350 degrees. Grease a 9-inch square baking pan with unsalted butter. Press the cookie dough evenly into the pan and prick with a fork. Bake for 15 to 20 minutes, or until the crust is set and light golden-brown.
1 tablespoon (8 grams) tapioca flour	
¼ teaspoon salt	
2 egg yolks	**3** Cool the crust completely on a wire rack. When the crust is cool, combine the sugar, cornstarch, tapioca flour, and salt in a medium saucepan and mix with a wire whisk until smooth. In a small bowl, combine the egg yolks and water, beat well, and then beat into the sugar mixture until smooth.
10 tablespoons water	
7 tablespoons lemon juice	
2 tablespoons butter	
½ teaspoon grated lemon zest	**4** Cook the egg yolk mixture over medium heat, stirring constantly with a wire whisk, until the mixture thickens and reaches 165 degrees. Remove from the heat and add the lemon juice, butter, and zest, beating well.
1½ cups white chocolate chips	
Three 3-ounce packages cream cheese, softened	**5** Place the white chocolate chips in a medium, microwave-safe bowl. Add 9 tablespoons of the hot lemon mixture. Microwave on low for 2 minutes and then remove and stir. Continue microwaving on low for 1-minute intervals, stirring after each interval.
	6 Beat all packages of cream cheese into the white chocolate chip mixture until smooth.
	7 Spread the cream cheese mixture over the cooled crust and top with the lemon mixture, spreading to cover. Cover and chill in the fridge for 4 to 5 hours to set. Cut into bars when cool.

Per serving: Calories 301 (From Fat 144); Fat 16g (Saturated 10g); Cholesterol 66mg; Sodium 305mg; Carbohydrate 37g; Dietary Fiber 0g; Protein 3g.

Rocky Road Bar Cookies

Prep time: 25 min • **Cook time:** 15–20 min • **Yield:** 16 bar cookies

Ingredients	*Directions*
½ batch Crisp Chocolate Roll Out Cookies (see Chapter 13)	**1** Prepare the Crisp Chocolate Roll Out Cookie dough, adding water along with the egg and vanilla in that recipe. Divide the batch in half; refrigerate or freeze half for later use.
2 tablespoons water	
⅔ cup coarsely chopped walnuts	**2** Preheat the oven to 350 degrees. Grease a 9-inch square baking pan with unsalted butter or nonstick cooking spray.
⅔ cup mini marshmallows	
⅓ cup semisweet or milk chocolate chips	**3** Press the cookie dough evenly into the pan. Sprinkle the walnuts, marshmallows, and chocolate chips on the dough and press in lightly.
	4 Bake for 15 to 20 minutes, or until the marshmallows are toasted and the chips are melted. Let the cookies cool completely on a wire rack before cutting into squares.

Per serving: Calories 137 (From Fat 69); Fat 8g (Saturated 3g); Cholesterol 14mg; Sodium 220mg; Carbohydrate 17g; Dietary Fiber 1g; Protein 2g.

Vary It! These cookies are perfect to take on a road trip. You can vary the topping according to your taste. Some people want some coconut on their Rocky Road. You can use different types of chocolate chips, too — peanut butter chocolate chips, white chocolate chips, or dark chocolate chips. All are scrumptious on these delightful bar cookies.

Apricot Crumble Bars

Prep time: 25 min • **Cook time:** 50 min • **Yield:** 24 servings

Ingredients	Directions
2 cups chopped dried apricots	**1** In a medium saucepan, boil the apricots and orange juice over medium-high heat for 5 minutes, stirring frequently.
2 cups orange juice	
¾ cup butter, softened	
⅔ cup packed brown sugar	**2** Reduce the heat to low and simmer the mixture until all the juice is absorbed but the apricots are still moist, about 15 minutes. Remove from heat. Purée the apricots in a food processor until smooth.
1 teaspoon vanilla	
1¼ cups minus 1 teaspoon (165 grams) Whole-Grain Flour Mix (see Chapter 10)	
1 cup minus 2 teaspoons (142 grams) White Flour Mix (see Chapter 10)	**3** Preheat the oven to 350 degrees. Grease a 13-x-9-inch pan with unsalted butter or solid shortening.
1½ cups gluten-free rolled oats	**4** In a large bowl, beat the butter until it's light and fluffy. Add the brown sugar and vanilla and beat for 3 minutes.
	5 Add the Whole-Grain Flour Mix, White Flour Mix, and oats and mix well. The dough will begin to form crumbs; keep mixing until smaller crumbs form.
	6 Press half of the oat mixture into the bottom of a prepared pan. Spread with the apricot filling. Top with the remaining oat mixture, pressing down lightly to flatten.
	7 Bake until lightly browned, about 30 to 35 minutes. Cool the bars on a wire rack in the pan and then cut into bars to serve.

Per serving: Calories 172 (From Fat 57); Fat 6g (Saturated 4g); Cholesterol 15mg; Sodium 5mg; Carbohydrate 29g; Dietary Fiber 2g; Protein 2g.

Tip: You can substitute a 12-ounce jar of apricot jam for the chopped dried apricots and orange juice mixture to save some time and effort.

Maple Syrup Shortbread

Prep time: 20 min, plus chilling time • **Cook time:** 25 min • **Yield:** 36 servings

Ingredients	*Directions*
⅔ cup grade B amber maple syrup	*1* In a small saucepan, bring the maple syrup to a boil over medium-high heat and reduce by half. This should take about 10 to 15 minutes. Remove from heat and let stand for 10 minutes.
½ cup unsalted butter, softened	
1¼ cups minus 1 teaspoon (165 grams) Whole-Grain Flour Mix	*2* Combine the cooled maple syrup, butter, Whole-Grain Flour Mix, White Flour Mix, baking powder, and salt in a mixer. Beat until well blended.
1 cup minus 2 teaspoons (142 grams) White Flour Mix	
½ teaspoon baking powder	*3* Wrap the mixture in plastic wrap and refrigerate it for at least 3 hours, until the dough is chilled.
¼ teaspoon salt	
	4 When the dough is ready to bake, preheat the oven to 350 degrees.
	5 Remove the dough from the fridge and roll to ¼-inch thickness between two sheets of plastic wrap.
	6 With cookie cutters, cut the dough into cookies. Place them on an ungreased cookie sheet and bake them until they're light golden-brown, about 10 to 12 minutes.
	7 Let the cookies cool on the sheet for 3 minutes and then move them to a wire rack to cool completely.

Per serving: Calories 67 (From Fat 24); Fat 3g (Saturated 2g); Cholesterol 7mg; Sodium 23mg; Carbohydrate 11g; Dietary Fiber 0g; Protein 1g.

Note: Sometimes you want to make a crisp cookie but you don't want to use sugar. The best syrup to use for this recipe is the grade B amber, which is darker and more flavorful than grade A. And it costs less, too!

Layered Chocolate Fruit Bars

Prep time: 20 min • **Cook time:** 25 min • **Yield:** 24 servings

Ingredients	*Directions*
16 Graham Crackers (see Chapter 18), crushed	*1* Prepare the Graham Crackers.
½ cup butter, melted	*2* Preheat the oven to 350 degrees. Spray a 13-x-9-inch baking pan with nonstick cooking spray.
1 cup milk chocolate chips	
1 cup semisweet chocolate chips	*3* Place the Graham Cracker crumbs in the bottom of the prepared pan. Drizzle evenly with melted butter.
1 cup dried cherries	
1 cup unsweetened coconut	*4* Top with both kinds of chocolate chips, cherries, and coconut, layering the ingredients evenly.
One 14-ounce can sweetened condensed milk	
	5 Pour the condensed milk over all.
	6 Bake for 23 to 28 minutes, or until the bars are light golden-brown and set. Cool completely on a wire rack and then cut into bars to serve.

Per serving: Calories 284 (From Fat 128); Fat 14g (Saturated 9g); Cholesterol 23mg; Sodium 66mg; Carbohydrate 38g; Dietary Fiber 2g; Protein 4g.

Vary It! You can substitute any type of dried fruit for the cherries. Use dried blueberries, dried cranberries, or finely chopped dried apricots. You can also use chopped nuts in place of the coconut. But stick with the 2 cups of chocolate chips; they're necessary to hold the bars together.

Double Chocolate Caramel Bars

Prep time: 25 min • **Cook time:** 28 min • **Yield:** 36 bar cookies

Ingredients	Directions
1 cup (123 grams) sorghum flour	*1* Preheat the oven to 350 degrees. Grease a 13-x-9-inch pan with unsalted butter and set aside.
½ cup minus 2 teaspoons (62 grams) brown rice flour	*2* In a large bowl, combine the sorghum flour, brown rice flour, white rice flour, xanthan gum, and cocoa powder. Mix well with a wire whisk until the flours are all one color.
⅓ cup plus 1 tablespoon (62 grams) white rice flour	
1 teaspoon xanthan gum	
⅓ cup cocoa powder	*3* Stir in the oatmeal, brown sugar, granulated sugar, baking soda, and salt and mix well.
2 cups gluten-free oatmeal	
1 cup firmly packed brown sugar	*4* Pour the melted butter and beaten egg over the mixture and mix with your hands until crumbly. Pat half of this mixture into the prepared pan.
½ cup granulated sugar	
1 teaspoon baking soda	*5* In a large saucepan, combine the unwrapped caramels and milk. Melt over low heat, stirring frequently, until the caramels are melted and the mixture is smooth. Pour over the crumb mixture in the pan.
¼ teaspoon salt	
1¼ cups butter, melted	
1 egg, beaten	
One 14-ounce package caramels, unwrapped	*6* Sprinkle with dark chocolate chips and top with the remaining crumb mixture; pat down gently with your hands.
¼ cup whole milk	
2 cups dark chocolate chips	*7* Bake for 23 to 28 minutes, or until the crust is set and the caramel is bubbling slightly around the edges.
	8 Cool on a wire rack and cut into bars when cool.

Per serving: Calories 223 (From Fat 94); Fat 10g (Saturated 7g); Cholesterol 24mg; Sodium 85mg; Carbohydrate 33g; Dietary Fiber 2g; Protein 2g.

Note: You can substitute other flours or starches for the flours called for; just be sure to use the same weight of the alternate flour. For instance, use 62 grams of sweet rice flour in place of the brown rice flour, not ½ cup minus 2 teaspoons of sweet rice flour, which weighs 72 grams.

Peanut Butter Brownies

Prep time: 20 min • **Cook time:** 40 min • **Yield:** 9 servings

Ingredients	Directions
2 tablespoons plus 1 teaspoon cocoa powder	*1* Preheat the oven to 325 degrees. Spray a 9-x-9-inch baking pan with nonstick cooking spray. Sprinkle with 1 teaspoon cocoa powder, shake the pan to distribute the powder evenly, and knock out the excess. Set the pan aside.
½ cup unsalted butter	
1 cup semisweet chocolate chips	
½ cup packed brown sugar	*2* In a large saucepan, melt the butter with 2 tablespoons cocoa powder and the chocolate chips over low heat, stirring frequently, until smooth. Beat in the brown sugar and granulated sugar and then remove from heat.
½ cup granulated sugar	
2 eggs	
½ cup peanut butter	*3* Add the eggs, one at a time, beating well after each addition. Beat in the peanut butter and then stir in the vanilla.
1½ teaspoons vanilla	
⅓ cup plus 1 tablespoon (44 grams) almond flour	
2 tablespoons (18 grams) sweet rice flour	*4* In a small bowl, combine the almond flour, sweet rice flour, xanthan gum, baking powder, and salt; mix with a wire whisk until the mixture is one color. Stir into the batter.
½ teaspoon xanthan gum	
½ teaspoon baking powder	
¼ teaspoon salt	*5* Spread the batter into the prepared pan and top with peanuts.
½ cup chopped peanuts	
	6 Bake for 30 to 40 minutes, or until a toothpick inserted near the center of the pan comes out almost clean, with a few moist crumbs sticking to it. Cool on a wire rack and then cut into squares to serve.

Per serving: Calories 455 (From Fat 273); Fat 30g (Saturated 12g); Cholesterol 75mg; Sodium 175mg; Carbohydrate 43g; Dietary Fiber 3g; Protein 9g.

Vary It! You can serve these brownies plain or top them with any type of chocolate or peanut butter frosting. For a super easy frosting, melt 1 cup semisweet chocolate chips with ⅓ cup peanut butter until smooth; pour over the brownies and let stand until set. Or make any standard butter cream frosting starting with ¼ cup butter and add ⅓ cup peanut butter. Beat until smooth and frost the cooled brownies.

Granola Bars

Prep time: 20 min, plus chilling time • **Cook time:** 45 min • **Yield:** 60 bars

Ingredients	*Directions*
1 cup unsalted organic butter	*1* In a large saucepan over low heat, melt the butter, brown sugar, honey, and almond butter, stirring until the mixture is smooth with an even texture.
¾ cup packed brown sugar	
½ cup honey	
12 ounces smooth or chunky almond butter	*2* Remove from heat and add the rolled oats. Stir until combined.
5½ cups gluten-free rolled oats	*3* Stir in the eggs, baking soda, salt, and vanilla until well combined.
2 eggs, beaten	
2 teaspoons baking soda	*4* Add the fruits, chopped nuts, coconut, and M&Ms. You can use any combination of any of these ingredients, as long as they add up to 4 cups.
½ teaspoon salt	
1 tablespoon vanilla	
4 cups diced dried fruit, chopped nuts, coconut, and M&M candies	*5* Cover the dough and let it chill overnight to let the oats absorb the eggs, butter, and almond butter.
	6 The next morning, preheat the oven to 300 degrees. Line two cookie sheets with parchment paper. Divide the dough between the cookie sheets and pat into an even layer about ½-inch thick.
	7 Bake for 20 minutes and then rotate the pans and move them around on the racks. Bake 20 minutes longer, until the bars are light golden-brown and set.
	8 Cool completely and cut into bars. Store in an airtight container at room temperature.

Per serving: *Calories 155 (From Fat 85); Fat 10g (Saturated 3g); Cholesterol 16mg; Sodium 71mg; Carbohydrate 16g; Dietary Fiber 1g; Protein 3g.*

Note: These granola bars are delicious as a quick snack or on a road trip. Keep them on your person at all times for when you get hungry but can't find a gluten-free food. Try to find only unsulfured organic fruits for the best flavor, texture, and nutrition. A nice combination is dried tart cherries, dried apricots, unsweetened flaked coconut, and dark chocolate M&Ms.

Honey Oat Bars

Prep time: 25 min • **Cook time:** 35 min • **Yield:** 32 servings

Ingredients

½ cup butter, softened

1 cup packed brown sugar, divided in half

½ cup plus 1 tablespoon plus 1 teaspoon (66 grams) almond flour

⅓ cup minus 1 teaspoon (41 grams) brown rice flour

2 tablespoons (20 grams) potato starch

½ teaspoon xanthan gum

½ cup butter

¼ cup granulated sugar

Pinch salt

½ cup honey

3 eggs

1½ teaspoons vanilla

6 Granola Bars (see page 233), crushed

⅔ cup semisweet chocolate chips

½ cup chopped walnuts

Directions

1 Preheat the oven to 400 degrees. Grease a 13-x-9-inch cake pan with unsalted butter and set aside.

2 In a medium bowl, combine ½ cup softened butter with ½ cup packed brown sugar and mix well.

3 In a small bowl, combine the almond flour, brown rice flour, potato starch, and xanthan gum; mix with a wire whisk until the mixture is one color.

4 Stir the almond flour mixture into the butter mixture to form a dough. Press the dough into the bottom and ½ inch up the sides of the prepared pan. Prick the crust with a fork and bake for 8 to 10 minutes, until light golden-brown. Remove from the oven and cool on a wire rack.

5 Meanwhile, make the filling. In a large pan, melt the butter over medium heat. Add the other ½ cup brown sugar, granulated sugar, and salt and mix well.

6 Add the honey, eggs, and vanilla and beat until combined.

7 Stir in the crushed Granola Bars, semisweet chocolate chips, and walnuts.

8 Pour over the cooled crust and bake for 20 to 30 minutes, or until the filling is set and light golden-brown. Cool completely on a wire rack before cutting into bars.

Per serving: Calories 158 (From Fat 76); Fat 8g (Saturated 3g); Cholesterol 31mg; Sodium 28mg; Carbohydrate 20g; Dietary Fiber 1g; Protein 2g.

Chapter 15

Pies and Pastries

In This Chapter

▶ Discovering a few tricks for making pies and pastries
▶ Baking some sweet pies and tortes

Many experienced cooks and bakers fear pies and pastries. Producing a flaky and light pie crust or a tender pastry may seem difficult, but it isn't — it just takes practice! A light hand with pastry, which is essential when making wheat-based pie crusts and pastries, isn't an issue with gluten-free recipes. That fact alone makes these recipes easier.

In this chapter we offer you recipes for different types of pie crust, ranging from a Mixed Nut Pie Crust you can use to make ice cream pies or custard pies to a Meringue Pie Shell that's naturally gluten-free. Tortes, a Pavlova recipe, and a fabulous recipe for Rugelach round out the chapter. (For classic pie crust recipes, including a Butter Pie Crust, Cookie Pie Crust, and Galette Pie Crust, see Chapter 17.)

Tips for Making Pies and Pastries

When you make wheat flour–based pie crusts and pastries, you must handle them very little to prevent a lot of gluten from developing. Wheat-based pie crusts need to straddle a delicate line between enough gluten development to produce the desirable flaky layers and too much gluten development, which makes the pastry tough. Gluten-free pie crusts and pastries are automatically tender. The trick is to make them flaky.

Here are some tricks for making the best pies and pastries:

- ✔ Keep all the ingredients cold. To make a flaky pie or pastry, the butter or other fat should remain as cold and as solid as possible. Then, when the pastry meets the hot oven, the butter melts quickly and creates steam, which puffs up the structure of the pastry, creating those flaky layers.

- ✔ If you don't use a scale to measure flours and mixes, always measure by spooning the flour or mix lightly into a measuring cup and leveling off the top with the back of a knife. See Chapters 4 and 5 for more info on measuring by weight and volume.

- ✔ Although you can handle this dough without fear of making it tough, try to keep your hands off as much as possible. You don't want to work the fat into the flour mixture so much that it loses its ability to create layers.

- ✔ Xanthan gum and guar gum are usually necessary when making pastries and pie crusts. Gluten provides the critical structure to create flaky layers. Without it, you need something to make the dough pliable. The Rugelach recipe uses gelatin.

- ✔ You can use any type of fat you'd like. Butter adds great flavor to pie crusts and pastries. Solid shortening makes for a tender pastry and works well for most recipes. Lard, that long-vilified fat, is actually pretty good for you as far as fats go. Its fat is mostly monounsaturated (the good kind). Leaf lard makes the flakiest pastry you'll ever eat.

- ✔ It's easiest to roll out pie crust between two sheets of waxed paper or parchment paper. Just tear off two sheets of the paper and rub your work surface with a damp paper towel so the paper doesn't slip around as you work. Sandwich the dough between the paper and start rolling.

- ✔ Roll from the center of the ball of dough out to the edges. Turn the dough around and roll as evenly as you can, making sure there aren't any spots that are thicker or thinner than others. You can get rings to put around your rolling pin that ensure an even thinness.

- ✔ Your crusts will have a better final shape if you chill the dough before rolling it out and then chill the shaped pie crust before filling it and baking. Give those fats a chance to solidify so they can create the layers you want. You can chill the crust in the fridge for at least an hour or put it in the freezer for 10 to 15 minutes.

Delicious Pie and Pastry Recipes

Enjoy these delectable recipes. And after you master pie crust, branch out! Look for pie recipes in other cookbooks and make them with your delicious, gluten-free, flaky, and tender pie crust. Experiment with different flour blends and enjoy the feel of watching dough come to life.

Mixed Nut Pie Crust

Prep time: 15 min, plus chilling time • **Cook time:** 10–15 min • **Yield:** One 9-inch pie crust

Ingredients	*Directions*
¾ **cup finely ground pecans**	*1* In a medium bowl, combine the pecans, almonds, almond meal, and brown sugar and mix well. Stir in the butter until blended.
½ **cup finely ground almonds**	
2 tablespoons almond meal	
1 tablespoon packed brown sugar	*2* Press firmly into the bottom and up the sides of a 9-inch pie pan. Cover and chill in the refrigerator for 1 hour.
¼ **cup butter, melted**	
	3 Preheat the oven to 350 degrees. Bake the pie crust for 10 to 15 minutes, or until set. Cool completely and then fill with any filling.

Per serving: Calories 177 (From Fat 157); Fat 18g (Saturated 5g); Cholesterol 15mg; Sodium 2mg; Carbohydrate 5g; Dietary Fiber 2g; Protein 3g. based on 8 servings.

Note: Fill this crust with any prepared pudding or a no-bake cheesecake filling. You can use any combination of ground nuts; just make sure they're finely ground. And don't skip the chilling step; it helps solidify the crust so the oils in the nuts don't separate.

Choosing pie pans

You can find several types of pie pans on the market. Pans made of metal conduct heat very well, so baked pie crusts brown more quickly and evenly. They don't break if you drop them (although they can dent), and you can put metal pie pans directly into the freezer from the oven. These pans can rust, so make sure you dry them thoroughly.

Glass pie pans hold heat longer, so the crust becomes a deeper brown color. It's also easy to check the doneness of the bottom crust because you can see it through the glass! But you must be careful with glass pans. They'll break if you drop them, and sudden and extreme temperature changes can make the glass explode.

Ceramic pie pans can be decorative and attractive. They also hold heat very well, so the crust becomes brown and crisp. But they can be heavy and also break easily.

Meringue Pie Shell

Prep time: 15 min • **Cook time:** 2 hrs • **Yield:** One 9-inch pie shell

Ingredients

1 tablespoon unsalted butter

1 tablespoon (8 grams) cornstarch

3 egg whites

Pinch salt

½ teaspoon lemon juice

11 tablespoons sugar

1 teaspoon vanilla

Directions

1 Preheat the oven to 275 degrees. Grease a 9-inch pie plate with unsalted butter and dust it with cornstarch. Shake out the excess cornstarch and set the plate aside.

2 In a medium bowl, beat the egg whites with salt and lemon juice until soft peaks form. Gradually add the sugar, 1 tablespoon at a time, until the meringue forms stiff peaks.

3 Beat in the vanilla. Spread the mixture evenly in the prepared pie plate, building up the edges and creating an impression in the center to form a shell.

4 Bake the shell for 1 hour and then turn off the oven and let the shell stand in the closed oven for 1 hour longer. Remove the shell from the oven and cool it completely on a wire rack.

Per serving: Calories 74 (From Fat 0); Fat 0g (Saturated 0g); Cholesterol 0mg; Sodium 38mg; Carbohydrate 17g; Dietary Fiber 0g; Protein 1g. based on 8 servings.

Vary It! You can vary this shell to add more interest to your pies. Add 2 tablespoons of cocoa powder along with the sugar for a chocolate meringue pie shell. Or add a teaspoon of grated lemon or orange peel for a citrus-flavored pie shell. For a mocha pie shell, add the cocoa and ½ teaspoon of instant espresso powder.

Note: Some people may think that this type of recipe in a gluten-free baking book is a "cheat." But meringue pie shells are delicious and easy to make, not to mention fat-free. If you enjoy the texture of light, airy, crisp meringue filled with a smooth and velvety filling, why not enjoy it?

Note: Fill this shell with everything from ice cream to pudding to mousse. It's used in Chocolate Angel Cheesecake Pie (see page 243) too. In fact, the three egg yolks left over from making this pie shell are just what's needed in the Chocolate Angel Cheesecake Pie recipe!

Pear Cranberry Tart

Prep time: 30 min, plus chilling time • **Cook time:** 65 min • **Yield:** 8 servings

Ingredients	*Directions*
½ **recipe Butter Pie Crust (see Chapter 17)**	*1* Prepare the Butter Pie Crust recipe. Press the dough into the bottom and up the sides of a 9-inch tart pan with a removable bottom. Cover and chill for 1 hour or overnight.
1 cup blanched almonds	
⅓ **cup superfine sugar**	
½ **cup organic cane sugar**	*2* Preheat the oven to 350 degrees. Place a piece of foil over the crust and top with pie weights or dried beans to keep the crust from puffing while baking. Bake for 20 minutes. Remove the crust from the oven and remove the foil and pie weights.
2 tablespoons water	
1 cup fresh or frozen cranberries (do not thaw)	
2 large ripe pears	*3* In a food processor, combine the almonds and superfine sugar. Grind until tiny crumbs form. Sprinkle the crumbs into the partially baked crust.
	4 In a small saucepan, combine the cane sugar and water and bring to a boil. Add the cranberries and cook until glazed, about 1 to 2 minutes. Don't cook until the cranberries pop. Set aside while you prepare the pears.
	5 Peel and slice the pears lengthwise into ¼-inch slices.
	6 Place the pears in a pretty pattern onto the almond layer. Drain the cranberries, reserving the glaze. Place the cranberries in the center of the pie and fill in the spaces between the pears. Brush the glaze from the cranberries over the fruit.
	7 Bake for 40 to 45 minutes, or until the pears are tender and the crust is golden-brown. Cool completely on a wire rack. Cut into wedges to serve.

Per serving: *Calories 337 (From Fat 138); Fat 15g (Saturated 4g); Cholesterol 15mg; Sodium 85mg; Carbohydrate 48g; Dietary Fiber 4g; Protein 5g.*

Chocolate Tartlets

Prep time: 30 min, plus chilling time • **Cook time:** 32 min • **Yield:** 24 tartlets

Ingredients	Directions
¼ cup butter, softened	**1** In a large bowl, beat the butter until it's light and fluffy. Add the Cookie Mix and cocoa powder gradually and beat until combined.
1¼ cups Cookie Mix (see Chapter 10)	
¼ cup cocoa powder	**2** Beat in the egg white and vanilla and beat for 1 minute. Scrape the batter onto a large piece of plastic wrap. Wrap up the dough and refrigerate overnight.
1 egg white	
½ teaspoon vanilla	
One 12-ounce package semisweet chocolate chips	**3** When you're ready to bake, preheat the oven to 350 degrees. Lightly spray 24 miniature muffin tins (two pans of 12) with nonstick cooking spray and set aside. Divide the dough into four pieces. Refrigerate the rest of the dough while you work with the first quarter.
1 cup heavy whipping cream	
2 tablespoons butter	
	4 Divide the first quarter of the dough into six pieces. Press one of the pieces into the prepared muffin tins, pressing against the sides and bottom to form a shell. Repeat with the second quarter of dough to fill the muffin tin; cover and refrigerate. Repeat with the remaining dough and then prick all the little shells with a fork.
	5 Bake the first pan for 12 to 15 minutes, checking halfway through and pressing down the dough if it puffs, until the shells are set. Let them cool in the pan for 5 minutes and then move them to wire racks to cool completely. Repeat with the remaining pan.
	6 In a large, microwave-safe bowl, combine the chocolate chips, cream, and butter. Microwave on 50 percent power for 2 minutes; remove the filling from the microwave and stir. Continue microwaving for 1-minute intervals, stirring after each interval, until the chocolate is melted and the mixture is smooth.
	7 Fill each little tartlet shell with the chocolate filling. Cover and refrigerate for 1 to 2 hours before serving.

Per serving: Calories 164 (From Fat 99); Fat 11g (Saturated 7g); Cholesterol 21mg; Sodium 152mg; Carbohydrate 18g; Dietary Fiber 1g; Protein 2g.

Pumpkin Pecan Cheesecake

Prep time: 40 min • **Cook time:** 35–40 min • **Yield:** 12–14 servings

Ingredients	*Directions*
4 ounces Graham Crackers (see Chapter 18), crushed	*1* Preheat the oven to 325 degrees. Butter a 10-inch springform pan and set aside.
⅓ cup plus ½ cup pecan halves	*2* In a food processor, combine the Graham Cracker crumbs and ⅓ cup pecans; process until crumbly. Add the light brown sugar and melted butter and pulse for a few seconds to blend. Place in a prepared pan. Press the mixture onto the bottom of the pan. Refrigerate for 20 minutes.
2 tablespoons light brown sugar	
1 tablespoon unsalted butter, melted	
½ cup firmly packed dark brown sugar	*3* In a small bowl, combine the dark brown sugar, cinnamon, ginger, cloves, and nutmeg.
2 tablespoons ground cinnamon	*4* Place the cream cheese in a large bowl. Beat with a mixer on medium speed until it's smooth and creamy. Gradually add the brown sugar mixture, beating until smooth.
1 teaspoon ground ginger	
¼ teaspoon ground cloves	
½ teaspoon ground nutmeg	*5* Add the eggs, one at a time, beating well after each addition and scraping down the sides of the bowl with a spatula.
16 ounces cream cheese, at room temperature	
3 eggs	*6* Add the pumpkin purée to the cream cheese mixture, beating until smooth.
1 cup pumpkin purée (canned or fresh)	*7* Scrape the batter over the pie crust and smooth the top.
2 tablespoons maple syrup	*8* Cover the cheesecake with ½ cup pecan halves in a circular pattern. Brush the maple syrup over the pecans.
	9 Bake for 35 to 40 minutes, or until just set and a knife inserted near the center comes out clean. Turn off the oven and let the cheesecake stand in the oven until completely cool.
	10 Cover the cheesecake and refrigerate it until ready to serve.

Per serving: Calories 309 (From Fat 198); Fat 22g (Saturated 10g); Cholesterol 100mg; Sodium 150mg; Carbohydrate 25g; Dietary Fiber 2g; Protein 6g.

Lemon Cream Pie

Prep time: 30 min, plus chilling time • **Cook time:** 20 min • **Yield** : 10 servings

Ingredients	Directions
½ cup plus 2 teaspoons (80 grams) **White Flour Mix (See Chapter 10)**	**1** Preheat the oven to 400 degrees. Spray a 9-inch pie plate with nonstick cooking spray.
⅓ cup (38 grams) coconut flour	**2** In a medium bowl, combine the White Flour Mix, coconut flour, Whole-Grain Flour Mix, brown sugar, and coconut and mix well.
¼ cup (34 grams) **Whole-Grain Flour Mix (see Chapter 10)**	
¼ cup packed brown sugar	**3** Add the softened butter and mix with a fork until crumbs form. Place in the prepared pie pan.
½ cup flaked coconut	
½ cup butter, softened	**4** Bake for 12 to 16 minutes, stirring gently every 4 minutes, until the crumbs are an even light golden-brown. Stir again, then let cool for 15 minutes. Press the crumbs into the bottom and up the sides of the pie pan to form a crust. Cool completely.
3 egg yolks	
¾ cup sugar	
½ cup lemon juice	
⅓ cup water	**5** Meanwhile, combine the egg yolks, sugar, lemon juice, water, and cornstarch in a heavy saucepan. Cook over low heat, beating frequently with a wire whisk until the mixture is thickened and smooth, about 3 to 5 minutes.
3 tablespoons (24 grams) cornstarch	
1 teaspoon finely grated lemon peel	
¾ cup white chocolate chips	**6** Remove the mixture from the heat and stir in the lemon peel and chocolate chips until the chips are melted. Let the mixture cool at room temperature for 1 hour.
Two 8-ounce packages cream cheese, softened	
⅔ cup heavy whipping cream	**7** Beat the cream cheese until it's light and fluffy. Gradually add the cooled lemon mixture until smooth, and then spoon into the cooled pie crust.
2 tablespoons powdered sugar	
½ teaspoon vanilla	**8** In a small bowl, beat the cream with powdered sugar and vanilla until stiff peaks form. Spread over the lemon filling. Cover pie and chill for 2 to 3 hours until set.

Per serving: Calories 550 (From Fat 345); Fat 38g (Saturated 24g); Cholesterol 163mg; Sodium 176mg; Carbohydrate 48g (Dietary Fiber 2g); Protein 7g.

Chocolate Angel Cheesecake Pie

Prep time: 45 min, plus chilling time • **Cook time:** 10 min • **Yield:** 8 servings

Ingredients	Directions
1 recipe Meringue Pie Shell (see page 238)	*1* Prepare the Meringue Pie Shell and cool completely.
¼ cup organic cane sugar	*2* In a medium heavy saucepan, combine the cane sugar, brown sugar, and unflavored gelatin and mix with a wire whisk. Stir in the cream, egg yolks, and salt.
⅓ cup packed brown sugar	
1 envelope unflavored gelatin	
½ cup light cream	*3* Place the pan over medium heat and cook, stirring constantly with a wire whisk, until the mixture starts to thicken and the sugar and gelatin completely dissolve, about 6 to 8 minutes. Don't let the mixture boil.
3 egg yolks	
⅛ teaspoon salt	
Two 1-ounce squares bittersweet chocolate, chopped	*4* Remove from the heat and add the chopped chocolate. Beat until the chocolate melts and the mixture is smooth.
Two 8-ounce packages cream cheese, softened	*5* Beat in the cream cheese using an electric mixer until the mixture is smooth and fluffy. Then beat in the vanilla. Chill this mixture in the refrigerator until it's smooth and thick, about 1 hour.
2 teaspoons vanilla	
1 cup heavy whipping cream	*6* In a small bowl, combine the whipping cream, cocoa powder, and powdered sugar. Beat until stiff peaks form.
3 tablespoons cocoa powder	
2 tablespoons powdered sugar	
	7 Using the same beaters, beat the cream cheese mixture until it's light and smooth. Fold in the whipped cream mixture.
	8 Spoon the mixture into the Meringue Pie Shell. Cover and chill for 3 to 4 hours before serving.

Per serving: Calories 537 (From Fat 350); Fat 39g (Saturated 23g); Cholesterol 193mg; Sodium 268mg; Carbohydrate 42g; Dietary Fiber 1g; Protein 9g.

Vary It! You can also serve this filling in graham cracker tartlet shells or in a graham cracker pie shell. It's also delicious layered with cookie crumbs and whipped cream for a parfait.

Pecan Pie

Prep time: 20 min • **Cook time:** 80 min • **Yield:** 8–10 servings

Ingredients	*Directions*
½ recipe Butter Pie Crust (see Chapter 17)	*1* Preheat the oven to 350 degrees.
3 eggs, beaten	*2* Place the Butter Pie Crust into a 9-inch metal pie pan. Line the crust with foil and add pie weights or dried beans to prevent puffing. Prebake the crust for 20 minutes.
¾ cup dark corn syrup	
¼ cup molasses	
1 cup sugar	*3* Remove the crust from the oven and carefully remove the foil and pie weights.
¼ cup butter, melted	
1 teaspoon vanilla	*4* In a large bowl, combine the eggs, corn syrup, molasses, sugar, butter, and vanilla and beat until combined.
2 cups pecan halves	
	5 Stir in the pecans until they're well-coated.
	6 Pour the pecan mixture into the pie crust.
	7 Bake for 55 to 60 minutes, or until a knife inserted 1 inch from the edge of the pie comes out clean.
	8 Cool the pie completely on a wire rack before slicing to serve.

Per serving: Calories 541 (From Fat 245); Fat 27g (Saturated 6g); Cholesterol 95mg; Sodium 155mg; Carbohydrate 74g; Dietary Fiber 3g; Protein 6g.

Note: If you want to take a bit more time and arrange the pecans in pretty concentric circles in the pie crust, reserve a bit of the egg mixture to spoon on the pecans just before the pie goes into the oven. Even the most careful arrangements can get a bit messy.

Decadent Chocolate Torte

Prep time: 20 min, plus chilling time • **Cook time:** 10 min • **Yield:** 16 servings

Ingredients	Directions
1 recipe Chocolate Sheet Cake (see Chapter 16)	*1* Bake and cool the Chocolate Sheet Cake.
8 ounces semisweet chocolate, chopped	*2* Line a 9-inch springform pan with parchment paper and set aside. Cut the cooled cake into 1-inch cubes and place them in a large mixing bowl.
1 ounce unsweetened chocolate, chopped	
8 ounces milk chocolate, chopped	*3* Place all the chocolate in a large, microwave-safe bowl and melt on 30 percent power for 2 minutes; remove and stir. Continue microwaving at 30 percent power for 2-minute intervals, stirring after each interval, until the chocolate is melted and smooth. Set aside.
1¼ cups heavy cream	
¼ cup butter	
	4 Combine the cream and butter in a medium, microwave-safe bowl. Microwave on high for 1 minute; remove and stir. Microwave on high for 1 minute longer, watching carefully in case the mixture boils over, until the butter is melted. Whisk the hot cream mixture into the melted chocolate.
	5 Pour 1¼ cups of the chocolate mixture over the cake cubes and mix with an electric mixer until the texture is even and very thick.
	6 Spoon and spread into the prepared springform pan. Press down on the top. Cover the remaining chocolate mixture and set aside at room temperature.
	7 Cover and chill the torte for 3 to 4 hours until it's cold and set. Run a knife around the sides of the pan and remove the sides.
	8 Pour the remaining chocolate mixture over the cake, spreading evenly to coat. Return the cake to the refrigerator to chill for another 1 to 2 hours before serving. Slice into thin wedges to serve.

Per serving: Calories 498 (From Fat 271); Fat 30g (Saturated 18g); Cholesterol 100mg; Sodium 117mg; Carbohydrate 58g; Dietary Fiber 4g; Protein 6g.

Chocolate Chip Pavlova

Prep time: 35 min • **Cook time:** 2 hrs • **Yield:** 8 servings

Ingredients

7 egg whites

⅛ teaspoon cream of tartar

Pinch salt

1½ cups organic cane sugar

1 tablespoon cornstarch

1 tablespoon raspberry vinegar

1 teaspoon plus 1 teaspoon vanilla

1 cup miniature chocolate chips

1¼ cups heavy whipping cream

3 tablespoons cocoa powder

¼ cup powdered sugar

1 cup raspberries

Directions

1 Preheat the oven to 275 degrees. On parchment paper, place a 9-inch round cake pan; draw a circle around the pan with a pencil. Turn the paper over and place it on a large cookie sheet.

2 Place the egg whites in a large bowl and let stand at room temperature for 20 minutes. Then add the cream of tartar and salt.

3 Beat until foamy, about 3 minutes, and then gradually add the cane sugar, beating until stiff peaks form. Fold in the cornstarch, raspberry vinegar, and 1 teaspoon vanilla, and then fold in the miniature chocolate chips.

4 Place the meringue inside the circle on the parchment paper; spread to form an even layer. Run a spatula around the sides of the meringue to make them straight.

5 Bake for 60 to 65 minutes. Then turn the oven off, crack open the door, and let the meringue sit for another hour.

6 Remove the meringue from the oven and slide it, with the parchment paper, onto a cooling rack; cool completely. Then gently peel the paper off the meringue and place the meringue on a serving plate; cover and store at room temperature.

7 When ready to serve, in a medium bowl, combine the whipping cream, cocoa powder, powdered sugar, and 1 teaspoon vanilla; beat until stiff peaks form. Pile the cream on top of the meringue and top with raspberries. Cut into wedges to serve.

Per serving: Calories 513 (From Fat 186); Fat 21g (Saturated 13g); Cholesterol 51mg; Sodium 85mg; Carbohydrate 81g; Dietary Fiber 3g; Protein 5g.

Rugelach

Prep time: 35 min, plus chilling time • **Cook time:** 10–15 min • **Yield:** 10 servings

Ingredients	*Directions*
1½ cups plus 3 tablespoons (248 grams) White Flour Mix (see Chapter 10)	**1** In a food processor bowl, combine the White Flour Mix, Whole-Grain Flour Mix, baking powder, sugar, salt, and gelatin; process until well blended.
½ cup plus 1 tablespoon plus 2 teaspoons (83 grams) Whole-Grain Flour Mix (see Chapter 10)	**2** With the processor running, drop the butter, cream cheese cubes, and vanilla through the intake chute. Let the dough work until it gathers into a squashy mass.
¼ teaspoon baking powder	**3** Turn off the processor, turn the dough over, and work it for another couple of minutes to ensure that the fat is incorporated into the flour mixture.
3 tablespoons sugar	
¼ teaspoon salt	
1 teaspoon gelatin powder	**4** Shape the dough into three equal balls. Wrap them in plastic wrap and chill them in the refrigerator for 30 minutes. While the dough chills, make the Rugelach Filling by combining all ingredients in a small bowl. Use 1 teaspoon per pastry.
4 tablespoons butter, cut into pieces	
8 ounces cream cheese, cut into 1-inch cubes	
1 teaspoon vanilla	**5** Take the dough out of the fridge and let it stand for 15 minutes. Preheat the oven to 425 degrees.
Rugelach Filling:	
½ cup finely chopped walnuts	**6** Roll out each ball into a 10-inch circle. Cut each into 8 to 12 pie-shaped pieces. Place 1 teaspoon of the filling in a circle ½ inch from the outer round edge of each pie-shaped piece of dough.
1 tablespoon sugar	
1 teaspoon cinnamon	**7** Roll the dough over the filling, rolling to the narrow tip. The filling may spill out a tiny bit, but those crispy parts are delicious.
1 pinch nutmeg	
	8 Place each Rugelach on a cookie sheet and bake for 10 to 15 minutes, until golden-brown. Cool them on the cookie sheet for 3 minutes and then move them to a wire rack to cool completely.

Per serving: Calories 292 (From Fat 150); Fat 17g (Saturated 8g); Cholesterol 37mg; Sodium 137mg; Carbohydrate 35g; Dietary Fiber 1g; Protein 4g.

Chapter 16

Cake and Frosting Recipes

In This Chapter

▶ Tips for making great cakes and frostings

▶ Checking out some cake and frosting recipes

A cake is a necessity for many celebrations. What would a birthday be without a layer cake, lavishly frosted and brimming with candles? People who must avoid gluten may think that they can only enjoy ice cream cakes from now on. Not with these recipes!

In this chapter we take a look at how to make the best cakes and frost them beautifully. We feature layer cakes, cupcakes, and Bundt cakes, with flavors ranging from the classic vanilla cake to a decadent carrot cupcake that's vegan!

So get out your mixer, mixing bowls, and cake pans and discover how easy fulfilling every cake craving can be with these delicious gluten-free recipes.

Making the Best Cakes and Frostings

Cake making and frosting is definitely an art and a science. These recipes are carefully calibrated for the best results: light and fluffy cakes (well, except for the Flourless Chocolate Cake) with a tender, even crumb. Follow the directions carefully, measure carefully, and mix and bake the recipes as directed.

Here are some tips for making the best cakes:

- Always grease the pans well. If you miss a spot, the cake will likely stick to that spot and may tear or break when it comes out of the pan. That's frustrating! Some recipes call for greasing and flouring cake pans. Put a teaspoon of any gluten-free flour in a greased pan and shake and tap the pan until the flour coats the entire surface. Tap out any excess flour into the sink.

- If you don't use a scale to measure flours and mixes, always measure by spooning the flour or mix lightly into a measuring cup and leveling off the top with the back of a knife. See Chapters 4 and 5 for more info on measuring by weight and volume.

- Cake doneness tests are very important. Check doneness by lightly touching the cake surface with your finger. If it springs back, it's done. Another doneness test is observing that the cake is pulling away from the pan sides. Some people think the cake is overbaked when this happens, but we think it's done — pulling away from the pan sides indicates that the structure is fully set.

- Cool sheet cakes in the pan. Layer cakes and Bundt cakes are often cooled in the pan for a few minutes and then turned out onto cooling racks to cool completely. The Angel Food Cake is cooled upside down because its structure is so delicate that it must be "stretched" as it cools so it doesn't collapse.

- To frost layer cakes, place one layer on the serving plate, rounded side down. Frost with about 1 cup of frosting. Place the second layer on the frosting, rounded side up. Frost the top of the cake and then gently ease the frosting over the cake's sides. Let the cake stand until the frosting sets before storing.

Delicious Cake and Frosting Recipes

Have fun with these delectable cakes, and don't be afraid to experiment (a little bit!) when you master a recipe. You can substitute plain water for the coffee in the Mocha Fudge Cake recipe for a fudge cake. Add some orange zest to Vanilla Cupcakes and frost with a buttercream frosting flavored with orange juice. Substitute apples for the pears in Pear Almond Yogurt Cake.

Sour Cream Almond Bundt Cake

Prep time: 30 min • **Cook time:** 60 min • **Yield:** 16 servings

Ingredients	*Directions*
2 tablespoons plus 4 teaspoons plus ¼ cup unsalted butter, melted	*1* Preheat the oven to 350 degrees. Generously grease a 12-inch Bundt pan with 2 tablespoons melted unsalted butter and sprinkle with the granulated sugar; set aside.
¼ cup granulated sugar	
¼ cup finely ground almonds	*2* In a small bowl, combine the ground almonds, sweet rice flour, ¼ cup packed brown sugar, and cinnamon. Mix in 4 teaspoons melted butter until crumbly; set aside.
¼ cup (37 grams) sweet rice flour	
¼ cup plus ½ cup packed brown sugar	
½ teaspoon ground cinnamon	*3* In a medium bowl, combine the White Flour Mix, Whole-Grain Flour Mix, ½ cup brown sugar, baking powder, baking soda, and salt and mix until the mixture is one color.
2 cups plus 1 tablespoon (307 grams) White Flour Mix (see Chapter 10)	
1¼ cups minus 1 teaspoon (165 grams) Whole-Grain Flour Mix (see Chapter 10)	*4* In a large bowl, beat the eggs, sour cream, ¼ cup melted butter, and almond extract until light and fluffy.
1 tablespoon baking powder	*5* Add the flour mixture and beat for 1 minute.
1 teaspoon baking soda	
½ teaspoon salt	*6* Pour the batter into the prepared Bundt pan. Sprinkle with the ground almond mixture and sliced almonds (if desired).
4 eggs	
1 cup organic sour cream	*7* Place on the bottom rack of the oven and bake for 30 minutes. Then turn the pan 180 degrees to even out the baking and bake for 25 to 35 minutes longer, until the cake is golden-brown and the top springs back when lightly touched.
2 teaspoons almond extract	
⅓ cup sliced almonds (optional)	
	8 Let the cake cool in the pan for 5 minutes and then gently remove it from the pan and cool it completely on a wire rack.

Per serving: *Calories 249 (From Fat 87); Fat 10g (Saturated 5g); Cholesterol 71mg; Sodium 251mg; Carbohydrate 39g; Dietary Fiber 1g; Protein 4g.*

Yellow Butter Cake

Prep time: 20 min • **Cook time:** 35–38 min • **Yield:** One 9-inch layer cake

Ingredients	*Directions*
1 cup unsalted butter, softened	*1* Preheat the oven to 350 degrees. Line two 9-inch cake pans with a circle of parchment paper and set aside.
2¼ cups sugar	
4 egg yolks	*2* In a large bowl, combine the butter and sugar and beat until fluffy. Add the egg yolks and vanilla and beat again.
1½ teaspoons vanilla	
4 egg whites	*3* In a medium bowl, beat the egg whites with ⅛ teaspoon salt until they're light and fluffy but not dry; set aside.
⅛ teaspoon plus ⅛ teaspoon salt	
1¾ cups plus 3 tablespoons (284 grams) White Flour Mix (see Chapter 10)	*4* In a large bowl, combine the White Flour Mix, Whole-Grain Flour Mix, baking powder, and ⅛ teaspoon salt. Mix until the mixture is a single color.
¾ cup plus 1 tablespoon (108 grams) Whole-Grain Flour Mix (see Chapter 10)	*5* Add half the flour mixture to the butter mixture and beat until combined. Add half the milk to the butter mixture and beat until combined. Repeat with the remaining flour mixture and milk.
2 teaspoons baking powder	
1 cup milk	
	6 Stir ⅓ of the egg white mixture into the batter to lighten it. Then gently fold in the remaining beaten egg whites.
	7 Divide the batter into the prepared pans. Tap the pans gently on a counter to remove larger air bubbles.
	8 Bake for 35 to 38 minutes, or until the cake springs back when lightly touched in the center and has started to pull away from the pan's edges.
	9 Let the cakes cool in the pan for 5 minutes and then turn them out onto a wire rack to finish cooling.

Per serving: Calories 398 (From Fat 193); Fat 21g (Saturated 13g); Cholesterol 137mg; Sodium 174mg; Carbohydrate 49g; Dietary Fiber 1g; Protein 5g.

Mocha Fudge Cake

Prep time: 40 min • **Cook time:** 55 min • **Yield:** 8 servings

Ingredients	*Directions*
1 large baking potato, peeled and chopped	*1* Preheat the oven to 350 degrees. Spray a 9-inch cake pan with nonstick cooking spray and set aside.
4 ounces dark chocolate, chopped	*2* Place the chopped potato into a large saucepan and cover it with cold water. Bring to a boil over high heat. Reduce the heat to low and cook until the potato is soft, about 18 to 22 minutes. Reserve 3 tablespoons of the cooking water; drain off the remaining water.
2 teaspoons instant coffee granules	
1 egg	
¾ cup sugar	
⅓ cup unsweetened applesauce	*3* Mash the potato in the saucepan until it's smooth and then add the chopped chocolate and instant coffee granules. Cover the pan and let the chocolate melt. Stir gently to blend and let cool.
1 teaspoon vanilla	
⅓ cup minus 1 teaspoon (42 grams) Whole-Grain Flour Mix (see Chapter 10)	*4* Beat in the egg, sugar, applesauce, and vanilla until smooth.
¼ cup (36 grams) White Flour Mix (see Chapter 10)	*5* In a small bowl, combine the Whole-Grain Flour Mix, White Flour mix, baking soda, and salt. Stir with a wire whisk until the mixture is all one color. Stir into the potato mixture.
½ teaspoon baking soda	
¼ teaspoon salt	
	6 Pour the batter into a prepared pan. Bake for 33 to 35 minutes, or until a wooden toothpick inserted into the center of the cake comes out clean.
	7 Cool in the pan for 10 minutes and then invert the cake onto a cooling rack. Remove from the pan and let the cake cool completely.

Per serving: Calories 162 (From Fat 49); Fat 6g (Saturated 3g); Cholesterol 28mg; Sodium 161mg; Carbohydrate 27g; Dietary Fiber 2g; Protein 2g.

Note: When you want a moist, fudgy cake and don't want to settle for something dry and unsatisfying, try this surprising cake. The mashed potato keeps the cake fresh and moist for days — if it lasts that long! You can frost this cake with any of the frostings from this chapter.

Vegan Carrot Cupcakes

Prep time: 15 min • **Cook time:** 25–28 min • **Yield:** 12 cupcakes

Ingredients	*Directions*
2 large carrots, grated	*1* Preheat the oven to 350 degrees. Grease 12 muffin tins or line them with paper liners.
1-inch piece fresh ginger root, grated	
¼ cup light olive oil	*2* In a medium bowl, combine the carrots, ginger root, olive oil, vanilla, applesauce, and raisins and mix well.
2 teaspoons vanilla	
1⅓ cups applesauce	*3* In a large bowl, combine the Whole-Grain Flour Mix, White Flour Mix, brown sugar, granulated sugar, baking powder, baking soda, salt, and cinnamon. Stir with a wire whisk until the mixture is one color.
½ cup raisins	
1½ cups minus 1 teaspoon (200 grams) Whole-Grain Flour Mix (see Chapter 10)	
¾ cup plus 1 tablespoon (120 grams) White Flour Mix (see Chapter 10)	*4* Add the wet ingredients to the dry ingredients and stir for 1 minute. Stir in the coconut.
⅓ cup packed brown sugar	*5* Fill the prepared muffin tins ½ full of batter.
⅓ cup granulated sugar	
1 tablespoon baking powder	*6* Bake for 25 to 28 minutes, or until the cupcakes begin to pull away from the sides of the pan. Let them cool completely in the muffin tins.
1 teaspoon baking soda	
½ teaspoon salt	
2 tablespoons ground cinnamon	
¾ cup unsweetened shredded coconut	

Per serving: Calories 254 (From Fat 79); Fat 9g (Saturated 4g); Cholesterol 0mg; Sodium 308mg; Carbohydrate 44g; Dietary Fiber 3g; Protein 2g.

Note: These cupcakes are tasty as is, but for a truly decadent treat, frost them with a vegan cream cheese frosting. Just substitute vegan cream cheese and margarine for the cream cheese and butter in any cream cheese frosting recipe, and don't beat the mixture more than 30 seconds.

Flourless Chocolate Cake

Prep time: 25 min • **Cook time:** 60 min • **Yield:** 16 servings

Ingredients	*Directions*
Two 1-ounce squares unsweetened chocolate, chopped	*1* Preheat the oven to 325 degrees. Grease a 10-inch springform pan with unsalted butter and line the bottom with parchment paper. Grease the parchment paper with unsalted butter. Wrap the outside of the pan with a large single sheet of heavy-duty foil (to prevent leaks) and set aside.
Two 1-ounce squares semisweet chocolate, chopped	
One 12-ounce bag dark chocolate chips	*2* Place the chocolate in a medium, microwave-safe bowl. Add the water, butter, and espresso powder. Microwave on high for 1 minute and then remove and stir. Continue microwaving for 1-minute intervals, stirring after each interval, until the mixture is melted and smooth, about 2 to 3 minutes.
½ cup water	
1 cup butter, cut into pieces	
1 teaspoon espresso powder	
½ cup packed brown sugar	*3* Beat in the sugars and cocoa powder and then let cool for 15 minutes.
⅓ cup granulated sugar	
¼ cup cocoa powder	
6 eggs	*4* Beat in the eggs, one at a time, beating well after each addition. Stir in the vanilla and ground white chocolate chips.
1 tablespoon vanilla	
½ cup white chocolate chips, finely ground	
Glaze:	*5* Pour into the prepared pan. Bake for 50 to 60 minutes, or until a thin crust forms on the top and the cake is just barely firm in the center.
1 cup milk chocolate chips	
3 tablespoons butter	*6* Remove the cake from the oven and let it cool on a wire rack for 15 minutes. Run a knife around the sides and invert onto a serving plate. Remove pan sides and pan bottom. Cool completely.
2 tablespoons honey	
1 teaspoon vanilla	
	7 To glaze, combine the milk chocolate chips, butter, and honey in a small saucepan over low heat. Cook and stir until smooth. Remove from the heat and stir in the vanilla; let cool for 15 minutes. Stir and pour carefully over the cake.

Per serving: Calories 417 (From Fat 264); Fat 29g (Saturated 18g); Cholesterol 120mg; Sodium 44mg; Carbohydrate 40g; Dietary Fiber 2g; Protein 4g.

Pear Almond Yogurt Cake

Prep time: 20 min • **Cook time:** 40 min • **Yield:** 10 servings

Ingredients	*Directions*
3 eggs	*1* Preheat the oven to 350 degrees. Spray a round, 10-inch, springform pan with nonstick cooking spray and set aside.
One 6-ounce container plain Greek yogurt	
⅓ cup light olive oil	*2* In a large bowl, combine the eggs, yogurt, oil, sugar, almond extract, lemon juice, and lemon peel and whisk until combined. Add the chopped pears and stir to combine.
⅔ cup sugar	
1 teaspoon almond extract	
1 tablespoon fresh lemon juice	*3* In a small bowl, sift the Whole-Grain Flour Mix, White Flour Mix, baking powder, baking soda, cardamom, and salt. Stir in the sliced almonds.
1 teaspoon grated lemon peel	
1 large pear, peeled, cored, and finely chopped	
1¼ cups minus 1 teaspoon (165 grams) Whole-Grain Flour Mix (see Chapter 10)	*4* Add the dry ingredients to the wet ingredients and stir with a large spoon just until well blended.
⅓ cup plus 1 tablespoon plus 1 teaspoon (61 grams) White Flour Mix (see Chapter 10)	*5* Pour the batter into the prepared pan and sprinkle with the raw sugar crystals. Bake for 35 to 48 minutes, until a toothpick inserted into the center comes out clean.
1½ teaspoons baking powder	
½ teaspoon baking soda	*6* Let the cake cool on a wire rack for 10 minutes and then run a knife around the edge of the pan. Carefully remove the pan sides; cool the cake completely before serving.
½ teaspoon ground cardamom	
¼ teaspoon salt	
½ cup sliced almonds	
2 teaspoons coarse raw sugar crystals	

Per serving: Calories 270 (From Fat 106); Fat 12g (Saturated 2g); Cholesterol 65mg; Sodium 146mg; Carbohydrate 37g; Dietary Fiber 2g; Protein 6g.

Note: This cake is wonderful served with a side of frozen yogurt or softly whipped cream. You can also drizzle it with a thin icing by mixing ½ cup gluten-free powdered sugar with 2 tablespoons almond milk. Drizzle over the cooled cake.

Vanilla Cupcakes

Prep time: 25 min • **Cook time:** 35–50 min • **Yield:** 6 servings

Ingredients	*Directions*
1 batch Cake Mix (see Chapter 10)	**1** Let the Cake Mix come to room temperature if it was frozen.
2 eggs, separated	**2** Preheat the oven to 350 degrees. Grease a 9-inch round cake pan with 1 tablespoon unsalted butter or line six muffin cups with paper liners; set aside.
½ cup milk	
1 teaspoon vanilla	**3** In a large mixer bowl, place the egg yolks, milk, vanilla, and Cake Mix. Beat for 3 minutes.
Pinch salt	
	4 In a small bowl, beat the egg whites until soft peaks form. Add the salt and beat until stiff peaks form.
	5 Fold the egg white mixture into the batter gently. Pour the batter into the prepared pan or muffin cups.
	6 Bake the cupcakes for 35 to 40 minutes, until they're golden-brown and set. Bake the cake layer for 48 to 50 minutes, or until the edges pull away from the sides of the pan and a toothpick inserted in the center comes out clean.
	7 Cool the cake in the pan for 5 minutes and then turn it out onto a wire rack to cool completely. Cool the cupcakes in the pan for 5 minutes and then remove them to a wire rack to cool completely. Store the cake in the fridge for up to four days.

Per serving: Calories 250 (From Fat 107); Fat 12g (Saturated 7g); Cholesterol 99mg; Sodium 101mg; Carbohydrate 34g; Dietary Fiber 0g; Protein 4g.

Tip: If you're going to store the cupcakes for a few days, add a spoonful of cherry or raspberry jam to each cupcake before you bake it. This helps keep the cupcakes moist a bit longer. The jam will drop down to the bottom, but that's okay.

Note: You can frost these cupcakes any way you'd like. For transferring them to school, individual cupcake holders are great.

Note: You can double this recipe to make a 9-inch layer cake or 12 cupcakes.

Clementine Cake

Prep time: 40 min • **Cook time:** 1 hr • **Yield:** 8 servings

Ingredients	*Directions*
3 clementines, cut into pieces	*1* Place the clementines, peel and all, in a saucepan and add water to cover them. Cook them over medium heat until they're tender, about 25 to 30 minutes. They're done when the peel is all the same color with no area of white. Let the water evaporate.
½ cup butter, softened	
4 eggs	
1 cup sugar	
1 cup minus 2 teaspoons (142 grams) White Flour Mix (see Chapter 10)	*2* Remove all the seeds from the clementines. Place the fruit in a food processor and process until very smooth and uniform.
½ cup blanched almond meal	*3* Measure out 1 cup of the clementine purée. Add the butter to the clementine mixture and let melt for 5 minutes.
1½ teaspoons baking powder	
¼ teaspoon salt	
	4 Preheat the oven to 350 degrees. Grease and flour a 10-inch springform pan.
	5 In a large bowl, beat the eggs at medium-high speed until they're thick and lemon-colored. Add the sugar, 2 tablespoons at a time, beating constantly. Beat for 5 minutes.
	6 Blend in half the White Flour Mix and the almond meal; beat for 1 minute.
	7 Add half the clementine and butter mixture and beat for 1 minute.

8 Repeat Steps 6 and 7, adding the baking powder and salt with the second addition of White Flour Mix.

9 Pour the cake mix into the prepared pan. Bake for 35 to 38 minutes, until the cake is set and a knife inserted just off center comes out clean.

10 Cool the cake completely on a wire rack and then run a knife around the edges. Remove the sides and serve.

Per serving: Calories 305 (From Fat 126); Fat 14g (Saturated 8g); Cholesterol 137mg; Sodium 178mg; Carbohydrate 44g; Dietary Fiber 1g; Protein 4g.

Note: Top this cake with whipped cream sweetened with a bit of powdered sugar, or frost it with a butter cream icing made with tangerine juice instead of milk.

Some cake topping and decoration ideas

You don't have to frost a cake! Sometimes a cake is good unfrosted, and an unfrosted square of cake is certainly easier to pack in a lunchbox. But if you don't want to make a frosting and don't want to serve a plain cake, there are easy ways to decorate your creation.

Put a couple of tablespoons of powdered sugar in a small sieve and shake it over the cake to decorate it. If you'd like, place a paper doily or stencil on the cake before you add the powdered sugar. Then remove the doily or stencil to reveal a pretty pattern.

A glaze is simply a thin frosting. Just combine a cup of powdered sugar with 1 to 2 tablespoons of orange juice, milk, or water. Stir until blended, and add ½ teaspoon vanilla or another extract such as orange extract. Spoon over the cake and spread into a thin layer.

Melted chocolate makes an excellent cake topping. Place 1 cup of semisweet chocolate chips in a microwave-safe, glass measuring cup. Microwave on high for 1 minute; remove and stir. Microwave for 1 to 2 minutes longer, stirring after each minute, until the chocolate is melted and smooth. Drizzle over the cake using a fork or the tip of a spoon. You can also put the chocolate into a pastry bag and pipe it over the cake.

Angel Food Cake

Prep time: 30 min • **Cook time:** 55 min • **Yield:** 10 servings

Ingredients	*Directions*
¼ cup (29 grams) tapioca flour	**1** Preheat the oven to 325 degrees.
¼ cup (40 grams) potato starch	
3 tablespoons (29 grams) sweet rice flour	**2** In a medium bowl, combine the tapioca starch, potato starch, sweet rice flour, cornstarch, xanthan gum, ⅓ cup granulated sugar, and powdered sugar. Mix well and set aside.
2 tablespoons (16 grams) cornstarch	
½ teaspoon xanthan gum	**3** In a large mixer bowl, combine the egg whites, cream of tartar, and salt. Start beating at low speed until foamy and then turn the mixer to high speed.
1 cup plus ⅓ cup granulated sugar	
3 tablespoons powdered sugar	**4** Gradually beat in 1 cup granulated sugar, 2 tablespoons at a time, beating until stiff peaks form.
13 egg whites, room temperature	**5** Beat in the vanilla and lemon rind.
¼ teaspoon cream of tartar	
⅛ teaspoon salt	**6** Carefully fold in half the flour mixture, trying to keep as much volume as possible. Then fold in the remaining flour mixture.
2 teaspoons vanilla	
2 teaspoons grated lemon rind	**7** Spoon the batter onto an ungreased 10-inch tube pan with a removable bottom.

8 Bake for 50 to 60 minutes, or until the cake is golden-brown and it springs back when lightly touched with a finger.

9 Cool the cake upside down on a wire rack.

10 To serve, run a sharp knife around the sides of the pan, both the outside and around the inner tube. Remove the outside ring of the pan. Then cut along the bottom of the pan, underneath the cake, and remove the cake. Store covered at room temperature.

Per serving: Calories 158 (From Fat 0); Fat 0g (Saturated 0g); Cholesterol 0mg; Sodium 30mg; Carbohydrate 39g; Dietary Fiber 0g; Protein 0g.

Note: Eggs separate more easily when they're cold, so separate the eggs right out of the fridge. Then let the eggs stand at room temperature for 30 to 45 minutes so they warm up before you start beating.

How to frost a cake

Frosting a cake takes some practice and skill, but it's not too difficult. To frost a sheet cake, just spoon or pour the frosting over the cake while it's in the pan. Use an *offset spatula* (the type with a bend in the blade) and spread the frosting evenly over the cake. You can use the tip of the spatula to make swirls and tips in the frosting.

To frost a layer cake, make sure the cake layers are completely cool. Tear off four 6-inch long pieces of waxed paper and place them on the cake stand or serving plate so there's a 5-inch empty square in the center. After you frost the cake, you'll gently pull these strips out so the cake stand stays clean.

Place one cake layer, top side down, on the waxed paper strips. The flat side of the cake will be on top. Place about one cup of the frosting in the center of the cake. Spread gently, just to the edges of the cake. Then place the second layer, top side up, on the frosting and press gently so the layers stick together. Place about a cup of frosting on the top of the cake and gently spread. Using an offset spatula (to help keep your fingers out of the frosting), scoop up some frosting and gently spread it on the sides of the cake. If frosting is left over, just pile it on! Or you can spread some frosting between gluten-free graham crackers (see Chapter 16) for a quick treat.

Angel food cakes are usually frosted with a glaze. Just pour the glaze over the cake. The glaze consistency should be fairly thin so it runs down evenly over the cake. You may need to use a spatula to spread the glaze evenly over the top. Let the glaze run down the sides of the cake. You frost Bundt cakes the same way.

Chocolate Sheet Cake

Prep time: 28 min • **Cook time:** 45 min • **Yield:** 16 servings

Ingredients	Directions
8 ounces 74% dark chocolate, chopped	**1** Preheat the oven to 350 degrees. Grease a 9-x-13-inch cake pan and set aside.
¾ cup cocoa powder	
1 cup minus 2 teaspoons (142 grams) White Flour Mix (see Chapter 10)	**2** In the top of a double boiler, melt the dark chocolate, stirring frequently, until smooth, about 4 to 6 minutes. Remove from the heat and cool to room temperature.
⅓ cup minus 1 teaspoon (42 grams) Whole-Grain Flour Mix (see Chapter 10)	**3** In a medium bowl, combine the cocoa powder, White Flour Mix, Whole-Grain Flour Mix, baking soda, baking powder, and salt. Stir until the mixture is one color and set aside.
½ teaspoon baking soda	
¼ teaspoon baking powder	
¼ teaspoon salt	**4** In a large mixer bowl, beat the butter until it's light and fluffy. Add the sugar gradually, beating constantly.
12 tablespoons unsalted butter, softened	
1½ cups sugar	**5** Add the eggs, one at a time, beating well after each addition until the egg is completely incorporated, about 2 to 3 minutes.
4 eggs	
1 teaspoon vanilla	**6** Add the vanilla.
1¼ cups sour cream	
	7 Add half the sour cream and beat well; then add half the flour mixture and beat well. Repeat.
	8 Fold in the melted and cooled chocolate.
	9 Pour the batter into the prepared pan, spreading evenly into the corners.
	10 Bake for 34 to 40 minutes, or until the center of the cake springs back when lightly touched. Cool completely on a wire rack.

Per serving: Calories 329 (From Fat 169); Fat 19g (Saturated 11g); Cholesterol 85mg; Sodium 110mg; Carbohydrate 40g; Dietary Fiber 2g; Protein 4g.

Cream Cheese Frosting

Prep time: 15 min • **Yield:** 8 servings

Ingredients	*Directions*
¼ cup unsalted butter, softened	*1* In a medium bowl, beat the butter until it's light and fluffy.
1¾ cups powdered sugar	
4 ounces cream cheese, softened	*2* Add the powdered sugar in three parts, beating well after each addition until fluffy.
2 tablespoons milk	
½ teaspoon vanilla	*3* Beat in the cream cheese until smooth and combined.
	4 Add the milk and vanilla; beat well until smooth and creamy. Use immediately or cover and refrigerate up to two days.

Per serving: Calories 205 (From Fat 97); Fat 11g (Saturated 7g); Cholesterol 31mg; Sodium 45mg; Carbohydrate 27g; Dietary Fiber 0g; Protein 1g.

Note: You can easily double this recipe to fill and frost an 8-inch layer cake or a 13-x-9-inch sheet cake. You may need to add more powdered sugar to reach the desired spreading consistency.

Note: Most food experts say that you should refrigerate any cakes or cookies that have cream cheese frosting because it's a perishable product.

Mocha Frosting

Prep time: 10 min • **Yield:** 9 servings

Ingredients	*Directions*
1 tablespoon hot water	*1* In a small bowl, combine the hot water and instant espresso powder and mix until dissolved.
2 teaspoons instant espresso powder	
½ cup (1 stick) unsalted butter, softened	*2* In a large bowl, beat the butter until it's light and fluffy. Gradually add the powdered sugar, beating well after each addition.
1 pound (3¾ cups) powdered sugar	
¼ cup cocoa powder	*3* Beat in the cocoa powder and espresso. The mixture will be very thick at this point.
4 to 5 tablespoons milk	
	4 Gradually add the milk, beating until the frosting is of desired consistency. Use to fill and frost one 9-inch layer cake.

Per 1 tablespoon serving: Calories 55 (From Fat 18); Fat 2g (Saturated 1g); Cholesterol 5mg; Sodium 1mg; Carbohydrate 10g; Dietary Fiber 0g; Protein 0g.

Note: The flavor of this frosting develops after it stands for a while. Make the frosting just after you put the cake in the oven, and let the frosting stand at room temperature, covered, while the cake bakes and cools. Beat it again just before spreading; you may need to add a little more milk, too.

Note: If you have leftover frosting, place dollops on a cookie sheet and freeze them until firm. Roll them into balls for truffles. They can be refrozen and then dipped into melted chocolate.

Vary It! You can use brewed espresso in this frosting recipe. Just substitute ¼ cup brewed espresso for the hot water, espresso powder, and milk. But the espresso powder does provide a stronger coffee flavor. A good brand is Medaglia D'Oro, available on Amazon.com.

Creamy Chocolate Frosting

Prep time: 20 min • **Cook time:** 3–5 min • **Yield:** 8 servings

Ingredients	Directions
2 tablespoons coconut oil	*1* In a large saucepan, combine the coconut oil, butter, and chocolate chips. Melt over low heat until smooth, stirring frequently, about 3 to 5 minutes.
½ cup butter	
1 cup semisweet chocolate chips	*2* Remove from the heat and beat in the cocoa powder and salt. Transfer the mixture to a large bowl.
6 tablespoons cocoa powder	
Pinch salt	*3* In a small bowl, combine the heavy cream, sour cream, and vanilla; whisk to combine.
¼ cup heavy cream	
⅓ cup sour cream	*4* Alternately add the powdered sugar and cream mixture to the melted chocolate mixture, beating well after each addition. You may need to add more heavy cream or more powdered sugar for desired spreading consistency. This recipe fills and frosts one 9-inch layer cake.
2 teaspoons vanilla	
3½ cups sifted powdered sugar	

Per 1 tablespoon serving: Calories 82 (From Fat 40); Fat 4g (Saturated 3g); Cholesterol 8mg; Sodium 5mg; Carbohydrate 11g; Dietary Fiber 0g; Protein 0g.

Note: Coconut oil is solid at room temperature; in fact, it's so solid that it's difficult to combine with the butter unless both are melted together. It gives this frosting a satiny texture. You can add more cocoa powder if you like a deeper chocolate taste.

Vegan Cream Cheese Frosting

Prep time: 10 min • **Yield:** 6 servings

Ingredients	Directions
8 tablespoons Tofutti cream cheese 8 tablespoons Earth Balance Buttery Spread ½ cup powdered sugar ¼ teaspoon almond extract	*1* Place all the ingredients in a medium bowl. Using a spoon, beat until combined. Don't use a mixer or the frosting will break apart and become oily.

Per 1 tablespoon serving: Calories 170 (From Fat 135); Fat 15g (Saturated 6g); Cholesterol 0mg; Sodium 188mg; Carbohydrate 8g; Dietary Fiber 0g; Protein 1g.

Maple Frosting

Prep time: 10 min • **Yield:** 4 servings

Ingredients	Directions
½ cup maple syrup 2 tablespoons gluten-free meringue powder ¼ teaspoon vanilla	*1* Combine all the ingredients in a medium bowl. *2* Beat with a mixer for 7 to 8 minutes, or until the frosting is fluffy and has the texture of marshmallow crème. Spread immediately on cake or cupcakes.

Per 1 tablespoon serving: Calories 30 (From Fat 0); Fat 0g (Saturated 0g); Cholesterol 0mg; Sodium 8mg; Carbohydrate 7g; Dietary Fiber 0g; Protein 0g.

Note: This is a wholesome variation on the classic seven-minute cooked frosting. Using prepared meringue powder means that you don't have to worry about raw eggs.

Note: This recipe is gluten-free, casein-free, and refined sugar–free. Wilton's Meringue Powder is gluten-free.

Buttercream Frosting

Prep time: 10 min • **Yield:** 8 servings

Ingredients	Directions
1 cup butter, softened 3½ cups gluten-free powdered sugar 2 tablespoons gluten-free meringue powder 2 teaspoons vanilla ⅛ teaspoon salt 4 to 6 tablespoons light cream	*1* In a large bowl, beat the butter until it's creamy. Gradually add 2 cups of the powdered sugar and the meringue powder, beating until fluffy. *2* Add the vanilla and salt and beat well. *3* Alternately add the remaining powdered sugar and the light cream. You may need to add more powdered sugar or more light cream for desired spreading consistency. *4* Beat the frosting at high speed until light and fluffy. This recipe will fill and frost a 9-inch layer cake or 24 cupcakes.

Per 1 tablespoon serving: Calories 107 (From Fat 55); Fat 6g (Saturated 4g); Cholesterol 17mg; Sodium 15mg; Carbohydrate 13g; Dietary Fiber 0g; Protein 0g.

Note: The meringue powder adds some body to this frosting recipe and makes it fluffier.

Vary It! To make this chocolate frosting, add ⅓ cup sifted cocoa powder. Increase the light cream to 5 to 7 tablespoons. For a mint frosting, add ½ teaspoon mint extract, omit the vanilla, and add 2 to 3 drops gluten-free green food coloring. For an orange frosting, add 2 teaspoons grated orange peel and substitute 2 tablespoons of orange juice for 2 tablespoons of the cream.

Part IV

Savory Gluten-Free Baking Recipes

The 5th Wave   By Rich Tennant

BAILIFF BAKER

All rise.

In this part . . .

Yes, there are savory baked goods! You can make whole-grain bread, crisp crackers, flaky biscuits, pizzas, calzones, soufflés, and casseroles with gluten-free flours and starches. These delicious yet easy recipes are so good that you can serve them to non-gluten-free friends and they won't be able to tell the difference!

Chapter 17

Batter and Dough Recipes

*Y*ou can use basic batters and doughs in so many ways. For example, after you figure out how to make the best type of dough for gluten-free calzones, you can fill them with hundreds of different combinations of ingredients. You can also vary the flours you use in these doughs and batters, as long as you substitute other gluten-free flours by weight, not by volume.

In this chapter we look at the basics of gluten-free batters and doughs. From a great pizza dough that's just like the pizzas you find in New York City to ethereal dumplings and flaky pie crusts, these recipes are what you've been craving.

Making the Best Batters and Doughs

Gluten-free batters and doughs are different from wheat batters and doughs. Because the flours don't contain gluten, you need to build structure in other ways. Combining flours and starches is the easiest and, really, the best way to make good doughs and batters.

Some doughs need gums or other additives simply because, even with high-protein gluten-free flours, you still need more structure. Adding whey, dry milk powder, or eggs can also help build structure.

To make the best gluten-free doughs and batters, follow these tips:

✔ Always mix the additives, such as xanthan gum or guar gum, into the dry ingredients before you add the wet ingredients.

✔ If you don't use a scale to measure flours and mixes, always measure by spooning the flour or mix lightly into a measuring cup and leveling off the top with the back of a knife. See Chapters 4 and 5 for more info on measuring by weight and volume.

✔ Mix the dry ingredients very thoroughly using a wire whisk. Mix until the dry ingredients are well-blended and the mixture is one color. Different gluten-free doughs have different colors, so mixing until the colors are blended is a good way to tell that they've been thoroughly combined.

✔ Be sure to beat the doughs and batters for the specified time period. Most gluten-free doughs and batters must be more aerated than wheat-based doughs. Beating works air into the structure of the dough so it can rise in the oven.

✔ If a recipe calls for a dough to be refrigerated, follow those instructions to the letter. Resting time lets the flours absorb more of the liquid in the recipe so the protein structure can develop.

✔ Use pans to shape most gluten-free doughs and batters. Most of these recipes are softer than wheat-based doughs. In fact, a kneadable gluten-free dough is very rare! Use loaf pans, jellyroll pans with sides, muffin tins, and cake and springform pans to shape doughs and batters.

Easy Batter and Dough Recipes

Remember that these doughs and batters are stickier than yeast-based doughs and batters. Use plastic wrap, parchment paper, or waxed paper to shape the doughs. You may want to line the pans with parchment paper or foil to make it easy to remove the baked goods from the pans. Be sure to remove breads and rolls from the pans as soon as they come out of the oven so they don't become soggy on the bottom and sides.

If your breads or other baked goods seem soggy or wet, you can remove them from the pan after they're set and firmed, put them on a wire rack in a baking pan, and bake for a few minutes longer. This removes excess moisture from the breads or rolls.

Enjoy using these basic recipes to make all kinds of breads, rolls, pizza, cookies, and desserts! Use your imagination to create fillings and add ingredients to change the flavor of these recipes.

Butter Pie Crust

Prep time: 20 min, plus rest time • **Cook time:** 20 min • **Yield:** 16 servings (two crusts)

Ingredients	Directions
½ cup plus 3 tablespoons (93 grams) Whole-Grain Flour Mix (see Chapter 10) ½ cup (80 grams) white rice flour ⅓ cup plus 2 teaspoons (56 grams) White Flour Mix (see Chapter 10) ⅓ cup plus 2 teaspoons (58 grams) sweet rice flour 1 teaspoon sugar ½ teaspoon salt Pinch baking powder ½ cup butter 1½ teaspoons apple cider vinegar ½ cup water 1 tablespoon tapioca flour	*1* In a large bowl, combine the Whole-Grain Flour Mix, white rice flour, White Flour Mix, sweet rice flour, sugar, salt, and baking powder and mix until the mixture is one color. *2* Using your hands, rub the butter into the flour, working it between your fingers until the mixture resembles sand with a few chunkier pieces. *3* Add the vinegar and stir. Add the water, a little bit at a time, stirring with your hands to incorporate the water. The dough should hold together with a gentle squeeze. You may need another tablespoon or so of water to reach this consistency. Every batch of flour has a different moisture content. *4* Divide the dough in half and form each half into a disc about an inch thick. Wrap the dough in plastic wrap and chill for at least 30 minutes. *5* Cover your work surface with a thin layer of tapioca flour. Unwrap one disc of dough and sprinkle it generously with tapioca flour. *6* Place the dough on the prepared surface. Roll very, very lightly with a floured rolling pin, using almost no downward pressure. The dough is very soft, so it should move gently, becoming flatter. Keep the dough and board sprinkled with tapioca flour. *7* Ease the crust into a 9-inch pie pan, trim the edges, and flute as desired. Bake according to your pie recipe. Repeat with the remaining dough, use the remaining dough for a top crust, or freeze the remaining dough for another use.

Per serving: Calories 229 (From Fat 107); Fat 12g (Saturated 7g); Cholesterol 31mg; Sodium 159mg; Carbohydrate 29g; Dietary Fiber 1g; Protein 2g.

Cookie Pie Crust

Prep time: 20 min, plus rest time • **Cook time:** 10–14 min • **Yield:** One 9-inch crust

Ingredients	*Directions*
⅓ **cup plus 1 tablespoon unsalted butter, softened**	*1* In a medium bowl, combine ⅓ cup unsalted butter and the Cookie Mix; stir until combined. Beat in the egg until combined.
1½ **cups Cookie Mix (see Chapter 10)**	
1 egg	*2* Place the dough onto plastic wrap and wrap it, forming it into a ball. Refrigerate the dough for 2 to 3 hours, until firm.
	3 Preheat the oven to 400 degrees. Grease a 9-inch pie pan with 1 tablespoon unsalted butter; set aside.
	4 Place the dough in the prepared pan pie. Press it into the bottom and up the sides of the pan, using plastic wrap as needed to help form the dough. Place the crust in the freezer for 10 minutes.
	5 Remove the crust from the freezer and prick it with a fork in several places. Bake it for 10 to 14 minutes, until the crust is light golden-brown and set. Check the crust halfway through baking time to make sure it's not puffing up too much. If it is puffing, use a fork to gently press down on the crust.
	6 Let the pie crust cool completely on a wire rack and then fill it with fillings.

Per serving: *Calories 200 (From Fat 90); Fat 10g (Saturated 6g); Cholesterol 51mg; Sodium 488mg; Carbohydrate 26g; Dietary Fiber 1g; Protein 2g.*

Note: This crust is ideal to fill with everything from ice cream to puddings to mousse. You can make any dessert recipe that calls for a baked pie crust with this recipe.

Note: You can use just about any cookie recipe to make a pie crust. Just press it firmly into the pie pan and chill it in the freezer before baking. You may want to weigh the dough down so it doesn't puff up in the oven. To do this, spray a 12-inch sheet of foil with nonstick cooking spray. Place the foil, sprayed side down, over the dough and press gently. Fill the foil with uncooked dried beans or pie weights. Bake for 8 to 10 minutes, until the dough is set. Remove the pie from the oven and gently remove the foil and beans or weights together. Bake the crust until it's light golden-brown. Remember, if you use dried beans, after the beans have been baked they won't soften, so you can't use them in a recipe. Save them to use as pie weights.

Galette Pie Crust

Prep time: 20 min, plus rest time • **Cook time:** 20 min • **Yield:** 6 servings

Ingredients	Directions
1 cup (148 grams) White Flour Mix (see Chapter 10)	**1** In a large bowl, combine the White Flour Mix, Whole-Grain Flour Mix (or brown rice flour), sweet rice flour, sugar, salt, and xanthan gum. Stir until the mixture is one color.
2 tablespoons (20 grams) Whole-Grain Flour Mix (see Chapter 10) or brown rice flour	**2** Add the cold butter and blend with a pastry blender or two knives until sandy crumbs form. It's fine if some of the butter is in slightly larger pieces.
1 tablespoon (10 grams) sweet rice flour	
1 tablespoon sugar	**3** Add the egg and citrus juice and beat until the dough forms a soft ball.
½ teaspoon salt	
¼ teaspoon xanthan gum	**4** At this point, you can make either one large pie crust or individual tarts. For individual tarts, divide into six balls. For one large tart, leave in one ball. Refrigerate for at least 2 hours.
6 tablespoons cold butter, cut into cubes	
1 egg	**5** When you're ready to bake, preheat the oven to 375 degrees. Place a ball of dough between plastic wrap. Using a rolling pin with steady pressure, roll the dough to a circle about 4½ inches in diameter for individual tarts. For a large pie, roll out the entire ball of dough into a 12-inch circle.
1 tablespoon lemon or lime juice	
	6 Place the dough onto a cookie sheet. You should be able to fit three individual tarts onto a standard cookie sheet. If you're making a large tart, just place it in the center of the cookie sheet.
	7 Fill, pleat the edges of the crust over the filling, and bake as your pie recipe directs.

Per serving: Calories 213 (From Fat 111); Fat 12g (Saturated 7g); Cholesterol 66mg; Sodium 206mg; Carbohydrate 26g; Dietary Fiber 0g; Protein 2g.

Note: A galette is a free-form pie made without a pie pan. Place the flat circles of dough on a cookie sheet, place about ½ cup filling in the center, and loosely pleat the edges of the dough over the filling, leaving the filling uncovered in the center. This is a classic French recipe.

Calzone Dough

Prep time: 15 min plus rest time • **Cook time:** 20–23 min • **Yield:** 4 servings

Ingredients

1 cup minus 2 teaspoons (142 grams) White Flour Mix (see Chapter 10)

½ cup plus 1 tablespoon plus 2 teaspoons (83 grams) Whole-Grain Flour Mix (see Chapter 10)

⅓ cup (38 grams) corn flour

2 tablespoons (20 grams) raw buckwheat flour

2 teaspoons olive oil

2¼ teaspoons (1 packet) active dry yeast

¼ teaspoon salt

1 cup warm water (102 to 103 degrees)

Filling ingredients: cheese; cooked chicken, sausage, ham, and vegetables; olives; and so on

Directions

1 Combine all ingredients in a large mixing bowl and beat for 2 minutes.

2 Cut a piece of parchment paper as long as your cookie sheet and place it on the cookie sheet.

3 Spread the batter over the parchment paper in a large rectangle. You can also spread the batter into a large circle.

4 Let the dough rise for 1 hour. Make the fillings during this time. You can use any combination of foods for the fillings, like olives, cooked sausages, mozzarella cheese, cooked chicken cubes, feta cheese, and cooked chopped onions. Don't use runny or liquid filling ingredients because the batter won't set if the filling is too wet.

5 Preheat the oven to 500 degrees.

6 Place the filling in ½ cup amounts on one side of the rectangle, lining up the filling evenly in four mounds with space in between.

7 Lift the parchment paper up and over the filing. Press down around the filling to seal the edges. Leave the parchment in place.

8 Bake the calzones for 15 minutes and then remove the parchment paper so the calzones can set. Bake the calzones for another 5 to 8 minutes, or until golden-brown.

Per serving: Calories 270 (From Fat 31); Fat 4g (Saturated 0g); Cholesterol 0mg; Sodium 147mg; Carbohydrate 59g; Dietary Fiber 3g; Protein 5g.

Note: Don't use any sauces in the filling because the dough is a batter. Sauces make the dough too wet, and it won't set and bake.

Crepe Batter

Prep time: 15 min, plus rest time • **Cook time:** 3 min • **Yiel**

Ingredients	*Directions*
⅓ cup (41 grams) sorghum flour	**1** In a medium bowl, co starch, sweet rice flou gum. Mix until the mix
¼ cup (40 grams) potato starch	
¼ cup (37 grams) sweet rice flour	**2** In a small bowl, beat the eggs with the butter, milk, and water. Add to the flour mixture and beat with a mixer for 1 minute.
¼ cup (35 grams) cornstarch	
¼ teaspoon salt	
¼ teaspoon xanthan gum	**3** Let the batter sit, uncovered, at room temperature for 20 to 30 minutes, until it thickens slightly. If you need to, you can refrigerate this batter, covered, overnight.
3 eggs	
3 tablespoons butter, melted	
1 cup milk	**4** When you're ready to cook, place an 8-inch nonstick skillet over medium heat. Coat the pan with butter.
¼ cup water	
⅓ ✱ 3/4 c mix	**5** Add ¼ cup batter to the skillet. Twist and turn the skillet so the batter evenly covers the bottom of the skillet in a thin layer.
	6 Cook the crepe until it sets, about 1 to 2 minutes. Carefully flip the crepe and cook for 30 seconds to 1 minute on the second side. Place the crepe on waxed paper to cool. Don't stack the crepes or they'll stick together.

Per serving: Calories 123 (From Fat 53); Fat 6g (Saturated 3g); Cholesterol 76mg; Sodium 90mg; Carbohydrate 14g; Dietary Fiber 0g; Protein 3g.

Vary It! You can use almond or soymilk instead of the cow's milk to make this batter casein-free. For dessert crepes, add 3 tablespoons sugar to the batter.

Note: You may need to add more milk or water after the batter has rested. The batter should be the consistency of thick cream. It must spread easily, because it starts cooking as soon as it hits the hot pan.

Note: Crepes freeze really well. Wrap each crepe in waxed paper or plastic wrap and place them in a freezer bag. Freeze up to three months. Thaw at room temperature and use as directed in your recipe.

in Batter

time: 20 min • **Cook time:** 30–33 min • **Yield:** 12 servings

Ingredients	Directions
1¾ cups plus 1 tablespoon plus 1 teaspoon (248 grams) Whole-Grain Flour Mix (see Chapter 10)	*1* Preheat the oven to 350 degrees. Grease muffin tins with cooking spray and set aside.
1 cup plus 3 tablespoons (177 grams) White Flour Mix (see Chapter 10)	*2* In a large bowl, combine the Whole-Grain Flour Mix, White Flour Mix, brown sugar, salt, baking powder, baking soda, cinnamon, and nutmeg and stir until the mixture is one color.
½ cup brown sugar	
½ teaspoon salt	
2 teaspoons baking powder	*3* In a medium bowl, combine the eggs, sour cream, oil, vanilla, and milk and beat well.
1 teaspoon baking soda	
1 teaspoon cinnamon	*4* Add the wet ingredients to the dry ingredients and mix well. At this point, you can add fruits or nuts as desired (see the note after the recipe).
¼ teaspoon nutmeg	
3 eggs	*5* Spoon the batter into the muffin tins.
½ cup sour cream	
½ cup vegetable oil	*6* Bake for 15 minutes, rotate the pan, and then bake 15 to 18 minutes longer, or until the muffins are golden-brown and a toothpick inserted into the center comes out clean.
1 tablespoon vanilla	
¾ cup milk	
	7 Cool the muffins in the pans for 5 minutes and then move them to wire racks to cool completely.

Per serving: Calories 292 (From Fat 124); Fat 14g (Saturated 3g); Cholesterol 59mg; Sodium 298mg; Carbohydrate 39g; Dietary Fiber 1g; Protein 4g.

Vary It! In Step 4 of the recipe, you can add 2 cups diced fruit, such as apples or pears, or ½ cup diced dried fruits like apricots, currants, or pineapple. Along with the fruit, you can add ½ cup chopped nuts, such as walnuts or pecans.

Vary It! For a vegan version, substitute 2 teaspoons ground golden flaxseeds and 3 tablespoons water for the 3 eggs. Substitute coconut or soy yogurt for the sour cream. Substitute rice, soy, almond, or hemp milk for the dairy milk.

Dumpling Batter

Prep time: 20 min, plus rest time • **Cook time:** 10 min • **Yield:** 8 servings

Ingredients	Directions
⅓ cup minus 2 teaspoons (46 grams) superfine brown rice flour	*1* In a medium bowl, combine the brown rice flour, tapioca flour, sorghum flour, millet flour, xanthan gum, baking powder, baking soda, and salt. Mix until the mixture is one color.
¼ cup (29 grams) tapioca flour	
¼ cup (32 grams) sorghum flour	*2* Work in the butter with your fingers or a pastry blender until the mixture looks like sand.
2 tablespoons (18 grams) millet flour	
1 teaspoon xanthan gum	*3* In a small bowl, combine the egg and buttermilk; beat well. Add to the flour mixture and stir until a dough forms. Let the dough stand for 20 minutes while you simmer some soup to use for the dumplings, or bring 4 cups of chicken broth or water to a simmer in a large saucepan.
½ teaspoon gluten-free baking powder	
½ teaspoon baking soda	
½ teaspoon salt	
3 tablespoons butter	*4* Use a Number 70 ice cream scoop or a tablespoon measure to make the dumplings. Dip the scoop into the simmering liquid and then into the dough. Drop the dough carefully into the liquid. Repeat until you use all the dough.
1 egg, beaten	
⅓ cup buttermilk	
	5 Cover the pot and simmer for 9 to 12 minutes. Don't lift the lid until 9 minutes has passed. The dumplings are done when they've puffed and a toothpick inserted in the center comes out clean.

Per serving: Calories 110 (From Fat 48); Fat 5g (Saturated 3g); Cholesterol 39mg; Sodium 268mg; Carbohydrate 14g; Dietary Fiber 1g; Protein 2g.

Vary It! This recipe is easy to vary. Add any kind of chopped fresh or dried herbs to the batter for more flavor. Use chicken broth, soymilk, or vegetable broth instead of the buttermilk; in that case, add ¼ teaspoon apple cider vinegar to the liquid.

Basic Pizza Dough

Prep time: 10 min, plus rest time • **Cook time:** 22–25 min • **Yield:** 6–8 servings

Ingredients	Directions
2¼ cups minus 1 teaspoon (300 grams) Whole-Grain Flour Mix (see Chapter 10)	**1** In a large bowl, combine the Whole-Grain Flour Mix, White Flour Mix, yeast, salt, and sugar. Mix until the mixture is all one color.
1¼ cups plus 1 tablespoon (196 grams) White Flour Mix (see Chapter 10)	**2** Add the olive oil and water and beat for at least 1 minute.
1 tablespoon active dry yeast	
1 teaspoon salt	**3** Immediately press the dough on a greased cookie sheet or a greased deep-dish pizza pan.
½ teaspoon sugar	
1 tablespoon olive oil	**4** Let the dough rise for 45 minutes. Preheat the oven to 425 degrees.
1¼ cups plus 1 tablespoon warm water	
	5 Place the dough in the oven for 10 minutes to partially bake it, remove, and add toppings to make a pizza.
	6 Return to the oven and bake 12 to 15 minutes more, until the toppings are hot, the cheese is melted and beginning to brown, and the crust is golden-brown.

Per serving: Calories 226 (From Fat 31); Fat 4g (Saturated 1g); Cholesterol 0mg; Sodium 390mg; Carbohydrate 46g; Dietary Fiber 2g; Protein 5g.

Note: To make individual pizzas, divide the dough into fourths. Partially bake each for 5 minutes and then bake for 10 to 12 minutes more after topping.

Note: This dough freezes well after partial baking. Shape the dough, let it rise, bake it for 10 minutes, cool it, and then freeze it. To use it, let it thaw at room temperature and then top and bake again.

Chapter 18

Biscuits and Crackers

In This Chapter

▶ Tips for working with biscuits and crackers

▶ A variety of delicious quick bread recipes

*T*he joy of biting into a warm biscuit or eating a crisp cracker with a glass of milk is no longer the stuff of dreams. These gluten-free recipes for treats that are usually made with wheat flour are easy and satisfying.

Biscuits and crackers are all made from doughs. Biscuits are usually made from soft doughs, and crackers are made from firm dough. The difference between the types of dough is in the amount of liquid in the recipe and how the dough is formed and shaped.

In this chapter you find basic recipes for these quick bread treats. After you master the technique of making biscuits and crackers, you can have fun experimenting in the kitchen. Try different flours, add different flavorings like cheese and herbs, or make a recipe heartier with nuts or spices.

Most of these recipes freeze well. Make sure that the breads are completely cooled before you wrap them for the freezer, and be sure to mark the package with the recipe name and date to avoid those unidentified mystery packages that float around in every freezer. Thaw these goodies by leaving them unwrapped on the countertop. You can rewarm them briefly in the microwave for a few seconds or in the oven for a few minutes. Serve with nut butters or regular butter for a wonderful treat.

Basic Rules for Biscuits and Crackers

Measure flour and other ingredients carefully, by weight if possible, as we mention in Chapters 3, 4, and 5, and mix the dough as directed. Measuring, building structure, and doneness tests are crucial to the success of these recipes. And if you can't use xanthan gum, raw buckwheat flour is a good substitute: Use 1 tablespoon of raw buckwheat flour and 2 tablespoons of water for ½ teaspoon of xanthan gum. As we mention in Chapter 5, you must grind your own raw buckwheat flour because the store-bought variety is toasted. Buy raw buckwheat kernels and grind them to a powder.

If you don't use a scale to measure flours and mixes, always measure by spooning the flour or mix lightly into a measuring cup and leveling off the top with the back of a knife. See Chapters 4 and 5 for more info on measuring by weight and volume.

Be sure the flours you use are the grind or texture the recipe specifies. If a recipe calls for super-fine flour and you can't find it, use fine flour or regular flour and grind it in the blender or food processor. Fine flours produce smoother dough with no grittiness. Sometimes you want more texture in a recipe, but sometimes, for a tender product, less texture is desirable.

Biscuits

Biscuits are quick breads, leavened by baking powder and/or baking soda. You make them by cutting a fat into flour and adding liquid until a soft dough forms. You can form biscuits in several ways. You can simply drop soft dough onto a cookie sheet and bake it; you can make these "drop biscuits" quickly and easily. Biscuits that you roll and cut with a cookie cutter require a little more finesse and the correct dough texture.

Crackers

Cracker dough is firm enough to roll out or shape into balls to flatten with a fork or the bottom of a water glass. For crisp crackers, some fat is necessary. The fat in crackers is what makes them crisp and flaky. Be sure that you mix the fat well with the flour before you add the liquid. And don't be afraid to handle this type of dough. Cut it into shapes with cookie cutters or make free-form crackers with a sharp knife.

Basic Buttermilk Biscuits

Prep time: 15 min • **Cook time:** 25–30 min • **Yield:** 12 biscuits

Ingredients	Directions
½ cup (78 grams) sweet rice flour	**1** Preheat the oven to 400 degrees. In a food processor or blender, combine the sweet rice flour and brown rice flour and process or blend until very fine. Pour into a large mixing bowl and add the potato starch, tapioca flour, sugar, xanthan gum, baking soda, baking powder, and salt.
½ cup (80 grams) superfine brown rice flour	
½ cup minus 1 teaspoon (80 grams) potato starch	
½ cup minus 1 teaspoon (58 grams) tapioca flour	**2** Using two knives or a pastry blender, cut in the butter until it's the size of tiny peas.
3 tablespoons sugar	
1 teaspoon xanthan gum	**3** Measure the buttermilk into a glass measuring cup and add the egg; beat until combined. Add all at once to the flour mixture and stir just until the liquid is absorbed. Let stand 5 minutes.
1½ teaspoons baking soda	
½ teaspoon baking powder	
½ teaspoon sea salt	**4** Using a spoon rinsed in cold water to prevent sticking, drop the biscuits the size of a golf ball onto ungreased cookie sheets, leaving about 4 inches between each biscuit. Bake for 25 to 30 minutes, or until the biscuits are light golden-brown. Cool on a wire rack.
6 tablespoons cold butter, cut into pieces	
1 cup cold buttermilk	
1 egg, beaten	

Per serving: Calories 153 (From Fat 60); Fat 7g (Saturated 4g); Cholesterol 34mg; Sodium 298mg; Carbohydrate 22g; Dietary Fiber 0g; Protein 2g.

Note: You can make your own buttermilk by putting 1 tablespoon of lemon juice or vinegar in a measuring cup. Add enough sweet milk to make ½ cup and let stand for 5 minutes. Use as directed in the recipe.

Spicy Cheese Biscuits

Prep time: 20 min • **Cook time:** 15 min • **Yield:** 8 servings

Ingredients	Directions
⅔ cup heavy cream	*1* Preheat the oven to 425 degrees. Line a cookie sheet with a Silpat (silicone) liner or parchment paper.
½ cup plus 1 tablespoon plus 2 teaspoons (83 grams) Whole-Grain Flour Mix (see Chapter 10)	*2* Place the cream in a large mixing bowl. Zero out the scale and measure each ingredient into the bowl.
⅓ cup plus 2 teaspoons (54 grams) White Flour Mix (see Chapter 10)	*3* Blend all ingredients together well. When the dough starts to come together, start kneading the dough.
2 tablespoons (20 grams) raw buckwheat flour	*4* Knead for 1 minute and then pat the dough on the Silpat liner into a circle ¾-inch thick.
½ teaspoon chili powder	
¼ teaspoon ground cumin	*5* Cut the dough into eight wedges with a sharp knife or bench knife. For soft edges, leave the wedges touching each other. For crisp edges, separate the wedges slightly.
1½ teaspoons baking powder	
½ cup shredded Mexican cheese blend	
	6 Bake for 12 to 15 minutes, until deep golden-brown. Move to a wire rack to cool completely.

Per serving: Calories 166 (From Fat 96); Fat 11g (Saturated 7g); Cholesterol 36mg; Sodium 132mg; Carbohydrate 16g; Dietary Fiber 1g; Protein 3g.

Vary It! You can make these biscuits with any kind of cheese and any seasoning. Use Cheddar cheese and ½ teaspoon dried thyme leaves for a different flavor, or try grated Gouda cheese with dried marjoram.

Note: Be sure you use raw buckwheat flour that you grind yourself from raw buckwheat groats. Store-bought buckwheat flour doesn't have the same thickening properties.

Herbed Cream Biscuits

Prep time: 15 min • **Cook time:** 15 min • **Yield:** 8 servings

Ingredients	Directions
1 cup plus 3 tablespoons (175 grams) White Flour Mix (see Chapter 10)	*1* Preheat the oven to 425 degrees. Line a cookie sheet with parchment paper.
¾ cup plus 1 tablespoon (110 grams) Whole-Grain Flour Mix (see Chapter 10)	*2* In a large bowl, combine the White Flour Mix, Whole-Grain Flour Mix, sugar, baking powder, and salt; stir until the mix is one color. Mix in the herbs.
2 teaspoons sugar	
2 teaspoons baking powder	
½ teaspoon salt	*3* Add the cream and mix well. The dough should be soft but pliable.
2 tablespoons minced fresh rosemary, tarragon, or other herbs	*4* On a board dusted with some more White Flour Mix, pat the dough out to ¾-inch thickness.
1½ cups heavy cream	*5* Cut out biscuits using a sharp-edged cutter. If you don't want scraps, cut the dough into 2½-inch squares.
	6 Place the biscuits on a prepared cookie sheet. Bake for 12 to 15 minutes, or until the biscuits are light golden-brown. Move to a wire rack to cool; serve warm.

Per serving: Calories 281 (From Fat 153); Fat 17g (Saturated 10g); Cholesterol 61mg; Sodium 258mg; Carbohydrate 32g; Dietary Fiber 1g; Protein 3g.

Ham and Cheese Muffins

Prep time: 20 min • **Cook time:** 23–25 min • **Yield:** 12 muffins

Ingredients	Directions
1¼ cups minus 1 teaspoon (165 grams) Whole-Grain Flour Mix (see Chapter 10)	**1** Preheat the oven to 350 degrees. Line 12 muffin cups with paper liners or grease them with nonstick cooking spray.
¼ cup plus 1 tablespoon (45 grams) White Flour Mix (see Chapter 10)	**2** In a large bowl, combine the Whole-Grain Flour Mix, White Flour Mix, baking powder, baking soda, and salt. Mix with a wire whisk until the mixture is one color.
1 teaspoon baking powder	
½ teaspoon baking soda	**3** In a small bowl, combine the eggs, oil, yogurt, milk, and Dijon mustard and beat until all the ingredients are combined.
½ teaspoon salt	
3 eggs	
⅓ cup vegetable oil	**4** Add the egg mixture to the flour mixture until well combined. Gently fold in the ham and cheese cubes.
⅓ cup whole milk plain yogurt	
⅓ cup milk	**5** Fill the prepared muffin cups, filling each ⅔ full.
2 teaspoons Dijon mustard	
½ cup diced ham	**6** Bake for 23 to 25 minutes, or until the muffins are golden-brown and spring back when lightly touched in the center. Cool them in the pan for 3 minutes and then move them to a wire rack to cool completely.
½ cup diced Colby or Cheddar cheese	
	7 Store leftovers in the refrigerator. You can rewarm them in the microwave on high for 10 seconds per muffin.

Per serving: Calories 174 (From Fat 96); Fat 11g (Saturated 2g); Cholesterol 64mg; Sodium 254mg; Carbohydrate 15g; Dietary Fiber 1g; Protein 6g.

Note: These muffins are delicious with a bowl of hot soup. They can even replace a meal. The Dijon mustard adds a nice kick, but you can omit it if you'd like.

Note: Because these muffins contain ham, you must store them in the refrigerator.

Sesame Seed Crackers

Prep time: 20 min • **Cook time:** 10 min • **Yield:** 48 crackers

Ingredients	*Directions*
1 cup plus 3 tablespoons (132 grams) almond flour	*1* Preheat the oven to 375 degrees. Line two cookie sheets with parchment paper and set aside.
½ cup minus 2 teaspoons (62 grams) brown rice flour	*2* In a large mixing bowl, combine the almond flour, brown rice flour, and tapioca flour; whisk until blended. Stir in the sesame seeds and sea salt.
¼ cup (29 grams) tapioca flour	
½ cup sesame seeds	*3* Using a pastry blender or two knives, cut in the butter until the particles are fine.
½ teaspoon sea salt	
¼ cup cold butter, cut into pieces	*4* In a small bowl, combine the egg white with 2 table-spoons almond milk. Whisk until foamy and then stir it into the flour mixture. Add more milk, tossing with a fork, a tablespoon at a time until you can form a dough by pressing it together. The dough should be moist but firm.
1 egg white	
⅓ cup almond milk	
More sesame seeds and sea salt	*5* Divide the dough in half and place each half on a prepared cookie sheet. Top with another sheet of parchment paper and roll out until the dough is ⅛-inch thick. Remove the top sheet of parchment paper. Repeat with the second half of dough on a second cookie sheet.
	6 Cut into squares or other shapes using a sharp knife, cookie cutter, or pizza cutter. Sprinkle with more sesame seeds and a bit of sea salt.
	7 Bake for 9 to 12 minutes, or until the crackers are light golden-brown. Cool the crackers on the cookie sheets for 3 minutes and then carefully move them to a wire rack to cool completely.

Per serving: Calories 42 (From Fat 28); Fat 3g (Saturated 1g); Cholesterol 3mg; Sodium 26mg; Carbohydrate 3g; Dietary Fiber 0g; Protein 1g.

Olive Oil Crackers

Prep time: 15 min • **Cook time:** 12–14 min • **Yield:** 48 crackers

Ingredients	*Directions*
2 cups (270 grams) Whole-Grain Flour Mix (see Chapter 10)	*1* Preheat the oven to 400 degrees. Line two cookie sheets with parchment paper or silicone sheets. Set aside.
3 tablespoons quinoa grains, rinsed if not pre-rinsed	
¼ teaspoon black pepper	*2* In a mixer bowl, using a dough hook, combine the Whole-Grain Flour Mix, quinoa grains, pepper, and onion powder; blend well with a wire whisk.
½ teaspoon gluten-free onion powder	
5 tablespoons olive oil	*3* Add the olive oil and water. Mix, adding more water if the dough seems dry, until a firm dough forms. Cover and let stand for 10 minutes.
½ cup warm water	
½ teaspoon sea salt	*4* Wet your hands with cold water and divide the dough in half. Press each half of dough onto each cooking sheet, making a thin layer. Prick the dough with a fork and cut it into pieces using a pizza cutter. Sprinkle with sea salt.
	5 Bake the crackers for 12 to 14 minutes, or until firm and light golden-brown. Carefully move the crackers to a wire rack to cool completely. Store in an airtight container at room temperature.

Per serving: Calories 36 (From Fat 14); Fat 2g (Saturated 0g); Cholesterol 0mg; Sodium 24mg; Carbohydrate 5g; Dietary Fiber 0g; Protein 1g.

Note: You may have to visit a health food store to find quinoa seeds. They're available online too.

Graham Crackers

Prep time: 40 min, plus chilling time • **Cook time:** 14 min • **Yield:** 44 s

Ingredients	*Directions*
3¾ cups minus 1 tablespoon (495 grams) Whole-Grain Flour Mix (see Chapter 10)	*1* Line a 9-x-5-inch bread pan with plastic wrap. Make sure the wrap fits into the corners so that the cookies will have rectangular edges.
3 cups minus 2 tablespoons (426 grams) White Flour Mix (see Chapter 10)	*2* In a large bowl, combine the Whole-Grain Flour Mix, White Flour Mix, sweet rice flour, cinnamon, baking powder, salt, and brown sugar. Mix until the mixture is one color.
½ cup plus 1 teaspoon (81 grams) sweet rice flour	
1 tablespoon cinnamon	*3* Add the butter and let the mixer run until the mixture looks like sand, about 2 to 3 minutes. Add the honey, vanilla, and water; beat for 1 minute.
1 tablespoon baking powder	
½ teaspoon salt	*4* Pat the mixture into the prepared pan. Cover with plastic wrap. Pat down the dough to make sure it doesn't have any air bubbles.
6 tablespoons packed brown sugar	
12 tablespoons unsalted butter	*5* Refrigerate overnight, or at least 2 hours, before slicing.
⅓ cup honey	*6* When ready to bake, preheat the oven to 400 degrees and line cookie sheets with parchment paper.
3 teaspoons vanilla	
¾ cup water	*7* Remove the top layer of plastic wrap and slice the dough into ⅛-inch slices. Place the slices on the prepared cookie sheets, leaving ½ inch space between each cracker. Dock the crackers by poking holes in the dough with a fork.
	8 Bake, two cookie sheets at a time, for 8 minutes. Then rotate the pans and bake 5 to 6 minutes longer, until the crackers are golden-brown.
	9 Remove from the oven and let stand on cookie sheets for 2 to 3 minutes; then move the graham crackers to wire racks to cool completely.

Per serving: *Calories 122 (From Fat 31); Fat 3g (Saturated 2g); Cholesterol 8mg; Sodium 54mg; Carbohydrate 23g; Dietary Fiber 1g; Protein 1g.*

Toasted Onion Buckwheat Crackers

Prep time: 20 min • **Cook time:** 60 min • **Yield:** 60 servings

Ingredients	Directions
1 cup raw buckwheat	**1** Preheat the oven to 350 degrees. Line two large cookie sheets with parchment paper and set aside.
1½ cups boiling water	
1 medium onion, finely chopped	**2** In a medium saucepan, stir the buckwheat into boiling water. Bring back to a boil and then turn the heat to low and simmer for 15 minutes, until the buckwheat kernels are very soft. Drain off the excess water, letting the buckwheat sit in the strainer for a few minutes. The drier the buckwheat, the crispier the cracker.
¼ cup golden flaxseeds	
¼ cup plus 1 tablespoon (49 grams) sweet rice flour	
1 teaspoon smoked paprika	**3** In a dry frying pan, cook the onion until it's well browned and the liquid evaporates, stirring frequently. Don't let the onions burn.
½ teaspoon salt	
2 tablespoons olive oil	**4** When the onions are completely browned, reduce the heat and add the cooked buckwheat. Cook for 1 minute; the mixture will begin to form a ball. Remove from heat.
	5 Grind the flaxseeds in a spice grinder or coffee mill until they're a fine powder.
	6 In a medium bowl, combine the flaxseeds, sweet rice flour, smoked paprika, and salt.

7 Add the flaxseed mixture and olive oil to the buckwheat mixture in the pan. Beat for 1 minute. The groats may get a bit mushy; that's fine.

8 Divide the dough in half. Spread out each half onto a prepared cookie sheet until the sheet is completely covered with dough. Score the dough into 2-inch squares.

9 Bake for 15 minutes and then rotate pans. Bake 15 minutes longer.

10 Remove the cookie sheets from the oven. Slide the crackers, with the parchment paper, directly onto the oven racks.

11 Bake 10 to 15 minutes longer, until the cookies are well browned and crisp. Move them to a wire rack to cool completely.

Per serving: Calories 20 (From Fat 7); Fat 1g (Saturated 0g); Cholesterol 0mg; Sodium 20mg; Carbohydrate 3g; Dietary Fiber 1g; Protein 1g.

Note: The baking time varies depending on the size of your cookie sheets and how thin you make the crackers.

Note: You may have to visit a health food store or co-op to find flaxseeds, although they're becoming more available in regular grocery stores. You can also find them online.

Soft Pretzels

Prep time: 30 min, plus rising time • **Cook time:** 10–12 min • **Yield:** 8 servings

Ingredients	*Directions*
1½ cups (199 grams) High-Protein Bread Flour Mix (see Chapter 10)	**1** In a large bowl, combine the Bread Flour Mix, White Flour Mix, and buckwheat flour; stir until the mixture is one color.
½ cup plus 2 tablespoons (93 grams) White Flour Mix (see Chapter 10)	**2** Add the remaining ingredients except the baking soda and coarse salt and beat for 2 minutes.
2 tablespoons (20 grams) raw buckwheat flour	**3** Form the dough into ropes by rolling on the counter to 14 inches long, about the diameter of a thick pencil.
1 tablespoon honey	
1 tablespoon vegetable oil	**4** Place each rope in the shape of a "U," and then cross the ends over the center to form a classic pretzel shape. Or, for simplicity's sake, just leave the pretzels in rods.
1 tablespoon active dry yeast	
1 teaspoon salt	**5** Place each pretzel on a square of parchment paper. Cover with plastic wrap and let rise 1½ hours. While the dough is rising, place 6 cups of water in a shallow pan. Add the baking soda. When 1¼ hours has passed, place the pan on the stove and bring the water to a boil.
½ cup plus 2 tablespoons water	
6 tablespoons baking soda	
3 tablespoons coarse salt	**6** Preheat the oven to 425 degrees. Place one pretzel at a time in the boiling water, parchment paper side down.
	7 Let cook for 1 minute and then flip the pretzel over in the water; remove the paper. Cook for 1 minute longer. Remove the pretzel from the water with a slotted spatula. Let drain for a few seconds. Discard the parchment paper square.
	8 Place the boiled pretzel on a greased cookie sheet and immediately sprinkle with some of the coarse salt. Repeat with remaining pretzels.
	9 After you finish boiling and salting all the pretzels, bake for 8 to 10 minutes, or until well browned.

Per serving: Calories 123 (From Fat 24); Fat 3g (Saturated 0g); Cholesterol 0mg; Sodium 1,553mg; Carbohydrate 23g; Dietary Fiber 2g; Protein 4g.

Crisp Pretzels

Prep time: 30 min • **Cook time:** 25 min • **Yield:** 16 servings

Ingredients	Directions
Recipe for Soft Pretzels (see page 292)	*1* Make the Soft Pretzels, except roll the dough a bit thinner. Form into 16 logs.
	2 Let the pretzels rise as directed and prepare water bath.
	3 Simmer each pretzel as directed in the Soft Pretzel directions.
	4 Preheat the oven to 375 degrees.
	5 When you finish boiling all the pretzels and sprinkling them with salt as directed, bake for 22 to 25 minutes, until the pretzels are deep golden-brown. Cool on a wire rack.

Per serving: Calories 123 (From Fat 24); Fat 3g (Saturated 0g); Cholesterol 0mg; Sodium 1,553mg; Carbohydrate 23g; Dietary Fiber 2g; Protein 4g.

Chapter 19

Savory Breads

In This Chapter

▶ Using some tips for making yeast and quick savory breads

▶ Baking some delectable savory bread recipes

When most people are diagnosed with celiac disease or gluten intolerance, the first thing that usually comes to mind is, "What about bread?" There's nothing like biting into warm bread, fresh from the oven, with a crisp crust and a melting interior. With these delicious recipes, you can still enjoy that wonderful treat.

In this chapter you find recipes for all kinds of savory breads, both yeast and quick breads. Chewy bagels, flavorful sourdough bread, crisp and light popovers, satisfying sandwich bread, and light and fluffy rolls can be part of your every-day menus.

After you master the basics, use these recipes to create your own treats. For instance, you can use the recipe for Parmesan Lemon Thyme Baguettes and make plain baguettes, or flavor the bread with chopped chives and grated Cotija cheese.

Basic Rules for Yeast and Quick Savory Breads

Gluten-free yeast breads are a bit different from wheat yeast breads. When substituting flours in these recipes, choose flours with a high protein content for the best structure. Nut flours, such as almond flour or hazelnut flour, are a good choice, and they mimic the nutty taste of wheat flour. As always, when substituting ingredients, use weight measurements instead of volume measurements.

To make the best gluten-free savory breads:

✔ Remember that you don't knead these breads. The "dough" is actually a soft or stiff batter.

✔ If you don't use a scale to measure flours and mixes, always measure by spooning the flour or mix lightly into a measuring cup and leveling off the top with the back of a knife. See Chapters 4 and 5 for more info on measuring by weight and volume.

✔ Let the dough rise only once. Because the structure is more delicate than wheat-based yeast breads, more than one rise weakens the web of protein and starch, which makes the structure too fragile to hold the air that gives yeast bread its texture.

✔ Always beat the batter for the time specified in the recipe. During this time, the flour absorbs moisture to develop the proteins, and the yeast is fully distributed throughout the bread.

✔ Always check the expiration date on yeast and baking powder before you start a recipe. Expired yeast won't rise, and expired baking powder won't give your breads the height you want.

✔ Check for doneness of savory gluten-free breads with an instant read thermometer and doneness tests. When breads are done, their internal temperature is 190 to 200 degrees, and the crust is deep golden-brown. The bread should pull away from the sides of the pan and sound hollow when lightly tapped.

✔ A few recipes in this chapter call for raw buckwheat flour, which isn't the same as the buckwheat flour you buy in packages. That buckwheat flour has been toasted. For these recipes, you must grind raw green buckwheat groats to a powder.

Delicious Savory Bread Recipes

After you master a recipe, you can vary it! Add herbs to your light and crisp Popovers, or use different herbs and cheese in Parmesan Lemon Thyme Baguettes. Add sun-dried tomatoes or different herbs to the Vegan Focaccia Bread. Then revel in the aroma of bread baking and enjoy every crisp, flaky, moist, and buttery bite! These breads are ideal for sandwiches, for snacking, and to add the finishing touch to just about every meal.

Vegan Rolled Oat Bread

Prep time: 20 min, plus rise time • **Cook time:** 60–70 min • **Yield:** 16 slices

Ingredients	Directions
1¼ cups plus 3 tablespoons (190 grams) High-Protein Bread Flour Mix (see Chapter 10)	**1** Grease a 9-x-5-inch loaf pan with unsalted butter or solid shortening.
1 cup minus 2 tablespoons (105 grams) gluten-free rolled oat flour	**2** In a bowl for a stand mixer, combine all ingredients. Beat on medium speed for 2 minutes.
⅔ cup gluten-free rolled oats	**3** Pour the batter into the prepared loaf pan.
¾ cup (100 grams) Whole-Grain Flour Mix (see Chapter 10)	**4** Let the batter rise in a warm, draft-free place for 1 to 2 hours, until the batter has doubled in size and is almost to the rim of the pan.
1 tablespoon sugar	
¼ teaspoon sea salt	**5** Preheat the oven to 350 degrees. Bake the bread for 60 to 70 minutes, or until the temperature registers 190 to 200 degrees. Cool the bread in a pan for 5 minutes and then turn it out onto a wire rack to cool completely.
1 tablespoon golden flaxseeds, finely ground	
1 teaspoon yeast	
1⅔ cups warm water (102 to 103 degrees)	**6** Let the bread cool completely before slicing.

Per serving: Calories 117 (From Fat 14); Fat 2g (Saturated 0g); Cholesterol 0mg; Sodium 37mg; Carbohydrate 23g; Dietary Fiber 3g; Protein 4g.

Note: Be sure to grind the flaxseeds to a fine powder. You use them to replace the eggs and the gums in this recipe. Keep a coffee grinder dedicated to this task in your kitchen, because nobody wants flaxseed-flavored coffee!

Note: Use golden flaxseeds in all your baking. The brown flaxseeds contain more chlorophyll and can turn your baked goods green. This may be festive for St. Patrick's Day but is otherwise off-putting.

Sandwich Bread

Prep time: 15 min, plus rise time • **Cook time:** 40 min • **Yield:** 8 servings

Ingredients	Directions
½ cup water	*1* Grease an 8-x-4-inch baking pan using nonstick cooking spray or unsalted butter and set aside.
½ cup milk	
2 tablespoons honey	*2* In a large mixing bowl, combine all ingredients. Beat at medium speed for 2 minutes.
2 tablespoons oil	
2 teaspoons salt	
2¼ cups minus 1 teaspoon (300 grams) Whole-Grain Flour Mix (see Chapter 10)	*3* Pour the mixture into the prepared pan, cover, and let it rise in a warm place until doubled, about 1 to 1½ hours.
1¼ cups plus 1 tablespoon (196 grams) White Flour Mix (see Chapter 10)	*4* Preheat the oven to 350 degrees.
1 egg	*5* Place the bread in the center of the oven. Bake for 35 to 40 minutes, or until the bread is golden-brown and the temperature is 190 to 200 degrees.
	6 Remove the bread from the pan and place on a wire rack to cool completely before slicing.

Per serving: Calories 281 (From Fat 51); Fat 6g (Saturated 1g); Cholesterol 29mg; Sodium 598mg; Carbohydrate 56g; Dietary Fiber 2g; Protein 5g.

Note: When you want a soft, simple sandwich bread, this is it. It slices perfectly and has a wonderful texture. This bread stays nice and soft for several days after baking because it's enriched with egg and milk.

Popovers

Prep time: 15 min • **Cook time:** 20–25 min • **Yield:** 12 servings

Ingredients	Directions
½ cup minus 1 teaspoon (58 grams) tapioca flour	*1* Preheat the oven to 450 degrees. You need a cast-iron popover pan, glass custard cups, or really sturdy muffin tins for these popovers to work. If you're using a cast-iron pan, heat it in the oven for at least 10 minutes and then grease it. Grease each cup very well because the batter needs to move easily in the pans to rise. Don't preheat the glass custard cups or the muffin tins.
½ cup (80 grams) white rice flour	
¼ cup (37 grams) sweet rice flour	
2 tablespoons (16 grams) sorghum flour	*2* In a large bowl, combine the tapioca flour, white rice flour, sweet rice flour, sorghum flour, xanthan gum, salt, and sugar and mix until the mixture is one color.
¼ teaspoon xanthan gum	
⅛ teaspoon salt	*3* Add the milk, melted butter, and eggs and beat for at least 2 minutes.
1 tablespoon sugar	
1 cup milk	*4* Pour the batter into the oiled pans (remember, the cast-iron pans should be hot).
2 tablespoons butter, melted	
3 eggs	*5* Bake for 20 to 25 minutes, until the popovers pop and are deep golden-brown.
	6 Remove the popovers from the pans immediately; eat them while they're hot with butter and jam.

Per serving: Calories 108 (From Fat 36); Fat 4g (Saturated 2g); Cholesterol 61mg; Sodium 50mg; Carbohydrate 16g; Dietary Fiber 0g; Protein 3g.

Vary It! For cheese popovers, add ¼ cup grated Parmesan cheese; omit the salt. Bake for the same time.

Egg-Free Yeast Bread

Prep time: 15 min, plus rise time • **Cook time:** 65–70 min • **Yield:** 32 slices

Ingredients	Directions
3½ cups plus ⅓ cup (500 grams) High-Protein Bread Flour Mix (see Chapter 10)	**1** Grease two 8½-x-4½-inch bread pans with solid shortening or unsalted butter.
3¼ cups plus 2 tablespoons (455 grams) Whole-Grain Flour Mix (see Chapter 10)	**2** In a large bowl, combine the High-Protein Bread Flour Mix, Whole-Grain Flour Mix, sugar, salt, xanthan gum, guar gum, and active dry yeast. Mix well with a wire whisk until completely combined.
2 tablespoons sugar	
1 teaspoon salt	**3** Add the water and stir until combined; then beat for 3 minutes.
2 teaspoons xanthan gum	
1 teaspoon guar gum	**4** Pour the dough into the prepared pans and cover them with plastic wrap.
1 tablespoon active dried yeast	
4 cups water	**5** Let the dough rise in a warm, draft-free place for 2 to 3 hours, or until doubled in size.
	6 Arrange the oven rack in the bottom third of your oven. Preheat the oven to 350 degrees.
	7 As soon as the loaves have doubled in size, bake for 30 minutes, and then rotate pans to ensure even baking. Bake 35 to 40 minutes longer, or until the temperature on an instant-read thermometer reads 190 to 200 degrees.
	8 Cool the loaves in the pans for 5 minutes and then move them to a wire rack to cool completely. Store them in an airtight container at room temperature. Use a serrated knife for slicing.

Per serving: Calories 110 (From Fat 8); Fat 1g (Saturated 0g); Cholesterol 0mg; Sodium 74mg; Carbohydrate 24g; Dietary Fiber 2g; Protein 3g.

Note: Simple, wonderful, plain bread is the one food most newly diagnosed celiacs covet. It can be so hard to find a tender loaf! This lovely, yeasty loaf slices like a dream, and you can slice it and freeze it for travel or to make delicious sandwiches for the school lunchbox.

Parmesan Lemon Thyme Baguettes

Prep time: 20 min, plus rise time • **Cook time:** 15–20 min • **Yield:** 8 servings

Ingredients	Directions
½ **batch Egg-Free Yeast Bread (see page 300)**	*1* Make the Yeast Bread dough as directed but stir in the thyme and Parmesan cheese.
1 tablespoon minced fresh lemon thyme	*2* Cut a piece of parchment paper the length of your baguette pan. Most baguette pans have two indentations to make two loaves at once. You'll fill both indentations with the batter.
¼ **cup grated Parmesan cheese**	
Sweet rice flour (about ½ cup; exact measurement doesn't matter)	*3* Sprinkle the parchment paper heavily with sweet rice flour. Place ½ of the dough onto the floured paper by spoonfuls, letting the balls of dough touch each other.
	4 Grab the long side of the paper and gently roll the bread away from you. The dough balls will begin to connect, to form the long narrow baguette shape. If this doesn't occur easily, press them together gently with your fingers.
	5 Continue to roll the baguette across the paper until it's completely covered with flour. Lift the paper to the baguette pan and gently roll the dough onto the pan. Repeat with the second half of the dough, rolling it into the second baguette pan.
	6 Cover the pan securely with plastic wrap to hold in the moisture as the bread rises. Let the bread rise in a warm, draft-free place until it doubles in size. Unwrap the pan and cut slashes across the baguette to allow for oven spring.
	7 Preheat the oven to 450 degrees. Place the baguettes gently into the oven and bake for 15 to 20 minutes, or until they're golden-brown and crunchy. The bread's temperature should be 190 to 200 degrees.

Per serving: *Calories 252 (From Fat 27); Fat 3g (Saturated 1g); Cholesterol 3mg; Sodium 223mg; Carbohydrate 51g; Dietary Fiber 4g; Protein 8g.*

English Muffins

Prep time: 20 min, plus rise time • **Cook time:** 20 min • **Yield:** 8 servings

Ingredients	*Directions*
2 teaspoons cornmeal 1 cup (131 grams) High-Protein Bread Flour Mix (see Chapter 10) ½ cup plus 1 tablespoon plus 2 teaspoons (89 grams) White Flour Mix (see Chapter 10) ¼ cup plus 2 teaspoons (41 grams) Whole-Grain Flour Mix (see Chapter 10) 3 tablespoons (30 grams) raw buckwheat flour 1 tablespoon plus 1 teaspoon sugar ½ teaspoon salt 2 teaspoons active dry yeast ¾ cup water	*1* Place eight 4-inch English muffin rings on a Silpat-covered (silicone) baking sheet. Sprinkle ¼ teaspoon cornmeal into the rings; reserve the rest for later.
	2 In a large bowl, combine the High-Protein Bread Flour Mix, White Flour Mix, Whole-Grain Flour Mix, buckwheat flour, sugar, salt, and yeast until the mixture is one color.
	3 Add the water and beat well by hand.
	4 Divide the dough evenly among the rings, smoothing the tops to level the batter. Sprinkle the tops with the remaining cornmeal.
	5 Cover the dough with plastic wrap and let it rise for ½ hour.
	6 Preheat the oven to 375 degrees. Bake the muffins for 20 minutes, or until the internal temperature registers 190 to 200 degrees. They won't brown; that happens in the toaster!
	7 Remove the muffins from the oven; let them stand for 2 minutes on the cookie sheet and then remove.

Per serving: Calories 139 (From Fat 8); Fat 1g (Saturated 0g); Cholesterol 0mg; Sodium 147mg; Carbohydrate 31g; Dietary Fiber 2g; Protein 3g.

Note: These are lovely to have on hand in the freezer. If you split them before freezing you can just drop them into the toaster and toast. They're delicious topped with a fried egg, a piece of Canadian bacon, and some Cheddar cheese. Broil until the cheese melts.

Bagels

Prep time: 30 min, plus rise time • **Cook time:** 15 min • **Yield:** 8 servings

Ingredients	*Directions*
1½ cups (199 grams) High-Protein Bread Flour Mix (see Chapter 10)	*1* In a large bowl, combine the High-Protein Bread Flour Mix, White Flour Mix, and raw buckwheat flour and mix until the mixture is one color.
½ cup plus 2 teaspoons (81 grams) White Flour Mix (see Chapter 10)	*2* Add the honey, oil, yeast, and ½ cup plus 2 tablespoons water and beat for 2 minutes.
2 tablespoons (20 grams) raw buckwheat flour	*3* Form the mixture into eight balls. Poke a hole at least 1 inch in diameter into the center of each ball.
1 tablespoon honey	
1 tablespoon vegetable oil	*4* Place each bagel on a 4-inch square of parchment paper. Place the squares on a cookie sheet. Cover the bagels with plastic wrap and let them rise for 1½ hours.
1 tablespoon active dry yeast	
½ cup plus 2 tablespoons plus 8 cups water	*5* While the bagels rise, prepare the water bath. Place 8 cups of water in a large pot; add the sugar. Bring to a boil over high heat.
2 tablespoons sugar	
Toppings: sesame seeds, poppy seeds, coarse salt	*6* Preheat the oven to 425 degrees.
	7 After the bagels have doubled in size, place them, one at a time, into the boiling water, paper side down. Boil for 1 minute and then turn, remove the paper, and boil 1 minute longer.
	8 Remove the bagels from the water with a slotted spoon; let them drain and place them onto a Silpat-covered cookie sheet. Sprinkle them with the toppings of your choice.
	9 Bake for 13 to 15 minutes, or until the bagels are deep golden-brown. Move the bagels to a wire rack to cool completely.

Per serving: *Calories 157 (From Fat 25); Fat 3g (Saturated 0g); Cholesterol 0mg; Sodium 2mg; Carbohydrate 32g; Dietary Fiber 2g; Protein 4g.*

Fluffy Hamburger Buns

Prep time: 30 min, plus rise time • **Cook time:** 20 min • **Yield:** 6 servings

Ingredients	Directions
2½ teaspoons active dry yeast ¾ cup lukewarm water	**1** In a small bowl, combine the yeast and water and mix. Let stand until foamy, about 5 minutes.
1 cup minus 2 teaspoons (142 grams) White Flour Mix (see Chapter 10)	**2** Meanwhile, combine the White Flour Mix, Whole-Grain Flour Mix, raw buckwheat flour, dry milk powder, sugar, and salt and mix until one color.
1 cup minus 1 tablespoon (125 grams) Whole-Grain Flour Mix (see Chapter 10)	**3** Add the yeast mixture and butter and beat together until the dough forms a soft ball.
5 tablespoons (50 grams) raw buckwheat flour	
3 tablespoons dry milk powder	**4** Divide the dough into six portions. Form each portion into a ball.
2 tablespoons sugar	**5** Place the portions into a greased support ring. (See note below for making support rings.)
1 teaspoon salt	
2 tablespoons butter, melted	**6** Let the dough rise in a warm place for 45 minutes. Brush it with oil or melted butter for a soft crust.
	7 Preheat the oven to 350 degrees. Remove the rings and place the pan in the oven.
	8 Bake for 20 minutes, rotating the pan once during baking time.
	9 Move to a wire rack to cool completely before slicing.

Per serving: Calories 247 (From Fat 48); Fat 5g (Saturated 3g); Cholesterol 13mg; Sodium 398mg; Carbohydrate 48g; Dietary Fiber 2g; Protein 5g.

Note: To make support rings, tear off a piece of foil 16 inches long. Fold it in half lengthwise and cut along this line. Fold the foil toward the center from one long edge about 1 inch at a time to form a long, 1-inch wide strip. Form a circle into hamburger bun size, or form an oval shape to make hot dog buns. Alternately, for hot dog buns, form the dough into rods and place in a greased 9-x-13-inch pan, not touching.

Sourdough Starter

Prep time: 10 min, plus rest time • **Yield:** 2 cups

Ingredients	Directions

Ingredients

583 grams brown rice flour

583 grams sorghum flour

583 grams millet flour

290 grams sweet rice flour

74 grams garfava flour

155 grams white bean flour

Directions

1 For Starter Mix, combine all the ingredients and mix them together until the mixture is one color. Store this mixture in an airtight container and use it to make the Sourdough Starter.

2 For the Starter, combine equal weights of the Starter Mix and water, such as 1 cup Starter and 1 cup water.

3 Let sit, uncovered, in a warm spot in the kitchen for three days, stirring the mixture once a day. You're trying to capture yeast spores that are naturally occurring in the air in your kitchen. You'll have more success with this process if you bake some yeast breads in the days before you create a Starter. The Starter is ready when it bubbles and it smells like bread baking.

4 When the Starter starts bubbling, hopefully by the third day, feed it with 1 cup Sourdough Starter and 1 cup water. Let it grow for a day and then feed it again. Repeat once more and the Starter is ready to use.

Note: Some experienced cooks use unwashed organic grapes in the Starter to give it a boost, but this can add chlorophyll to your Starter. Try capturing wild yeast first by using just this flour mixture and water.

Sourdough Bread

Prep time: 30 min, plus rise time • **Cook time:** 35 min • **Yield:** 24 servings

Ingredients	Directions
150 grams potato starch	*1* Using a scale to measure the ingredients, combine the potato starch, tapioca starch, sorghum flour, sweet rice flour, sugar, salt, xanthan gum, and guar gum in a large mixing bowl for a stand mixer. Mix until the mixture is one color.
150 grams tapioca starch	
140 grams sorghum flour	
35 grams sweet rice flour	
30 grams sugar	*2* Stir the Sourdough Starter to mix in any liquid that may be floating on the top. Add the starter and water to the flour mixture.
10 grams salt	
20 grams xanthan gum	*3* Beat on high for 5 minutes. The bread will change from a mass of soft dough to one with some bounce. The dough will look like strands on the sides of the bowl and will gather on the beater.
10 grams guar gum	
1500 grams Sourdough Starter (see page 305)	
½ cup water	*4* To form a boule, place half the dough on a parchment paper square. Use a spatula to smooth and shape the dough into a ball. Repeat with the second half of dough.
Course sea salt (optional)	
	5 Lift the paper holding the balls and place them into a bowl a little bit smaller than the pot you'll use for baking. Cover with plastic wrap and place in a warm spot to rise.
	6 Let the dough rise for 4 hours, or until it doubles in size. You can refrigerate the dough instead; it will rise there for 12 hours. If you refrigerate the dough, bring it to room temperature before baking.
	7 Remove the dough balls from the bowl using the paper. Using a sharp knife or razor blade, cut slashes into each loaf. Create two parallel lines on either side of the balls, turn them 90 degrees, and slash two more lines to form a square on top. These slashes allow for oven spring.
	8 Place an 8-cup ovenproof pot into the oven and preheat both to 450 degrees.

9 When the oven is preheated, carefully remove the pot from the oven with oven mitts.

10 Remove the lid and place the bread dough into the pot, keeping it attached to the paper. Sprinkle with coarse sea salt, if desired, and replace the lid. Put the pot in the oven and set the timer for 35 minutes.

11 When the timer goes off, check the bread's temperature. It should be 190 to 200 degrees and look deep golden-brown. If the bread isn't brown enough, remove it from the pot, place it on the oven rack, and bake it for 5 minutes longer. Let the bread cool on a wire rack.

12 For baguettes, sprinkle a piece of parchment paper or Silpat with sweet rice flour for a crisp crust or millet flour for a softer crust.

13 Divide each half of dough into a long log and sprinkle them with a bit more sweet rice or millet flour.

14 Using the paper, extend and roll the dough into a long baguette shape. Roll onto a baguette pan. Repeat with the other half of the dough.

15 Let the dough rise as directed for the boule, wrapping the pan in plastic wrap.

16 Preheat the oven to 450 degrees. Remove the plastic wrap. Add the bread and bake for 15 minutes.

17 Reduce the heat to 400 degrees, rotate the pan, and bake for 15 minutes more.

18 Test the bread; it should be 190 to 200 degrees and look deep golden-brown. Bake 5 minutes longer if the bread tests done but isn't brown.

19 Move the bread to a wire rack to cool completely.

Per serving: *Calories 254 (From Fat 16); Fat 2g (Saturated 0g); Cholesterol 0mg; Sodium 165mg; Carbohydrate 56g; Dietary Fiber 4g; Protein 6g.*

Rosemary Parmesan Pull-Apart Rolls

Prep time: 30 min, plus rise time • **Cook time:** 40 min • **Yield:** 12 servings

Ingredients	*Directions*
One batch Sourdough Bread (see page 306)	*1* Make the the Sourdough Bread but don't let it rise yet.
1 cup grated Parmesan cheese	*2* On a large plate, combine the Parmesan cheese and pepper.
½ teaspoon black pepper	*3* Stir the rosemary into the Bread dough.
3 tablespoons fresh minced rosemary	*4* Prepare a 12-cup Bundt pan by spraying with nonstick cooking spray.
Extra virgin olive oil or melted butter	*5* Scoop the balls of dough using a Number 70 (⅓ cup or DP-12) ice cream scoop. Drop each ball into the cheese mixture and roll to coat.
	6 Place each ball into the prepared pan in one layer. Drizzle with a bit of extra virgin olive oil or melted butter.
	7 Repeat with the next layer of dough, placing each ball of dough on the junction of two rolls below. Drizzle with more oil or butter. Repeat until all the dough is used.
	8 Cover the dough with plastic wrap and let it rise for 8 to 10 hours, until doubled.
	9 Preheat the oven to 425 degrees. Cover the pan with foil and bake for 35 to 40 minutes, or until the internal temperature is 190 to 200 degrees.
	10 If the rolls aren't brown enough, remove the foil and bake 5 minutes longer.

Per serving: Calories 540 (From Fat 50); Fat 6g (Saturated 2g); Cholesterol 5mg; Sodium 455mg; Carbohydrate 112g; Dietary Fiber 7g; Protein 15g.

Soft Egg Bread

Prep time: 30 min, plus rise time • **Cook time:** 50 min • **Yield:** 8 servings

Ingredients	Directions
2¼ cups minus 1 teaspoon (292 grams) High-Protein Bread Flour Mix (see Chapter 10)	**1** Grease an 8-x-4-inch bread pan with unsalted butter and set aside.
1⅓ cups minus 1 teaspoon (177 grams) Whole-Grain Flour Mix (see Chapter 10)	**2** In a large bowl, combine the High-Protein Bread Flour Mix, Whole-Grain Flour Mix, sugar, yeast, and salt and stir until the mixture is one color.
¼ cup sugar	
1 tablespoon active dry yeast	**3** Add the eggs, butter, and water and beat well until combined.
1¼ teaspoons salt	
3 eggs	**4** Pour the mixture into the prepared pan. Cover with plastic wrap and let rise for 1 hour.
¼ cup butter, melted	
½ cup water	**5** Preheat the oven to 350 degrees. Bake for 45 to 50 minutes, or until the internal temperature registers 190 to 200 degrees.
	6 Remove from the pan and cool completely on a wire rack before slicing.

Per serving: Calories 297 (From Fat 84); Fat 9g (Saturated 4g); Cholesterol 95mg; Sodium 391mg; Carbohydrate 47g; Dietary Fiber 4g; Protein 9g.

Note: This tender bread is like challah. For a nice change of pace, incorporate ¼ cup dried currants into the dough before rising.

Vegan Focaccia Bread with Kalamata Olives

Prep time: 30 min, plus rise time • **Cook time:** 30 min • **Yield:** 12 servings

Ingredients	Directions
¼ cup golden flaxseeds, finely ground	*1* Combine the ground flaxseeds and buckwheat flour in a large mixing bowl with warm water. Beat for 1 minute to develop the structure because these ingredients act as gums in this recipe.
½ cup (80 grams) raw buckwheat flour	
1¼ cups warm water	*2* Stir in the White Flour Mix, Bread Flour Mix, salt, sugar, and yeast and beat for 1 minute.
1 cup minus 2 teaspoons (142 grams) White Flour Mix (see Chapter 10)	
1 cup plus 1 teaspoon (133 grams) High-Protein Bread Flour Mix (see Chapter 10)	*3* Use one tablespoon of oil to grease a 9-x-13-inch baking pan. Use another tablespoon of oil to grease your hands.
¼ teaspoon salt	*4* Gather the soft dough and press it into an even layer in the pan. It should fill the pan completely.
2 tablespoons sugar	*5* Sprinkle the dough with rosemary and olives, pushing gently into the dough. Drizzle with the remaining 2 tablespoons of olive oil.
1 tablespoon active dry yeast	
4 tablespoons olive oil	
1 tablespoon chopped fresh rosemary	*6* Cover the pan with plastic wrap and let the dough rise 1 hour.
⅓ cup pitted kalamata olives	*7* Preheat the oven to 400 degrees. Remove the plastic wrap and sprinkle the dough with coarse sea salt (if desired).
Coarse sea salt (optional)	
	8 Bake on the lower oven rack for 15 minutes and then rotate the pan and bake 15 minutes longer, until the temperature is 190 to 200 degrees. Remove the bread from the pan to cool completely before cutting it into squares.

Per serving: Calories 176 (From Fat 73); Fat 8g (Saturated 1g); Cholesterol 0mg; Sodium 166mg; Carbohydrate 25g; Dietary Fiber 2g; Protein 3g.

Vary It! You can use chopped reconstituted or oil-packed sun-dried tomatoes, any grated cheese, or finely chopped cooked meats in place of the olives. Use other herbs, too.

Chapter 20

Pizzas, Savory Pies, and Calzones

*E*veryone loves pizza. There's nothing like picking up a piece of hot pizza with a crisp yet tender crust and biting into oozing cheese and savory toppings. With these tasty recipes, you can enjoy this classic treat whenever you want. Savory pies include quiches and pot pies. And calzones are stuffed pizzas, filled with mouth-watering ingredients. Gluten-free pie crusts make these treats enjoyable again. These easy recipes are designed to maximize a crisp and flaky crust while matching it with healthy and satisfying fillings.

Tips for Making Pizzas and Pies

Just as with savory yeast and quick breads, gluten-free pizza and pie crusts are a bit different from yeast crusts. Pizza crust is a stiff batter, similar to yeast bread doughs, but the preparation method is different.

You've probably heard of pizza stones. This product is literally made of stone. It heats up quickly and holds heat so the pizza crust has a wonderful crackly bottom. For best results, get one! You can find them at kitchen supply stores, big box stores, and even some large supermarkets.

Here are some tips for making pizzas, pies, and calzones:

- Gluten-free pizza doughs use more yeast than wheat-based pizza doughs, and the dough rises just once on parchment paper.

- If you don't use a scale to measure flours and mixes, always measure by spooning the flour or mix lightly into a measuring cup and leveling off the top with the back of a knife. See Chapters 4 and 5 for more info on measuring by weight and volume.

- Make sure the pizza stone is very hot. An oven takes only 10 minutes to heat, but the racks and oven walls aren't at the correct temperature until at least 20 minutes have passed. Pizza stones take at least 20 minutes to heat up to the correct temperature.

- You must bake the crust before adding the toppings. And don't overload the crust with lots of sauce and toppings. This pizza is New York style, which means the crust is crisp but bendable. If you add tons of sauce, meats, and cheeses, you can't pick up a piece and bend it in half to eat it in the classic manner!

- You can vary main dish pies in many ways. Use different vegetables, meats, and cheeses for quiches. You can make quiche with pork sausage, leftover vegetables, and any cheese you'd like, or use shrimp and asparagus for an elegant version.

- Make gluten-free calzones using a stiff batter formed on parchment paper. The filling for these calzones can't be too liquid or the batter will dissolve. And don't overfill calzones! Too much filling just bursts out of the calzone and makes the crust wet.

- A few recipes in this chapter call for raw buckwheat flour, which isn't the same as the buckwheat flour you buy in packages. That buckwheat flour has been toasted. For these recipes, you must grind raw green buckwheat groats to a powder.

Easy Recipes for Pizzas, Pies, and Calzones

These recipes are the most fun to vary. After you master the perfect pizza crust, you can top it with just about anything. Take a look through some gourmet cookbooks or browse the Internet for topping ideas. Goat cheese, smoked salmon, grilled shrimp or steak, roasted vegetables, lots of cheeses, tofu, and chicken are all great pizza toppers.

You can make main dish pies, too, with just about any meat, cheese, or vegetable. And calzones are the perfect easy recipe for using up leftovers. Enjoy these crisp and crusty treats.

Vegan Pizza Crust without Gums

Prep time: 20 min, plus rising time • **Cook time:** 20 min • **Yield:** 8 servings

Ingredients	Directions
½ cup plus 1 tablespoon plus 1 teaspoon (81 grams) Whole-Grain Flour Mix (see Chapter 10)	**1** In a large bowl of a stand mixer, combine all ingredients. Beat with the paddle attachment for 2 minutes. The dough will be soft and spreadable, like frosting in texture.
1 cup minus 2 teaspoons (142 grams) White Flour Mix (see Chapter 10)	**2** Cut a piece of parchment paper to fit a 10-inch pizza stone for a thick crust. Spread the dough onto the parchment paper. If you don't have a stone, just line a cookie sheet with parchment paper and spread the dough to its edges for a thin crust.
½ teaspoon salt	
⅓ cup (38 grams) corn flour	
2 tablespoons (20 grams) raw buckwheat flour	**3** Let the dough rise in a warm place for 1 hour. You can reduce the rising time to 30 minutes, but the dough won't be as puffy.
2 tablespoons extra virgin olive oil	**4** Preheat the oven and pizza stone together to 500 degrees. This may take as long as 20 minutes; make sure the stone is very hot.
2¼ teaspoons dried yeast (1 packet)	
1 cup warm water	**5** Slide the parchment paper with the dough onto the hot stone. If you're using a cookie sheet, just place it in the oven.
Toppings of your choice	
	6 Bake for 10 minutes, until lightly browned. If any areas get very puffy, poke them with a fork.
	7 Top with tomato sauce or pesto and other pizza toppings.
	8 Bake for 10 minutes longer. Cool for 2 to 3 minutes before cutting.

Per serving: Calories 148 (From Fat 35); Fat 4g (Saturated 1g); Cholesterol 0mg; Sodium 147mg; Carbohydrate 28g; Dietary Fiber 1g; Protein 2g.

Cornmeal Pizza Crust

Prep time: 20 min • **Cook time:** 25–30 min • **Yield:** 8 servings

Ingredients	Directions
¾ cup yellow cornmeal	*1* Preheat the oven to 425 degrees. Put the pizza stone in the oven to heat while you make the dough.
⅓ cup minus 1 teaspoon (49 grams) sweet rice flour	
⅓ cup plus 1 teaspoon (46 grams) millet flour	*2* In a large bowl of a stand mixer, combine the cornmeal, sweet rice flour, millet flour, corn flour, and raw buckwheat flour; mix until the mixture is one color.
⅓ cup (38 grams) corn flour	
3 tablespoons (28 grams) raw buckwheat flour	*3* Add the remaining ingredients and beat with the paddle attachment for 2 minutes.
2 tablespoons extra virgin olive oil	*4* Cut a piece of parchment paper to fit a 10-inch pizza stone for a thick crust. Spread the dough onto the parchment paper. If you don't have a stone, just line a cookie sheet with parchment paper and spread the dough to its edges for a thin crust.
1½ teaspoons baking powder	
½ teaspoon baking soda	
½ teaspoon salt	
1 cup water	*5* Slide the parchment paper onto the hot pizza stone or put the cookie sheet in the oven.
Toppings of your choice	
	6 Bake for 15 minutes, remove, and top with toppings.
	7 Return to the oven and bake for 10 to 15 minutes longer, until the crust is browned and the toppings are hot and melted. Cool for a few minutes before cutting.

Per serving: Calories 146 (From Fat 37); Fat 4g (Saturated 1g); Cholesterol 0mg; Sodium 296mg; Carbohydrate 25g; Dietary Fiber 2g; Protein 3g.

Note: Cornmeal adds great crunch to this simple pizza crust. This crust is a good choice for dinner in a hurry because you don't have to wait for the dough to rise. Top it with anything you like!

Tex-Mex Pizza

Prep time: 30 min • **Cook time:** 35 min • **Yield:** 8 servings

Ingredients	*Directions*
1 recipe Cornmeal Pizza Crust (see page 314)	*1* Preheat the oven to 425 degrees. Prepare the Cornmeal Pizza Crust and bake it for 10 minutes, then set aside.
½ pound gluten-free ground pork sausage	
1 small onion, chopped	*2* In a large saucepan, cook the ground pork sausage with the onion, garlic, and jalapeño pepper until the sausage is thoroughly cooked, about 5 to 7 minutes, stirring to break up the sausage. Drain well.
2 cloves garlic, minced	
1 jalapeño pepper, minced	
1 cup gluten-free refried beans (from 16-ounce can)	*3* Stir in the refried beans, taco sauce, chili powder, salt, cumin, and red pepper flakes. Remove from heat.
½ cup gluten-free taco sauce	
2 teaspoons gluten-free chili powder	*4* Spread the bean mixture over the crust and top with the cheeses. Bake for 15 to 20 minutes, or until the crust is golden-brown and the cheeses are melted and starting to brown.
½ teaspoon salt	
½ teaspoon cumin	
¼ teaspoon crushed red pepper flakes	*5* While the pizza is baking, combine the avocado, tomato, and green onion.
1 cup shredded Cheddar cheese	*6* Let the pizza cool for 3 to 5 minutes before cutting it into wedges to serve. Top with the avocado mixture.
½ cup shredded Pepper Jack cheese	
1 avocado, peeled and diced	
1 ripe tomato, chopped	
¼ cup chopped green onion	

Per serving: Calories 412 (From Fat 164); Fat 18g (Saturated 7g); Cholesterol 35mg; Sodium 859mg; Carbohydrate 49g; Dietary Fiber 9g; Protein 15g.

Note: To make your own chili powder, combine 1 teaspoon ground cumin, 1 teaspoon dried ground chiles, 1 teaspoon smoked paprika, 1 teaspoon ground oregano, 1 teaspoon garlic powder, 1 teaspoon salt, 1 teaspoon onion powder, ½ teaspoon black pepper, and ½ teaspoon cayenne pepper. Blend well and store in an airtight container. And make sure all these ingredients are gluten-free too!

Meat and Vegetable Pasties

Prep time: 40 min, plus rest time • **Cook time:** 50 min • **Yield:** 8 servings

Ingredients	Directions
1 cup (123 grams) sorghum flour	*1* In a large bowl, combine the sorghum flour, tapioca flour, sweet rice flour, 1 teaspoon salt, sugar, baking powder, and gelatin or xanthan gum. Cut in the shortening until large crumbs form.
¾ cup (94 grams) tapioca flour	
½ cup (78 grams) sweet rice flour	
1 teaspoon plus ½ teaspoon salt	*2* Add the water until the dough forms a ball. Let rest, covered, for 1 hour.
1 tablespoon sugar	*3* Roll the dough out to ¼-inch thickness. Using a 6-inch saucer, cut out circles of dough.
½ teaspoon baking powder	
½ teaspoon unflavored gelatin or 1 teaspoon xanthan gum	*4* For the filling, melt the butter in a large skillet over medium heat. Add the beef and cook until browned, about 3 to 4 minutes.
1 cup solid shortening	
¼ cup ice water	*5* Add the turnips, potatoes, carrots, and onion. Cook for 10 to 12 minutes, until the vegetables are crisp-tender. Add ½ teaspoon salt, parsley, and pepper; cool for 15 minutes.
1 tablespoon butter	
1 pound boneless sirloin, cubed	
½ cup cubed turnips	*6* Preheat the oven to 400 degrees. Put ½ cup filling on one side of each circle of dough. Fold the dough over to cover the filling and crimp the edges. Place on a cookie sheet.
½ cup cubed potatoes	
½ cup cubed carrots	
1 onion, diced	
2 tablespoons minced parsley	*7* Bake for 35 to 40 minutes, or until golden-brown.
¼ teaspoon pepper	

Per serving: *Calories 475 (From Fat 268); Fat 30g (Saturated 8g); Cholesterol 37mg; Sodium 499mg; Carbohydrate 41g; Dietary Fiber 2g; Protein 15g.*

Vary It! For a vegetarian pasty, omit the beef and butter. Add 2 cloves minced garlic and ¼ pound mushrooms, chopped, to the vegetable mixture. Cook the vegetable mixture in 1 tablespoon olive oil until it's crisp-tender and then proceed with the recipe.

Pepperoni Pizza

Prep time: 30 min • **Cook time:** 26–30 min • **Yield:** 6 servings

Ingredients	Directions
1 recipe Basic Pizza Dough (see Chapter 17)	**1** Preheat the oven to 425 degrees.
1 small onion, chopped	**2** Prepare the Basic Pizza Dough and press it onto a cookie sheet. Let it rise. While the dough is rising, make the filling.
2 cloves garlic, minced	
1 small green bell pepper, chopped	
1 tablespoon olive oil	**3** In a medium, microwave-safe bowl, combine the onion, garlic, bell pepper, and olive oil. Microwave on high for 2 minutes; remove and stir. Microwave on high for 1 minute longer.
One 8-ounce can tomato sauce	
2 tablespoons gluten-free tomato paste	
2 tablespoons yellow gluten-free mustard	**4** Stir the tomato sauce, tomato paste, mustard, Italian seasoning, salt, and pepper into the onion mixture.
½ teaspoon dried Italian seasoning	**5** Put the dough in the oven and bake for 10 minutes.
½ teaspoon salt	
⅛ teaspoon pepper	**6** Remove the dough and spread the sauce over the crust. Top with the pepperoni slices in a single layer. Sprinkle with the cheeses.
One 3-ounce package gluten-free pepperoni slices	
1 cup shredded mozzarella cheese	**7** Return the pizza to the oven and bake for 13 to 18 minutes longer, or until the crust is golden-brown and the cheese is melted and beginning to brown.
½ cup shredded Cheddar cheese	

Per serving: Calories 414 (From Fat 154); Fat 17g (Saturated 7g); Cholesterol 36mg; Sodium 1,289mg; Carbohydrate 53g; Dietary Fiber 4g; Protein 15g.

Tip: Hormel pepperoni is gluten-free. Be sure to check the label of any pepperoni you buy to make sure it doesn't contain gluten.

Roasted Vegetable Pizza

Prep time: 35 min • **Cook time:** 11–28 min • **Yield:** 6 servings

Ingredients	*Directions*
1 recipe Basic Pizza Dough (see Chapter 17) **2 large ripe tomatoes** **1 zucchini, thinly sliced** **2 large portobello mushrooms, thinly sliced** **1 large bell pepper, sliced ¼-inch thick** **2 tablespoons plus 2 tablespoons extra virgin olive oil or kalamata olive oil** **3 ounces fresh basil leaves** **8 ounces (2 cups) grated mozzarella cheese (optional)** **Salt and pepper to taste**	*1* Preheat the oven to 450 degrees. Prepare the Basic Pizza Dough. Put the dough on a cold cookie sheet, stretching and patting so it fits the pan. Let it rise while you prepare the vegetables. *2* Remove the core from the tomatoes and slice them ¼-inch thick. Prepare all the vegetables. *3* Place the vegetables on a cookie sheet and coat with 2 tablespoons of the oil. Roast for 5 to 10 minutes, or until the edges start to brown. Remove them from the oven and set them aside. *4* Gently rub the remaining 2 tablespoons oil into the dough. *5* Place the basil leaves on the dough in a single layer and arrange the vegetables on top. Top with the cheese (if desired). *6* Bake for 6 minutes for a no-cheese pizza. Bake for 15 to 18 minutes for a pizza with cheese, until the cheese melts and browns. *7* Let the pizza cool for 3 minutes before cutting to serve.

Per serving: Calories 343 (From Fat 116); Fat 13g (Saturated 2g); Cholesterol 0mg; Sodium 496mg; Carbohydrate 54g; Dietary Fiber 5g; Protein 7g.

Vegetable Cheese Calzone

Prep time: 40 min • **Cook time:** 45 min • **Yield:** 4 servings

Ingredients	Directions
1 recipe Basic Pizza Dough (see Chapter 17)	*1* Make the Basic Pizza Dough and divide it into four parts. Roll out each piece onto a piece of parchment paper into a 10-inch circle.
2 tablespoons olive oil	
1 red bell pepper, diced	*2* In a large skillet, heat the olive oil over medium heat. Add the bell pepper, zucchini, and spinach and cook until soft, about 8 to 9 minutes. Let cool completely.
1 zucchini, diced	
1 cup frozen chopped spinach, thawed and well drained	*3* Divide the vegetable mixture among the dough circles, leaving the outer inch of dough filling-free.
½ cup grated mozzarella cheese	
¼ cup grated Parmesan cheese	*4* Top each circle with 2 tablespoons mozzarella cheese, 1 tablespoon Parmesan cheese, 1 tablespoon kalamata olives, and 2 tablespoons artichoke hearts.
¼ cup sliced kalamata olives	
½ cup chopped artichoke hearts	*5* Fold one side of the calzone over the other and crimp well around the edges.
	6 Let rise for 30 minutes. Preheat the oven to 425 degrees.
	7 Bake the calzones for 35 to 40 minutes, until well browned.

Per serving: Calories 507 (From Fat 167); Fat 19g (Saturated 5g); Cholesterol 15mg; Sodium 922mg; Carbohydrate 76g; Dietary Fiber 5g; Protein 14g.

Vary It! Use your favorite vegetables in this easy recipe.

Spinach Quiche

Prep time: 25 min • **Cook time:** 50 min • **Yield:** 8 servings

Ingredients	Directions
1 recipe Butter Pie Crust (see Chapter 17)	**1** Preheat the oven to 350 degrees. Line a 9-inch pie pan with the Butter Pie Crust; refrigerate.
1 tablespoon olive oil	
½ large onion, minced	**2** In a large skillet, heat the olive oil over medium heat. Add the onions and cook until translucent, stirring frequently, about 5 minutes. Add the spinach and continue to cook, stirring occasionally, until the spinach wilts and the liquid evaporates, about 3 to 5 minutes. Remove from the heat.
1 pound fresh spinach, washed and chopped	
8 eggs	
½ cup light cream	**3** In a large bowl, beat the eggs until they're light and fluffy. You want to get as much air into the eggs as possible so the quiche rises well.
¼ teaspoon salt	
¼ teaspoon pepper	**4** Stir in the cream, salt, and pepper and beat to combine.
½ cup shredded havarti or Swiss cheese	
	5 Place the pie crust on a cookie sheet. Arrange the spinach mixture in the bottom of the crust.
	6 Pour the egg mixture slowly over the spinach mixture. Top with the cheese.
	7 Bake for 40 to 45 minutes, or until the quiche is browned and set. Let the quiche cool for 5 minutes and then cut it into wedges to serve.

Per serving: Calories 403 (From Fat 215); Fat 24g (Saturated 12g); Cholesterol 261mg; Sodium 435mg; Carbohydrate 37g; Dietary Fiber 4g; Protein 12g.

Note: You can substitute 1 pound of frozen, chopped spinach, thawed and very well drained, for the fresh spinach. Be sure to sauté the spinach with the onions until the liquid evaporates or the quiche will be soggy.

Mini Pancetta Quiches

Prep time: 20 min • **Cook time:** 25 min • **Yield:** 36 servings

Ingredients	*Directions*
2 tablespoons (16 grams) cornstarch	*1* Preheat the oven to 425 degrees. Spray 36 mini muffin cups with nonstick cooking spray and set aside.
2 tablespoons (14 grams) tapioca flour	*2* In a blender or food processor, combine the cornstarch, tapioca flour, milk, cream, eggs, salt, thyme, and pepper. Blend until smooth and set aside.
¾ cup milk	
⅓ cup heavy cream	
3 eggs	*3* In a medium skillet, heat the olive oil over medium heat. Add the pancetta; cook and stir until the cubes are crispy, about 5 to 7 minutes. Add the shallot, cook for 2 minutes, and then drain well on paper towels.
½ teaspoon salt	
1 teaspoon dried thyme leaves	
⅛ teaspoon pepper	
1 tablespoon olive oil	*4* Divide the pancetta mixture and fontina cheese among the mini muffin cups.
6 ounces diced pancetta	
1 shallot, minced	*5* Spoon about 1 tablespoon of the egg mixture into each mini muffin cup, over the pancetta mixture. Sprinkle each mini quiche with a bit of Parmesan cheese.
1 cup shredded fontina cheese	
¼ cup grated Parmesan cheese	
	6 Bake for 15 to 20 minutes, or until the quiches are light golden-brown and set.
	7 Let the quiches cool in the muffin tins for 5 minutes and then run a sharp knife around the edge of each mini quiche and remove from the tin. Serve warm.

Per serving: Calories 37 (From Fat 26); Fat 3g (Saturated 1g); Cholesterol 21mg; Sodium 95mg; Carbohydrate 1g; Dietary Fiber 0g; Protein 2g.

Vary It! You can use just about any filling and any cheese in these tiny crustless quiches. Some chopped cooked chicken or tiny shrimp would be delicious. Use vegan cheese, Cheddar cheese, Swiss cheese, or Gouda cheese.

Asparagus Quiche

Prep time: 20 min • **Cook time:** 2 hrs • **Yield:** 6 servings

Ingredients	*Directions*
2 cups long-grain brown rice 5 cups water	*1* Preheat the oven to 350 degrees. Grease a 10-inch springform pan and set aside.
¼ cup (39 grams) sweet rice flour ¼ cup plus 2 tablespoons olive oil	*2* In a large saucepan, combine the brown rice and water. Bring to a boil over high heat.
1 pound asparagus, ends trimmed 9 eggs	*3* Reduce the heat to low, cover the pan, and simmer for 35 to 40 minutes, or until the rice is soft. Drain the rice if necessary. Cool for 15 minutes.
1 cup unsweetened soy, rice, or hemp milk	*4* Add the sweet rice flour and ¼ cup olive oil to the rice. Press into the bottom and up the sides of the prepared pan. Place the pan on a cookie sheet.
	5 Bake the rice crust unfilled for 20 minutes.
	6 On a large baking sheet, combine the asparagus and 2 tablespoons olive oil and roll to coat. Bake for 15 to 20 minutes, or until the asparagus is tender.
	7 Let the asparagus cool for a few minutes. Chop the stems finely until you reach 3 inches from the tip end. Leave the tips whole.
	8 Arrange the chopped asparagus stems in the pie shell. In a large bowl, beat the eggs with the milk until smooth. Pour over the asparagus stems in the crust. Top with the reserved asparagus tips in a pretty pattern.
	9 Bake for 45 to 55 minutes, or until the quiche puffs, turns brown, and is firm in the center. Cool slightly, remove pan sides, and cut into wedges to serve.

Per serving: Calories 504 (From Fat 215); Fat 24g (Saturated 5g); Cholesterol 319mg; Sodium 114mg; Carbohydrate 55g; Dietary Fiber 5g; Protein 17g.

Spinach and Goat Cheese Stuffed Rolls

Prep time: 30 min, plus chilling time • **Cook time:** 25 min • **Yield:** 6 servings

Ingredients	Directions
4 ounces goat cheese with herbs, crumbled 8 ounces frozen chopped spinach, thawed and very well drained ¼ teaspoon pepper 1½ teaspoons active dry yeast 1½ teaspoons sugar ½ cup plus 1 tablespoon plus 2 teaspoons (83 grams) Whole-Grain Flour Mix (see Chapter 10) ½ cup minus 1 teaspoon (71 grams) White Flour Mix (see Chapter 10) 2 tablespoons (20 grams) raw buckwheat flour or ¾ teaspoon xanthan gum ¼ teaspoon salt 1 egg ¼ cup butter or butter-flavored shortening 2 tablespoons water	**1** In a medium bowl, combine the goat cheese, spinach, and pepper until combined. Place the mixture onto plastic wrap and form it into a 10-inch-long log. Chill the log while you make the dough. **2** For the dough, in a large bowl, combine the yeast, sugar, Whole-Grain Flour Mix, White Flour Mix, buckwheat flour (or xanthan gum), and salt and mix until the dough is one color. **3** Add the egg, butter or shortening, and water and beat well for 1 minute. **4** Roll the dough onto parchment paper to ½-inch thickness, a 12-x-6-inch rectangle. Chill the dough for a half hour to let it rise slightly and firm. **5** Preheat the oven to 425 degrees. **6** Remove the dough and goat cheese filling from the fridge. Remove the plastic from the goat cheese log and place the log in the center of the dough. Flatten the cheese mixture slightly. **7** Fold in the ends of the dough and then the sides to encase the filling. Leave a gap at the center so the filling shows. **8** Bake for 15 minutes, rotate the pan, and bake 10 to 12 minutes longer, or until the crust is golden-brown. Let the roll cool completely before slicing to serve.

Per serving: Calories 263 (From Fat 132); Fat 15g (Saturated 9g); Cholesterol 71mg; Sodium 240mg; Carbohydrate 27g; Dietary Fiber 2g; Protein 9g.

Note: Make sure that the spinach is really well drained. Squeeze the spinach until no more liquid comes out. Press it in a kitchen towel or between paper towels to make sure it's really dry.

Chicken Pot Pie

Prep time: 40 min • **Cook time:** 60 min • **Yield:** 8–10 servings

Ingredients	*Directions*
½ recipe Butter Pie Crust (see Chapter 17)	**1** Preheat the oven to 425 degrees. Grease a deep dish metal pie plate or shallow casserole dish and place it on a cookie sheet.
3 tablespoons butter	
⅓ cup (53 grams) sweet rice flour	**2** Prepare the Butter Pie Crust and roll it out in a circle large enough to cover the pie plate or dish; refrigerate.
½ cup dry white wine	
1 cup milk	**3** For the sauce, melt the butter in a medium saucepan over medium heat. Add the sweet rice flour and cook for 1 minute. Add the wine and cook until the wine evaporates, about 3 to 5 minutes. Add the milk and chicken stock, whisking constantly until smooth, about 3 to 5 minutes.
1 cup chicken stock	
4 tablespoons olive oil	
3 boneless, skinless chicken breasts, diced	
1 large onion, diced	**4** Simmer the sauce until it thickens, about 3 to 4 minutes. Remove it from the heat and set aside.
3 carrots, diced	
3 celery stalks, sliced	**5** For the filling, in a large saucepan, heat the olive oil over medium heat. Add the chicken and onions and cook, stirring, until the chicken is done and the onions are crisp-tender, about 6 to 8 minutes.
¾ cup green peas	
1 teaspoon chopped fresh thyme	
2 tablespoons minced fresh parsley	**6** Add the carrots and celery and cook another 2 to 3 minutes.
	7 Place the chicken mixture into the prepared pan plate. Top with the peas and herbs.
	8 Pour the sauce over the chicken and vegetables and top with the pie crust.
	9 Immediately place the cookie sheet/pie plate into the oven. Bake for 10 minutes, reduce the heat to 350 degrees, and bake 25 to 30 minutes more, until the crust is golden-brown and the filling is bubbly.

Per serving: Calories 357 (From Fat 178); Fat 20g (Saturated 8g); Cholesterol 59mg; Sodium 294mg; Carbohydrate 31g; Dietary Fiber 3g; Protein 15g.

Chapter 21

Casseroles, Soufflés, Crepes, and Dumplings

In This Chapter

▶ Following some tips to make the best baked entrée recipes
▶ Serving up casseroles, soufflés, and crepes

*O*n a cold or rainy night, nothing's more comforting than pulling a bubbling casserole from the oven. But can you still enjoy dumplings, bread-topped casseroles, and soufflés on a gluten-free diet? Yes!

In this chapter, we concentrate on recipes for hearty casseroles, luscious crepes, ethereal soufflés, and hearty, creamy dumplings. These recipes focus on chicken, beef, ham, and cheese as the savory base for corn bread and herbed bread toppings. And we include vegetarian and vegan entrée recipes as well.

These recipes are perhaps the easiest to adapt. Vegan cheeses work well in these recipes because they need more moisture to become creamy and rich, and casseroles and soufflés are very moist. You can substitute shrimp for chicken, ground pork for ground beef, or turkey for ham. After you master the soufflé, you can make it with cheese, shrimp, chicken, or vegetables. Crepe fillings are a wonderful way to use up leftovers. And you can serve an oven pancake with fruit for brunch or with a rich beef gravy for a hearty dinner.

Tips for Making the Best Entrée Recipes

Although these recipes are a bit more tolerant than most gluten-free baking recipes, you still need to follow some rules. Measure carefully, using weight for the flours. Timing is important; many of these recipes won't wait for people to get to the table, so have your guests waiting for the finished dish!

- For casseroles topped with biscuits or bread, add the batter or dough while the filling is very hot. Start baking the bread as soon as it touches the casserole ingredients or the bottom will be soggy.

- If you don't use a scale to measure flours and mixes, always measure by spooning the flour or mix lightly into a measuring cup and leveling off the top with the back of a knife. See Chapters 4 and 5 for more info on measuring by weight and volume.

- Soufflés seem scary, but they're really quite easy. You just make a white sauce, add cheese and beaten egg yolks, and then fold in beaten egg whites. Gluten-free soufflés are delicate; you should serve them immediately. They begin to fall about a minute after they come out of the oven. But even when fallen, they taste delicious!

- For crepes, make sure the filling is thick. A filling that's too runny may make the crepes too fragile and they won't hold together. Filled gluten-free crepes don't reheat well, so plan on eating them all when first made.

- Gluten-free dumplings are lighter and more fragile than wheat-based dumplings. Don't simmer them longer than the recipe states. And be sure to drop the dumplings into simmering water, not boiling. Keep a lid on dumplings while they cook, and don't peek until you reach the minimum time. To test dumpling doneness, spoon one out of the pot and cut it open with a knife. The inside should be hot and not doughy.

Quick and Delicious Entrée Recipes

Entrées are the most tolerant of all baking recipes. You can substitute just about anything for most of the ingredients in these recipes. Use turkey or ham instead of chicken. Vary the spices and cheeses. Use different vegetables. You can even make miniature casseroles or individual pot pies for a nice change of pace.

And when you create a new recipe, be sure to write it down! You won't be able to remember all the details of your wonderful new creation. Now let's make some delicious main dishes perfect for serving to family and friends.

Chicken Corn Bread Bake

Prep time: 25 min • **Cook time:** 55 min • **Yield:** 8 servings

Ingredients	Directions
2 tablespoons olive oil	*1* Preheat the oven to 350 degrees. Spray a 13-x-9-inch glass baking pan with nonstick cooking spray and set aside.
1 onion, chopped	
2 cloves garlic, minced	
1 cup sliced button or crimini mushrooms	*2* In a large skillet, heat the olive oil over medium heat. Add the onion and garlic and cook and stir until crisp-tender, about 4 minutes.
1 red bell pepper, chopped	
4 cups cubed, cooked chicken	*3* Add the mushrooms and red bell pepper and cook and stir until tender, about 4 to 6 minutes longer. Stir in the chicken, thyme, sage, salt, pepper, and cayenne pepper and remove from heat.
1 teaspoon dried thyme leaves	
½ teaspoon dried sage leaves	
1 teaspoon salt	
⅛ teaspoon black pepper	*4* Crumble the corn bread into a large bowl and toss with the Cheddar cheese. Add the chicken mixture and stir to mix.
⅛ teaspoon cayenne pepper	
One 8-x-8-inch pan Hearty Corn Bread Mix (see Chapter 10), baked and cooled	*5* In a small bowl, combine the chicken broth, sour cream, eggs, and melted butter and mix well. Pour over the corn bread mixture and stir gently to combine.
1 cup diced Cheddar cheese	
One 14-ounce can ready to use chicken broth	*6* Pour the mixture into the prepared pan and top with the Parmesan cheese.
1 cup sour cream	
2 eggs	*7* Bake for 40 to 50 minutes, or until the top is light golden-brown. Let stand for 10 minutes before serving.
¼ cup butter, melted	
¼ cup grated Parmesan cheese	

Per serving: Calories 1,012 (From Fat 468); Fat 52g (Saturated 27g); Cholesterol 220mg; Sodium 1,331mg; Carbohydrate 104g; Dietary Fiber 9g; Protein 37g.

Tex-Mex Corn Bread Bake

Prep time: 30 min • **Cook time:** 55 min • **Yield:** 8 servings

Ingredients	*Directions*
2 tablespoons olive oil	*1* Preheat the oven to 375 degrees. Grease a 9-x-13-inch glass baking dish with butter.
1 onion, chopped	
3 cloves garlic, minced	*2* In a large skillet, heat the olive oil over medium heat. Add the onion, garlic, and jalapeño pepper and cook and stir until crisp-tender, about 5 to 6 minutes.
1–2 jalapeño peppers, minced	
1 pound lean ground beef	
½ pound gluten-free pork sausage	*3* Add the ground beef and pork sausage. Cook, stirring with a fork to break up the meat, until the meat is browned, about 6 to 8 minutes. Drain off the excess fat.
One 15-ounce can gluten-free refried beans	
One 15-ounce can kidney beans, rinsed and drained	*4* Add the refried beans, kidney beans, tomato sauce, salsa, chili powder, cumin, and pepper to the skillet. Stir to combine and bring to a simmer. Reduce the heat to low and simmer for 10 minutes, stirring occasionally.
One 8-ounce can tomato sauce	
1 cup salsa	
2 teaspoons chili powder	*5* Meanwhile, in a large bowl, combine the cornmeal, brown rice flour, corn flour, baking powder, baking soda, and salt. In a medium bowl, combine the eggs, sour cream, buttermilk, and Parmesan cheese; add to the dry ingredients and mix just until combined.
1 teaspoon ground cumin	
¼ teaspoon black pepper	
1¼ cups yellow cornmeal	
¼ cup minus 1 teaspoon (31 grams) brown rice flour	*6* Pour the hot beef mixture into the prepared dish and top with the cornmeal mixture. Bake for 25 to 35 minutes, until the corn bread is light brown and set.
⅓ cup (38 grams) corn flour (masa harina)	
1 teaspoon baking powder	
1 teaspoon baking soda	
½ teaspoon salt	
2 eggs	
1 cup sour cream	
¾ cup buttermilk	
⅓ cup grated Parmesan cheese	

Per serving: Calories 646 (From Fat 193); Fat 21g (Saturated 8g); Cholesterol 96mg; Sodium 1,260mg; Carbohydrate 84g; Dietary Fiber 12g; Protein 29g.

Cheeseburger Casserole

Prep time: 25 min • **Cook time:** 50 min • **Yield:** 6 servings

Ingredients	*Directions*
1 tablespoon olive oil	*1* Preheat the oven to 375 degrees. Spray a 2-quart casserole with nonstick cooking spray and set aside.
1 onion, chopped	
3 cloves garlic, minced	*2* In a large skillet, heat the olive oil over medium heat. Add the onion and garlic and cook for 5 minutes, stirring frequently. Add the ground beef and cook, stirring to break up the meat, until the beef is browned, about 6 to 8 minutes. Drain off the fat.
1¼ pounds lean ground beef	
One 8-ounce can tomato sauce	
2 tablespoons tomato paste	
⅓ cup ketchup	*3* Add the tomato sauce, tomato paste, ketchup, mustard, thyme, salt, and pepper and simmer for 10 minutes.
¼ cup mustard	
1 teaspoon dried thyme leaves	
Salt and pepper to taste	
1¼ cups minus 1 teaspoon (165 grams) Whole-Grain Flour Mix (see Chapter 10)	*4* Meanwhile, in a medium bowl, combine the Whole-Grain Flour Mix, White Flour Mix, baking powder, and ½ teaspoon salt.
⅓ cup minus 1 teaspoon (45 grams) White Flour Mix (see Chapter 10)	*5* In a small bowl, combine the eggs, butter, and milk and beat until combined.
1 teaspoon baking powder	
½ teaspoon salt	*6* Stir the egg mixture into the flour mixture just until combined.
2 eggs	
⅓ cup butter, melted	*7* Stir the cheese cubes into the hot beef mixture and pour into the prepared casserole. Spoon the batter onto the beef mixture in six sections. Sprinkle with Parmesan cheese.
⅓ cup milk	
4 ounces Cheddar cheese, cubed	
3 tablespoons grated Parmesan cheese	*8* Bake for 25 to 30 minutes, or until the topping is light golden-brown and set.

Per serving: *Calories 583 (From Fat 309); Fat 34g (Saturated 16g); Cholesterol 180mg; Sodium 972mg; Carbohydrate 40g; Dietary Fiber 3g; Protein 30g.*

Note: The mustard flavor is strong in this recipe. If you love mustard, you'll love it! If not, reduce the mustard amount to 1 to 2 tablespoons.

French Onion Soufflé

Prep time: 30 min • **Cook time:** 55 min • **Yield:** 4 servings

Ingredients

1 tablespoon plus 3 tablespoons unsalted butter

2 tablespoons grated Parmesan cheese

5 eggs

1 onion, chopped

2 cloves garlic, minced

1 tablespoon (8 grams) sorghum flour

2 tablespoons (18 grams) brown rice flour

2 teaspoons (6 grams) cornstarch

¾ cup light cream

½ cup gluten-free beef broth

½ teaspoon salt

¼ teaspoon white pepper

1 cup shredded Cheddar cheese

½ cup shredded havarti cheese

¼ teaspoon cream of tartar

Directions

1 Preheat the oven to 350 degrees. Grease a 2-quart soufflé dish with 1 tablespoon butter, sprinkle with Parmesan cheese, and set aside.

2 Separate the cold eggs, placing the yolks in a small bowl and the whites in a large bowl. Set aside.

3 In a medium saucepan, melt 3 tablespoons butter over medium heat. Add the onion and cook and stir until the onion is golden-brown, about 12 to 15 minutes. Add the garlic and cook for 2 minutes.

4 Add the sorghum flour, brown rice flour, and cornstarch; cook and stir for 2 minutes.

5 Add the light cream, broth, salt, and pepper; cook and stir until the mixture thickens.

6 Add the cheeses and stir until melted; remove from the heat. Beat the egg yolks into the onion mixture and set aside.

7 Add the cream of tartar to the egg whites; beat until stiff peaks form.

8 Stir ¼ of the egg whites into the onion mixture to lighten. Then gently fold the remaining egg whites into the onion mixture.

9 Immediately pour into the prepared dish. Bake for 30 to 40 minutes, or until the soufflé is puffed and golden-brown. Serve immediately.

Per serving: Calories 507 (From Fat 365); Fat 41g (Saturated 23g); Cholesterol 373mg; Sodium 824mg; Carbohydrate 14g; Dietary Fiber 1g; Protein 22g.

Note: Substitute chopped cooked chicken for the onions or use finely diced ham or cooked ground beef. Add chopped jalapeños and Pepper Jack cheese for a Tex-Mex Soufflé.

Vegetarian Herb-Topped Biscuit Casserole

Prep time: 45 min • **Cook time:** 50 min • **Yield:** 8 servings

Ingredients	*Directions*
1 recipe Herbed Cream Biscuits (see Chapter 18)	*1* Preheat the oven to 400 degrees. Grease a 9-x-13-inch pan with nonstick cooking spray. Prepare the biscuits and set aside.
2 tablespoons plus ¼ cup olive oil	
1 onion, diced	*2* Cook the 2 tablespoons olive oil and onion in a large frying pan over medium heat for 1 to 2 minutes, until the onion starts to soften. Add the sweet potatoes, russet potatoes, and zucchini. Cook and stir until the potatoes begin to brown, about 8 to 10 minutes.
2 sweet potatoes, peeled and diced	
2 russet potatoes, peeled and diced	
1 zucchini, diced	*3* Add the red bell pepper, mushrooms, and garbanzo beans and cook for 1 minute longer. Pour into the prepared pan.
1 red bell pepper, diced	
1 cup sliced button or crimini mushrooms	*4* In another medium saucepan, heat ¼ cup olive oil over medium heat. Add the garlic and cook for 30 seconds, until the garlic is fragrant.
1 cup rinsed and drained garbanzo beans	
3 cloves garlic, minced	*5* Stir in the sweet rice flour and cook for 30 seconds. Add the rosemary and milk and cook over medium heat, stirring constantly with a wire whisk, until the gravy is thickened and smooth, about 5 to 6 minutes.
3 tablespoons minus 1 teaspoon (27 grams) sweet rice flour	
2 tablespoons minced fresh rosemary	*6* Pour the gravy over the vegetables in a casserole dish and immediately top with the biscuits.
2 cups milk or light cream	
	7 Bake for 25 to 30 minutes, until the casserole is bubbly and the biscuits are golden-brown. Serve immediately.

Per serving: *Calories 513 (From Fat 248); Fat 28g (Saturated 13g); Cholesterol 69mg; Sodium 390mg; Carbohydrate 62g; Dietary Fiber 5g; Protein 9g.*

New Orleans Shrimp Casserole

Prep time: 50 min • **Cook time:** 40 min • **Yield:** 4 servings

Ingredients	Directions
½ recipe Butter Pie Crust (see Chapter 17)	**1** Prepare the Butter Pie Crust, roll out into a 10-inch circle, and refrigerate.
¼ cup butter	
½ cup chopped celery	**2** Preheat the oven to 425 degrees.
1 onion, chopped	
3 cloves garlic, minced	**3** In a large skillet, melt the butter over medium heat. Add the celery, onion, garlic, and red bell pepper; cook and stir until crisp-tender, about 5 to 6 minutes.
1 red bell pepper, chopped	
2 tablespoons (18 grams) sweet rice flour	**4** Add the sweet rice flour, White Flour Mix, celery salt, pepper, and paprika; cook and stir for 2 minutes.
2 tablespoons (20 grams) White Flour Mix (see Chapter 10)	
½ teaspoon celery salt	**5** Add the wine or chicken broth and tomatoes. Cook, stirring occasionally, over medium heat until thickened, about 3 to 5 minutes.
¼ teaspoon black pepper	
½ teaspoon paprika	
¼ cup dry white wine or chicken broth	**6** Add the shrimp to the mixture; cook and stir for 4 to 5 minutes, until the shrimp curl and turn pink. Stir in the peas and Cheddar and Gouda cheeses; remove from the heat and pour into a 2-quart casserole dish.
One 14-ounce can diced tomatoes, undrained	
3 cups 30-count uncooked peeled shrimp	**7** Immediately top with the Butter Pie Crust; crimp the edges if desired. Sprinkle the crust with Parmesan cheese.
1 cup baby frozen peas, thawed	
1 cup shredded Cheddar cheese	**8** Bake for 18 to 23 minutes, or until the casserole is bubbly and the crust is golden-brown.
½ cup shredded Gouda cheese	
2 tablespoons grated Parmesan cheese	

Per serving: Calories 727 (From Fat 351); Fat 39g (Saturated 24); Cholesterol 317mg; Sodium 1,161mg; Carbohydrate 55g; Dietary Fiber 6g; Protein 41g.

Classic Chicken and Dumplings

Prep time: 55 min • **Cook time:** 55 min • **Yield:** 8 servings

Ingredients	Directions
5 slices bacon	*1* In a large, heavy saucepan, cook the bacon until crisp, about 8 to 10 minutes. Remove the bacon from the pan, crumble it, and refrigerate it. Drain all but 1 tablespoon of bacon fat from the pan.
2 tablespoons olive oil	
1 onion, chopped	
3 cloves garlic, minced	*2* Add the olive oil to the pan and heat over medium heat. Add the onion; cook and stir until tender, about 5 minutes.
1½ cups sliced carrots	
1 cup chopped celery	
10 boneless, skinless chicken thighs, chopped	*3* Add the garlic, carrots, and celery; cook and stir for 3 minutes.
3 cups gluten-free chicken broth	*4* Add the chicken thighs; cook and stir for 5 minutes, until browned.
1 bay leaf	
1 teaspoon salt	*5* Add the chicken broth, bay leaf, salt, poultry seasoning, thyme, and pepper; bring to a simmer. Cover the pot, reduce the heat to low, and simmer for 20 minutes.
½ teaspoon poultry seasoning	
1 teaspoon dried thyme	
⅛ teaspoon black pepper	
1 recipe Dumpling Batter (see Chapter 17)	*6* Make the Dumpling Batter and stir the parsley into it.
3 tablespoons chopped parsley	*7* Remove the bay leaf from the chicken mixture and then add the peas, cream, milk, and reserved bacon; bring to a simmer.
2 cups frozen peas, thawed	
1 cup light cream	
1½ cups milk	*8* Stir the lemon zest into the chicken mixture and then drop the dumplings by tablespoons into the pot. Cover and simmer for 9 to 12 minutes, until the dumplings are cooked through. Serve immediately.
1 teaspoon grated lemon zest	

Per serving: Calories 421 (From Fat 237); Fat 26g (Saturated 11g); Cholesterol 132mg; Sodium 1,105mg; Carbohydrate 22g; Dietary Fiber 2g; Protein 24g.

Mushroom Stroganoff Crepes

Prep time: 40 min • **Cook time:** 40 min • **Yield:** 6 servings

Ingredients	Directions
12 Crepes (see Chapter 17)	**1** Prepare the Crepes and set them aside.
1 tablespoon butter	
2 tablespoons olive oil	**2** In a large saucepan, combine the butter and olive oil over medium heat. Add the onion; cook and stir for 3 minutes.
1 onion, chopped	
2 cups chopped button mushrooms	**3** Add all the mushrooms; cook and stir until the mushrooms are browned and the liquid evaporates, about 10 to 12 minutes.
1 cup chopped porcini mushrooms	
1 cup chopped shiitake mushrooms	**4** Add the garlic, salt, thyme, pepper, and beef broth and stir well.
2 cloves garlic, minced	
1 teaspoon salt	**5** Add the cream cheese; stir over low heat until the cheese melts and forms a smooth sauce, about 3 to 5 minutes. Remove the pan from the heat and stir in the sour cream and Worcestershire sauce. Let cool for 15 minutes.
1 teaspoon dried thyme leaves	
⅛ teaspoon black pepper	
½ cup gluten-free beef broth	
Two 3-ounce packages cream cheese, softened and cubed	**6** Preheat the oven to 350 degrees.
¼ cup sour cream	**7** Divide the mushroom mixture among the Crepes. Roll up the Crepes, enclosing the filling. Place them in a 13-x-9-inch glass baking dish. Sprinkle with parsley.
1 tablespoon gluten-free Worcestershire sauce	
¼ cup chopped parsley	**8** Cover the pan with foil and bake for 15 to 20 minutes, or until the Crepes are hot. Serve immediately.

Per serving: *Calories 448 (From Fat 272); Fat 30g (Saturated 16g); Cholesterol 193mg; Sodium 771mg; Carbohydrate 35g; Dietary Fiber 2g; Protein 11g.*

Vary It! If you can't handle casein, use soft tofu in place of the cream cheese and omit the sour cream. Use olive oil in place of the butter.

Chicken Pepper Crepes

Prep time: 30 min • **Cook time:** 35 min • **Yield:** 4 servings

Ingredients	Directions
8 Crepes (see Chapter 17)	*1* Prepare the Crepes and set them aside. Preheat the oven to 350 degrees.
2 tablespoons butter	
1 tablespoon olive oil	*2* In a large saucepan, combine the butter and olive oil over medium heat. Add the onion; cook and stir for 5 minutes, until tender.
1 onion, chopped	
1 red bell pepper, chopped	
2 tablespoons (20 grams) sweet rice flour	*3* Add the bell pepper; cook and stir for 3 minutes.
⅔ cup gluten-free chicken broth	*4* Add the sweet rice flour; cook and stir for 1 minute. Add the chicken broth, milk, tarragon, salt, and white pepper; bring to a simmer over low heat. Cook until thick, about 5 to 7 minutes.
¼ cup milk or almond milk	
1 teaspoon dried tarragon	
½ teaspoon salt	*5* Stir in the chicken.
⅛ teaspoon white pepper	*6* Fill the Crepes with the chicken mixture and roll them up. Place them in a 2-quart baking dish.
2 cups shredded cooked chicken	
	7 Cover the Crepes with foil and bake for 12 to 16 minutes, or until hot. Serve immediately.

Per serving: Calories 504 (From Fat 246); Fat 27g (Saturated 12g); Cholesterol 233mg; Sodium 708mg; Carbohydrate 36g; Dietary Fiber 2g; Protein 29g.

Vary 1t! This recipe is so easy to change. Use leftover cooked turkey or ham instead of the chicken. Use dried thyme or basil instead of the tarragon. Use fresh herbs instead of dried. Add other vegetables, too: chopped mushrooms, asparagus, peas, and green beans are all delicious.

Skillet Puffy Pancake

Prep time: 30 min • **Cook time:** 35 min • **Yield:** 6 servings

Ingredients	Directions
4 tablespoons butter	**1** Preheat the oven to 450 degrees.
1 cup diced apples or pears	
1 recipe Popovers (see Chapter 19)	**2** Melt the butter in a cast-iron skillet in the oven. Remove the skillet from the oven and add the fruit to the butter; spread evenly over the bottom of the skillet.
1 teaspoon cinnamon	
	3 Make the Popover batter as directed, adding 1 teaspoon cinnamon.
	4 Pour the batter over the fruit.
	5 Bake for 30 to 35 minutes, until well browned and puffy. This pancake will collapse when removed from the oven; that's normal! It still tastes wonderful.

Per serving: Calories 296 (From Fat 141); Fat 16g (Saturated 9g); Cholesterol 142mg; Sodium 102mg; Carbohydrate 35g; Dietary Fiber 1g; Protein 6g.

Vary It! You can make this a savory recipe, too. Omit the cinnamon. Use cooked onions and garlic, or cooked and drained ground beef instead of the diced fruit. Serve the pancake with heated maple syrup or with salsa. Or sprinkle it with cheese as soon as it comes out of the oven.

Potato Puff Casserole

Prep time: 40 min • **Cook time:** 50 min • **Yield:** 6 servings

Ingredients	*Directions*
1 cup water	**1** Preheat the oven to 400 degrees. In a medium saucepan over high heat, bring the water, ½ cup beef broth, and butter to a boil. Remove from the heat and add ½ teaspoon salt and the cream or milk. Stir in the potato flakes until mixed.
½ cup plus 1 cup beef broth	
3 tablespoons butter	
½ teaspoon plus ½ teaspoon salt	
½ cup light cream or whole milk	
1½ cups gluten-free dried potato flakes	**2** Beat 1 egg and egg white into the potato mixture. Stir in ½ cup plus 1 tablespoon (83 grams) White Flour Mix and baking powder and set aside.
2 eggs	
1 egg white	**3** In a large skillet, cook the ground beef and ground pork with onion and garlic until the beef and pork are browned, stirring to break up the meat, about 8 to 10 minutes. Drain.
½ cup plus 1 tablespoon (83 grams) plus ¼ cup plus 1 teaspoon (40 grams) White Flour Mix (see Chapter 10)	
1 teaspoon baking powder	**4** Add ¼ cup plus 1 teaspoon (40 grams) White Flour Mix and cornstarch to the beef mixture; cook and stir over medium heat for 1 minute.
1 pound ground beef	
½ pound ground pork	**5** Add 1 cup beef broth to the beef mixture; cook and stir for 2 minutes until thickened. Add the ketchup, mustard, sour cream, ½ teaspoon salt, and marjoram leaves to the beef mixture; bring to a simmer.
1 onion, chopped	
3 cloves garlic, minced	
2 tablespoons (18 grams) cornstarch	
3 tablespoons gluten-free ketchup	**6** Pour the beef mixture into a 2½-quart casserole. Immediately drop the potato mixture by tablespoons over the beef mixture. Beat the remaining egg in a small bowl and brush over the potato puffs.
1 tablespoon gluten-free mustard	
1 cup sour cream	**7** Bake for 30 to 40 minutes, or until the potato puffs are golden-brown.
1 teaspoon dried marjoram leaves	

Per serving: *Calories 559 (From Fat 293); Fat 33g (Saturated 17g); Cholesterol 117mg; Sodium 930mg; Carbohydrate 41g; Dietary Fiber 2g; Protein 26g.*

Two Potato Frittata

Prep time: 30 min • **Cook time:** 75 min • **Yield:** 12–14 servings

Ingredients	*Directions*
8 eggs	**1** Preheat the oven to 350 degrees. Grease a 13-x-9-inch pan with unsalted butter and set aside.
2 teaspoons dried oregano or 6 sprigs fresh oregano, leaves removed	
1 teaspoon salt	**2** In a large bowl, beat the eggs, oregano, salt, and pepper. Add the milk and tapioca flour and mix well; set aside.
½ teaspoon black pepper	
2 cups milk	**3** Grate the yams and potatoes using the coarse side of the grater. Mix the potatoes together in a large bowl.
1 tablespoon (8 grams) tapioca flour	
2 large garnet yams	**4** Press ⅓ of the potato mixture into the prepared pan. Top with ½ of the spinach and ½ of the feta cheese.
2 large russet or Yukon Gold potatoes	
One 10-ounce package frozen chopped spinach, thawed and drained	**5** Add another ⅓ of the potato mixture, the remaining spinach and feta cheese, and the last ⅓ of the potato mixture.
12 ounces feta cheese, crumbled	**6** Pour the egg mixture slowly over all. Make sure the oregano is evenly distributed.
	7 Cover the pan with foil, bake for 1 hour, and then remove the foil and bake for 15 to 20 minutes more, until the top is browned. Cut into squares to serve.

Per serving: *Calories 236 (From Fat 98); Fat 11g (Saturated 6g); Cholesterol 172mg; Sodium 606mg; Carbohydrate 23g; Dietary Fiber 3g; Protein 12g.*

Note: You can make this dish ahead of time and then reheat it in a 375 degree oven for 10 to 15 minutes. It's perfect for a brunch or late breakfast.

Part V
The Part of Tens

The 5th Wave   By Rich Tennant

"What do you think of my cookie dough – pastry bag or caulking gun?"

In this part . . .

In this final part, we give you ten tips for successful gluten-free baking and point out ten sneaky places where gluten can hide.

Chapter 22

Ten Important Gluten-Free Baking Tips

*T*o make the best gluten-free baked goods, you need to know some specific methods and tips. Alternative flours just don't behave the same way as wheat flour in batters and doughs. When you understand these tips and tricks, they'll become second nature.

Remember that baking is a science. Recipes are formulas, and the language of baking is like the language of any science. When you understand that accuracy matters and you know how gluten-free batters and doughs perform, you'll be able to relax and enjoy the art of baking.

Always Weigh Flours and Starches

The biggest breakthrough in gluten-free baking was weighing flours and starches. Gluten-free flours and starches all have different weights, and everybody measures differently! You can even see this on the Food Network. One chef measures by scooping the measuring cup into the flour, another stirs the flour and then scoops, and a third measures the proper way — by spooning flour into the cup.

Because gluten-free flours have different weights, weighing by volume almost always gets you into trouble. Take a page from European bakers, who've been weighing flour for years. Buy a simple scale and learn how to use it. Your gluten-free treats will be delicious, with a light and tender crumb.

Consider Weighing All Other Ingredients

As long as you have the scale out, why not measure all the ingredients by weight? It takes some practice, but measuring ingredients by weight is actually faster than measuring by volume. Just zero out the scale between each ingredient addition and keep track of what you've added by marking it off on the recipe. You don't have to fumble with cup measures, tablespoon measures, and liquid measuring cups. Cleanup is easier! And your baked goods will be even better, because every single ingredient will be perfectly measured every single time.

Remember That Gluten-Free Doughs Are Like Batters

The second gluten-free baking breakthrough, after weighing ingredients, was realizing that gluten-free flours absorb more water than wheat flour. In other words, they need more hydration. That means gluten-free doughs are more like stiff batters. If you use enough gluten-free flour so the dough is stiff enough to knead, the bread or pizza crust will be as hard and dense as a brick.

You must handle these batters differently, too. You probably need to stock up on more baking pans because gluten-free doughs must be contained until the structure sets. Have fun choosing unusually shaped pans. You can find heart-shaped muffin tins and cake pans, fluted and scalloped Bundt pans, and even fun mini Bundt pans to shape your delicious gluten-free treats.

Increase Flavorings

Because gluten-free doughs are like batters, with more liquid, the flavors can sometimes be diluted. Many gluten-free bakers like to add more flavorings to compensate. Especially at first, gluten-free flours may taste different, and many of them have strong flavors, so adding more flavors can help.

Just about any sweet recipe benefits from doubling the vanilla. You can increase spices, and you can substitute fruit purées and juices for some of the liquids in a recipe. Brown sugar adds more flavor than granulated sugar. And any recipe with coconut, sour cream, shredded vegetables, or nuts has more flavor.

Bake with Room-Temperature Ingredients

A general rule of baking is that all ingredients should be at room temperature. This is important for gluten-free baking, too. Ingredients combine more quickly and more smoothly when they're about the same temperature. Room-temperature eggs beat to a higher volume. Room-temperature butter blends well with other ingredients and is easier to beat.

Take butter out of the refrigerator a couple of hours before baking. Eggs need refrigeration to stay safe; put them in warm water for 5 to 10 minutes before you add them to a recipe. If you freeze or refrigerate gluten-free flours, let them stand at room temperature for 30 to 40 minutes before starting the recipe. When you use room-temperature ingredients, you'll find that batters and doughs are smoother and easier to work with and your baked goods have a better texture.

Beat It!

You always have to handle wheat flour carefully so the gluten doesn't overdevelop. Gluten-free flours don't have that problem! You can beat a delicate dough without having to worry about a tough end product.

In fact, most gluten-free recipes call for beating the batter for a good 2 to 4 minutes. Doing so incorporates air into the batter, creating air pockets that make that tender and fine crumb of the best baked goods. When a recipe calls for beating a batter for 5 minutes on high, don't skip or scrimp on the time.

As a caveat, when a recipe calls for letting the dough rest in the refrigerator for hours, don't skip this step either! Gluten-free flours need time to hydrate, or absorb liquids. Read recipes carefully before you begin and plan for resting and chilling times.

Calibrate Your Oven

Any baker needs a tightly calibrated oven. It doesn't matter how well you measure ingredients, develop the dough, or flavor the recipe; if you put it into an oven that's off by 25 degrees or more, the recipe is going to fail.

You may be able to calibrate your oven yourself. Read the owner's manual to see whether this is possible. If the manual doesn't have calibrating instructions, call a professional! Don't fool around with gas or electrical equipment unless you know what you're doing.

Get the Pan into the Oven Quickly

You can manipulate gluten-free flours more than wheat flours, but that delicate structure can also lose the air you've worked so hard to get into the batter. Don't let gluten-free batters and doughs leavened with baking powder or baking soda sit around after you put them in the pan or mold; get them into the oven quickly! Even yeast doughs benefit from a quick entry into the hot oven, creating the perfect oven spring for a light and tender bread.

Get the Breads out of the Pan Quickly

When your breads and cakes have baked to golden-brown perfection, get them out of the pan quickly! Because gluten-free baked goods have more liquid than wheat baked goods, they can steam while they sit in the hot pan. That makes for soggy and tough crusts. For the best gluten-free baked goods, remove them quickly from the pan and place them on a rack to cool.

In fact, some breads benefit from a quick trip back into the oven after you remove them from the pan. For a crisp crust on baguettes or pizza, put them back, right on the oven rack, for a minute or two.

Don't Toss Your Mistakes

Everyone has disasters in the kitchen. Maybe something went wrong in measuring, or you forgot an ingredient, or you added too much of another. When everything fails and your gluten-free bread turns into a brick, don't throw it out! Cut it up, process it in a food processor, and voilà! Instant bread crumbs you can use to coat chicken or make a meatloaf.

Sometimes gluten-free breads and cookies improve when they're refrigerated or frozen. If your brownies are too hard or gummy, freeze them and then serve them cold.

Don't let mistakes and disasters discourage you and don't give up! You'll most likely learn something from a recipe disaster, and that will make you a better baker.

Chapter 23

Ten Sneaky Places Where Gluten Can Hide

*A*fter you realize the necessity of eating gluten-free, you must become a detective. You must carefully examine every single processed food item because gluten can lurk in the strangest places. In the processed food world, gluten is used as a thickener, a stabilizer, an emulsifier, and something called a "flow agent."

In this chapter we list many of the most common sneaky places gluten can hide. You know that you must always read labels on every product every single time you buy it. Be vigilant. Manufacturers change formulas for products every day! Something that was gluten-free yesterday may not be gluten-free tomorrow. And even though one product in a company's line may be gluten-free, not all are. For instance, although Butterfinger candy bars are gluten-free, Butterfinger Crisp candy bars contain gluten!

Companies don't usually use the term *gluten* on product labels, although they must identify wheat because it's one of the eight main food allergens. Wheat is used as a stabilizer, thickener, and texture enhancer in many products. But gluten is also found in barley and rye. Other grains are cross-contaminated in the growing rotation of crops or in handling and processing.

Be sure to check out Chapter 8 for different words that wheat can hide behind and the most common places gluten can hide. Print out a list of these words and terms and post them prominently in your kitchen. After a while, ferreting out hidden gluten will become second nature.

Lunch Meats

Many processed lunch meats contain gluten. Companies add wheat starch and wheat protein to these meats for texture and flavor. Cold cuts, pepperoni, hot dogs, and sausages are all suspect. Read the labels carefully and call the manufacturer to inquire about ingredients if you aren't absolutely sure the product is free of wheat and gluten.

If you also follow a vegetarian diet, be especially cautious. Most of these products are based on wheat gluten, and vegetarian "lunch meats" are a big slab of gluten. Some tofu-based lunch meats exist. For a good substitute if you're vegetarian, make your own vegetarian and gluten-free sandwich fillings.

Your best bet may be to forgo lunch meats and processed meats altogether and just cook your own meat. Sliced cooked turkey and chicken really taste better than slippery lunch meats anyway!

When you buy deli meats, you must be extra careful! If someone purchases a gluten-containing lunch meat and the deli slices it, and then you come along and have a gluten-free lunch meat sliced on the same machine, your gluten-free meat will be contaminated. Ask whether the deli has a separate slicing machine for gluten-free meats. If it doesn't, buy a chunk of the gluten-free meat (make sure the knife and cutting board have just been washed) and slice it yourself at home.

At the time of this writing, these companies state that their meat products are gluten-free:

- Applegate Farms
- Boar's Head
- Columbus
- Diestel
- Freybe
- Jones Dairy Farm
- Niman Ranch
- Some Hormel products, especially the Natural Choice line
- Some Jennie-O products

But still check the label every single time you buy lunch meats or any other product!

Condiments

Many condiments — such as ketchup, mustard, mayo, chutney, and salsa — can contain gluten. These products use wheat starch or wheat as a thickener and stabilizer. You must read every label every time you buy these products. Also keep an eye on the labels of pickle relish, hot sauce, and Asian condiments such as oyster sauce, plum sauce, and soy sauce.

Visit the websites of companies such as Heinz, Annie's, Arrowhead Mills, and Hodgson Mill for a complete list of gluten-free condiments.

Malt vinegar is one type of vinegar that isn't gluten-free because it's not distilled. This vinegar is made with barley, one of the forbidden grains.

Of course, you can make your own condiments. Homemade mustard is especially delicious when made from just mustard seeds, water, and vinegar. And homemade salsas, especially when made from more exotic ingredients such as blueberries or kiwi, are very special. Most large cookbooks and most online recipe sites have a recipe for these foods.

Food Colorings and Flavorings

It's hard to believe that something as innocuous as food colors and flavorings can contain gluten, but there you are. One of the worst offenders is caramel food coloring produced outside the United States. All U.S. manufacturers use corn or wheat to create caramel color. If they use wheat, they must declare it on the package because it's one of the eight main allergens.

As of this writing, here's where the largest companies that make these products stand on the gluten-free spectrum:

- ✔ McCormick food colorings are certified gluten-free.
- ✔ Wilton, one of the largest manufacturers of food colorings and flavorings, doesn't have a production plant dedicated to gluten-free products, although gluten isn't included in its products.
- ✔ Cook's Flavoring makes gluten-free extracts and natural flavorings, including orange, anise, and lemon extracts.
- ✔ Nielsen-Massey makes all gluten-free liquid extracts.

Spices and products that contain only one ingredient don't have a label; you don't need to worry about whether they're gluten-free.

Alcoholic Beverages

Alcoholic beverages aren't required to have an ingredient label, so determining whether the product is gluten-free is difficult. Here's what we know about alcoholic beverages.

Some alcohols are made from wheat, rye, or barley. Rye whiskey is distilled, leaving the proteins behind in the residue. Some beers contain wheat and most beers contain barley; the fermentation doesn't alter the gluten, so gluten-intolerant folks can't drink typical beer. Still, you can find some delicious gluten-free beers on the market. They're made from sorghum, buckwheat, rice, wild rice, and corn.

Bard's was the first gluten-free beer made in the United States. It's a craft-brewed beer made from malted sorghum, hops, yeast, and water. Lakefront's New Grist and Anheuser-Busch's Redbridge are gluten-free beers made from sorghum.

Some wines are processed with wheat gluten. Apparently, gluten doesn't appear in the final product, but if you're very sensitive, check with the winery before imbibing. Some vodkas are made from wheat, but companies that make these products claim, again, that the distillation removes all gluten. But watch out for any alcoholic beverage that has flavorings added back to the finished product. Make sure each of these ingredients has no gluten before enjoying these products.

And remember that, as you're recovering from the effects of gluten, you should avoid alcoholic beverages altogether. They're hard on your body and contain no real nutrients. In the early stages of eliminating gluten, you're trying to get your body to recover.

Candy and Chocolate

Though you'd probably like to think that candies and chocolate don't contain gluten, unfortunately, that's not true. Many candies have gluten in the form of malt, and other candies may have wheat starch to thicken them or act as stabilizers.

Obviously, malted milk balls, such as Whoppers, are on the no-no list. Other gluten-containing candies that may be a surprise include Nestle Crunch Bars and Milky Way bars. There's that malt again! Twizzlers are another no-no because they contain wheat starch.

Any candy that contains a cookie or a crunchy substance is automatically suspect. Twix, Kit Kat, and Butterfinger Crisp bars have wheat flour. The Wonka Bar, Wonka Oompas, and Pretzel M&Ms all contain gluten. Before you eat a candy or chocolate, always read the label. If you're unsure about the ingredients, contact the company.

But you can find some gluten-free candies and chocolate, including regular M&Ms, Snickers, Dove chocolates, Baby Ruth, Oh Henry!, Jelly Belly jelly beans, Hershey's Kisses, and Tootsie Rolls.

Vitamins and Supplements

Vitamins and supplements are probably the last thing you think of when you're purging your home of gluten. But gluten can lurk in these products. Many companies use starch and modified food starch as emulsifiers and stabilizers in many supplements and vitamins. And natural vitamin E products are often made from wheat germ oil.

Fortunately, companies that make vitamins and supplements are required to list all ingredients on the label. Still, cross-contamination can occur, even if no gluten is used in making the product.

Some of the supplement lines that are guaranteed gluten-free (at least as of this writing) include Thorne, Vital Nutrients, Nature Made, The Sisters' Supplements, Bio-35, and Country Life. For more information about gluten-free vitamins and supplements, visit www.glutenfreedrugs.com.

Medications

Medications can contain gluten. One of the first things you need to do after a diagnosis is to inform your pharmacist and all your doctors and healthcare providers that you can't have any gluten. They should all put notes in their computer systems about your diagnosis.

Fever reducers, painkillers, anti-inflammatory drugs, and cold medicine are usually gluten-free, but don't count on it. Antibiotics and other prescription drugs may be gluten-free, but that isn't guaranteed.

Read the label, and to be really sure, look up the medication in the Physician's Desk Reference (in print, or online at www.pdr.net). There, you'll find the name and phone number of the drug's manufacturer. Call and find out about the gluten status of the product you need.

Marshmallows

Marshmallows aren't made with gluten, but the sticky marshmallow mixture is poured into molds coated with a starch or flour, and this flour may contain gluten. Even if the starch or flour is gluten-free, cross-contamination within the factory is a consideration.

Kraft says that its marshmallows are gluten-free. Lundberg, Elyon, and Campfire marshmallow brands are gluten-free as well, and AllerEnergy makes a gluten-free and corn-free marshmallow (the company uses rice syrup instead of corn syrup).

Self-Basting Poultry

Self-basting chickens and turkeys are known as "enhanced" meats. They're injected with a solution that can contain flavor enhancers, salt, water, and "approved substances." This solution can increase the poultry's weight by 15 percent! The fact that you must read the label for a whole chicken is frustrating, but that's the world we live in.

Any meat that's treated with something called a "solution" can contain gluten. Even the words "natural" and "organic" don't mean that the poultry is gluten-free. After all, gluten is "natural," and there are sources for "organic" gluten. Always look at the label on poultry products. If it says "injected with a solution" or lists any ingredient other than "chicken," be safe and don't buy it.

Makeup and Lotions

The main ingredient that causes problems in many shampoos, lotions, and lip balm is wheat germ. Oats are often used in these products, too. Brands such as Aveeno aren't gluten-free, simply because of the cross-contamination that can take place in its production plants.

Putting gluten-containing products on your sensitive skin can be problematic. Dermatitis herpetiformis, a painful skin rash, is frequently linked with celiac disease.

You can find some wonderful gluten-free lines of cosmetics, including Afterglow and Pangea. Look for them in specialty stores and online.

Index